Arpeggio of Redwings

Chesapeake Seasons:
A Guide to Joy

by Audrey Y. Scharmen

New Bay Books

Arpeggio of Redwings
Chesapeake Seasons: A Guide to Joy
by Audrey Y. Scharmen

Editor
Sandra Olivetti Martin
New Bay Books
Fairhaven, Maryland
NewBayBooks@gmail.com

Cover Illustration: "Blackbirds among the Cattails"
by Peg Scharmen Lynch

Design by Suzanne Shelden
Shelden Studios
Prince Frederick, Maryland
sheldenstudios@comcast.net

Library of Congress Cataloging-in-Publication Data
ISBN   978-1-7348866-0-3

Printed in the United States of America
First Edition

•

*To Audrey's "little people,"
her grandchildren:*

*John, Fred, Frank, Sarah, Becca & Will
Adria & Pablo
Becky, Lisa & Hank
Selah & Marta*

*And her "extra-little people,"
her great-grandchildren:*

Leah, Gwen, Nour & Edwin

Her greatest delights and hope for the future.

*With endless gratitude to
Sandra Olivetti Martin
without you, Audrey might never have taken
pen to paper to write these stories.*

Leave then, such simple precious things,
that they may begin again . . .

— A. Y. S.

FOREWORD

Dear Reader:

The reflections of Audrey Scharmen will put your life in order. Not permanently, as their author would have confided, had she and you the moment to talk over these stories. But for her in the moment of writing and you in the moment of reading—and we only live in the here and now—you'd both find your place in nature's way.

In these stories, you'll understand arpeggios of redwings as you regain a child's sense of wonder.

These are stories to be taken as seasonal tonics to accompany your springs, summers, autumns and winters. Read, reflect and refresh your notion of what kind of place this world is.

You need not read them only once; They'll be just as good next year. Their magic is inexhaustible.

I read the first of them a quarter century ago as one of the wonders swept onto the shore of my new newspaper, born *New Bay Times*, by a generous and unpredictable Chesapeake Bay tide. Audrey found us quickly. Her first reflection—then titled "Bermuda High," now "Caught in the Doldrums"—appeared July 29, 1993, the eighth issue of our first volume.

It was a natural match. What's a writer without an audience but a voice calling out in the wilderness? *New Bay Times* gave a home to writers like Audrey, who wanted to speak of our times and place. She'd written for other publications and local papers. But *New Bay Times*, a storyteller's paper, was as right for her as the spot she and her USAAF pilot husband Merrill had created for their retirement, on the shores of Mill Creek, which feeds into the Patuxent River, which leads into Chesapeake Bay.

New Bay Times gave her a place—and promised her thousands of readers for every word she wrote. We wanted her just as she was, writing as often as she chose, and we did not ask her to change.

Periodically for a dozen years, Audrey's reflections appeared to remind me—and our readers—that daily life, which seemed to have succumbed to routine, in fact unfolded around us with spectacle and miracles.

Read her personal catalogue of miracles in "A Prayer for the New Millennium." Among them are "the arpeggios of redwings" that give us the title for this book. That Prayer, as she wished, was read at her funeral.

Compiling them in this book all these years later, they come to me so fresh and startling that I slap my cheek and ask, World, what have I been missing?

The ailment—missing life's point—is as perennial as the cure: Audrey's well-tempered meditations.

I'm not the only reader shocked into clarity by Audrey's writing. Her "local columns"—as they were called in contest parlance—won first place three years running in the Maryland, Delaware, D.C. Press Association's editorial competition.

Readers from different newspapers across the country did each year's judging. Yet for those years—1998 to 2000—Audrey rose like the cream.

Weekly readers wrote—that week or many weeks later, on a second chance encounter—to tell me that Audrey had knocked their socks off, again.

"I've not seen the cedar waxwing in Bay Country. Then, the morning after I read Audrey Scharmen, a flock of about 40 descended on my crepe myrtle and holly bushes, devouring seeds and berries in a fury. If I'd not read the article, I might not have paid so much attention to all of this activity just outside my window," Kathleen Wilson wrote. "Thanks for reminding us of the beauty in our own back yards."

You'll share Wilson's thrill in "Snowflakes and Cedar Waxwings: Ordinary magic enchants my garden."

A quarter century later, a young man—who had not been born when Audrey wrote about waxwings—told me he wanted to grow up to write as well as she did. That was University of Maryland journalism student Brad Dress, an intern whose assignment included tracking down all Audrey's stories.

Through this book, other generations can continue to be enchanted by the ordinary magic of Audrey's writing.

It's your turn now.

Sandra Olivetti Martin

Sandra Olivetti Martin
Editor
Fairhaven, Maryland

Table of Contents

Spring

	Audrey Remembered	13-18
1.	Rejuvenation	21
2.	Winter's Perfect Ending	23
3.	It Was a Bad Winter	25
4.	Of Eagles and Politicians	29
5.	The Seasons Are Misaligned	33
6.	Spring Fever	35
7.	Now We Begin Again	39
8.	Gone Wild as Wisteria	41
9.	Spring Is on Her Own	45
10.	The Hippies Had the Right Idea	49
11.	First Communion	51
12.	This Earth Day, I Am Alive	55
13.	Against the Tide	57
14.	Things Just out of the Dark	61
15.	Lilacs at Last	63
16.	My Oracle	67
17.	Mama Was a Realist	69
18.	Visited by a Comet	73
19.	Keeping Faith	75
20.	Ducks and People	79

Summer

	Audrey Remembered, Marta	82
1.	Luna Moth at Flower Moon	85
2.	The Unwelcome	87
3.	Accounting for Summer	91
4.	My Granddaughter's Future Husband	95
5.	St. Francis of Summer	97
6.	Caught in the Doldrums	101
7.	Spiderlings	103
8.	The Moon's Flower	107
9.	Visitations of a Strange Summer	109
10.	Elegy for a Chesapeake Fish House	113

Autumn

	Audrey Remembered, Lisa	116
1.	Little Girl Found	119
2.	Autumn Sharpens Our Senses	121
3.	Autumn's Winged Blossoms	125
4.	On Finally Seeing Pikes Peak	127
5.	The Condition of Our Old Boat	131
6.	We Walk in the Footsteps of Ghosts	133
7.	Clinging to Autumn's Shirttail	137
8.	Transformation	141
9.	Another Autumn, Another Crisis	143
10.	Despite Armistice Day	147

Winter

	Audrey Remembered, Becky	150
1.	Running Pine in the Winter Woods	153
2.	Refugees: An Unfinished Portrait	156
3.	The Gift	159
4.	Arpeggios of Redwings	161
5.	Let There Be Trees	163
6.	Glory Be to January	165
7.	Desperate Measures	169
8.	My Oracle: Epilogue	171
9.	Tidings of False Cheer	175
10.	The Promise of Things Beautiful	179
11.	The Logic of Crows	181
12.	Accidentals	185
13.	What Have I Done with My Life?	187
14.	My Granddaughter at 16	189
15.	Eavesdropping on February's Stage	193
16.	This Will Be the Year	195
17.	Kite Flying	199
18.	On My 79th Birthday	201
19.	Snowflakes and Cedar Waxwings	205
20.	False Spring	207
21.	Then Comes February	211
	Audrey's Valedictory	213
	Acknowledgements	215
	Photo Credits	217

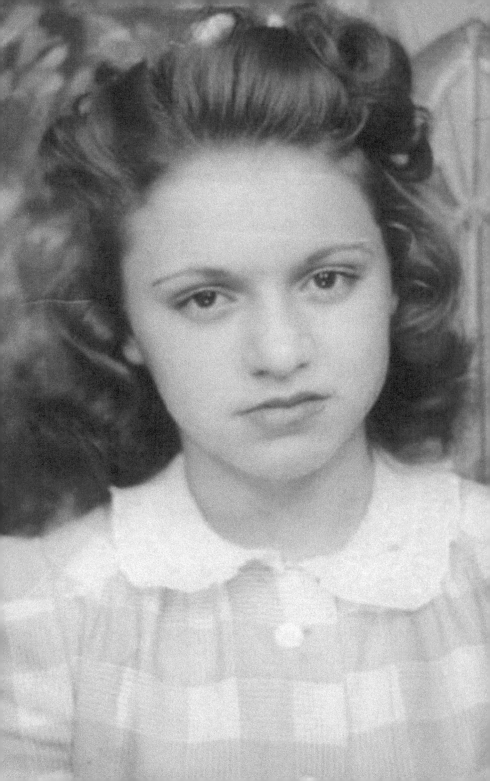

∞ *Audrey Remembered* ∞

Peg Scharmen Lynch
Daughter

Born in 1927, raised in the midst of the Dustbowl and Great Depression in Topeka, Kansas, Audrey Yvonne Frost left high school at the age of 16 to help support her family during World War II. Throughout her life, she related stories of working at the Topeka Army Air Forces Base Exchange alongside all the people who stepped in for the war effort. In that turnstile city, where many young soldiers were leaving their homes, family and country for the unknown, she witnessed the first drama that imprinted her soul, a clash of innocence meeting maturity.

In 1946, she married Merrill Scharmen, a career military pilot, who became a veteran of three wars and the father of her four children. She had been blessed with family, friends and fortune, faithfully fulfilling her duties as a military wife, mother and citizen. But war fatigue was disguised in Air Force glamor to sustain valor and democracy.

With most of her life spent stationed in the Southwest desert, she and my father finally retired along the shoreline of Chesapeake Bay. It was an oasis for the all the creativity that had been stored in her mind and heart. Here the casings of persistence and grit gave way to her writing and painting, her love of nature and gardening and reconnected her to joy.

One of the last conversations I had with my mother was on a sunny late afternoon. We sat with rainbows swirling on the walls of her room from a single suncatcher hanging in the window.

"Mom, what is your fondest memory from childhood?"

She had many, but her favorite was having a secret hideaway under an enormous cedar tree where she could retreat with her book box and writing tablets. Here she could escape in her daydreams and quiet her mind from the hectic hubbub of seven cherished siblings. Here the boughs absorbed the noise ...

I invite you to sit under that tree ...

∞ *Audrey Remembered* ∞

Michael Lynch
Son-in-Law

I first met the writer of this book at the annual Christmas Eve bash that was the Scharmen family tradition. Audrey had a martini and a smile on her round, Swedish face as her daughter, my future wife, introduced us. Her *joie de vivre* was clear to see, the welcome so genuine and unreserved, we clicked from the moment we met amongst the wreaths of dried flowers as a breathtaking magenta and indigo sunset unfurled out the picture window.

The small house where she and Merrill—you meet him in these pages as her "roomie" and "consultant"—had retired sat atop a finger of land overlooking a deep-water creek, with a view to the wild shore opposite: forested, red clay cliffs with the slash of fallen trees where osprey, swan and merganser found refuge. You'll get to know this Chesapeake Country setting well as you read.

The crabapple tree in her front yard gained mythic status, for its prodigious size and age and profusion of pink blossoms each spring—and for the rabbits who grazed beneath it and the owls and doves and occasional hawk who perched on its branches. It was the centerpiece of her small Eden, where she observed the comings and goings of the seasons, the ever-changing cast of flora and fauna, the sights, sounds and smells that were the true, deep, yet simple joys of a well-lived life.

Audrey was a delightful, cantankerous, intelligent, complex person who felt life and saw the world with an intensity that was exhilarating and exhausting, for her and those around her.

She was a wonderful grandmother who exalted in all her progeny's progeny. Among thirteen were our two daughters, Selah and Marta, to whom Grandma Audrey was a force of nature and a companion in long strolls through the fields and marshes, beaches and forests of Southern Maryland, marveling with them at the flowers, shells, birds and berries they encountered. They were imbued with her love of and respect for nature, always clear-eyed, acknowledging the brutality, death and decay that was as much a part of this great mystery as the exquisite beauty, serendipity and voluptuousness she chronicled so well in her writing.

A woman ahead of her time, she rued that she was born too soon as she watched the women of her children and grandchildren's generation have opportunities that she never had, that she wished for dearly, and I think reached for, successfully, with her writing.

A reader as well as a writer, Audrey introduced me to nature writing beyond the staples of Thoreau and Emerson: Aldo Leopold's Sand County Almanac and Annie Dillard's Pilgrim at Tinker Creek, and maybe most cherished, the great American poet Mary Oliver, with whom she shared a haunted background and deep, nuanced communion with "the family of things."

In Audrey's words and stories, I'm certain you will find that same solace and fellowship "in the promises of things beautiful."

∞ *Audrey Remembered* ∞

Tom Scharmen
son

Welcome to this milestone moment when we are at last privileged to share this volume of my mother's many voices. I hear her voices so clearly when reading this collection of her conversations and observations, a beautifully assembled but modest sampling from more than 100 notebooks she left behind. But then, I am privileged to hear her voices even when not reading her words.

I remember her distinctive play-acting narrative voice she used when reading us bed-time stories. I hear her critical voice, scorning political foolery or applauding incisive thinking. I hear her disciplinarian voice shake a finger at our youthful behavior and her proud voice praising our childhood achievements to friends. I hear her anger and also her singing. I hear her laughter and also her doubtful hesitancy. I hear her love and even her occasional sad reluctance to speak.

Even in her late 80s, I was always amazed when I would call her on the phone and hear the clear bright voice of a 20-year-old.

Listen closely. Her voices are woven with overtones that enrich the meanings and subtly share the feelings. Some are obvious, such as her undefeated humor, her sensitive respect towards the non-human biology of our planet, her awe and acceptance of new discoveries, or her sense of time, history and family. But some are possible to miss, such as her innate reverence for social justice, her biting ironic juxtapositions, or her transparency with hidden places in her heart.

Her words — and the moods she invokes with them — are but one example of the prolific creative art of a girl who never finished high school. The best of Audrey's paintings were sold to all kinds of buyers or given to family. You will see a couple of samples in this volume. But imagine if we could have included recordings of her singing the songs I can still hear, in a voice that borrowed from and rivaled Sarah Vaughan, Sam Cooke, Ella Fitzgerald, with a combo of musicians at a local nightclub!

But, dear readers, it is her love for words and writing and especially reading that she instilled most deeply in her children. We had to work hard to keep up with her voracious and diverse devouring of literature written by women and feminists, Native Americans and naturalists, best sellers, historians and the classic authors. As pre-teens, we were reading MacKinlay Kantor, Carson McCullers, Margaret Fuller, James Baldwin and Elie Wiesel.

I hope her writings and her voices will be an inspiration for us all to read and reread, to open our minds to learning, to share what we think and to add our own voices to the conversation.

Spring

1
Rejuvenation

For an ageless infusion
of March energy, fly a kite

In some countries, kites are flown at a mid-January festival in celebration of the passing of the sun from Capricorn into Aquarius, when the gods are awakening from their long sleep. Winter kite-flying is an ancient ritual I can understand. In this especially gray time of year, when little snow has come to soften the hues and define the drab season, I feel a need to seek the shore and fly a kite.

To fly is to embrace the very soul of Nature. The ritual is rejuvenating. With each launching there is an immediate infusion of energy throughout the body, a heightening of the senses.

The first time I sent a kite aloft was on a Maryland beach beside a summer sea at dusk, with a full moon peering over one of my shoulders and the great orange sun setting on the other. Kites buzzed all around the beach and lay about the sand like enormous fallen butterflies. Most were fancy kites with complicated controls manned by real astronauts. Mine was simply a single-line Delta, a small, graceful, silken little thing with very long tails, its stripes of bright primary colors a reflection of the scene. It had the look of an Aztec god as it snapped smartly in a sharp wind, soared high and swayed sensually in the darkening sky. I was struck with wonder.

A 40-ish friend, wearing a bikini and rollerblades, remarked that the kite was perfect: one even a child could fly. Her words failed to diminish my joy and feeling of accomplishment. I was a child. I, in my late 60s and recovering from a serious illness that had left me with a lame leg, I—who had been told by those who know about such things, that I might never walk properly again—did not dwell on what I could not do but only on what I could. I might never ride a bike again or wear a pair of roller blades (or a bikini). But I would stand barefoot in warm velvet sand in the glow of the sun and the moon and fly a kite.

It was something I had longed to do all my life. As a child of seven, tagging behind my older brothers with homemade kites slung smugly over their shoulders, I had begged to fly, but that was a part of their secret power they would not share with a mere girl-child. So I stood alone in the middle of a shorn field and watched them from afar. I shivered in the cold spring wind until distracted suddenly by the muffled cries of sandhill cranes high overhead in tangled skeins that filled the wide Kansas sky. I followed the birds until they drifted from sight.

Sixty years later, I eventually grew stronger, and with the help of my best friend—a real flyer—I graduated from single-lines to a dual-control stunt kite, a beginner's Luna I can easily handle alone. It performs with wonderful enthusiasm and a powerful sound like that of swans' wings when they fly very low overhead.

Kiting is a whole new way of communing with Nature: with winds, clouds, gulls and osprey. With each launching comes always that feeling of déjà vu, of rebirth. Perhaps that is why kite-flying is called Fishing for Angels.

March 1, 2001

2
Winter's Perfect Ending

No more snow!

Gosh, I love winter. Snow is falling. Designer snow. A marshmallow snow like that in the movie *A Wonderful Life*. Perfect, happy-ending snow.

I gaze contentedly from my window at the creek that lies beyond. Graceful amethyst rivulets zigzag through floating islands of frosted ice. The usual accessories of the winter scene—assorted gulls and a pair of swans—drift lazily as if arranged by some benevolent entity with impeccable taste.

The door-side scarecrow on my porch wears an elegant mantel of white over her shabby dress. A colorful inaugural greeting is clasped tightly in her arms, and the face of the anointed one smiles frostily from its frame.

All is well. It is the weekend. I haven't anyplace I need to be but here in my cozy house. I will do homemade. I start the cookie dough and set the marrow bones to simmer for soup. I go out to feed the colorful birds nuzzling the panes from a window-side perch, beady little eyes gazing expectantly at me. They are eager for the gourmet seed I serve on special occasions. They are dear pampered creatures.

On the phone, I swap weather conditions with a friend who lives a few hours northeast. No need to check the weather channel and endure negative reports by perky blondes in designer ballcaps standing out in parking lots and on turnpikes. Whatever is happening in my friend's part of Pennsylvania will soon come down this way. It's as simple as that. Weather really is so predictable.

She and I exchange extravagant adjectives about the snow, which is softly falling now in a carefully orchestrated manner. She reports that a flock of robins just vacated her yard an hour before. I exclaim that they are already here! Right in my backyard! And isn't that some sort of record for bird flight, for heaven's sake? She agrees and we hang up.

Returning to my window view, I find that the snowflakes have metamorphosed into steely pellets of sleet. The fluff has flown, and I hear the ominous pinging of a dreaded wintry mix against the window panes. The birds have fled with my euphoria.

Reality is cold and calculating. Within minutes, winter's visage has turned gray and hateful.

I dial Pennsylvania for another report. My friend says the branches are bent with ice outside her window. At that moment, the phone goes dead. Our aged furnace makes an audible lurch and a grunt, like someone being kicked in the stomach, as it rattles to a stop. Silence descends. Darkness and cold settle into every corner where lingers the scent of half-baked cookies. Out in the creek, the swans are little islands racing Bayward through the amethyst maze. The gulls are gone.

My cell phone rings. It is Pennsylvania calling. A grim voice says: *Gawd I hate winter.* I agree.

March 3, 2005

3

It Was a Bad Winter

Consider it a new beginning

As a protest against life and everyone in it, I had intended to remain wrapped in a down cocoon until spring.

"If it weren't for global warming, we would really be in trouble," said my roommate, in the aftermath of one of the killer storms that held Southern Marylanders hostage for most of February.

My roomie has a wonderful way of finding something positive in every catastrophe. He is that kid who received a bag full of horse manure from Santa years ago—and is still looking for the pony. Thank goodness for people like him. They make up for us pessimists.

Thus at noon he coaxed me from my room, where I had intended to remain until spring when, I hoped, this vendetta of winter directed at me would end. And besides, it was a great way to lose weight.

I yelled at him to give me some *good* news even if he must lie. But honesty is another of his sterling traits, and he told me that our power company had never heard of Drum Point and we would never have electricity again. Before he retreated hastily from my darkened room, he left me a pail of hot bath water and told me the sun was shining.

During the long, brutal siege of powerless gray days, the sun had not once come to our aid. Neither had the old reliables that help us through the last dark weeks of winter. No crocuses. No lilac spikes of rosemary blossoms. Even the snowdrop—the true symbol of hope, the small white flag of truce—was long past due.

The ice would remain for a while, but it was dripping. It was yielding to the powerful sun. Disoriented people were milling about in the streets squinting at the bright light, but now a sense of hope softened the madness in their eyes. They knew we could make it with the sun on our side.

Forgive. Forget, I tell myself. Consider it a new beginning. A chance to be rid of the relics that died quietly in the freezer. Petrified leftovers; all that bluefish we have been passing off for years as faux crab cakes and bass to out-of-town house guests.

I'll start life over with brand new veggies. Toss out the capers and the tiny gift jars of corncob jellies and the moldy wedges of weird cheeses that have hung around the fridge waiting for a party.

Beyond my window, a spunky boat plows her way up the creek with another boat in tow. I watch her waver as she rounds marker No. 9 in the ice. She quits, backs up, revs her engines and roars right through the mess merrily on her way. She is the metaphor for our winter ordeal.

March 7, 1994

4

Of Eagles and Politicians

At close range we show our frailties

In June of 1782, the Continental Congress selected the bald eagle as the emblem of our nation and made it the central figure of the United States of America. At that time, Benjamin Franklin remarked that no bird with such bad habits should represent the country. William Bartram described the bald eagle, in his diaries of April 1773, as an "execrable tyrant who supports his assumed dignity and grandeur by rapine and violence, extorting unreasonable tribute and subsidy from all the feathered nations." In other words, the eagle is not popular in birdland.

There are still some who question the choice of a notorious predator and sometime-felon with perpetual bad breath as our representative. Actually, considering the shenanigans of some politicians since Ben's time, the eagle seems an appropriate choice.

Ironically, they who bestowed the honor failed to create laws to protect the eagle. Not until the latter part of the past century was such protection provided, albeit inadequately: There are loopholes, called variances, that allow the powers-that-be to overrun his habitat almost at will. Thus, even though the eagle has rebounded, the national bird is said only to have "stabilized—probably plateaued" here in our region.

In the 1970s, when we thought his kind might expire, there was some discussion of a successor. Who would carry Jupiter's thunderbolts in his stead? The popular dove, long a cliché for love and peace, is a hypocrite, said to be quite vicious beneath its perfectly groomed plumage. A blue jay is all bluff and empty rhetoric. The raven is majestic and articulate but is said to consort with seers.

Thus the eagle remains on the seal regardless of an occasional lapse of morals. But what the heck, everyone does it. Right?

When I came to live here on the Chesapeake, 20 years ago, sightings of eagles were few. Old-timers who had seen them waddling about the beach, or clomping about on residential rooftops munching on an enormous fish, entertained us with such droll tales.

Then, one spring day, an eagle came into my midst. At the tip of a tall oak in my neighbor's yard, he perched and preened for half an hour while we watched at close range. Regal and unruffled, he ignored an angry flock of crows and gulls protesting his presence. When finally he took flight, his broad wings were wide as our country lane where he flew very low for a block before taking to the blue yonder. He was huge, his white head luminous as moonlight.

I was reminded then of a close encounter, in 1964, with that other wily politician, Lyndon B. Johnson. He stood on the running board of a sleek black limo as it slowly cruised the tarmac of an airbase runway. He smiled and waved and paused often to shake hands with many of the small group gathered there. He was Texas-tailored and booted, his trademark white Stetson dazzling in the California sunlight. No matter our politics: We all were pushovers for his brand of showmanship.

To see an eagle soar is to see power and freedom in action and to understand why his supporters of 1782 fought for him as their choice. To see an eagle at close range is to overlook his frailties.

But, with eagles as with politicians, few is probably better. It would not do to see such a specimen relegated to the status of common nuisance, just one of the masses. And a local power line bearing a shoulder-to -shoulder flock of eagles would not be a good thing.

March 14, 2002

5
The Seasons Are Misaligned

Yet the constellations emerge

in their proper places

There is chaos in the garden where camellias have languished since Christmas: throughout the long, wet weeks of winter, their rosy heads heavy with rain, their satin leaves sparkling with droplets, their presence untimely.

Azaleas bloomed prematurely as well, their biological clocks in shambles, their blossoms sparse and puny.

In place of the cold, clean scent of lingering snow, we had an eerie fragrance of sweet alyssum, the sharp pungency of pelargoniums and flowering arugula from a porch-side plot. Over all was the musty odor of fecundity, of too many things growing out of turn in a strange, extended autumn.

Wizened little violets, ragged and unkempt, roamed aimlessly beside the fences. They had lost their place to sprouts of sedum quite out of sync. The daffodils came early and are stressed, their yellow heads bowed on stems too fragile to support them.

They are tired. They needed weeks of deep sleep beneath a blanket of snow: the rejuvenation of defined seasons, deep-snow winters, ebullient springs, hot summers and chill autumns.

So does their caregiver. She is unaccustomed to pulling weeds and nursing newborns in early March. She has old muscles and stiff joints with too many miles on them.

Is it too late to apologize to Mother Earth for our misdeeds and ask her to line up the seasons neatly, to put them back where they once were? This is what the caregiver mutters as she creeps about the muddy beds, trying to restore order, floundering on soggy ground made even more unstable by the wanderings of the wakeful ones tunneling beneath. They have not slept either; they too need a long rest, she grumbles.

In gathering twilight, she glances anxiously above, at a naked bough on a tall tree where hang the remains of an enormous wasp nest stripped of its silken shroud by maddened winds that prowled the shore all winter in search of a blizzard. The nest is a wondrous work, a simple paper mache structure that has survived the violence of the past season.

The architecture is of another time, a nether world, its perfectly symmetrical rows of cells like those of an ancient cliff dwelling—or a spaceship.

She imagines a thousand pairs of sleeping eyes within the amazing incubator and she wonders what wild winged things it will spawn in the coming spring—if there be a spring.

The daylight lingers, she sees the constellations emerge from their proper places and hears from the nearby marsh the joyful noise of peepers.

And the hive moves subtly to and fro in the windless garden.

March 19, 1997

6
Spring Fever

What's the tonic
for an overdose of euphoria?

On a cold March day she kneels in her garden, sowing summer, dreaming of yellow and white and blue blossoms of Dutch iris filling every bare place beneath the crabapple tree where the things who live deep beneath ate all of last year's crop. They had waited until the plants were in full May bloom, then devoured the root of each one, dragging the carcasses down into their cavern, leaving only a neat empty hole where each iris had stood.

They will not be back, she mutters, ignoring the phantom rustlings beneath the soil where she digs. This year the bulbs will multiply and naturalize like a scene from an English countryside, just as she has always imagined. They will thrive and grow old with her and generations of flowers will live on and on long after she has gone. They will be her legacy.

This year she will be prepared for all catastrophes. She will do all the things for her garden that experts suggest. She will back her car up to the edge of the yard and attach a hose to the car's exhaust pipe. She will block all exits to the subterranean tunnels and flood them with a lethal dose of carbon monoxide, sending the destructive critters painlessly into oblivion.

When the grass begins to brown, she will feed it a tonic of beer, molasses and household ammonia and grow the greenest yard in the entire neighborhood. She will kill all weeds by dosing them with vinegar and her roomie's Beefeater gin. Weekly shots of Jack Daniels will enhance her container plants. A big crop of four o'clock flowers

will bloom all summer amid the perennials to poison the Japanese beetles. These are good things, and environmentally correct. So say the experts.

And she must not forget the bottle of fox urine. Frequent sprinklings kept the rabbits from her flowers all last summer and attracted, as well, a real fox during the following winter to relocate them.

It has taken her years of heartbreaking experiences to acquire all this wisdom. She has done her homework. Actually, gardening is simply a matter of common sense and logic, she muses.

She gazes about the garden where spring is, despite the blustering cold. There, in the creek, is the cry of a solitary loon and the caroling of redwing blackbirds from the marsh beyond. A Carolina wren has slept each wintry night in a pine wreath on the porch. Bluebirds flit in and out of their house by the shore, and small rose finches—eternal optimists—fly about with nesting materials in their beaks. Flurries of snowflakes fall like ghost petals from the barren boughs of the apple tree, and crocus blooms nearby with the last of January's snowdrops.

Two mute swans fly very low over the garden, the whirring of huge wings like those of a great hummingbird. One swan in pursuit of the other, planning a legacy.

This season can be hazardous to one's health. She has overdosed on euphoria. Her serotonin level soars and combines with a smidgen of latent dementia to spike an onset of spring fever. So she returns to her cozy lair to mix a soothing tonic. What shall it be? Sulfur and molasses, dandelion greens or some tender new cattail shoots? What is best for an aged Pisces person, still fruitful with strong-rooted tendencies?

What do the experts say?

March 22, 2001

7

Now We Begin Again

Well–diggers staged an offensive
against my small village

The day of reckoning has come. Things are greening, beginning to bud, and it is time for me to go back into my yard and face the damage of the Great Well Debacle.

It began with last summer's drought, when my roomie became concerned about the source of our water supply. Many of this rural community's wells were failing, and he decided we had better replace our 50-year-old well before it was too late.

Not to worry, said I. There is lots of water left in that place where it all comes from. As I turned on a faucet to make my point, the water came rushing forward.

His pained expression was sufficient response. So the well people were called, and they came to assure us that a new one would be a simple procedure: Just remove a section of the picket fence, a narrow trench would go here, the well head there, and so on. Neat. No problem. Such nice guys.

Then came a rainy day in September with a procession of machinery grand enough to stage an offensive against a small village. This would be only the first stage. Others would follow at intervals. The dogwoods were bobbed, several sections of fence removed, very deep ruts were cut in the lawn and an impressive crater was rimmed with piles of dirt containing remains of my dear departed cat's grave, half the roots of my very old crabapple tree and a mass of pulverized perennials. The yard appeared to have been bombed and strafed. Even a patch of periwinkle I had declared invincible was demolished.

It had taken years to create this humble garden with an authentic colonial ambiance that can be accomplished only with total dedication to indifference by the gardener. It took the diggers only moments to destroy it all.

I had planted aristocratic European lilies one year. The directions had seduced me: Care Free! (My kind of goods. I go for wash and wear. Precooked. No complicated instructions; I never read them. It simply makes sense just to wait until something goes wrong). The soil was drought-dry that autumn, so hard I was certain I heard my lilies mutter "Mein Gott! This is no garden, it's a !#*! parking lot!" But they stayed, and they had grown and blossomed. Now this.

My only rose bush was a survivor. It fled to the top of a tall conifer in a sheltered corner where it dropped blood-red petals well into winter. The tree is a perfect trellis, though I hadn't known the poor rose was a climber.

Now I join the walking wounded amid grave-like little hillocks in the yard: clumps of dazed and disoriented daffodils in full bloom; the rose bush proudly showing tiny leaf buds. I clutch a clod of soil in my upraised fist and I shout madly, bravely, (as Scarlett in the devastated fields of Tara): "As God is my witness, we will never be thirsty again!"

And I grasp a rusty shovel and begin.

March 23, 2000

8
Gone Wild as Wisteria

Spring exudes the
hallucinogenic scent of purple

Many autumns past, a tornado swept across this point of land where I live on Mill Creek near Solomons Island. It snapped off the tops of big pines as if they were saplings. Ugly splintered trunks were left all along the lane, and for weeks the residents sawed and dug up stumps.

However, one neighbor chose to leave the tall remains of a ragged stump standing in her yard. She planted a wisteria vine next to it, and the following spring it was engulfed in a drift of purple blossoms and graceful green tendrils. It was a highlight of the season that always left us neighbors a bit crazy. Some say, you know, that the scent of purple is hallucinogenic.

That is the way of the prolific wisteria, And so it was that a scraggly old loblolly was for many years after, a reigning beauty of spring on our lane. It was eventually felled by a callous 'dozer, but it is a legend still.

In one of John Burroughs' books, *Ways of Nature*, is an amazing account of the odyssey of a honeysuckle vine that found its way through a crack in the window of the naturalist's study one summer day. It crept about the sills and ventured finally into the center of the room where it "beckoned" (according to the author) for support. By late October, it had bridged three of the 10 feet between it and safety, before it fell to the floor. Burroughs believed it "knew there was a support somewhere near, and it tried all ways to find it."

It is a wonderfully eerie account of the stamina of a vine and the wiles of Nature. A touching tale. I think of it always when watching the wanderings of wild clematis and very old rambler roses.

Yes, we all are aware of the aggressive behavior of "bad" botanicals on the "wanted" lists, such outlaws as kudzu and honeysuckle. It is probably only a matter of time until wisteria, with her wandering ways and strangling tendencies, ends up on the post office wall. But gosh, she is so beautiful.

Meanwhile I will continue to admire her as I travel the back roads of Bay Country in spring. In many parts of the rural south, her handiwork is remarkable along unlovely roads. She feeds hungrily on neglect, climbing in and out of derelict houses, festooning the sagging rooftops with billowing hillocks of purple petals. The vines seemingly snap up eyesores as soon as they appear. When spurned, she simply rambles aimlessly on through the woodlands in a wide wake of lavender.

Imagine the potential of such a vine: It could be the perfect solution to non-biodegradable roadside litter. Let's try turning it loose in a tire dump, or among the decaying cadavers of old cars that slumber beside our highways or crowd a neighbor's yard. Better still, let's train it to wander through all the abandoned strip malls of our suburbs.

Soon is the time of violets, lilac, paulownia and the incredible wisteria, the many hues of purple. But do not breathe too deeply of the powerful scent. It may be hazardous to your health.

April 12, 2001

9
Spring Is on Her Own

Like me, she's one more year

without a cat

A goose-feather snow fell in the first week of April as the greening apple tree in my yard clutched anxiously its nosegays of buds and softly complained. But beneath the boughs, the ground was still merry with periwinkle and a lone tulip prepared to bloom on the grave of my cat.

Spring had always been his favorite season. He had the look of a new lamb as he romped happily about the yard. There were birds to stalk, rabbits to harass and moles to excavate from their catacombs under the lawn. His expertise endeared him to local gardeners, even those who professed to hate cats.

There were boats to oversee. His stubby tail and awkward gait were the traits of his unique breed. He was Manx, descended from islanders, and the sea was in his blood.

That we discovered when he was young, on the October day when a big wooden sloop, bound for Europe, tied up at our dock beside the creek. She was *Amantha*, well groomed and still beautiful in her golden years. The captain was a young Heathcliff, the crew a lovely German woman, her child and a cat. They were a cast of romantic characters straight from the pages of a novel. Our cat was fascinated with them, and he spent every evening of that chill week with all of us huddled around the wood-burning stove in *Amantha's* cozy main cabin listening to sea tales.

Then they were gone: Mere acquaintances who had sailed into our lives and quickly off again into a stormy autumn, leaving us to yearn.

Winter was long and boring, and when spring came our cat took to haunting the dock with a look of longing on his funny, pointed face. He was such an unlikely sailor. One could not imagine him in the boots of a swashbuckler: He was so proper and portly, with ordinary short white fur and varicolored spots. If he had been able to speak, I suspect it would have been with the subtle accent of a British butler.

All that summer he was restless and melancholy and neglected his gardens. He got into trouble on the docks. He boarded boats without permission and took lengthy naps in the captains' quarters. He prowled the gunwales and fell often into the creek. He was a clumsy swimmer, and a ramp had to be built for him.

Once, he was accidentally locked inside a boat for several days, in an old sloop that resembled *Amantha*. Some nights, he would crouch on a low piling and bat at fireflies for hours. And he took up with unsavory critters, nocturnal possums and raccoons. He even kept company with a young skunk for a while. They were sometimes seen at dawn sitting together beside the lane.

Finally he settled down, stayed home nights and seemed content with summer mole patrol and days of dock-dreaming. He slept away the hated winters, and he lived to a ripe old age.

He died in springtime some years ago. A true Gaelic, he was buried on St. Patrick's Day. The Royal Dragoons' Bagpipers played for the service while March blustered about the shore, scattering Amazing Grace notes all the way across the cold blue creek where the first transient sloop of the season lay at anchor.

Now the apple tree moans as rowdy grackles move in amid her blossoms. Rabbits nibble at the new sprouts of phlox, and giant moles happily uproot the periwinkle.

Spring is on her own.

April 13, 2000

10
The Hippies Had the Right Idea

We skeptics neglected
the recycling of good intentions

Once upon a time, before the first Earth Day, there lived in my house one of the hippie kids of that era. He was raised in California in the age of the flower children, and his clothing and hairstyles were considered weird by some of our new Maryland neighbors—as was his high regard for the environment. His appearance was of no concern to me. He was a promising college student raised with a good set of values and high ideals, and so I listened.

I, too, was passionate about Nature, albeit naively so, never questioning the state of her health or beauty. And I became a kind of apprentice to the Hippie. We talked of global warming and recycling. We rescued doomed saplings from the path of bulldozers and transplanted them in other sites that had been devastated by builders. We planted in our yard a vegetable garden and edible flowers.

He taught me to compost leaves and clippings and kitchen refuse. They would evolve into a magic potion to be used to nurture the gardens, he said. (My mother had done something similar in her 1930s' gardens. She also had recycled tin cans and plastic bread wrappers and meat grease.) There is nothing new under the sun, I told the Hippie.

By late summer, my compost heap had become a wart on the pampered green visage of suburbia. It attracted feral cats. (Thus we added cats to our list of recyclables and kept a couple as house pets.) The neighbors suggested the compost be beautiful or be gone—and they insinuated the Hippie could use some tending as well.

I must admit the hippies had the right idea. We skeptics simply got too late a start. All the passion and lofty talk of Earth Day is meaningless unless everyone participates—and we didn't. We neglected the recycling of good intentions. Thirty years later there are roaming truckloads of debris still in search of permanent rest. And the environment faces far more serious threats.

The compost heap seems a frivolous measure in this new age. But I still tend it. It is therapeutic, a part of the maintenance of normalcy, part of a life-giving process that has existed since the beginning of time. My wire bin resides, discreet as a mushroom, behind a hydrangea bush in my side yard. There are no raw kitchen scraps, no predatory cats. The smug gardening magazines tell me the compost will spawn lush blossoms and a lawn to rival any chem-treated yard in the neighborhood. Alas, that is not quite so. But my weeds are really green.

So where have all the hippies gone? They grew up to become useful citizens: teachers and lawyers and stuffy congressmen. Mine is conventionally shorn and tailored now, but he harbors still those weird ideas about the environment. After college, he tended for many years a public health clinic in a primitive village of a faraway country. He lived off the land and taught in the area's first school, which he helped establish. He is one who heard, quite young, what Denis Hayes, organizer of Earth Day 1970, called "the cry of the Earth and came to heal her." Now as an epidemiologist for the state of New Mexico, he ministers still to our sick old planet and the recycling of precious leavings.

April 18, 2002

11
First Communion

Nature spoke to her in a voice
so familiar she might have heard it
on the morning of her birth

In the dim light, the little girl slipped quietly as a cat from her bed, her small brown feet padding across the cold linoleum to the closet where hung her first new Easter dress. A sleeveless, lilac dotted Swiss organdy, it had long black grosgrain ribbon streamers that hung from the gathered bodice all the way to the hem. She felt a shiver of delight as she slipped the silky frock over her naked skin. She was forbidden to wear it for play, but today she simply must.

She opened the screen door, taking care not to squeak it, and sat down on the porch step in the rose-streaked dawn. There was the soft sweet moaning sound she knew intuitively to be that of birds, so familiar she might have heard it first on the morning of her birth. Not really a song but rather a kind of liturgical lament. (It was unlikely she would have known the meaning of such words at her tender age, but who can say for sure?)

The yard was abrim with daffodils and violets not yet fully abloom, awaiting hesitantly the sun. Their fragrance was everywhere, mingling with the mounting sob of the mourning doves. She hugged her knees to her chest, the wonderful full skirt of her dress enveloping her legs.

Throughout childhood, she would hear in the constant voices of doves an echo of that first encounter. It was there in a snowfall of perfect flakes. In her secret oasis of green grass beneath flowering boughs of a sapling peach, new and unblemished as she. And in the boughs of a very old cherry tree where she gathered summer's fruit. It was an awareness that compelled her to scribble tributes to her small world in her very first journals that, alas, were lost as she grew older.

It was then she began to take such moments for granted as life overtook her and priorities of adulthood demanded precedence. But a subtle nuance of nature permeated everything she wrote throughout those years.

And there came, long after, another Easter, in another place far removed from that of her childhood. There she found again, in a humble little garden beside the blue Chesapeake where she had come to stay, the essence of that time long past.

She discovered it at dawn in a newborn poppy with a broken bud shell cupped in pink petals still wrinkled from sleep. In the gnarled boughs of an ancient and ailing crabapple tree where tiny tips of magenta spoke of resurrection. And in the soft, sweet litanies of doves.

There she reaffirmed her vows in the first of many odes to the gentle side of nature. She saw, she listened, and she has never ceased.

April 20, 2000

On the back of this photo Audrey has written "My french dress from the 4th street rummage shop '34 or '36?"

12

This Earth Day, I Am Alive

And perennial as wineberries

The daffodils beside my fence bloom very early each year. This winter I hurriedly picked a small bouquet before a mid-February snowfall, certain the rest would not survive the night. They did. Only slightly bowed, they bounced right back with the first rays of morning sun in the melting snow. They are as all things that live here in my yard beside the creek: sturdy nonconformists.

Now with spring well established they are fresh and abundant, and they toss merrily in the sharp wind that follows me along the lane. I am on my way to inspect a patch of wineberries nearby, the last of many that once lined our lane. Progress has taken a toll of such things, and this clump is especially vulnerable now, located as it is on a choice corner lot.

I catch sight of the thicket and my heart quickens as I see familiar graceful canes flushed rose with a delicate fuzz that identifies their kind, a lone touch of color in the grey landscape. But I note with alarm the small mound of raw soil and some freshly cut trees, signs of a perc test, which heralds the destruction that precedes construction.

It is inevitable, I murmur, as I kneel on the hard cold ground to lop a tip of a cane for my own perc test. I see the wonderful green within the stem, and there is the sharp prick of a sticker through the worn leather of my glove. It is a good thing, this strong urge of life in us both.

I pause to recall a steamy July day last summer when my young houseguest came running excitedly into the house to fetch a basket and declare that the wineberries down the lane were ripe. I told her to pick enough for a cobbler as I rummaged quickly in the pantry for the proper ingredients.

She is my youngest grandchild, who introduced me long ago to wineberries and taught me how to distinguish them from the more common variety of wild ones. Their fruit is juicier and much larger, said she. And the canes are all covered with rosy fuzz to disguise the vicious stickers. She is a born wood-nymph, raised beside the towpath along the Delaware River's shore in Pennsylvania where all things thrive in the rich black soil.

I close my eyes to summon the image of her as a toddler, all golden and new as the pup that bounced alongside her at the edge of the berry patch. She gleefully picked and shared berries at random with the pup, and both went to bed that night with a tummy-ache. Even at that tender age she knew where her range hens laid their eggs and just where grew the finest morels. She is a willowy teen now, yet not too sophisticated to run barefoot through the woodlands in search of precious things.

Dessert was a great success that day last summer, with only a few scraps of fluted leaves and a couple of teensy winged creatures (necessary additions to an authentic wild cobbler) amid the berries and cream.

The cold seeps into my knees; it is time to leave, and I rise clumsily from the patch, an aged arthritic wood sprite trying not to attract the attention of curious passersby. I limp homeward with the scent of warm cobbler and a sweet Bay summer hovering in my memory, and I whisper a plea to those in charge of perc tests and bulldozers: Err here. Err there. But let the berries be ...

April 21, 2005

13
Against the Tide

*In the azalea orgy of Bay Country
spring, I made a garden of common
descendants of humble immigrants*

I first met azaleas in the spring garden of a deserted plantation in Alabama where they had grown untended for many years. It was a fairy tale kind of place, the azaleas so tall that they met high overhead, forming a pastel tunnel of color over a weedy brick path strewn with petals. As I wandered through the froth of blossoms, I vowed to someday own some of the beautiful flowers.

I went on to live in a succession of barren places. Brown places where azaleas appear only in florists' shops and where we stacked and painted tumbleweeds green for a Christmas tree and sowed a lawn of gravel and cactus. Indoors, I raised a 10-foot philodendron, and some sort of weird plant once sprouted in the floorboards behind my sofa. That was the extent of my gardening.

When, finally, I left the desert to live in the South again, I arrived in the midst of spring, smack in the middle of azalea time. Up and down the lane paraded southern belles in pastel gowns, the marvelous azaleas, the darlings of all local gardeners. The yard I had acquired had only a couple of scrawny trees and a crop of wiregrass and dandelions. But no matter, I would simply raise a big family of azaleas. It must be easy, I thought. Everyone was doing it. Everywhere was a frenzy of azaleas, a kind of Bay Country bacchanalia.

So I became a faithful participant in the spring ritual, only to have the fruit of my labor die in infancy, to see their tiny fluffy bonnets wither and fade in the beds. I was cursed and barren. I was the only one in my neighborhood without an azalea. Grief spawned envy and humiliation as I failed again and again. Knee-deep in blossoms, my neighbors smugly asked, why?

I retreated indoors to the comfort of the lanky philodendron, and we discussed alternatives: We could return to the desert where we fit in, or we could go back to the nursery and adopt some of the other poor plants that lay forgotten in their beds.

Thus I took home phlox and daisies and lilies and other common things that haven't an aristocratic ancestor to their name. They are not the coveted progeny of princesses descended from a sun goddess. No esteemed botanist scaled a sheer mountainside in a far-away county to bring them to us. They are the descendants of humble immigrants who came here in the holds of ships and wagons. We are kindred.

They love my yard. They revel in the heat of the humid tidewater summer and blossom in untidy profusion where an azalea would never dare show her fragile face.

So it is that I have coped. Yet sometimes in the midst of the orgy of blossoming that is Bay Country spring, I yearn still for my very own azaleas ...

April 29, 1997

14

Things Just out of the Dark

My legs are roadkill
and potholes returned to light

This is the season of beautiful things, of daffodils and snowdrops and crocus, of promises just out of the dark, dank places where they have lain dormant all the long winter awaiting the nurturing warmth of the sun.

Alas, it is also the season of legs: ungainly spindly sprouts covered with fuzz and goose bumps searching for sunlight to make them beautiful again. But there is no promise in a pair of ancient legs, no blossoming or rebirth.

When you first take them bare into the spring light, what you see is what you get. They are like roadkill and potholes—the unlovely harbingers that never improve.

It is always a shock when I unveil the legs for the first time each spring. You see, I always thought old age was a self-induced condition. (That is the logic of youth.) I thought I was immortal.

I can't imagine what went wrong. When I tucked them away last autumn (in baggy jogging pants that have never known a good sweat) the legs didn't look bad. We did what we always do in winter. Nothing. We crept listlessly about the house and occasionally (on a bad day) kicked things with the attached feet.

We perfected the art of retrieving small objects from the floor with the toes, so we wouldn't have to rise often from our fireside chair. Sure, the legs spent a lot of time bent at the knees in front of the TV. (It snowed a lot, remember? They weren't about to go outside for a walk and break a femur or something—they are fragile, of indeterminate age: somewhere between golden and badly tarnished.)

Mine couldn't go to aerobics with all the other old legs, for they have flunked every class in the tri-county area. They have never known right from left.

Life is unfair. For example, when I was young the bikini had just been invented and I couldn't wait to wear one. But I and the legs were too skinny. Then suddenly, we were too plump. Just how do these things happen, for heaven's sake?

Logic says that during the transition there must have come a time when we were perfect. Did it happen in the middle of the night? Did we sleep right through it? Whatever, I never got to wear a bikini.

So here we are, putting on our short shorts, preparing to intrude on another season. But I've heard a rumor that's making me nervous: It seems these ugly sprouts are so prolific they have been declared a blight on the greening of America. The lawn service companies have put them on their hit list along with chickweed and dandelions and other exotic species that don't match the zoysia and the azaleas: If they aren't green, if they won't bloom, they're out of here.

April 30, 1996

15
Lilacs at Last

Their time is too brief

Spring came early this year. When I returned to Bay Country in mid-April from several weeks away, I found it in full swing. The crabapple tree beside the creek was already dropping its petals and the daffodils were past. My neighbor's azaleas sprawled beside the fence, gaudy undulating entities in full bloom, spilling color everywhere.

(I own no azaleas. They have found my yard unsuitable, except in blossomtime when they slip their bonds and slide between the pickets and flaunt a kind of in-your-face arrogance to remind me of what is missing from my simple garden.)

No matter. I had eyes only for a lanky lilac that has been freeloading in my yard for a decade. Something was wrong: It was covered with flowers, great clusters of lavender.

The bush was a gift from a dear neighbor. I carried it home on a sweltering summer afternoon, the tall, limp, form cradled like an overgrown child in my arms, its dangling limbs trailing in the dusty lane. It was the offspring of a full-figured beauty that had long presided over her garden. Thus I had high hopes for the foster child as I carefully propped it in a hole beside the fence.

I fantasized about all the lilacs I had known long ago: spectacular specimens that filled dooryards and cellar holes along Kansas country roads. But my bush remained lethargic, bringing forth only a few blossoms in spring as if to justify its existence. Finally, last year,

I came close to destroying it. Instead, I pruned it brutally and let it be. All winter, the naked grey stick-figure outside my window stared accusingly each time I peeked around the casement.

Now it stood tall and fully foliaged and crowned with royal purpose. I walked slowly through the rain to bury my face in a wet clump of fragrance to realize the fulfillment of a fantasy. And I recalled the petite lady who had given me the bush: she, in yellow boots and rain slicker, tending in all sorts of weather the flowers and wild ducklings that were her greatest joy.

She has gone now, the garden abandoned. But the dowager lilac was heavy with blooms this past spring and her flowers thrived still along the lane. In gardens of friends are her lilies and violets and yucca—and nests of ducklings. And there is cherished autumn clematis from the vines that covered her small pavilion beside the cove where she liked to sit at dusk listening to the sleepy conversation of mallards and watching late summer hummers flit among a galaxy of luminous starflowers.

I mourn the passing of lilacs. Their time is much too brief. They could not linger for Memorial Day. But soon there will be pink roses and laurel—and autumn garlands of stars—to grace a new grave in the country cemetery nearby.

April 2000

(unpublished)

16
My Oracle

Though we change with the world,

we are both amazingly sturdy

I brought her home one autumn day, quite on impulse: a sweet-faced scarecrow the size of a seven-year-old child. She was clad in baggy burlap knickers and a blue plaid shirt the same shade as her big painted eyes, and she wore a dainty straw hat. I gently secured her to the light-post in my front yard where she would gaze past a border of sprawling chrysanthemums to a blue cove across the lane where swans coasted among rafts of colored leaves. I tied a pumpkin to her arm and readied her for Halloween.

I expected she would disintegrate in the blustery weather, but she is amazingly sturdy. In December I traded the pumpkin for a jaunty red-peaked Santa hat and gave her a sheaf of frosted pine boughs for the Christmas season. She wore a valentine in February and a bouquet of daffodils on the first day of spring. She is my harbinger of seasons and special events.

Summer passed, hot and dry, and there came the horror of 9/11. She proudly accepted a new American flag like all the others on our lane, and it remains a constant. We bonded—life is pretty dull here in the sticks—and she has become a sounding board for one who is accustomed to talking to herself here in this wilderness of apathy where I reside.

War was imminent, and during the months of negotiations that ensued she became a sly effigy in a mask and cowboy hat. A series of placards pinned to her shirt expressed our views (hers and mine) of opposition. The messages changed quickly from: NO WAR to GOD BLESS OUR TROOPS ... and finally, in capitulation, simply a plea for PEACE.

But no one heard. Thus she stands now, shed of the grim disguise and wearing red, white and blue ribbons on her dilapidated straw hat. Stress has aged her moon-face, but her flag flies bright and fresh as ever. She is cast as a grieving mother presiding over a small headstone at her feet, which reads: REST IN PEACE. So she will remain at her post through Mother's Day and Memorial Day. She will don a gold star soon to symbolize loss, a sacrifice faced by parents since time began. Politicians make wars. Our kids do battle.

I am grateful my kids returned safely from their wars. Many years—and wars—have passed since my son fought fiercely in the A Shau Valley with the 101st Airborne troops in the spring of his 21st birthday. In that same period—1968 to 1969—his father, a bomber pilot and combat veteran of World War II and a professional warrior, came safely home as well from combat in Vietnam.

I have taken the liberty of quoting from The Washington Post—and the works of Shakespeare—these appropriate lines:

> He that outlives this day and sees old age
> Shall stand on tiptoe when this day is named.

Growing up as I have, surrounded by professional warriors, I have noted that our veterans often are overlooked when the smoke of battle has cleared and the parades have passed by—even when they stand on tiptoe.

May 1, 2003

17
Mama Was a Realist

*Despite myself, I have not
wasted her lesson of practicality*

Each spring, I remember Mama when I first go into my tiny dooryard with eager plans for my garden. I remember her when I prowl the local greenhouses where I hover over mandevillas or fondle some jasmine—then move quickly away.

Mama was a realist; she originated the word *practical*. She raised a passel of kids in the midst of a Dustbowl and a Depression. Her garden consisted only of edible things. If it couldn't be eaten, she didn't plant it.

I was a child with a fierce passion for flowers and color, and I would rush to the nursery to buy fragile little seedlings of something exotic and Southern for her on every special spring occasion, hoping that she might transform our sun-cracked yard into a real garden. Like the neighborhood dooryards where flowers crowded petal to petal in summer, where lived generations of perennials whose ancestors could be traced back to the first Conestoga.

Mama always graciously accepted my gifts and dutifully planted them in the hard ground, where they promptly disappeared. All her green-power seemingly went into the oasis of vegetables. Precious water was reserved only for them.

Some migrant moonflowers managed to establish a camp beneath the dining room windows, and an itinerant mock orange bush bloomed clandestinely beside the porch. A colorful colony of portulaca lived quietly among the little wooden crosses of the pet cemetery in the back yard, where our cats lay in eternal sleep. (The life expectancy of a Depression cat was brief.) But the remaining yard resembled the sad sepia scenes one often sees in photographic exhibits of grim-faced children and Midwestern moonscapes of the 1930s.

Mama was a woman of culture. She played piano beautifully by ear. Just whistle a few bars and she would produce the entire score (as the saying goes). Yet she actually traded the old upright one spring for a coop and a clutch of chicks (to go with the veggies). In fact, she was always swapping things. There were no heirlooms to haggle over when she died. She had made so many trades that the surviving pieces were all strangers to us.

Years later, when Nature acquired a more positive attitude toward the Midwest and we children had all grown up and left, Mama swapped the home place for a cottage on the edge of town. There she grew roses on an arbor and daffodils and a wonderful alley of peonies in the midst of a lush green lawn. She had a proper glider swing and a healthy cat. But no veggies.

Mama follows me still to the local nursery, where exotic plants, like schoolyard vendors, beckon from every corner. I just say no and leave, laden with utilitarian daylilies and hardy herbs—plus a few packets of moonflower seeds and some portulacas. Teetotalers, all.

The past few years of droughty Bay Country summers have revived my respect for the ancient well in my yard. But lately, I've begun to hear a ghostly voice that gently suggests I simply dump the flowers and plant instead some okra and greens and perhaps acquire a couple of hens—and that banty rooster I have always wanted.

May 6, 1999

18
Visited by a Comet

I shared six weeks of Hale–Bopp's
2,533–year orbital cycle

The quintessential comet, the wanderer of the 20th century, has gone on without me.

I first saw it in early March. It hung over the creek right outside my bedroom window: highly visible, looking roundly pregnant. With its short tail of tentacles like that of a sea-thing, Hale-Bopp seemed a great pulsating phosphorescent cone-jelly, another iridescent flower of the Chesapeake night.

It was a week before I would see it again. By then it was sylph-like, as if it had indeed given birth, its gossamer tail long and trailing as the veil of a bride.

We lost touch as it moved about and clouds drifted in and out. But in early April, it came just after dusk to peer into a westerly window. Posed high above the black limbs of trees, it seemed smaller, more distant, but stunning still, sometimes with star-baubles entangled in its gauzy raiment.

I quickly became one of the abnormally obsessed; a last look at bedtime was a treasured ritual. Often, I lingered late on the front porch, watching and shivering in a chill blizzard of apple blossoms that inexplicably opened weeks too soon. Nothing had ever altered the cycle of the old tree, but there was confusion—disorder— in this spring.

On many nights, the stars shone like spotlights and the sky glowed with the eerie luminescence of a full moon even when it was still just a cold sliver in the bare boughs of an oak tree. Orion lingered as if awaiting something as Big Bopp presided.

The Flower Moon waxed full, then faded with April and the comet. The night sky returned to normal and spring went on about her business at a hurried pace.

And in secret woodland places where cults of wildflowers had waited with bated breath—deep in damp holds of ravines like earthbound arks—choice specimens of Solomon's seal, bellwort, maypops, trout lilies and wood sorrel resumed blossoming in a great rush of relief.

Belief, in the absence of compelling evidence, is called faith ...

May 20, 1997

19
Keeping Faith

In Flanders field the poppies blow
Between the crosses, row on row
That mark our place ...

And so it was that we buried him on a perfect May morning—an auspicious day just past the 20th anniversary of the end of the Vietnam War and just before the half-century commemoration of V.E. Day—in the holy burial ground at Arlington National Cemetery. In that garden of stone, the rolling hills are awash in springtime with blood-red azaleas and the bittersweet notes of the bugler's Taps.

Overhead, rumbling Hueys in parade dress—the shining black airborne hearses of Nam—saluted the brave Marine who had come late to join the other members of his platoon in this Flanders field. The awesome wounds he sustained in Nam had taken longer to bring him down; his war had taken longer to win.

Afterwards, I went home to plant poppies in my small garden. Misshapen little tubers, each with a crimson promise, would be a front-yard memorial to a friend and his fallen comrades. There were just enough bulbs for a single platoon (if I didn't plant them wrong-side up).

In Greek mythology, there are many tales of beautiful young men who died in the springtime of life and returned as flowers. Some of the earliest heroes were said to have been sacrificed by elders who believed their blood would make the barren land fruitful. The elders were comforted by the scarlet acres of poppies that sprang up—in justification of the sacrifice or a convenient coincidence—to blanket the scene of the slaughter.

As time passed, people could not recall the details. All that was cruel would be forgotten. They would declare that the earth hadn't needed the blood of those young men after all. It was just a sorry mistake.

So what about all those fields of blood-red flowers, those oceans of poppies?

The more things change, the more they stay the same. Here we are, thousands of years later, sowing seeds still. Watching the retrospective groveling of past policy makers. Hearing the threats of scholars who would rewrite history and lose our heroes among the pages of self-righteous rhetoric. And so it goes.

But on this Memorial Day, I will do as I always have. I will perform loving rituals of remembrance, honoring my heroes with flags and flowers in little country cemeteries.

If ye break faith with us who die
We shall not sleep, though poppies grow
In Flanders fields.
—John McCrae

May 25, 1995

20
Ducks and People

Neither make easy neighbors—

On the heels of spring came courting mallards to my yard. One drab little brown hen waddled up the hill from the creek with a swaggering drake in full spring splendor. They checked out the prime real estate under the azaleas and the spreading juniper while I watched with apprehension, hoping they wouldn't choose the barrel on the dock where the geraniums grow—where crows held last year's company picnic.

Little did I know what I was in for when I came to live with ducks. They seemed so charming at first. But mallards are not the best of neighbors: They are capricious and unstable like—well, like people.

The hen is a real control freak. She sweetly selects a site and builds the nest; then, in a fit of post-partum rage, kicks out the drake when the clutch is completed. This makes him angry, and he often returns with rowdy peers who behave in an irresponsible manner, resulting in some carnage and a lot of non-consensual acts of a disturbing nature. All this right outside my window.

Often a hen disappears in the melee and never returns to her newborn ducklings, who wander the neighborhood untended until, one by one, they are all gone. We are talking anguish here: lots of wailing and hand-wringing by us shore-dwellers.

One summer we adopted a day-old duckling abandoned on our doorstep. When we sought advice from an expert on such things he told us to let it be. Leave it to nature. We asked if he thought that should be the rule for all starving little ones worldwide. Are we to ignore famine victims? How about oil spills? He hung up on us.

So, with the help of a small dog who cuddled and attempted to nurse it, we tended the duckling until it was grown. We shed tears when it flew happily away.

That was the same summer a hen died soon after her clutch was hatched in a neighbor's yard and (I am not making this up), the drake returned to raise the youngsters.

We are seeing fewer ducklings in our creek each year. Refuge is scarce on our bulkheaded tributaries where predatory creatures, chemicals and indifference are taking a toll.

Thus, despite the anguish and aggravation—the charges of anthropomorphizing—I suppose we shall continue to "upset the balance of nature" by offering friendship and emergency care to the ducks, by sharing amiably a habitat which, after all, belonged to them in the first place.

May 26, 1994

∞ *Audrey Remembered* ∞

Marta Lynch
Granddaughter No. 13
Daughter of Peg Scharmen Lynch and Michael Lynch

I remember grandma as a BLT and Dr Pepper for lunch on a hot, heavy summer day. I remember grandma as the only other family member who would do her nails with me. She always said I had her hands.

I remember grandma showing me off to her friends, when I caught a tree frog in the retention pond behind her nursing home. She said, "Marta, you should have been a naturalist."

She didn't know I was in the midst of an existential-career-change crisis. A month after she died, I started a new job as an Urban Farmer and Environmental Educator. She's with me whenever I take a moment to appreciate the natural world, which is a lot these days.

I never got to tell her the significance of her words, but I think she knows.

Summer

1

Luna Moth at Flower Moon

Opportunity is a brief moment

A full Flower Moon—pearl with a golden aura—hung high over the tall pines beside the country lane where I live. Midnight was warm and sullen, heavily scented with honeysuckle and laurel, pale and silent. The season was yet too new for the racketing of summer insects.

Long ago such a night would have been filled with the melancholy calls of whippoorwills. A century and a half ago, they were so numerous on the mid-Atlantic coast that Thoreau was said to have named this final moon of spring the Whippoorwill Moon. Alas, they seek the solitude of deep woodland and seldom are heard where progress has drastically altered their habitat.

While mourning the demise of whippoorwills, I probably missed the debut of a Luna Moth, the loveliest of all the great American silk moths. She craves the moon's light, and so do I. Awakened by the same energy, led into the white night by an inexplicable force, we may have crossed paths in some shadowy place. For that is where I found her the morning after.

She may have been drawn to the sweetgum tree that towers above my yard. (This tree, much disliked by many for its pesky seeds the size of golf balls, affords a spectacular autumn coat of many colors unequaled by any other.) Whatever: There she lay at dawn in the damp grass, her sea-green gossamer wings imprinted with the mark of the moon and edged in mauve; the swallowtails scarcely marred. Her plump little body, white and furry and perfect, with golden feather-like antennae above onyx eyes; the legs intact and peacefully folded in death.

I held her gently in my hand and felt blessed to have found this ephemeral moonchild from the pages of a fairy tale.

A sister contributor to New Bay Times wrote recently of me in a brief bio: "She waits for her stories, and when they come fluttering like a butterfly she scribbles them down before they disappear." Perhaps. But too often I am victimized by daydreams or moon madness. I miss more butterflies than I catch. And so, the elusive Luna.

The pale moth shares now a shelf beside my desk with an entire collection of mummified mementos: untold tales of sand and sea and woodland, of aborted inspiration and opportunity lost.

June 22, 2000

2

The Unwelcome

Value is weighed in the scale of righteousness

The paulownia tree in my yard beside the creek scattered its faded blossoms all about the hillside and on the gray-green water where a quartet of newborn swans came to feed with their proud parents.

A family of mute swans was a lovely sight amid ripples of purple petals. The adults were extremely vigilant, and the male rose suddenly to chase away a pair of Canada geese who came too close. In a snow-flurry of feathers, he returned to his brood and they lingered in the dappled shade of the tree.

I was told many years ago by one who knows about such things that the paulownia—which turns out to be highly valued for its wood—is a trash tree. I went ahead and planted it anyway. The expert was right. The tree creates an amazing amount of lavender litter and the sweet violet scent of its fluted flowers drifts brazenly into every open window of my house on soft May nights.

There were no trees on this land when we bought it 20 years ago. They all had been bulldozed by the previous owner, who left only an ancient crabapple with careless habits. It tosses pink petals in every direction in spring and in autumn drops its golden fruit all over the ground, which attracts such winged nuisances as yellow grosbeaks and cedar waxwings.

All my teenage trees have a dark side. Nearby is a sweetgum with seedpods like huge spiked ball bearings; a sloppy locust whose wormlike spring tassels shed and clog the down spouts; and some untidy dogwood with

psoriasis. I clean up after them all—just as I have always done for my roomie, my children, my pets and other cherished essentials who also have a dark side.

Now I must go down to greet the swan family beside the shore and inform them they are pests, near top on a list of environmental nuisances with a dark side. They are accused of destroying the submerged aquatic vegetation of the Chesapeake (what little we humans have chosen to leave for them). SAV is their main diet.

They trust me, thus I advise them to fly away home, wherever that may be. But they do not know about migration. They were brought here against their will. They have no other home. I mention ethnic cleansing and collateral damage, catchy all-occasion euphemisms for the new millennium coined by those in charge of everything.

The little swans frolic unaware, ignoring me while their mother beams and father hisses threateningly as if he understands every word. I speak of ancestors who came here against their will and of those already here, for centuries, and how they were relocated. But the swans soon grow bored with my sermonizing and paddle serenely away through the fragrant trash of the paulownia.

I watch them disappear around a bend of the creek, all asparkle in morning sunlight, and I wonder if they might escape relocation and simply be allowed to fade gradually away—like the beaches, the woodlands and the shellfish, whose fate has been decided too by those who know about such things.

July 1, 1999

3
Accounting for Summer

We are resilient—until we are not

The woman is at work in her garden on a summer day. There is a scent of sea from the creek that is lazily lapping the bulkhead. Offshore, a transient trawler crouches in the heavy heat. The scene is blurred bottle-green with humidity. Like California summer smog, she muses.

She frets because she has yet to see a baby mallard in the creek this season. Mute swans paddle beside the shoreline, and she can see that one of their quartet of young is missing. She wonders if the others will survive the onslaught of hot-rodding personal watercraft, the latest man-made threat to this popular Bay tributary and its occupants.

She kneels among the daylilies, humble field flowers that have invaded her garden and grown tall and disorderly. Their blooms have faded, their time is past, and so she prepares to trim them to make way for the hybrids, those she calls every-other-daylilies. They are disciplined summer bloomers and uniform in height. Thus for a brief time, the row beside the fence will look as a proper garden should.

There are gaps among the perennials, and she fills them with slightly bedraggled plants she has brought from the garden shop. They have a weary post-solstice appearance. Nothing is sadder, she thinks, than these shopworn flowers no one wants: plants with a withered expression of disillusion. But they will rebound, she says, as she tucks them snugly in place.

Gardening is solitary, and so the woman does a lot of musing aloud, to no one. Much miscellaneous trivia passes in review.

Summer is good. Crabs are scarce but sweet and heavy this year. The garden has never looked so good (but that isn't saying much; it is, after all, a simple one). There have been nurturing rains to prepare it for the cruel whims of July. The yard burgeons with newly fledged birds. There are thrush, titmouse, cardinals, and a second batch of bluebirds is hatching in the house beside the creek. This is her first year to see a young titmouse: tuftless, skinny, gawky and curious as first graders on a field trip. Each creek-summer brings new surprises.

She wistfully recalls the recent fledging of one more grandchild who graduated from university. His was a circuitous route to the podium, as harrowing as a baby bird's. His father, too, had taken the long way to his college graduation 30 years before, one that led through Southeast Asia and the A Shau Valley. Thus they all felt a rush of gratitude to be present at this one.

She idly wonders why she has never seen a killdeer here in lower Calvert County. They are abundant in the meadows of St. Mary's County just across the river. And there are meadowlarks there as well. None here. Why?

When she was in old Ocean City last month, a pair of killdeer bobbed happily about the wide lawn of a big white frame house where she vacations. According to her hosts, the birds are regulars there in the bustling, congested area at Seventh and Baltimore streets a block from the seaside boardwalk. The birds lay a nest amid the bluestone of an adjacent parking lot where passersby look out for them. (It really does take a village.)

The hatchlings immediately flee their nest for the alley behind, and they obviously survive there amid moonflowers and rambling roses and sparse patches of tall weeds, surrounded by horrendous traffic.

Silly birds: They could be in Rehoboth or Bethany for heaven's sake. But the woman, too, is a honky-tonk sort of old bird who prefers the surreal summer symphony of that beach town to any other. And so she understands.

Summer is a time of resilience, she remarks (she likes to philosophize). And she lays her trowel aside and wipes her brow and spies the first Japanese beetles of the season on the ragged leaves of her favorite bee balm plant.

Well, so much for resilience, says she, as she reaches for the bug spray.

July 5, 2001

4

My Granddaughter's Future Husband

The perfectly matched pair of dragonflies met over Venus flytraps

A small girl with sea green eyes who has come to spend part of a Chesapeake summer at my house says, "Grandma, what you need are some Venus flytraps to get rid of these tiny flies you complain about."

Then the wise womanchild carefully explains that such plants are carnivorous and catch wee winged pests in their leaf lobes and digest them. She says all they do is sit on the windowsill and eat.

What a clever common-sense solution, and well worth a try, I muse. I have been plagued for years by obnoxious summer insects that resemble fruit flies, whose source may have been a wheel of Mennonite cheese (delicious!) brought here from down Mexico way by one of my grown kids.

Anyway, they have resisted all manner of preventive measures. They ride on one's eyelashes, crawl into the ears and gawdknows where else. I don't even want to know what happens when one disappears into a nostril; I have read far too many tales about parasitic insects.

So it is over the river and into the new Lowe's store on opening day for the little girl and me; and there in a fairyland of miniature succulents is an entire colony of tiny flycatchers, sly and smug and menacing even in their smallness. There, as well, is another bright green-eyed child like mine.

He is perhaps nine (as she is), a tall and handsome lad and very articulate, and soon we are engaged in an animated conversation about fruit flies. (He includes me as if I were a regular person, not just someone's old-geezer grandma.) He has had much success with these plants, and he shows us how to choose one with large lobes and upright stems. The two nature-wise children have an instant rapport. They are as a perfectly matched pair of beautiful dragonflies.

We put three plants into our cart as he disappears into the crowd. Wait, I shout, but he is quickly gone. This is all too serendipitous. The two children are made for each other, and I want to call him back and ask where he might be in 2010.

But of course I do not. We add a hammock to our purchases and head home.

The flytraps are comfortably ensconced on the windowsill in the back kitchen, happily munching. The fruit flies decrease in number overnight—and seemingly have lost interest in my orifices.

As for the green-eyed girl, she is on the beach in search of the "teeniest ever" carapace of an infant horseshoe crab, and the largest of sharks' teeth. Or she is wandering down a country lane where the sweetest wineberries grow.

July 27, 2000

5

St. Francis of Summer

She is one with this gull she watches

The small girl, her eyes reflecting the sea beyond, sits amid the maze of sandcastles and moats she has created on this sullen summer morning. Above the boardwalk, kites in glorious colors gasp for air; and in the far distance she sees the faint outline of a Ferris wheel so tall that one can see all the way across to England. A sign says so.

Her older cousins have grown bored with the castles and left her for the surf. She watches them slither like seals in the bottle-green shallows where a sand bar stretches.

All around her is a vast, gaudy carpet of sunbaked bathers as far as the eye can see.

And everywhere are the gulls. Ubiquitous birds of the coastal summer. Crowds of crying, restless things. Many, gray and grizzled old men; few, fresh and new. Charming panhandlers; shopping-center gulls who forsake marshes of grass and mallows for the largesse of beach and boardwalk.

All morning they have milled about the little girl's castles, stalking her pet hermit crabs, staying always out of reach. But there is one who lingers close, young and new as she, not beach-wise. He wears a stunning black cap and orange bill, delicately curved. He is white and shiny as satin. His eyes are sparkling onyx.

She is a child of Nature, with sea-eyes and sun-burnished skin golden as a pecan's shell. She has grown up with country roads and intuitively knows already, at the tender age of seven, where to find the first violets, ripe wineberries and fairy-rings of morels—and how to rig

a sling for a crippled chicken. Hers is a deep respect for the small creatures of her world.

She is one with this gull whom she closely watches. He is likely (in bird years) the same age as she. There is a bond and she covets him, longs to pick him up and pet him. But he moves quickly, gingerly away. Thus, she plots to accomplish the feat.

Nearby is her cup of French fries, grown cold and sandy, a favorite of beach birds. She spreads a sodden towel across her lap, covering all but her head, and lays a path of fries from the edge of the towel to a spot where her hands are hidden. And she sits still as a statue while the bird gradually shortens the path. Eventually, he follows the trail to its end and right into her arms, where she wraps him carefully and cradles him gently and carries him back to the cottage.

She and her excited clutch of cousins, talking all at once, recount the story of the capture as they hand him happily to me where I sit on a porch in a patch of pink mallows. With a sense of wonder, we pass him from one to another. He is calm and friendly with that innate trust of the very young. He shows us his lovely red, pointed tongue, and we marvel at his fragility. Tough little sea bird, sleek as a rose petal, weightless as down.

With a gentle nudge, the child releases him, reaching high as her short arms allow. And we clap and cheer as he rises jubilant on shining wings from out of the mallow.

Nature has indeed bared her soul to us all, and our hearts soar along with the gull—over the alley and the steep rooftops of weathered old clapboard houses and to the sea.

August 20, 1998

"St. Francis of Summer" earned Audrey her initial first place in Maryland, Delaware, D.C. 1998 competition, the Oregon Press Association judging.

6
Caught in the Doldrums

It happens every summer

These are the times that try the very soul of a sailor. These are the times when a choice part of the Chesapeake summer is swept into the doldrums and clasped in the relentless grip of something called a Bermuda High, an area of stagnant air that may strangle the entire Atlantic Coast for weeks.

I pay no mind to inclement weather. What's the use, say I. What will be will be and there's nothing I can do about it. I just use as my guideline the seaman's ditty that goes: Dark sky at night—sailor's delight, (or is it red sky at dawn? Oh well—you know the one I mean). Anyway I have this kind of kinship with Nature (she has her own reasons for her actions and we should support her) and I often side with her (she being a sister and all) except, of course, when she really gets out of hand. Then I become irritable. And she did go a little too far with this recent Bermuda High thing.

You see, I had plans. And all of a sudden this stifling weather interfered. But the problem (according to my consultant on weather) is that it takes a real jolt to get rid of that kind of high. The ingredients are: (says my consultant) a nuclei, a lifting action and moisture. The makings of a major storm. I have to wonder if it is worth a hurricane just to clear the air. Isn't there an easier way? Can't we come up with something else, I asked my consultant?

His rather pained reply was unintelligible—made so by mine. I reminded him that there was our old cruiser, with her carburetor newly rebuilt and her steering cable replaced at much expense and labor, languishing at the dock—impatiently tugging at her lines and shrugging off swallows—all dressed up and nowhere to go, so to speak. (She had planned to be bound for some distant Chesapeake tributary by now.) I asked the consultant just what he intended to do about her.

He replied that we would just have to forget the cruise until Nature decided how to rouse that supine jet stream from its stupor without wreaking too much havoc. And, he added, she (a sister and all) would probably take her own sweet time doing it. (This is one sarcastic consultant.)

Golly, I wouldn't like to be responsible for such decisions. Wouldn't you hate to be in Mother Nature's shoes?

So it was that I spent a precious part of summer awaiting the arrival of the nuclei, the lifting action and the blessed moisture. I roamed the beach, hoping for some sign of a horizon long lost in a milky-green Bay where rafts of jellies drifted and workboats listlessly trolled. In my wilting yard, the banshee wails of cicadas declared the end of the world while the dock swallows went right on teaching their young to fly; and goldfinches frolicked merrily in the hardy zinnias—gathering seeds and nesting material—their faith unshaken by a simple drought.

In due time Mother Nature made a sensible decision about the Bermuda High. She scoured the sky and restored the horizon and stirred up a breeze to ruffle the water and left a promise of gentle rain. She accomplished in short all the things she does so well (on a good day). All those things we Chesapeake people covet but simply take for granted—when they are there.

Gasping days of drooping sails and drying things. It happens every summer ...

July 29, 1993

7
Spiderlings

In autumn ritual, perfect tiny creatures
spin skyward on buoyant silk

Spiderlings drift lazily above the autumn garden, a melancholy place of fragile things: wan daisies, fading phlox and browning lilies. Fine serpentine threads hang from the yellowing boughs of the crabapple tree and wave from the seeding zinnias. They are gossamer umbilicals, clinging to my hair and following me about.

It is said that nearly all spiders emigrate by air. The babies, no larger than a pinhead, spin silken strands to propel them skyward as soon as they hatch. They are as the down of dandelions, ballooning just a few yards or, according to some records, as high as 20,000 feet above the earth. It is part of Nature's plan, a perfect ploy to perpetuate. They must go far from home for the first hunt, and if they stay too long in the nursery they will become bored—and hungry—and eat one another.

Alas, the ritual of the newborn is requiem for their mother. In the midst of the aging flowers, where little crab spiders linger late in ragged roses, are shrouds of tattered silk, husks of the summer tenders of webs that hang now in ruin. Ariadna, Argiope, Zygiella: They are gardeners with beautiful names that belie their features. Their names spin images of a nether world, conjuring visions of fairy tales.

Stirred by a morning breeze that lifts gently the spiderlings to safety is the frail corpse of a great black and yellow Argiope, swathed in gauze, presiding still over

the lilac spikes of speedwell beside the fence. One of her kind was the nemesis of my childhood, who guarded jealously my favorite summer gardens. Argiope still has my respect. The weeds grow high beside her once-elegant web.

Nearby is the veiled tomb of the small rotund one who lived summer-long among the pink geraniums, who rose at dusk to weave a magic orb on the moonlit porch for a small audience of children. They watched her amazing artistry while weaving webs of their own, tangled tales of spiders we have known: of a brown recluse in an innocent garden of yellow jasmine; of the black widows, glittering onyx gems that haunted our house on a faraway desert; and of a comical furry tarantula that left a patch of wild verbena to become a friendly house-pet for a while.

I told them of the ghostly arachnids that roamed an old stone house deep in a tropical canyon in Mexico where I once stayed. I never saw them but sensed their presence everywhere—in courtyard gardens of cascading flowers, in the dewy ruins of a web in a mango tree, in the scattered remains of a meal in a dark corner of the kitchen.

They are the silent ones. One hundred thousand species are believed to share our world.

Thus I bless the vigilance of Nature, who has saved a few for my garden. She made possible this autumn ritual of perfect tiny creatures borne on buoyant silk, the gauze of Mary that legend says came from the shroud of the Virgin on her assumption into heaven.

Let us wish them a prosperous journey, said the great naturalist J. Henri Fabre.

For what would a garden be without its spiders?

August 20, 1997

8
The Moon's Flower

They rise like ghosts of my childhood

In the midst of a sultry night, I slip out into the darkness to see the flower. She is the first of the season. Her fragrance, sweetly Southern, mingles with the salty scent of the Bay. The half moon has set and the sky throbs with stars; a conversation of crickets is punctuated with the squawks of a restless heron in the shallows nearby.

Born of a beloved bud laboring long in the rose-streaked dusk, ephemeral babe brought forth in a convulsive crescendo of cicadas, the powerful prelude to a lullaby ...

I look warily for the large spider who summers here on the porch. She is busily tidying her web of trophies; thus she pays me no mind. I keep an eye out for the black snake who lives in the yard, and hope he is not nocturnal. He is a friendly creature, but I want no chance encounters.

Since summer's advent (when I plant each year the odd beanlike seeds of moon vines in garden corners and clay pots) I have awaited this moment. I have tended them zealously—protected them from predatory bunnies and beetles—and watched the tendrils climb patiently skyward in search of the mother. With gentle nudges and occasional boosts from me, they are propelled to the balcony, to the pinnacle of a flagpole there, which marks the end of their odyssey.

They are special, blooming as they do in the ashen remains of August. They bear saucer-size moons, luminous, cool and pristine as their namesake, each etched appropriately, mysteriously, with a star. They seem oblivious of drought, their enormous leaves fresh and green in a landscape that has been withered by a great golden orb and bleached dry as the spider's prey.

The flowers are ghosts of my childhood, the same that blossomed beneath my bedroom window throughout the dust-bowl summers of the 1930s. They flourished in a sun-cracked yard where seldom grew anything, their heavy fragrance drifting whitely as an apparition through the darkened rooms of the weathered old house.

So it is, here in another time, another place, they bloom again outside my bedroom. And here, still, is a child's sense of wonder in the presence of ephemera.

Abandoned by the night in a pale mauve dawn, a dying blossom in a shadowed bier, mourned by Argiope, a great green moth and the face of a child damp with tears ...

August 23, 2001

9
Visitations of a Strange Summer

Wonder meets the wonderful

These are the mad dog days of summer, I grumble, as I sit on my porch on a sweltering afternoon and watch strange beetles creep dazedly from fissures in my sunbaked yard. They are big insects the color of dull jade and marked with burnished gold. Are they simply cicadas in a stage I am unfamiliar with? Or are they mutant harbingers of Armageddon?

The butterflies in my garden seem fragile and faded as old quilt blocks. The perennials along the fence are deformed by drought and vicious winds. The blue basil I planted last year has returned in the guise of lilac bergamot, which is okay with me because that wild fragrant herb is what I wanted in the first place but couldn't find anywhere in spring. My garden consultant tells me the basil may have "morphed." That is a scary thought. But who am I to question it? It has been that kind of summer.

Over in the corner of the yard the old apple tree is amazingly green despite the heat. Beneath the spreading boughs are a birdbath and a damp patch of periwinkle vines where lives a box turtle. It is a magical tree, a haven of rarities. One winter it hosted a flock of yellow grosbeaks; in another, dozens of flower-eating golden waxwings during a late snowfall.

Suddenly there is a flurry of birds in and out of the boughs. A crazed mockingbird—the neighborhood terrorist—is stirring up trouble. He screams and all the other birds fly about hysterically. So I rush to see what is going on, expecting to find one of their own in crisis.

A false alarm, I mutter, as the birds flee and all becomes very quiet. I pause to peer up into the canopy of tangled branches. There, staring back at me, only a few feet above, is a trio of fuzzy grey owlets. Three cunning catlike faces with enormous yellow eyes. One swivels its head constantly as if it has just discovered how to do it, and I am Alice in Wonderland. Nearby, a russet-hued parent, handsomely feathered and with tiny white horns, keeps one eye on the brood and the other on me. She is only slightly larger than the petite babes. (My intuition told me she is female.)

I am seeing something unique. Little screech owls. My first. I have since learned that they are congenial, can see in brightest sunlight, are fond of water and have been seen bathing in backyard birdbaths. They like apple trees and eat cicadas. So!

Whatever has drawn them, I will them to stay. It is the sort of neighborhood I would choose to nest in if I were an owl. It is close and cluttered. There are few tall trees, some of which have been altered by recent development. But it is a peaceful peninsula surrounded by water and there is a perfect dead hollow tree across the lane, thoughtfully spared by the new owner of the property. The owls may have been born there on the shore.

I summoned my friend, my roomie, to snap photos and assist with an interview with the little cat-owls. (That is one of many colloquial names for them.) They moved confidently about the boughs during the afternoon, and the parent eventually assumed a position (of annoyance?) on the trunk of the tree where she resembled a perfect carving, so rigid was she. Toward dusk, she grew restive and the family conversed in soft trills and tremulous purrs as they gathered together and flew off into the afterglow of sunset.

The babes returned, alone, a few nights later, pausing curiously at the backyard birdbath and perching briefly on the eave of our house. Lightning flickered on the western horizon as the sky darkened. A molten-gold moon, one night from full, rose determinedly over the trees in a race with gathering clouds. As a long-awaited rain moved in, the moon disappeared with the owls.

The owls have not come again. But they are near. I have heard their shrill little cry in the pre-dawn stillness of the creek shore. Sometimes I step outside to answer.

August 29, 2002

10
Elegy for
a Chesapeake Fish House

So venerable, so vulnerable

The building clings stubbornly to its place beside the wide mouth of a river that feeds into the Chesapeake. It is a typical crab house, purveyor of Bay bounty, a very old sprawling farm structure once encircled by wetlands of willow and mallows and rushes. Now the wetlands are occupied by new upscale buildings with trendy Palladian windows like arched eyebrows that lend a perpetual expression of disdain to the facades. They stare haughtily at the shabby old-timer, as if questioning his right to be there.

The old place has a wonderful wraparound porch with wooden tables where we sit in summer to watch the river run. It is a friendly refuge where mallards, rowdy as small children, race about the table legs and mingle with diners. These ducks are descendants of those we first met many years ago on this porch, hatched amid the pink petunias and marigolds in whiskey barrels beside the front door.

At sunset, we watch the gaudy remnants of the day promenade across the horizon, littering the water with glittering scraps and casting a rosy glow on a lone egret bound homeward. The mallards, suddenly grown sedate at twilight, murmur drowsily as they make the final rounds of tables and greet patrons or pause to annoy the gull with the broken wing who is mending here on the porch.

Schools of stripers come to beg at the railing where the waves bound off the pilings. They are big beautiful fish, frolicking on the surface as they snap up breadcrumbs. We lean precariously over the rail to marvel at their behavior: nobility begging like feral cats at the fish house door.

So it is that we linger longer than usual on our last night beside the river, in the glow of starlight with a hint of autumn in the air, to ponder the fate of fish houses and porches, of crabs and oysters and beggar stripers. So much a part of the Chesapeake is this venerable building: a kind of earthbound reef long nurtured by spot and roe and megalops. A refuge of mallards and mending gulls, a place of torn screens and picnic tables spread with faded oilcloth, a homely place redolent of crab and creosote and cigarettes. A way of life.

When we return next summer to this broad, wandering stream with the sweet breath of the sea, there may be only the crowd of Palladian faces to greet us—triumphantly blocking our way to the tomb of an old friend, one we took too much for granted.

August 30, 1995

⌒ *Audrey Remembered* ⌒

Lisa Smith, Granddaughter No. 8
Daughter of Debbie Scharmen Smith and David Smith

My fondest memories of Grandma Audrey are related to nature. Sitting in her garden watching hummingbirds, rescuing turtles from the road and musing about the daily soap opera playing out among the creatures in her yard. She's the one who taught me that bald cypress trees are most beautiful in the dead and drab of winter, and a black widow spider's life is worth fighting for.

Her influence is apparent in her children, who raised their own to also marvel at and respect nature. Now that I am older, I realize the value of growing up in a family that casually personifies plants and animals. The idea of a plant being ornery or a tree being wise was never a foreign concept. I've come to find that the world benefits from the personification of nature, and people tend to hesitate to destroy something that they no longer consider an "it."

I still make time to sit and watch the soap opera playing out among the hummingbirds in my backyard, and think of her often.

Autumn

1
Little Girl Found

She had hidden in my granddaughters

She attends a weekly art class at a senior center where she produces portraits in pastels, a wonderful medium of chalk in lovely colors that, when rendered on rough paper, resembles delicate watercolor.

Her classmates ask why she always paints the same subjects: little girls doing various things, holding an armload of ducklings, grasping a struggling calico cat, or snuggling a great Cochin hen with a fluffy tutu of golden feathers. The classmates murmur that all the portraits resemble her. She should try something else as well, such as landscape or still life, they say. But she continues to recreate from photographs of her little grandgirls. *Perhaps I am searching for something,* she murmurs.

She once was that small person, and she has tried often to contact her in meditation, at night when sleep is slow to come, or while daydreaming in a hammock on a perfect summer day. The child lurks within, so why can she not be summoned, she wonders.

She remembers her in summer as a skinny kid walking to the last day of school, toting an enormous bouquet of flowers for her teacher. She is sobbing because the iris all have broken necks and the blowsy roses are dripping petals rapidly.

She sees her gathering grasshoppers on the riverbank to sell to fishermen, dropping the bugs into a green Mason jar and whining because they are spitting brown juice on her clean dress.

Or perhaps she is readying her firecrackers for the big day having hoarded them for weeks in a box beneath her bed where she has hidden them from her brothers. She counts carefully the ladyfingers and sorts black tablets that will become curly charcoal snakes when lighted with a match, fragile things that crumble in a slight breeze and soil her hands. Her passion for neatness always has been a point of derision from her siblings, long before it acquired an acronym and a cure.

So now she has discovered the chalk and set out on an odyssey. It is the velvety soft kind her brothers once used to scribble on the sidewalks. She never joined in. She paints happily and recklessly with the messy stuff, which gets under her nails and on her face. But she doesn't even care. Her OCD is in remission, and she has finally summoned the little girl in the process. Subtle traces of her are in each rendition.

She sits among them as she writes and they stare down from dusty frames, all big-eyed little women with Mona Lisa smiles. Not a marketable painting in the lot. No matter. They have served a purpose.

September 1, 2005

2
Autumn Sharpens Our Senses

We grow alert to what is here
and what is going

Around the autumnal equinox, the season reveals itself in subtle ways. No matter the place, autumn's advent is defined by a certain aura that brings a quickening of the senses—anticipation tinged with melancholy. And so it is here in Chesapeake Country.

The goldenrod blooms and the first crimson leaf from my ash tree appears magically on the front doormat—like a calling card—filling me with unease. I need to grasp summer's shirttail as it slips away. I need to see the golden meadows of late summer cosmos, the crimson-eyed rose mallows thick in the salt marshes, the wild clematis that wanders restlessly along wooded bands. I need to follow the haunting summer song of the Chesapeake that beckons me seaward.

We unslip the *Cardinal* for our cruising adventure.

Crossing the Bay to launch from Crisfield on the rising tide, we thread our way through the winding marshes of Broad Creek and across capricious Pocomoke Sound toward a 10,000-acre wetland Eden, Shad Landing, in Pocomoke River State Park.

A thin river winds a dark and deep course from the Sound to Snow Hill through 30 scenic miles of salt marshes until dwindling to a trickle a few miles from the waters of Chincoteague.

This is the Pocomoke River, a mystical place where great hardwoods and feathery cypress conjure fantasies of wood nymphs and fairies. Eagles, herons, kingfishers, flycatchers and warblers thrive in this opulent wilderness. Such spots aren't to be hurried; this is a slow day's cruise.

Our old Chris-Craft cruiser takes us all the way to the upper river. She is well behaved, maintaining a leisurely pace and controlling her wake to keep from disturbing the delicate shoreline and tributary tranquility. The *Cardinal* clears bridges that bar tall-masted sailors. If the captain keeps a sharp eye out, she'll also avoid the sand barges that travel back and forth between Shelltown and Pocomoke City.

Fair-weather cumulonimbus clouds in a bright blue sky accompany us all the way. At Shelltown, a tiny village at the mouth of the river, least terns rise up from a tottering dock. They dip and soar with the elegance that has earned them the name sea swallows. Through the wide mallow-marshes of silken grasses and satin flowers, they follow us until the river narrows and the forest closes in. Suddenly the terns are gone.

My first glimpse of the other cardinal comes just beyond the city.

This cardinal is a flower, our only red lobelia—so rich a shade the entire plant is often stained with it. It may be a survivor of warm eons before the glacial epoch, for biologists believe that hotter suns than ours made that intense color. The flower's flamboyant hue, brighter even than scarlet, make it a seductive beacon wherever it grows.

It grows sparsely on the Western Shore, but here in the shallows of the Pocomoke it has found an idyllic haven where it may keep its feet wet and its flowers crowned with sunlight. Thus it blooms in stunning profusion well into autumn.

Lush mallows, golden water lilies, jewelweed, blue pickerelweed and exquisite gypsy clematis share the late-summer scene. All along the river the sweet fragrance of this wild flowing vine hovers over the dusky water. It clambers everywhere amongst the ragged pines trailing lavish garlands of lacy white blossoms as if determined to beautify, singlehandedly, the entire shoreline.

We spend nearly a week in the upper Pocomoke, dinghying amidst the floating islands of flowers and listening to the lamentations of cicadas. When we reluctantly head home, the trip back down the river is just as idyllic. Amid the cypress knees, flocks of Canada geese talk of autumn, and crimson sparks amid the trees speak of a pending conflagration. Autumn in this vast forest is spectacular.

I recall a line from Thoreau:

How early in the year it begins to be late.

September 9, 1993

3
Autumn's Winged Blossoms

Bouquets of monarchs and golden birds cling
to threadbare stems

Now is the time of winged blossoms—a kind of resurrection of a dying garden—when butterflies and golden birds come to brighten an untidy plot.

I have left the dried remains of August standing in the yard to feed the goldfinches that are still raising their young. So it is that the seeding sunflowers—threadbare plants with withered petals and bowed heads, which no respectable gardener would claim—are graced daily with new yellow flowers.

Butterflies come to cover the scars of phlox and sedum and near-nude rose bushes that send forth still a few tattered blossoms. Bouquets of monarchs and yellow swallowtails cling to the fragile stems.

Pokeberry bushes that crept into the yard midsummer were allowed to stay. Their blight-free foliage, graceful burgundy stems and lacy white blossoms freshen the ragged garden, and the plump purple berries are a tempting attraction for migrant birds. I once saw, alongside an autumn county road, just such a bush covered with cedar waxwings like great golden flowers. They paid me no mind when I stood an arm's length away. I could have picked them from the branches and carried them home in a basket so sated were they with fruit.

One of my pokeberry bushes has grown in just one season to a height of 10 feet. It has the girth of a sapling and wears a disguise of white star clematis. My neighbor eyes it anxiously as it hangs over her fence.

Winged blossoms love wild things. The clematis is full of the largest bimbo-bees I have ever seen, shiny black-and-yellow button blossoms. And several years ago, a late autumn vine of fox grapes draped on a loblolly beside the road attracted a rare rosy dozen of pine grosbeaks. They lingered long while I watched at close range. Later, a neighbor tidied up the easement, and the grape vines have never returned. Nor have the rosy birds.

Perhaps I will add grape vines to my garden next year—and some milkweed, too.

So gather your bouquets of autumn blossoms while you may, of butterflies and golden birds and perhaps a ruby hummer or two. No need to tidy the garden; the black frost will tend to that much too soon.

September 17, 1998

4

On Finally Seeing Pikes Peak

And the stories I imagined while waiting

She was 10. Her lean little frame tanned from summer, her straight dark hair sun-streaked and newly bobbed. She wore a starched cotton dress that was too long and new shoes from the secondhand store. The shoes were molded in the shape of the previous owner's feet—alas, very unlike her own. But Mama assured her she would grow into them eventually.

She was as tall and gangly now as the sunflowers beside the dusty path to school, and the realization left her feeling melancholy, blue as the giant morning glories that clung to the flower stalks. She was dreading the first day of school and The Essay: the inevitable annual account of What I Did Last Summer.

She had never been more than 40 miles from home. Her aunt, who lived in nearby Kansas City, invited her each summer for a brief visit, and it was great. Auntie lived in a fine house on Cherry Street. One could see the glow of the city from there. Mama said she was "well to do." Her house had a screened sleeping porch on the second floor, kind of like sleeping outside, but without the discomfort of pesky insects. That was her room for the duration of the visit, and she also got to drink all the Pepsi she wanted.

Auntie took her to Loew's Midland Theater downtown, the most elegant place she had ever been: all gilt trim and red velvet draperies. They sat in the balcony in plush loges and watched a movie. On the drive home, through a rough part of town, she saw old men sleeping on the sidewalks. Auntie told her they were winos and please not to stare.

Thus she had written about it last autumn. Her jaded classmates liked the part about the winos, but they yawned and snickered through the rest. Their dads worked for the railroad and had free family passes for vacations. They traveled all the way to Colorado and California in fancy Pullman cars. Some even had been to the Chicago Stockyards. How could she compete with that, forheavensake?

She complained angrily to Mama and demanded to know what the heck was Pikes Peak where all those kids claimed to have been. Mama said to pay them no mind. Anyway, she added slyly, there is no such place.

This year Auntie had been ill and there had been no trip to the city. She would just have to write about the family reunion she had attended in a pretty country churchyard nearby where there were rambling roses everywhere and a creek for wading. Her cousins had come all the way from Tonganoxie and Lyndon, and the aunts made wonderful Concord grape pies and special fried chicken, from scratch.

She sensed a good tale there. She had watched often the cruel ritual of preparing the hens for cooking—the wringing of necks and scalding of feathers—and she always ran away before it was finished.

But it was impressive, and she would embellish a bit. (That was one of the new words she had discovered recently.)

So she assembled a plot in her mind as she strolled on through the blue morning that suddenly glowed rose. She always was happiest when composing.

The story was a smash hit. Those snotty kids were mesmerized by a gruesome description of decapitated chickens and voodoo rites and a near drowning in the creek. Mama was angry when she read it, but teacher gave it an A-plus.

Life passes quickly after one turns 10. And so the little girl grew up and married a traveling man and they lived in many places—but never near Pikes Peak. Then suddenly last summer, a very old woman by then, she suggested they stop by there on a trip West.

It was okay, but really no big deal. She and the white-knuckled driver and their dog had dizzy spells at the summit, and it was cold and slushy and very crowded.

She wished she could have seen it when she was 10.

September 19, 2002

5

The Condition of Our Old Boat

He says she should be repowered.
Shouldn't we all? I say.

She is a Chris-Craft Commander 32 with a Fiberglas hull her captain declares is the same design as the gunboats that patrolled the Mekong Delta in '68. The year she was launched; the year he spent in 'Nam.

Twenty years later she came to him—both past their prime by then—and since then they have gone a lot of miles together. He is still in pretty good shape, but she languishes dockside, despondent, not really wanting to go anywhere or do anything. She has taken to breaking down often under stress. Most recently in 100-degree heat on a summer Saturday in the rough rapids near Sandy Point on the Patuxent.

That comes with age, I tell her. It's time to slow down. I say not to worry; she can still lead a useful life as an extra bedroom. She can spend her golden years at the dock with friends who love her. She creaks complainingly in response.

I ask her if she has a living will. Her captain/doctor (although one of the best in his field) has pumped a lot of time and money into her bilge. *Is that what she really wants?* I inquire.

Then I confer with him, the master mechanic, who speaks of past treatments, of new points and risers. I have never learned captainese and his terms are so much Greek to me, but I nod sagely and acknowledge his thoroughness, his expertise.

Then he says she should be repowered. Well, shouldn't we all, I say. She needs a double transplant, he says. I say let her go peacefully; such drastic surgery will be painful and expensive for all of us. He says I have lost faith in his doctoring. I remind him that it was just last year that I designed and sewed a fitted sheet for the unwieldy cushions of her V-bunk. If that wasn't faith, what was it?

How old is she in people years? I shout. And he puts on his gloves and stalks back into the examining room.

In a state of denial he bought her, just last month, a new fish finder. Why? I whined. She is too old and infirm to troll and all the fish have psoriasis anyway. He replied that she has many miles left in her—and so have the fish.

So I capitulate. Who could possibly undermine such optimism? Even though I see major heartbreak in his future, I admire his determination.

He postpones surgery and applies more Band-Aids and lots of hope: his faith as unfaltering as the cadence of cicadas that herald the end of the season, the winding down of cruising time. The days grow cool and crystalline on the Chesapeake and the old Chris-Craft strains at her tethers when he finally says—yet again—she's as good as new and ready to go.

October 8, 1997

6

We Walk in the Footsteps of Ghosts

Point Lookout has seen too much

to rest in peace

Here on Point Lookout there is a pall of sadness over the last bittersweet days of October. Empty is the osprey nest atop a piling just offshore. Now departing terns, who summer nearby, cry as they sweep low over the white lighthouse guarding this southernmost tip of Maryland's Western Shore.

Bordered on the east by the Chesapeake Bay and on the west by the broad Potomac, Point Lookout is nowadays a 500-acre state park, a favorite of fishermen, campers and nature lovers. Migrant flocks seek cover in the wide marsh. Clouds of transient monarchs pause to graze the goldenrod.

Yet this is a shore with a dark past.

On the path beside the river, golden leaves scurry beside me and crackle underfoot. The path is deserted, yet I pause often to peer over my shoulder because I am walking in the footsteps of ghosts.

My path leads through the well-trod grounds of the Union Army's Civil War Camp Hoffman. By war's end in April 1965, 52,000 men had come through this notorious prison site—the North's largest. Twenty thousand Confederate soldiers were interned here, in a space prepared for half that number. Nearly 4,000 perished under appalling conditions.

Today's pine-scented path meanders to the fort and stockade. At the shadowy glade where the prison pen once stood, some imagined presence draws my glance

sharply to the dark corners. The path continues toward a swampy place where smallpox victims were isolated; today, I do not hear their cries for help. Abruptly, the path ends at the burial ground. These dead have found little rest.

They have been interred and disinterred and moved so often about the camp that only the skulls remained intact. The Civil War made the Point a hospital for Union troops. After the Battle of Gettysburg in 1863, the Rebel camp was added. But long before that grim chapter, this had become a dark shore.

Leonard Calvert, the first governor of the Maryland colony, died young here, on land settled in the early 1600s as part of St. Michael's Manor. His son drowned nearby in Calvert Bay. Virginia Indians raided in 1648 and 1681, killing many of the settlers. After the Civil War, the tradition continued. Many a soul has been lost in shipwrecks on this vulnerable stormy shore, including two dozen who drowned when the steamer *Express* broke up on the beach near the lighthouse in a storm on the night of October 22, 1878.

Horror has mounted on horror until you can feel, hear and see its traces. Point Lookout, says world-renowned parapsychologist Hans Holzer, is the most haunted place he has ever visited.

Wandering apparitions appear on pathway and beach. Ghost lights flicker far out on the water on moonless nights. Perhaps they are the lanterns of prisoners who drowned, attempting to escape in makeshift boats. Until the 1920s' hotel was razed, guests complained of visitors who walked in and out of closed doors. The lighthouse is still visited by a woman, seemingly locked in a basement room, who cries for hours and scratches at the door. A golden-haired young man hides in a closet beside the steps to the light tower.

At one campsite on the grounds of the former smallpox hospital, a bully ghost compels campers to loud, agitated action.

During the past century, the Chesapeake has reclaimed over half of the land once occupied by Camp Hoffman—as if to erase the blight. Few relics remain. If you search, you'll come upon a few reconstructed remnants and impersonal historical markers. Most poignant is the fine, small Civil War museum nestled in a meadow of mallows and plumed phragmites. Here you'll find letters, diaries and pictures: the cherished goods soldiers carry into battle. The tangibles are inadequate; the ghosts are eloquent.

A few nights before Halloween each year, rangers, psychics and local historians recount the stories of those who linger here into eternity. Nature and artifice add eerie effects: Herons squawk in the shallows; a fox barks across the river; the throbbing white light of a strobe illuminates the pale faces of soldiers who re-enact wartime scenes.

October 21, 1993

[136]

7

Clinging to Autumn's Shirttail

October ends in golden rain

Clinging to autumn's shirttail, I follow a brook through the piney woods where jewelweed gleams still along the banks. A few tall spikes of turtlehead remain. Some believe that a sprig of these rare ivory blossoms, so like their namesakes, offer protection from bewitchment.

The path swarms with frogs, black elfin creatures barely an inch long that utter an eerie unfroglike yip as they scramble away. Crows jeer from the treetops, and I guiltily snatch a single magic blossom from the turtleheads, hurrying from the woods into the morning sunlight.

The murmur of the brook becomes an exclamation as it tumbles across the sand and into the broad Chesapeake. Offshore, a lone workboat, like some sea-going pied piper, leads a crowd of gulls across the water. The towering cliffs that rim the beach are streaked with wet ribbons of color: raw sienna and ochre and dusky mauve. Velvet moss and ragged clumps of goldenrod cling to the glistening facade.

Last night's storm has felled a centenarian sycamore. It lies upended on the sand with the rusty gold of its final autumn clinging to bone-white limbs mottled with age. In its time I suspect it has seen log canoes, royal warships, merchants and marauders ply a pristine Bay—teeming with fish —beneath a sky black with waterfowl.

Shouldn't someone say a few words over this noble giant? Not many of its kind remain.

Suddenly the morning stillness is pierced by a sharp report, like that of a gunshot, and a section of a cliff falls nearby. The invading Bay is continuing the disinterring of millennia. In this small portion of soil, with the musty scent of a tomb, are remnants of the Chesapeake's ancestral home: shark teeth, crocodile bones and exotic shells from a tropical sea. They mingle now with relics of the present: rubber sandals, rusting beer cans, plastic bottles and glittering shards of glass. Our legacy—our enduring fossils.

I imagine such treasures being peddled from the back of a pickup truck on a roadside far in the future. Or perhaps at some New Age version of a flea market. I see them languishing in a stuffy museum surrounded by admirers ...

A breeze comes racing along the beach, leaving a scent of death on the fresh salty breath of the Bay. The arcing sun has warmed the carcass of a she-crab nearby; she points a limp claw, tipped with gaudy red, at the smooth water where a murky surf gently rocks a trio of big rotting stripers.

The sun wanders behind a cloud, and the air grows chill. The gulls abandon the workboat and come to scavenge, wildly laughing as they squabble over the stripers. Why is there no mirth in the laugh of a gull? And I turn back toward the woodland trail where the crows, suddenly grown somber, follow me homeward in the golden rain of autumn leaves.

October 26, 1994

8

Transformation

How to become a witch

The old woman was a recluse without a real job. She was a free-lance writer whose days were spent indoors at a word processor spinning tales of gardening. She was a loner who came out only in the dusky part of the day to sit in her messy garden among disheveled and withered things.

Actually she knew nothing of gardening. Her columns were all about why to garden, not how. Her flowerbeds were slapdash plots nurtured only by hope and fantasy, neither of which ever lasted through summer. She wistfully longed to be a real gardener, to hang out with those who belonged to clubs and knew the proper names for flowers and never resorted to the vulgar colloquialisms she used such as snotweed, knotweed and pissenlit.

Alas, she simply hadn't the knack. There was, however, in a dark corner beneath her old crabapple tree, an inexplicably green and healthy patch of periwinkle vines, and it was there she came as the white-hot haze of the Bay Country summer blushed pink with sunset and one could almost see across the creek. There was the feeble song of hot cicadas and a ghostly scent of ragged herbs and four o'clocks spared by a terrible drought. There were goldfinches swinging on tattered sunflowers beside the birdbath. They brought a semblance of normalcy to a summer gone bad.

Then her patch of green came under surveillance by angry neighbors: A furry terrorist had roamed the waterfront community since spring and eaten what little was left by the drought. He never came to her yard. But why should he? she mused. It wasn't exactly a Whole Foods kind of place. No self-respecting scavenger would want to dine there.

The neighbors declared that her periwinkles hid the lair of the terrorist. It is there, below in a maze of tunnels, they cried. The woman laughed and imagined a cozy labyrinth of cunning groundhogs in ruffled aprons and pantaloons, like those in children's books of yore.

But her peers did not think her remarks amusing. A kind of hysteria set in, and evenings brought a crescendo of angry voices and a flickering of torches to the shadowy woodland along the shore. She grew uneasy and hoped the Dog Days madness would soon end.

And it was there, in that controversial patch of periwinkle one night—as the day melted into darkness and no rain fell and a great red Thunder Moon rose in a clear sky over the creek—that she saw the bud: A single enormous pulsating pod among satiny leaves and ready to burst into bloom. She knew it must be a rarity—a night-blooming cereus kind of plant—that just might assure her acceptance into any garden club in the county.

So she filled a rusty sprinkling can with precious water, hope and fantasy (and a generous spoonful of Miracle Grow) and lavishly fed the burgeoning bud. And she was never seen again.

There came, soon after, the rains of three successive hurricanes to drown the terrorist and restore the creek-shore gardens. All but the garden of the old woman, which remains a sad, abandoned place where no birds come and nothing grows—except a patch of periwinkle guarded by an ancient crabapple tree.

October 28, 1999

9
Another Autumn, Another Crisis

The soldier's wife gets back to normal

The pontificators tell us to get back to normal—whatever that is. When was it anyway? Was it a three-day weekend? I think I may have missed it. Perhaps I was out of town. Maybe I simply slept through it one day.

On my television screen is the new normal. I see a precious girl, sevenish, swathed in robe-like garments and gathering yellow bags on a barren desert. The disembodied voice of a newscaster tells me the packages are foodstuffs dropped from the sky courtesy of the USA. On her head she balances a large orange bundle and smiles shyly at the camera as the voice goes on to say that the food gifts include Pop-Tarts, and the Afghan children seem to love them.

Thus I recall another autumn, another crisis, long ago: My own little girl sat with her brothers at the kitchen table in a small house on a desert airbase where we lived in the Southwest United States. It was the time of the Cuban Missile threat. Her father was a pilot, commander of a B-52 bomber, bearer of that era's latest designer weapon. He had gone off on air alert to fly a long and dangerous mission, and she was sad. She refused to eat her supper, and I scolded her with that old chestnut of a tale about war-torn countries and starving children who had no food at all. She began to sob as she replied: "Please Mama, send them this pea soup."

I couldn't help but smile at the wonderful simplicity of her logic as I comforted her.

That war didn't happen. Her daddy came safely home, and her life returned to "normal."

So it was that I went recently looking for some old familiar normal along my favorite backroads. I found flocks of monarch butterflies at Point Lookout State Park, and I wandered among them through the marsh where frothy white clouds of groundsel blossoms were a fantasy setting for the scarlet-winged blackbirds. No, they didn't sit on my hat nor did they perch on my hand. Actually they were as skittish as I on that perfect day. They too had come in the wake of a storm, their journey interrupted, and now they seemed unwilling to trust the sense of serenity that prevailed there.

The haunted old lighthouse at Point Lookout wailed a mournful warning to sailors just as it has for a century plus. I lingered a while and left to trail through the tawny marshes of nearby Cornfield Harbor, where pink gerardia lined the paths through comforting sameness. I headed back home.

There is a nagging sense of insecurity that leads me quickly home now on these autumn evenings.

We went out at sunset to sit on the porch of the small blue house where we live in the towering shadow of a nuclear power plant and its neighbor, a liquid natural gas facility, which, incredibly, is awaiting reactivation along with the blessing of those who control such decisions. In the yard there were golden finches feeding as always in autumn amid a raggedy patch of seeding zinnias beside the fence. They were oblivious to the scarecrow that presides there and waves a small American flag. We watched quietly the silver glint of fighter planes circling and landing at the big airbase across the river. On their way to sea, we mused. And so, it seems, they were.

November 1, 2001

10
Despite Armistice Day

Our offspring keep going to war

My outdated dictionary states that Armistice Day was to commemorate the anniversary of the cessation of hostilities of World War I.

Such a quaint phrase. Equally quaint is the fable that The Great War ever was "the war to end all wars." But that is what was taught to us in elementary school. That is why we celebrated that date each year, said the teachers. We believed them—with reservations. Actually it sounded just too pat to me, even at my tender age.

That November date is still on the calendar, but it has never become important enough to have its own three-day-weekend. In 1954, it was quietly changed to Veterans Day and, along with the veterans, eventually was relegated to the past and mostly forgotten.

At an early age, I began to question the wisdom of grownups. My intuition surfaced when our teacher talked of wars of the past. Lots of wars. One of the first pieces she read that impressed me was Robert Southey's poem "After Blenheim." It was a gripping story of a battle fought in a Bavarian village beside the Danube in 1704. Old Karl's grandchildren are gathered about the doorstep of his cottage in the midst of the battleground where thousands had perished so long before. He is explaining the presence of a human skull found by the children in the freshly tilled soil of a garden nearby. His is the story of his father, a survivor of the war.

When Karl's horrific tale is concluded, he jubilantly remarks: "Great praise the Duke of Marlborough won, and our good Prince Eugene!" Little Wilhelmine declares that the war was "a very wicked thing." Old Karl replies: "Nay. It was a famous victory." Young Peterkin then asks: "But what good came of it at last? The old man repeats stubbornly: "Why—I cannot tell. But 'twas a famous victory.'

I can imagine Old Karl telling them not to worry, to just bury the skull, run off and play.

We kids were to hear many unsatisfactory answers to our questions along the way to war. We read of the failure of the League of Nations, which was formed by grownups as a kind of council-fire where representatives of all nations would come to negotiate and mediate, then demonstrate. If we had been around when it was conceived in 1920, we could have told them it would never work.

Grownups have abandoned all logic and common sense and realism in their dealings with one another. Those in charge of war refuse to reckon with human nature. Reason is replaced by greed and a great lust for power.

Now we see the gradual demise of the U.N. as another example of failure. In the 1930s, when we were learning our first lessons about war, a pompous, posturing little despot far across the sea was planning his version of war to end all war, and my generation would receive a special invitation to participate—along with Wilhelmine and Peterkin. The rest is history. The past is prologue.

And still the grownups are telling us kids not to worry Just shut up and run and play.

On my desk is a faded sepia photo of my dad in the khaki uniform of The Great War. He was prepared to go, but he wasn't called up. But his offspring have been going to wars regularly ever since. He is smiling from the snapshot, tall and handsome and very grand in puttees and a jaunty broad-brimmed hat. He is the image of his great-grandsons. So young. Just right for war.

November 7, 2002

∞ *Audrey Remembered* ∞

Becky Cordero, granddaughter No. 7
Daughter of Debbie Scharmen Smith and David Smith

Grandma was, is and always will be a tangle of sights, sounds, smells and savors. She, and by extension the home she offered as respite from the normal day's hustle and bustle, remains a sharp contrast within my memories, like bright rubies and sapphires kept safe in a display cabinet that's a bit dusty and dingy: too good, too pure, too wonderful.

The sights of her bird feeder, perched at the top of the tall hill that led down to Mill Creek, the sounds of the classical station she played during the afternoons, the smells of the Christmas Eve dinner she always had prepared on the best night of the year, the savors of the homemade strawberry jam we would sit and make at the dining room table. Everything awash in the natural light that steamed through the casement windows that lined the back of the house, framed by the thick green shag carpet that still makes me think of a beautiful, peaceful meadow. A younger me loved that carpet so much that I would make carpet angels when left to my own devices.

The home she made brought the beauty of nature inside, a blessing for my pale skin that would seem to burn almost immediately. There was a magic in the air there, something that, to this day, makes me long for more time in that safe, sacred space. It is not unlike what I feel looking at beautiful photos of the countryside, the beach, the mountains, the ocean or even a Bob Ross painting.

Grandma was the caretaker of the most beautiful place, a place she cultivated and grew for all of us so lucky to call her ours. I hope that you can experience even a fraction of this by reading the works she created, sitting at her typewriter while nestled in the corner of the sitting room, next to the fireplace and in full view of those same casement windows that lined the back of the house, overlooking the tall hill that led down to Mill Creek.

Winter

1
Running Pine in the Winter Woods

Christmas gifts from prehistory

Between the last leaf and the first snow, the woodlands are bleak indeed. It is then I am grateful for the conifers and holly, the winter greens of Bay Country. And the wonderful running pine that comes into its own at this time.

I first saw it years ago in early November as a miniature forest of delicate green fronds covering the leaf litter. All about were tiny candelabra from which rose puffs of golden dust, like smoke, as I tiptoed carefully through the ankle-deep patch. The candelabrum contains the spores of the plant, so ancient it is listed in botanicals just behind the horsetails.

It is lycopodium complanatum, known colloquially as crowsfoot, groundcedar, and Christmas green. Its tendrils are the beloved garlands that adorn the mantles and doors of Bay Country homes at this season. Like stuffed hams and oysters, they are essential trappings of a Southern Maryland Christmas.

The fine powder produced by the plant is unique. Also known as vegetable brimstone, it is flammable and was used centuries ago in the early stage plays of Shakespeare to create special effects. A palmful, tossed into the air and ignited, will produce dazzling streaks of blue-tinged lightning. I have tried this in my fireplace and it is truly the stuff of wizards.

Vegetable brimstone was also used in the manufacture of the first firecrackers and as a source of illumination for early flash photography as well as a soothing remedy for chafes and wounds. The spores are so uniform in size that they were employed as a standard in microscopic measurements. It is believed that cannel coal was formed by prehistoric deposits of such spores.

We take the greens of our winter woods so for granted, I muse as I gather some holly and cut aromatic boughs from an old juniper. I covet the garlands of running pine, but it is becoming scarce in our woodland. Thus I leave untouched the only patch that grows nearby.

As I walk back to the trail, I see satin leaves of wintergreen peeping above the tarnished gold of autumn, with tips of the foliage of rare cranefly orchids and uncommon ferns, so I linger to admire them and the fronds of the running pine, which do so resemble the claws of the crows that scold from the treetops. And I ponder the destiny of such botanicals, which have lived here on Earth for millions of years and have blessed the barren forests of many Christmases past.

December 7, 2000

2

Refugees: An Unfinished Portrait

In an exquisite burst of naiveté,
I had imagined their salvation

Last year before the crisis of 9-11, I began work on a portrait of an Afghan woman and her infant, a pair of refugees ...

> *The fruit tree is bare*
> *the rose bush a thorn*
> *and the ground bitter with stones.*

Through the advent of winter—that time of foxes, frosted leaves and falling stars—autumn's flowers clung stubbornly to life in my garden beside the creek. Purple sage and red zinnias mingled with rosemary's pale lilac blossoms and gray boughs. Now the petals are fading fast on drooping stalks that straggle single-file like worn warriors along the fence.

At dawn I peer out at them from my bedroom window, and I listen warily, as I have come to do each morning of the unsettling year just past. All is calm. There in the cold light of a rising sun is silence: the sound of peace under siege. The sun briefly floods the creek with a bloody glow, and a new day begins.

They tell us this will be a "new war," a provocative tag, I muse. Like a pitch for a new product, it conveys the notion that if we liked the old we are bound to love the new—still on the drawing board at this writing.

I finish dressing and prepare to leave for class: I study art one day a week in a studio up-county. There, with a group of mutually creative friends, I attempt to summon images of people from rough paper and a flurry of pastel chalk dust; and I see my subjects evolve from ghostly fetal figures into fully formed humans, to whom I always become inextricably bound during the process. In my case, that process can be as lengthy as the gestation period of an elephant.

So it was I began work on a portrait of an Afghan woman and her infant, a pair of refugees I sketched from a color news photo that had caught my eye and filled me with sadness. (War is so much more terrifying in color than in black and white, I thought, as I worked.)

The mother is clothed in the dusty muted hues of my doomed garden, her face a reflection of anguish. Only a hint of color and a bit of tarnished silver thread are visible on her ragged cloak. She clasps the child snuggly, defensively. He wears a cunning peaked hat with all the jellybean colors of a patchwork quilt, lovingly pieced by hand, bright and new as he. His expression is one of uncertain wonder and the instinctive trust of the innocent. He is a bud in a garden where nothing thrives.

The portrait of these refugees stands, still, against the wall of my room. In an exquisite burst of naiveté, I had imagined their salvation as I called them forth on my easel. But of course, that is unlikely now. This is, after all, their normal life: one of endless wandering and strife on a barren plain that stretches far beyond.

Tonight there is no moonlight
but a new star opens like a silver trumpet over the desert
Tonight in a nest of ruins the babe is laid.

December 11, 2002

3
The Gift

An unbroken circle

of memories—with room for more

Several years ago, my child gave me a wreath for Christmas. It was braided from the bare vines of fox grapes that grew in the woods behind her house and interwoven with golden ribbons from a Christmas past. She decorated it with ivy and the dried pods of a trumpet creeper. With an apologetic shrug, she shyly said that she hadn't any money for gifts that year.

It was beautiful—the size of a hula-hoop—and I hung it proudly on the wall above the fireplace.

Soon after the holidays, she moved far away from us and I found myself tucking precious bits of that last Christmas amid the vines of her wreath that still hung above the fireplace. A few sprigs of baby's breath from a wilted holiday arrangement; a garland of creeping fern with weathered feathery fronds like spun gold, its tiny candelabra seedpods glittering in the firelight.

In the bleak weeks of January, I added some scarlet lichens found alongside the lane and a delicate branch from a primrose bush, a fairy kind of plant with miniature brown seed boxes imprinted with a perfect rendition of its flower, carved by some elfin hand. It is a conversation piece among small children who come to visit, still believing in the little people of the forest.

In February, I added a rose, a pale pink flower fragile as porcelain, salvaged from a birthday bouquet sent from afar. And there are some early snowdrops and a pair of pressed daisies from the bier of a friend.

The wreath remains, year after year. In springtime, it wears briefly the first violet and perhaps a spray of flowering quince. Summers provide birds' nests, a piece of an abandoned wasp nest and the exotic seedpod of an enormous Southern lotus. Someone once brought from the beach several kelp pods resembling large beetles carved from onyx. They creep amid the burgeoning collection that clings to the vines.

In autumn, the children find perfect specimens that have been embalmed by summer heat in shed or garage: a bumblebee mummy, a cerulean dragonfly and a monarch butterfly. They hang them happily on the wreath. And there are birds' eggs, fallen intact in late summer storms.

Now, in another Christmas season, I tuck holly amid the vines and add glittering ribbon rosettes from a golden-wedding cake to this treasured gift, an unbroken circle of memories—with room, still, for more ...

December 16, 1996

4
Arpeggios of Redwings

My prayer for a new millennium

There is a young soul in this worn old receptacle.

Whoever is in charge of such things: Give it to a golden child with a lean tall barefoot mother in a flowered dimity dress. A woman with Nordic eyes and sun-bleached hair and a lilting laugh.

Leave them a dusty country road where blue morning glories and sunflowers embrace. A road that leads through riverside fields where plump sweet potatoes lie deep in rich black soil, waiting to be dug.

Leave a cottonwood to be scaled and a rippling waist-high sea of grass, brimming with meadowlarks, to explore beneath the wide clean sky where crows converse.

Leave a vintage green mason jar to fill with autumn-drowsy crickets and the last of summer's grasshoppers for fishermen on the riverbank who will pay a penny for each.

Leave arpeggios of redwings amid fuzzy cattails in the backwater where mother and child primly tuck up their skirts and wade happily hand in hand.

Leave some ripe black walnuts to be carried home with late roses and sweet potatoes bundled in folds of dimity.

Leave then such simple precious things, that they may begin again.

January 6, 2000

5
Let There Be Trees

They enhance the view

This place where I live—on the shore of a wide deep creek near the Chesapeake—is part of a great scar carved into the woodlands back in the 1950s long before I came here. No rules or regulations existed then to prevent the first builders from bulldozing everything in their path. And many did—without a thought of those who would come after.

There are no trees but the ghosts of wild dogwoods, laurel and enormous hardwoods and pines on these pampered green slopes where houses bump elbows amid ubiquitous gardens of azaleas. Thus, a couple of years ago, I planted in this yard beside the creek a pair of knee-high sapling paulownias, little long-legged princesses that grew quickly tall and slender and produced their first flowers last spring.

A neighbor said my trees spoiled the waterfront view.

Quite the opposite, they enhance the view—and the environment. Before planting those trees, I envisioned blue water through purple clouds of fragrant spring blossoms; sultry summer shimmer of bottle green beyond the big cool leaves; and skim-ice framed by graceful grey boughs in winter. I conjured an entire royal family eventually holding court here on this shore years hence. I imagined a resurrection of those phantom forests, a kind of arboreal memorial to those slaughtered ones. My paulownias, woodland goddesses of fertility, would bring me this.

And I considered the new settlers who came recently to live on the other side of the creek. They look at this monotonously bulkheaded and barbered side. Their dwellings fit snuggly into the woodland in harmony with Nature.

They have unselfishly preserved the white blossoms of spring and blazing hues of autumn; the thicket of pines where a trio of herons roost and an eagle sometimes perches; the ragged banks that have housed generations of sassy kingfishers and the grassy shallows where a great white egret summers.

Now, in winter, in the rosy dawn—before the wind rises; before the buffleheads and loons come with an entourage of gulls to stir up the creek; and before a lone waterman's boat rouses from slumber to stagger sleepily toward the Bay—images of primitive Indian Shamans, exotic animals and fierce warriors seem to lie along that far shoreline. They are reflections of the bare bones and broken limbs of trees, of silken bronze grasses and the fine earthy tones of the raw banks. They are eerie reproductions of a past when Nature was revered.

And over on this shore two bluebirds perch in the first glow of the morning sun on the crown of a princess—one that has grown tall enough now to cast her first reflection in the creek ...

January 6, 1994

6
Glory Be to January

For pink ice, pearly opalescence
and the purple prose of golden waxwings

The holidays are past, their glow diminished, and we must quickly adjust or succumb to the dark side of winter.

Nothing is left in the bottom of the bowl but shells and Brazil nuts. The chocolate box is bereft of soft centers. Tinsel wanders listlessly about the house looking for a tree. It winks from corners and slithers along the baseboards or clings like a kitten to my shoulder.

Outside the window, the accessories of winter are all white and gray: ragged clouds, satin swans and gulls with the shiny plastic sheen of penguins. Only holly—the beautiful burning bush of the Chesapeake woodland—adds color to a monochromatic scene.

The New Year should come with spring, I muse; winter is no time to begin anew. The holiday has wrung me of all color, too. In fact, I am so tired and numb I find I have been walking around for days unaware of a pine needle embedded in my big toe.

Then one day I awaken to dawn on the pink-iced creek, a sky the pearly opalescence of an abalone shell. I watch a flock of buffleheads—funny little clowns of winter water—dive for breakfast, and I note that the ubiquitous gulls are providing a new act each day: everything from graceful ballet to raucous duck brawls.

Masked golden waxwings come midday to plunder the poke bushes of frozen fruit. They fill the air with the shrill sound of Cracker Jack whistles and dribble purple prose all over my new car.

The sunset, which stands unchallenged by any other season, floods the cove with a tidal wave of brilliance, brushing the tips of trees with autumnal rose. At nightfall, the shore is aglow with giant candles as dock lights appear suspended on pillars of gold and silver in the quiet water. The interlopers we consider such a summer nuisance are welcome in the black of winter.

Tomorrow or the next day may bring a wet sticky snow to turn shiny green leaves of magnolia into snowflowers, white and lily-like, lovely as June.

So it is, as the writer Dorothy Wordsworth said, "a pleasure to the real lovers of nature to give winter all the glory they can, for summer will make its own way and speak its own praises."

January 8, 1997

7

Desperate Measures

Planting a forest in time of hardship

At a recent holiday party, a group of women was discussing some really deep subjects—all that intellectual stuff that women love to share with one another. This time the topic was what happens to old Christmas trees left on city lots or streets after the big day.

Now, the trees are probably all sent to recycling centers, but in my time (way back there someplace) they were put out, like old dogs, to wander the streets in packs until Easter when they simply disintegrated.

Actually, my mother told me when I was about seven, that they often were seen after dark as hairless changelings following disobedient children who refused to come home on time for supper. (I still peer over my shoulder when I am out late during their time abroad.)

The women's discussion grew quite intense at that gathering, before the topic switched from the fate of holiday trees to that of Halloween pumpkins. But that is another story.

That very night at three o'clock—the hour when great plots are born to writers—I recalled a tale of abandoned Christmas trees and what befell them in a small community long ago.

I am one who has always loved trees. I grew up with wonderful singing cottonwoods, enormous hemlocks with little caves beneath the spreading branches, weeping willows and forests of pine. They were important to me, yet I took their presence for granted. Then, suddenly, when I was grown and the mother of three young children, the man of our house transported us to an isolated air base in the Southwestern United States where no trees grew.

We arrived shortly before Christmas, when the stark flat moonscape at the edge of the Chihuahuan desert was already bleak with winter. No snow would fall on that arid plain, I was told. There would be no white-frosted pines and ebony branches dipped in silver. Rocks and thorny shrubs and a single crooked sapling maple were all that grew in our new yard.

Right after the holiday, the father/husband left for temporary hardship duty in some exotic place where lush tropical things grew. He would return in three months, said he, and the children and I (even the dog) fell deep into depression.

Colored lights were gone from the windows of the community and the trees, stripped of finery, thrown into the drab yards to roll restlessly about and cling to the curbings with a band of tumbleweeds. I stared hard at them and realized there was a way to make us all happy— and restore some dignity to the homeless trees, as well.

So we spent that day with the bitter wind, gathering up the trees. As I dug holes in the concrete-like dirt of the back yard, the children staggered home with firs of all sizes. Some trees were bedraggled and bald, some trailed mangled tinsel, but most were still fresh and green as the forests of home.

We planted them in a sheltered spot away from the bully wind, and at day's end there stood a mini-forest proud and tall outside the window. It remained through Twelfth Night and on to Candlemas. Until spring arrived faithfully—just as it always has—everywhere.

January 11, 2001

8
My Oracle: Epilogue

Our war was lost,
and it was yet to end

In early autumn, my oracle collapsed beside the lamppost in my yard where she had presided for many seasons: a ragged little scarecrow, fellow activist, alter ego and oracle. A great storm brought her down.

I had watched the war we both had opposed become a deadly scavenger hunt with mounting casualties. In late summer, I was still preaching and proselytizing as I crawled about the flower beds at the feet of the oracle and grappled angrily with alien weeds.

She listened silently and commiserated, offering ambiguous and obscure comments in a quintessential oracular way. But the gardening that had always been a source of solace for me was no longer a comfort. My anger suddenly was the key weapon of my personal war against everyone. My own Weapon of Mass Destruction.

And so there came a tempest to shove a seething summer into the grasp of winter. The trees along the shore where I live were traumatized, autumn was canceled and the sparse foliage on battered limbs turned black and shriveled.

In the midst of it all lay the oracle amid the dead of the garden, gray as the rough waters that slapped viciously at the creek shore. On her faded gingham blouse a tattered sign, the last of a series, said simply: SNAFU. It was her final comment on the war. She who had been

my only sounding board for months was indeed gone. We were weary of empty rhetoric. Our war was lost, and it was yet to end.

She lay in state with summer on a weathered bench beneath the wounded apple tree. The tree itself was so disoriented, so confused, it had begun to send out pink nosegays of spring blossoms among the yellowed leaves and fruit on its broken boughs. A proper wake was held amid the ruins of the storm, scattered like peaked teepees all about, and the oracle was spirited away to that place of eternal rest, a vast acreage where clouds of gulls drift whitely above like miniature angels sadly surveying the accumulation of a wasting society.

It was inevitable that I would suffer trauma as well. I was suddenly stricken and taken away to recover in another place of angels, caring ministrants of casualties and castoffs alike.

When I returned, I found the garden stark and bleak, healing and humbled as I. The first frost had come and gone and winter was well advanced; the old apple tree was recovering nicely. The bedding-down of summer had been brutal. Perennials were cut to the ground beside the fence, leaving only the Mexican sage, prone but pointing pentacles of purple skyward, as if determined to complete the life cycle come hell or high water.

A rambler rose that had lived several years at the tip of my 50-foot conifer had been snatched from its perch, still in partial bloom. There was the subtle scent of June in wrinkled crimson petals left behind, and a promise of green in the decapitated canes in a corner of the yard.

With the new year came an aura of benevolence to the scene. The rosemary bush, gray symbol of hope and remembrance, prepares as usual for winter bloom beside the porch; her limbs mended, her aged ugliness a kind of disheveled beauty. Skim ice gathers in the crannies of the creek shore outside my window, and last spring's swans coast nearby. They have lost the gray feathers of infancy.

They are full-blown and dazzling, flaunting youth and persistence—and optimism—in the cruel face of adversity while they await the end of their war. They are the perfect metaphor for survival.

January 15, 2004

9

Tidings of False Cheer

My Oracle and I dissent

Winter has swept the last traces of color from the creek shore, and the view is a mere negative of autumn past. A lone mute swan bobs ghostlike in a setting of skeletal trees and black water.

A new scarecrow stands now beside my front door in a cloud of scent amid the rosemary bush that defies the season. She is Oracle 2, a replacement for the one who was my voice of dissent until she fell prey to storm and stress.

The successor already shows the scars of Halloween and Election Day, two equally scary occasions bravely endured. Her campaign poster is gone, and she bears on her burlap breast a red, white and blue badge proclaiming Proud to Vote. A crumpled Santa hat perches atop her yarn curls. Her broad smile denies the bitter disappointment of defeat. There is still the gaudy ritual of the inauguration to endure, and I sense a subtle slump of her thin shoulders.

Winter days are dusk barely diluted, and I peer through the gloom and down a narrow lane where bright banners wave from the porches of neighbors. Cocktail glasses and confetti embossed on rippling silk are little icons announcing the new year. A rumpled campaign poster peeks from beneath a bush, and a faded turkey banner hangs limply from a post nearby.

The perennial icons blossom with the changing seasons. There are bunnies for Easter and flowers for Mother's Day and birthday cakes for family members. Appearing sporadically on the same porch is even a special silhouette of a kissing couple on a flag.

"Look at that," I exclaim to my dog. "Nobody in this community has a raggedy scarecrow as a spokesperson. Our PR is a flop. No one pays attention. We need some of those banner things to spread our message." The dog nods agreement and goes back to sleep.

These people are talented, I muse. They make these things. I can do that. I have a sewing machine, if I can find it. I am a faithful fan of Martha Stewart, and I follow her reruns. I really miss her since she went away. But I never got around to doing any of her projects. They all look so hard. Being a homemaker is really hard.

Besides, I am more a Phyllis Diller type left over from the 1950s. (Anyone out there remember her? I wonder where she is. Was she spirited away, as well, to that place where audacious females who dare to become rich and famous CEOs are taken?)

We were inventors, scientists, Phyllis and I. We did hydroponic gardening in our refrigerators long before Disney discovered the process. And didn't we find the very first deadly strains of Ebola in the dark corners of a common laundry hamper? Of course we did. But others took all the credit. Life is unfair.

I sigh as I see all the windows on the lane twinkling clean in the gloom. Mine are plastered with leafblow. The banner ladies' chrysanthemums are properly plumped in uncluttered yards and still abloom. Mine sprawl like drunken strumpets beside the mossy fence. (What the heck is a strumpet? I must look it up someday.)

So I resolve to become organized. I will change my values, my morals and my politics. I will wash my windows and plump my posies. I will sew. My banners will spout reality. They will be beautiful but practical. I will have one to herald each new war. One to announce the first winter blizzard. One to represent the debut of hurricane season, plus satin portraits of each name. Lifesize? I see commissions. I smell money.

No flowers. No bunnies. And you can forget about that hokey kissing couple. That's not gonna happen on my front porch. Look for our website: badnewsbanners.com. Happy New Year from me and the oracle.

January 6, 2005

10
The Promise of Things Beautiful

Miss Katherine sends
a poinsettia to restore my faith

Here in the vestibule of my house, devoid now of holiday trappings, stands a poinsettia that followed me home, so to speak, during the Christmas season a year ago. It was a humble little grocery-store plant snatched off a shelf on my way to the checkout stand. It was an impulsive decision by one who had sworn not to be seduced ever again by big scarlet blossoms and a good buy. Those fickle flowers that promise so much, then simply collapse after the holiday.

But this one did not. This plant had some of the right stuff, and it bloomed brazenly on through February. So instead of ending up on the compost heap, it was granted a stay on the windowsill in the utility room with a straggly geranium and a browning aloe. They expired soon after, but the poinsettia remained green and lush even after it had dropped its flowers.

Spring came and the poinsettia was given a special corner of the patio that overlooks the creek. There it was replanted in a large container with caladiums and alyssum for company, and it settled happily in for the summer and grew tall and full-figured. It spent August alone while I vacationed elsewhere and a kind neighbor tended it sporadically. The plant was undemanding and congenial.

When winter threatened, the caladiums wilted. The poinsettia had grown so large I hadn't the heart to abandon it to the elements. Thus it was moved inside to a corner of the garage where a row of windows provided excellent diffused light all day. It seemed not to mind the unlovely surroundings amid years of clutter. Poinsettias, after all, are from hardy stock. I have seen them in riotous bloom in brown yards of poor Mexican villages in winter, where they and the chickens provided the only color in a barren landscape. And in arid southern California, where I once lived, they sometimes grew in thick hedges.

As the poinsettia approached her second Christmas I saw that the tips of the limbs were tinged with red; and the hue grew deeper and spread each day to other leaves. It was going to bloom for me, and as Christmas Eve grew near it did indeed develop six perfectly respectable flowers.

I recalled my beloved second grade teacher who actually had owned a real poinsettia back in the 1930s. It was as tall as I and my classmates, and the first any of us had seen. She was Miss Katherine Lund, pretty and willowy and redheaded as her flower, which she brought to share with us in a gloomy classroom of the two-storied red brick schoolhouse on a bleak Kansas prairie. There it languished all through the winter, a miracle of scarlet blossoms, the most exotic we could imagine. We worshipped it like a cult of small dryads. It bloomed on through Valentine's Day, its red flowers outstanding amid white paper doilies and frosted window and snowy vistas beyond.

So here again is just such a poinsettia in the making: Miss Katherine, incarnate, come to restore my faith in the promises of things beautiful.

January 17, 2002

11
The Logic of Crows

Things different from us
have no right to be in our midst

In winter, the crows own this creek shore where I live.
They patrol from dawn to dusk looking for interlopers,
wild things that are different from them—creatures
that have no right as far as they are concerned to be in
their midst. They quarrel constantly, rise early and stay
up late so as not to miss anything, and often at dawn
their raucous cries summon me from my bed to find yet
another surprise outside my window.

Sometimes it is an eagle they have discovered in the
tip of a tree across the creek, and they will not rest until
they rout him from his perch. In exasperation, he usually
leaves the tree and flies about with the crows in a blasé
sort of way, as if to placate them so they will let him be.

On a recent morning it was a fox, walking unconcernedly along the bulkhead as they harassed him. An old
paulownia tree on the bank—so lovely in other seasons,
so naked and vulnerable now in winter—was black with
crows loudly cussing and discussing. The fox paused
several times to gaze up in wonder.

He was small and elegant, his pale coat rose in the first
rays of sunlight that painted the creek and transformed
him briefly into a fantasy, his pink bushy tail a changeling
prince's plume. He was the very first fox I had ever seen
in my yard.

During the cold weeks that followed, he came sporadically, along the same route with the contingent of crows,
at last turning suddenly to dash up a hill, into the woods

and out of sight. One morning he came before dawn, in graceful black silhouette. The crows awaited and sounded an alarm.

He seemed healthy and energetic. Yet, when I told a friend about the sightings, he suggested we call animal control. The fox is obviously ill, said he, or he would not be here among humans.

But where else could he be? We are everywhere, I replied. His attitude saddened me. His is the logic of crows, I muttered.

Donald Stokes' *Guide To Nature In Winter* assured me that foxes often live near humans. So it was, a few days later when a light snow had fallen during the night, I found tracks along the bulkhead and walked beside them until they disappeared amid the reeds of a marsh.

On my way home, a line of mute swans passed overhead, and I paused to watch them fade from sight. At this very moment, I mused, an environmental task force is deciding their fate. There is nothing left to say in defense of the swans. No matter how beautiful, there simply are too many. So say those who know about such things.

I must not become too emotionally involved with this fascinating fox. Nor with bluebirds and eagles whose numbers have increased, just as the swans have, in the 20 years I have lived here on this shore. How long before they too are declared a nuisance and acquire their very own task force?

We humans are as crows: shadowy bellwethers standing guard over Nature's excesses while oblivious to our own.

January 18, 2001

12
Accidentals

We, too, might be odd,
uncommon, perhaps rare

It is said that the great hope of a birdwatcher is to see an accidental, a foreign species—like the yellow-breasted chat that made a Christmas visit to Fairhaven this year—that has strayed into your region. I once knew a woman whose pet peacock ran off into the Maryland woods with a flock of wild turkeys. He wore a red bandanna around his neck. Might he be classified as an accidental? Certainly uncommon, I would suppose. Perhaps rare?

Anyway, he is one I would really like to see; he would have top billing on my lifelist.

I suspect most accidentals are migratory males of the species who simply refuse to stop and ask for directions when they become lost. Thus they are found in unlikely places, wandering aimlessly and wearing that expression of unconcern that says *Of course I know where I am!*

Here in Bay Country I have come across such birds: A glossy ibis flew low over the bow of our boat one summer day as we cruised the lower Chesapeake. A flock of yellow grosbeaks came to my yard one snowy day, and pink pine grosbeaks stopped by in autumn to dine on wild grapes beside the lane. During a stormy February, a rare blue grosbeak was seen here on the creek shore, where he lingered for several days. Near Point Lookout on the lower Potomac, a variety of glorious warblers often come ashore in an autumn storm and remain for a while to feed amid thickets of goldenrod and myrtle in the marsh. They are quite tame: I once watched a lone cerulean warbler feed there just a few feet away from where I stood.

One winter when my roomie and I traveled South, we had many close encounters with uncommon birds: In a Florida swamp we saw the parula warbler a ranger had reportedly spotted there a few days before. We had no witnesses; thus our sighting was met with condescension back at the visitor center. Were we not properly rumpled? Were our shoes too white? Perhaps we lacked the look of credibility, but the thrill of seeing such a bird in the wild lingers still.

In the Everglades, wood storks were not where they were supposed to be. Instead they were slogging around in a mud puddle next to a rest stop, behaving like commoners despite their great celebrity. Overhead was an enormous spiraling cloud of purple swallows that darkened the sky: an unusual occurrence, we were told.

Over on the Gulf Coast, the roseate spoonbills we had looked for in the wetlands wandered instead over the elegant grounds of a private residence beside the road. We found a trio of wood ducks in an artificial pond just outside the door of a cocktail lounge and mute swans (quite scarce back then) in a grubby lake of a housing development. A great horned owl cavorted at dusk in a tall pine beside a busy restaurant near a shopping mall.

If those southern birds kept a lifelist of sightings, the description of me and my companion might have read thus: *A rare pair. Neat plumage inconsistent with the usual ragged olive-drab vest markings of that species. Female has pointed silver crest, skinny long legs and very white feet. Male is short, rotund and in a molting phase. Accidentals?*

February 1, 2001

13
What Have I Done with My Life?

In praise of the simple pleasures
of blessed sameness

I write often about the blessings of sameness, the succession of seasonal simple pleasures that come and go in my Bay Country back yard. My words express my gratitude for serenity. But one reader told me (with more than a tinge of the form of sarcasm called enantiosis) that my life sounded so "exciting" he could hardly wait to hear more.

His words left a wake of discontent. Perhaps I had too high a regard for sameness, I mused. Perhaps I should be sprinting from one place to another in frenetic pursuit of excitement, wearing one of those T-shirts with the message Been There Done That.

Outside my window, this fragile winter day is like an icicle: so cold and crisp and crystal clear that it may shatter at any moment. Across the creek, the sky is darkening and a great swirling cloud of gulls caught in the last flight of the sun are like giant snowflakes. Along the shore, six swans swim in single file like a ballet troupe in perfect unison.

Now that is pretty dull stuff. I should be racing sports cars or climbing the Andes, not spending my golden years on such sameness. I am about to become a septuagenarian (a state akin to sameness) and what have I done with my life?

I spent my youth as a stay-at-home mom. Nobody does that anymore. In fact, I eventually was forced into leading a double life, telling tall tales to strangers who asked at parties what I do. I have been a trial lawyer, a rocket scientist and a best-selling author. I lie well. That's what I do.

So it is that I dwell on the critic's comments and become more agitated. It is that time of year. This is called pre-birthday syndrome. It is dangerous, and there is no pill for it.

Suddenly from the TV (which I had turned to for distraction) comes a voice excitedly discussing dust mites. A renowned scientist is saying (sort of) that dust mites are responsible for killer plagues that now threaten us all. We must bring back the art of vigorous cleaning or die.

Well! I know dust mites. I am a veteran of guerrilla groups who stalked them throughout the 1950s all over the United States. Armed only with our dainty vacuum cleaners and white gloves, feminine intuition and a fierce maternal instinct, we held all kinds of critters at bay while the world snickered.

My generation controlled hordes of exotic bacteria until we were forced to go to work at real jobs.

Now the good doctors imply that we were more than mindless drudges who wasted our talents tending children and fighting dust mites. We were pioneers. Like Rachel Carson. Like Madame Curie. We, who toiled long with no recognition (as is the way of visionaries) may now form clubs, sue for back pay, hold reunions and erect our own monument carved from granite and standing tall with other noble warriors on the Mall.

Suddenly I am so weary from excitement that I have to lie down. So I turn off the TV and lapse into blessed sameness. A nap is a fine simple pleasure.

A loon calls from the creek and the rising moon is contemplating full ...

February 4, 1997

14
My Granddaughter at 16

She is a rare and endangered species,
near full–fledged

She was born on a gray day in midwinter when snowdrops bloomed beneath the bare limbs of the crabapple tree and mute swans came to this tributary of the Chesapeake for the very first time. As if to welcome her arrival, they appeared at our dock just minutes after: a pair with golden bills and glowing pearly plumage right out of a fairy tale. Such swans were uncommon to our area then.

She was special, too. She became my companion on the woodland trails of Southern Maryland at a very early age, and she nurtured my awareness of nature with the sense of wonder only a child has. Well, she was shorter than I: Small people live closer to the earth, seeing subtleties of seasons that tall folk miss. Children amble. One must amble to fully appreciate the natural world.

By the age of four, she was highly opinionated, amazingly verbose, and she had a remarkable memory. Her motto—one she often repeated to me when I walked too fast—was a favorite phrase I taught her from a book by naturalist Hal Borland: *Nature reveals her secrets not to those who hurry by.*

Thus it was she who first pointed out to me the flowers of the pawpaw trees that I long sought: dark purple blossoms cleverly concealed beneath the leaves of the limbs. It was she who first spotted the elusive wild pink orchid beside a trail at Flag Ponds, and she who noted the cunning mitten-shape of a tulip poplar's yellow autumn leaves.

One late summer day in a boggy place, we examined a cardinal flower, an uncommon species with petals so rich and red the entire plant is often stained with it. We spoke of endangered things and how they are threatened by those who must possess them—and consequently destroy them—because they are rare and beautiful. She exclaimed—with the simple common-sense logic of a little woman—that they needn't pick the wildflowers. They could just take them home in their heart and cherish them always, as she would.

When she was five, she loved to drape herself in old silken scarves and dance about the yard in a shower of petals carefully gathered from summer roses past their prime. Her interests were many: She was dancer, botanist, vet, actress, writer, artist and connoisseur of swans by the time she turned six.

I was fortunate to share those years, but such time is quickly spent and she eventually moved away with her parents to another place far from the Chesapeake.

The swans stayed on to establish a dynasty in this small tributary, where they preside as royalty throughout all seasons. And so it was, on a recent midwinter day, they came by to commiserate and remind me that it was her 16th birthday.

She is the same little girl, grown tall now, but examining still with discerning eyes her vast world. She is a scholar and athlete who paints botanicals and loves math; an eager student and a budding scientist.

She is a rare and endangered species, near full-fledged.

February 11, 1999

"My Granddaughter at 16" earned Audrey her second, and consecutive, first place in Maryland, Delaware, D.C. 1999 competition, the South Carolina Press Association judging.

15
Eavesdropping on February's Stage

Nothing much happens here
but mortal drama of weather and the birds

Here in winter the creek outside my window is polished cobalt. An incoming tide has left a wake of open water where buffleheads feed. The clownish little ducks are toy-size, satiny white and black. They are skittish—and rightfully so—as suddenly an eagle appears, its great wings spread to full length in an awesome display of power as it dips into their midst. The agile ducks react quickly, diving under the dark surface, and the eagle misses his mark.

This is a time of grayness with bitter winds sharp as the eagle's talons. The feeder outside my window is immediately deserted in the shadow of the predator. The feathers of a blue jay, left by a kestrel who hunts daily at dawn in my yard, drifts about the dun-colored grass, and the eagle vanishes over the treetops. The golden waxwings will not return today, nor the bluebirds that fed with them.

I scan the opposite shore for touches of color. There are none. But in the sepia woodland, the summerhouses emerge. In other seasons, they are barely visible in a shroud of deep foliage. Now they are revealed in all their splendor. I note, as well, the bare bones of yet another new one rising from a raw scar amid the leafless trees.

They are enormous dwellings, the habitat of those seduced by summer into retirement on the creek shore. Now in this inhospitable season, they are unoccupied.

This is a rural area where nothing much happens in winter. Radio reception consists of a choice of country or classical static. Cell phones stutter and blur, and cable is unstable. And there is snow. Thus folks grow restless here and, like migrant birds, fly off to their homes in other places, returning only sporadically to the creek.

The lonely houses are fascinating. They have all the new-age trappings of well-loved abodes—except for people. Sophisticated electrical systems are cleverly designed to discourage intruders. Lights flash on at dusk, the many ells and gables illuminated in varied sequence. Blue light of television screens flickers through uncurtained windows, and electric candles adorn windowsills on some nights as if an elegant party is in progress. But no one is there.

When the first snow comes to define the topography, the graceful contours and frosted conifers, and the creek lies solidly blanketed in white, the blue shadows of dusk rescue this die-hard resident of all seasons from monochromatic oblivion. The opposite shore seems a stage then, a kind of Twilight Zone production replete with intriguing props and ghostly drama. The actors can only be imagined as the deserted McMansions become Jay Gatsby's place, postwar Tara, the Bates Motel and Manderley.

When midnight arrives, blue lights and golden dim in perfect unison, the darkened houses retreat into the skeletal trees and another beautifully gloomy gray day ends here on a winter shore where nothing much ever happens ...

February 12, 2004

16
This Will Be the Year

Euphoria is always
somewhere in a garden

On a gloomy day comes a package from a friend who lives now in the far Wisconsin woods where, she says, the snow lies deep and clean and the rare arbutus slumbers beneath. I sigh as I glance out at the monotonous landscape of our drab winter.

The package contains precious bergamot with pink petals of summer clinging still to the fragrant dried sprigs. Enclosed are instructions for brewing a tea to heal my bronchitis, and there is a bouquet of white sage to burn in the incense pot to cleanse the premises of negativism. So it is, with health and attitude improved, I will make it through the dragging days of an eerie season.

Outside my window, the mockingbird is protecting a pitiful cache of dried pokeberries in the bleached boughs of the shrub. He flies frantically from backyard to front, where he claims rights as well to the withered fruit of a crabapple tree. There are frequent air strikes from starlings and cedar waxwings, and he is losing the battle. He could easily win with support from a few friends. Alas, he has none.

Bluebirds are bickering over ownership of the single birdhouse, and two pair of mallards noisily debate squatters' rights to a meager supply of corn. Gentle finches and wrens and chickadees eat their fill while ignoring the melee.

In the front yard, it is quiet when I go out to clear away the dead stalks of flowers. Rosettes of green

and spikes of daffodils are showing beside the fence. An ancient rose vine that fled the well-diggers a spring or so ago has made it to the top of a very tall conifer where, last autumn, it bore an amazing bunch of scarlet blossoms at the pinnacle: a red flag of victory from one who survived many a crisis to reach the summit.

There is a scent of crushed herbs amid the gray dampness there on the porch where I linger. Euphoria kicks in (it is always somewhere in a garden, no matter the season) and I dream of the summer to come. Like the old climber (we are about the same age in rose years), I should strive now for the pinnacle.

This will be the year I landscape the small dooryard with slate pavers and plant in all the cracks creeping thyme with perfect blue flowers and the fragrance of Provence. This will be the year when 300 plugs of zoysia sprout in bare corners where we planted them last spring. They still must be down there someplace, for heavensake.

Beside the porch, I make note of an evening primrose that should have blossomed in June but came instead in December. A squirrel has rearranged the sweet violets. The crazy coral honeysuckle has bloomed all winter. Thus I make a promise to be a more attentive gardener. I will grow bergamot and white sage, and my perennials will be of uniform height and compatible colors.

I will conquer my nemesis, the computer, and join the ranks of real writers. I will assemble my nature columns and they will become a book. One simply must have faith. It's a good thing. (Didn't Martha Stewart say that?) What the heck! "It's never too late to be what you might have been." (George Eliot said that.)

"Time to temper the euphoria with a bit of despondency and a good dose of negativism. It's called reality." (Audrey Scharmen said that.)

February 14, 2002

17
Kite Flying

Our dual lines are a bond with eternity.
We grasp them tightly and reach for the sky,
wanting never to let go

In late winter on a deserted shore, gulls write haiku along the water's edge where the sea has licked the sand clean and smooth as silk. A cloud of skittish sanderlings come to add a verse, then wheel and rise into the air.

Away from the water, the sharp wind is just a breeze wandering among the dunes, rippling the tips of phragmites, following a trail of fence posts that stagger toward the distant horizon where dim shapes of skyscrapers cluster.

Perfect carapaces of crabs and a fisherman's seine lie high on the sand, where winter waves and wind have left them unscathed. Nearby is a strand of whelk cases strung together like dried apple slices, though not so fragrant. These are rare treasures a scavenger will not find in summer.

This is the time, the place to fly. A blue place. Sky, sea and kites all the glorious hues of cobalt. The very air an icy breath of Mentholatum.

We seek the sea's edge where the fierce polar-bear-wind roams in winter. He rushed to attack, this bully that tears at our hats and shoves us forward, thinking our frail aged bodies an easy mark. But he is mistaken and our booted feet do not fail us. We are a pair of nimble old seabirds, our long skinny legs suddenly limber and surefooted.

The kites leap eagerly from our hands and soar overhead, infusing us with their strength and enthusiasm. They are wild winged things that tremble in our hands and lead us in a strange spastic dance of swiveling hips and torsos, a dance of our youth. Their dual lines are a bond with the universe, with eternity. We grasp them tightly and reach for the sky, wanting never to let go, wanting to soar along like the band of curious gulls, small avian angels that have come to join them in an aerial ballet.

And so the day goes, and ebbs. An arcing sun casts kite shadows in the shallows, dark shapes of manta ray and sea snake. The sky darkens, gulls walk the beach as ordinary birds now, the sea has wandered in to erase the poetry. Our time of communion is past.

We reluctantly reel in the kites and cradle them in our arms, along with the seine and shells of summer. Leaving the sea behind, we head homeward, knowing this day will not come again.

Days are ephemeral as a snowflake—with no two alike.

February 19, 1998

18
On My 79th Birthday

Who will authenticate Julia
when I am gone?

Just six, moonfaced and petite, she stood tiptoe to peer into the coffin where her tall, slim grandmother lay in a gauzy cloud of fabric the very shade of peaches and cream. Her mother said it was a negligee, a sort of nightdress. The little girl, accustomed to seeing her grandmother always in drab cotton garments, was fascinated by such elegance. The image would remain vivid throughout her long life.

More than sadness, she felt a sense of wonder, a curious indefinable emotion. Her grandmother's hair was loosened from its familiar bun and lovingly brushed to a sheen, heavy and black and barely streaked with silver. The dark slanted eyes slept, black lashes brushing the high cheekbones and tawny skin that defined her bloodlines. Shawnee? Osage? Kansa? No one would ever be certain. It was whispered that she was a squaw who married a maverick Englishman. Her grandchild, instinctively proud of her heritage, would never come to understand the cruel intricacies of racism.

As she clung to the side of the bier, she recalled summer nights and sounds of crickets in her grandparents' neat lamp-lit house. She remembered washing her bare little feet at the outdoor pump in the glow of fireflies on nights when she was permitted to sleep over, and falling asleep quickly afterward with her cousins on a pallet spread on the floor. It was a shotgun house. Three narrow rooms,

one behind the other in single file. A row of the sturdy homes—some of which still stand—were built for railroad men who labored in car barns and yards just down the street, beneath a viaduct that arced above a maze of rusting tracks and machinery. Her father was one of five children born and raised in the tiny dwelling in the early 1900s.

Shortly before death, her grandmother had given the child a rare gift for her birthday: a ragged little Bible and a unique cast-iron paperweight rooster she had cherished. Many years later when the grown woman asked what had become of them when she left home, her mother replied that she had sold them to the local sheeny-man, along with other discarded toys. Mama hadn't been one to collect things.

Thus she has only her memories of that brief time with Julia. Not even a photograph remains. Her older siblings barely recall their paternal grandmother, and the younger ones were born after she died. The precious tales gleaned from her father during his life have been all but disclaimed by the family genealogist, newly empowered by computer technology. However, she considers his information unreliable in comparison to what is in her own head and heart, and she clings stubbornly to her memories.

All are gone who share my special memories of her, and soon I will be, as well. Then who will authenticate Julia? she muses.

The moon is gone from the face that stares back from her mirror. But the sepia-tone visage there—all nooks and crannies and angles—reflect the dark eyes of Julia: deep-set and subtly slanted above high cheekbones revealed now by time and travail. She is comforted.

February 22, 2006

19

Snowflakes and Cedar Waxwings

Ordinary magic enchants my garden

It's what I like to do in the first snowfall: flap giddily about the yard, catching snowflakes on my tongue. But on a recent morning, I was walking sedately to the mailbox through the fluffy flakes, trying not to lose control, determined to create a more dignified image.

Suddenly, from out of my crabapple tree, came a cloud of cedar waxwings, swooping and dodging in all directions in some crazy kind of aerial ballet—as they do when they are drunk on elderberries. But I saw that they weren't drunk; they were sipping snowflakes, catching them neatly on tiny tongues.

I lost it. I shouted at a passerby on the lane that the birds were eating the snowflakes, and it was the first time I had ever seen them do that—although it is said they do.

Then I began a garbled account of how birds do really weird things ... Like the trio of sledding crows I saw in my backyard one winter. They took turns sliding down a teensy snow bank. I told her about the flock of gulls that perched clumsily in the ash tree last summer and ate all the berries. That was an unusual feat for birds who do not like to sit in trees.

I babbled. On and on I went until the woman laughed derisively, backed away and ran off down the lane.

I shouted at her not to come back here. This is an enchanted cove, a place where strange things occur ... where images of witches often appear on the cutbanks that rim the water ... and where, in summer, magic flowers open at dusk along the lane, great yellow nocturnal blossoms where giant moths sup.

As I wandered about the yard snapping at snowflakes, I wanted to tell her that cedar waxwings are the stuff of fairy tales. They are masked golden Gypsies, marked with a red stigmata on each secondary blue wing and a stripe of molten yellow on the tip of their tail. They drift from place to place, seemingly with no set migration patterns. It's not unusual for some to show up in Central America at the very same time in mid-winter as other flocks are arriving in Chesapeake Country.

They cast wondrous spells wherever they go. In May, they come back to my crabapple tree to bask in a pink bower of blossoms, passing petals back and forth to one another in a unique courting ritual. It is said they become so tame during nesting season that they will accept offering of yarn and string from the human hand. They sometimes pluck hair from a woman's head to weave into their nests.

I would tell her that if she were to see them at their most beautiful in a heavily laden elderberry thicket, clinging like golden butterflies to the dark purple pentacles amid the scarlet and apricot of autumn shrubs, she need beware. She could become enchanted and be tempted to gather them like flowers and carry them home. And they just might let her ...

She certainly should be told that it is unwise to scoff in sacred places.

February 23, 1995

20
False Spring

*Among our species, only perennials
possess the secrets of everlasting life*

*The snowdrop is the herald of flowers
Sent with its small flag of truce
to plead for its beleaguered brethren ...*

In the final days of February came a spring-like day when winter seemingly released its grip on the Chesapeake shore. Drifts of snow melted and the ditches ran full beside the country lanes.

The day proved to be an interlude after all, but I pretended otherwise as I went eagerly about the yard, sweeping away debris from the flowerbeds. There were daffodils with tissue-wrapped buds already tinged with yellow. Amid dry stalks of herbs was lavender, indifferent in summer, but showing tiny shoots now. A tall bush of middle-aged rosemary appeared robust. Hidden beneath her spreading branches were traces of bergamot, sage and even a pot of exotic curry with new life.

Beneath the apple tree, snowdrops clung to the wet black trunk, their bell blossoms pure as the snow that had just revealed them. They are lone survivors of an established patch that grew for years on the grave of my cat. All were rudely disinterred in an autumn storm of upheaval waged by well-diggers and dumped with a mass of clay into a battered plot of periwinkle vines that encircles the apple tree. The missing flowers are still entombed far below; it is likely they will appear in time. That is the nature of hardy bulbs. They are eternal. Would that the old cat possessed their secrets of everlasting life.

In the bare boughs overhead is a warbler who has wintered here on the shore. He is a loner, perhaps strayed from his flock and blown off course in a late autumn gale. During a recent storm, a fierce wind tossed him against my window. When I rushed to his aid he lay in the snow on his back gasping for life, and I believed he would die. He was small and weightless in my bare hand as I placed him gently into a brown paper grocer's bag and carried him into the warmth of my house. He huddled there for an hour or so at the bottom of the bag, calm and alert and curious all the while. Suddenly he arose and flew confidently and strongly about the room and out through the open door that led to his world. He is with us still, the only one of his kind at the feeder, easily identified as a myrtle warbler by his distinctive yellow markings.

In a corner of the porch, I sit in a lopsided wooden rocker as old as I and watch the day fade. There I am snug and safe as a stunned bird in a brown bag. There I am soothed by the symbolism and serendipity all around. There in the dusk the snowdrops glow like small beacons of hope as the warmth of a faux spring day grows chill and the fragrance of herbs follows me indoors.

A new dawn is shadowy with familiar specters. It is frigid, with a wintry mix on its breath, and I see from the window a dozen mature mute swans sailing benignly, bravely, downstream. It is unusual to see such a large group in this creek, and a pair of local swans pause to peer curiously as they pass.

They are our beleaguered brethren. Why are they flocking? Have they a plan? Or are they simply resigned to their fate, as we.

February 23, 2006

21
Then Comes February

The lull between the fierceness of winter and the gentleness of spring.

The Leyle is an herbe whyth a whyte floure.
And though the levys of the floure be whyte,
yet shyneth the lykeness of gold.

That first virginal lily is said to have evoked such jealousy in Aphrodite, who claimed issue from the whiteness of sea foam, that she had a golden pistil set in the center of the flower. Lilies come now in every color, but they still tote that pistil.

A lily came to me at Christmas from a friend. I was pleased, but skeptical, as I gazed at the plastic pot where a ragged circle of flower-flesh protruded from gray parched soil. I am not skilled at nurturing lifeless things: They need to be green and abloom when they fall into my hands. Even so, their survival rate will be low.

The instructions that came with her suggested she have some sun and be watered sparingly. Come midwinter, she would rise and bloom suddenly and dramatically. Sure she will, I mused, and I put her on a windowsill in the keeping room, a cool place with morning sunlight. And there she sat, abandoned, well into the new year.

No sun came and winter turned cruel. Eagles drove our winter flock of buffleheads and other sea ducks from the creek outside my window where they fed. Diving and swooping low each morning, the big birds so terrified them that they took flight in great disorderly groups and were gone. The creek was barren, green ice crept across the water and the cold settled in with vengeance.

The lily shivered on the sill and showed no signs of doing anything dramatic. I gave her a sip of water and let her be.

There came snow, a howling blizzard with sculpted drifts that covered the windows. A total eclipse of the moon occurred during a brief pause in the storm, casting a copper glow to add to the eerie drama of winter gone mad. Ice followed to sheathe the shore in deadly glass and blow low the trees. With some help from the sun, bands of squirrels appeared the morning after to dismantle the Russian scene with a kind of fury, scurrying about the limbs and filling the air with small glittering explosions. By the time of the rosy sunset, the trees had regained dignity and the events of the past weeks seemed a fantasy.

And there came February. She: the lull between the fierceness of winter and the gentleness of spring. She: born on the cusp with bewildering traits of both seasons.

She banished the snow, and Canada geese came to dine on green grass shoots beneath the paulownia tree beside the creek. A trio of mute swans flew low over the water, necks stretched to full length, like sleek white arrows shot from Cupid's bow. Obviously they were engaged in some sort of mating ritual, as there was much quarreling and hostility in the pursuit. (It is said, you know, that birds begin to pair off on Valentine's Day.)

The sea ducks returned without the eagles, and all appeared normal on the shore for the season. The lily had produced a tiny tip of a bud, its sepals pulsating gold peering shyly from the bulb-nest. And snowdrops bloomed outside the window: Fair maids of February, heralds of flowers, symbol of hope.

Then came snowflakes like pale petals drifting from the sky. Lazily, charmingly, hypocritically.

February 24, 2000

Audrey's Valedictory

Listen to Your Muse

Mine was missing for weeks. Gone. Presumed dead. Yet she has been here all along—or so she says. It was I who was faithless. I who fell prey to apathy. I who failed to feel her gentle nudging of the psyche.

For she is always everywhere. She is a composite of all the daughters of Zeus, the very visage of nature.

She is the face of the new-blown poppy in my garden, pink and wrinkled and wet with clinging bits of bud-shell. She is all the faces of the newborn swans, seven small, pale shadows of the parents who brought them proudly to our dock, here on the creek, on a misty Mayday morning.

She is the buxom bee that hovers in front of my face, one of a swarm of fat carpenters dripping sawdust as they methodically dismantle the deck where I lounge in the sun. They are cartoon bees, cunning black satin clowns with enormous eyes that stare disconcertingly into mine until I turn anxiously aside.

The song of my Muse is the bittersweet cry of an osprey and the boisterous racket of Canada geese who stage an on-going territorial dispute with mute swans in a neighboring cove. Hers is the rare dance of eagles I saw alongside the shore where they came briefly together low over the water, then soared high above the woodlands and out of sight. Lovers? Rivals? Who knows? (She didn't say.)

She is the swan that fed along the shore on a recent bright blue day. Contentedly tipping up, with fat ruffled rump and paddles waving frantically in the air as she dove for tender sprouts of aquatic grasses.

My Muse reminded me that she never left my side throughout a long illness several years ago. She was there in the guise of tiny golden birds and an old tabby cat who flitted comforting in and out of a dreamlike world. (They provided the inspiration for a very favorite story, so she says.)

She is the cardinal who comes to beg seeds at dusk, who sits on the garden bench just an arm's length away. She is the face of the magical moonflower and the gold of an evening primrose. She's the choreographer of fireflies. She is the drama, the dance, the music of Bay Country.

Though one has sorrow in their soul, yet when the servant of the Muses sings, at once dark thoughts are forgotten and troubles not remembered.

So she says. So listen to your Muse.

June 25, 1997

Acknowledgements

Audrey Scharmen reveled in things short-lived: the momentary, the fleeting, the ephemeral. Her writing flourished in that realm as well, as newspaper stories that opened your eyes or touched your heart as you read them, then made a table covering for your crab feast. What a pity, you might think, as you dumped a pot of steaming crabs on a story that moved you. But if you save every ephemeral delight, you're on the road to hoarding.

Nature, however, gives us a different kind of ephemera: perennial flowers that pop up in early spring, adding a beauty mark to winter's hold-out days, then disappear— only to return next year.

Audrey's writing was in that class: perennial reflections on life lived in the moment. They return to light in this book, many after a quarter century in the winter of memory, thanks to the editorial assistance of family members. Daughter Peg Scharmen Lynch created the cover drawing, introduced Audrey and plucked the book's title from a favorite of Audrey's stories. Son-in-law Michael Lynch oversaw the project, contributed photos and a further introduction to Audrey, hunted for illustrations, and edited and proofread Audrey's stories. Also contributing were Audrey's son Tom Scharmen, and grandchildren Marta Lynch, John Scharmen, Becky Cordero and Lisa Smith.

The project began not long after Audrey's death, on February 17, 2017, as the Scharmen clan sought to gather the entirety of her writing for Bay Weekly.

That hunt had to be wedged into the schedule of a fast-running weekly newspaper. I'd gather pieces in rare spare moments, searching our temperamental online indices, for stories that appeared after 1998. Those stories could simply be copied, cut and pasted. Finding stories published before 1998—before our web presence (www.bayweekly.com) gave us an online index—took hunting through bound volume books and retyping or, even more complex, finding ways to make old floppy disks accessible to ever-changing new technology.

Over the years, two salaried Bay Weekly interns, Leah Lichtenstein and Brad Dress, helped assemble those collections.

As founder and editor of Bay Weekly, I kept faith with the intention. After the sale of our family paper and my retirement on January 3, 2020, the project came to life. I completed and verified the collection, and the Scharmens and Lynches jumped in, proofreading, writing, envisioning title and cover art and finding illustrations. Many of the illustrations are photos taken by Audrey's husband Merrill Scharmen; others are Audrey's paintings.

We owe many thanks to artist and book designer Suzanne Shelden, who, with patience and vision, worked with us to create this book. Liz Barron, our marketing consultant, stepped in with expertise we lacked.

Arpeggio of Redwings is a Chesapeake Bay Anthology, the debut publication of New Bay Books, a limited edition publishing house newly established by Bay Weekly founders Sandra Olivetti Martin and William Lambrecht. Michael and Peg Scharmen Lynch have our deep gratitude as founding investors.

Sandra Olivetti Martin
Editor

Photo Credits

Page 01: Blackbirds Among the Cattails, by Peg Scharmen Lynch, artist, courtesy of the Scharmen Family

Page 04: Waves at Dawn, oil painting by Audrey Scharmen, artist, courtesy of the Scharmen Family

Page 08: Lenten Roses, photo by Suzanne Shelden

Page 12: Audrey at 14, photo courtesy of the Scharmen Family

Page 13: Audrey Scharmen, photo courtesy of the Scharmen Family

Page 20: Flying Kites at Ocean City, photo courtesy of the Scharmen Family

Page 26: Icy Trees on the Creek, photo courtesy of the Scharmen Family

Page 28: Flying Bald Eagle, photo courtesy of Jean Beaufort, public domain

Page 32: Wasp Nest, photo courtesy of Michael Lynch

Page 36: Audrey's Crabapple Tree, photo courtesy of the Scharmen Family

Page 38: Country Garden, photo courtesy of the Scharmen Family

Page 42: Wisteria Blossom, photo by nnattalli, Shutterstock

Page 44: *Amantha*, photo courtesy of the Scharmen Family

Page 48: Tom Scharmen, Adria Christina Scharmen (age 2), Veronica Scharmen in 1983, photo courtesy of the Scharmen Family

Page 52: Audrey in Her French Dress, photo courtesy of the Scharmen Family

Page 54: Wineberries, photo courtesy of Michael Lynch

Page 58: Azaleas, photo by Suzanne Shelden

Page 60: Daffodils, photo by Suzanne Shelden

Page 64: Lilacs, photo by Suzanne Shelden

Page 66: Audrey's Scarecrow, photo courtesy of the Scharmen Family

Page 69: Audrey's Mother and Family, photo courtesy of the Scharmen Family

Page 71: Night-Blooming Cereus, photo courtesy of Michael Lynch

Page 72: Hale-Bopp Comet, photo by a.v. ley, Shutterstock

Page 77:   Arlington National Cemetery, photo courtesy of the
          Scharmen Family

Page 78:   Duck on Bird Feeder, photo courtesy of the Scharmen
          Family

Page 81:   Dutch Irises, photo by Todd Boland, Shutterstock

Page 84:   Luna Moth on Purple Clematis, Steven Russell Smith,
          Shutterstock

Page 88:   Visiting with Swans, photo courtesy of the Scharmen
          Family

Page 90:   Daylily, photo by Maryka, Shutterstock

Page 93:   Blue Crab, photo courtesy of the Scharmen Family

Page 94:   Venus Fly Traps, photo by y.a. konstant, Shutterstock

Page 98:   Marta and Gull, photo courtesy of the Scharmen Family

Page 100: Old Boat, photo courtesy of Michael Lynch

Page 104: Orb Spider, photo courtesy of Michael Lynch

Page 106: Moonflower, photo courtesy of Michael Lynch

Page 110: Two Little Owls, photo courtesy of the Scharmen Family

Page 114: Tommie's Crab House, photo courtesy of the Scharmen
          Family

Page 118: Portrait of Selah, pastel by Audrey Scharmen, courtesy
          of the Scharmen Family

Page 124: Monarch Butterfly, photo by Suzanne Shelden

Page 129: Pikes Peak Decal Souvenir, mfg. by Lindgren - Turner Co.,
          Spokane, Washington

Page 130: Chris-Craft Boat, photo courtesy of the Scharmen Family

Page 134: The Old Hotel on Point Lookout, photo by Hank Curtis

Page 136: *Point Lookout, Md - View of Hammond Genl. Hospital &
          U.S. Genl. Depot for prisoners of war.* , ca. 1864. Mar. 2.
          Photograph. https://www.loc.gov/item/2003656672/.

Page 138: Calvert Cliffs View, photo by Suzanne Shelden

Page 140: Groundhog, photo by Rabbitti, Shutterstock

Page 144: Point Lookout State Park, photo courtesy of the Scharmen
          Family

Page 146: Unnamed American WWI Soldier, photo courtesy of Susan
          Law Cain, Shutterstock.

Page 152: Diphasiastrum digitatum, Southern Ground Cedar, photo
          by Jeri Brand, Shutterstock.

THE LAND
THAT TIME
FORGOT

THE LAND
THAT TIME
FORGOT

Edgar Rice Burroughs

FALL RIVER PRESS

New York

FALL RIVER PRESS

New York

An Imprint of Sterling Publishing
387 Park Avenue South
New York, NY 10016

This 2012 edition published by Fall River Press
Introduction © 2012 by Mike Ashley

ISBN 978-1-4351-3440-9 (print format)
ISBN 978-1-4351-3913-8 (ebook)

Distributed in Canada by Sterling Publishing
c/o Canadian Manda Group, 165 Dufferin Street
Toronto, Ontario, Canada M6K 3H6
Distributed in the United Kingdom by GMC Distribution Services
Castle Place, 166 High Street, Lewes, East Sussex, England BN7 1XU
Distributed in Australia by Capricorn Link (Australia) Pty. Ltd.
P.O. Box 704, Windsor, NSW 2756, Australia

For information about custom editions, special sales, and premium and
corporate purchases, please contact Sterling Special Sales at 800-805-5489 or
specialsales@sterlingpublishing.com.

Manufactured in the United States of America

2 4 6 8 10 9 7 5 3 1

www.sterlingpublishing.com

CONTENTS

Introduction · vii

PART I
The Land That Time Forgot · 3

PART II
The People That Time Forgot · 113

PART III
Out of Time's Abyss · 221

Map of Caspak · 327

Glossary · 329

About the Author · 334

Burroughs's Lost World

Although Edgar Rice Burroughs is best remembered for creating Tarzan, the three short novels that make up *The Land That Time Forgot* are generally regarded as amongst his best work. Unlike his earlier works, many of which developed into series as they progressed, these were written specifically as a trilogy, allowing Burroughs to provide three different perspectives on an amazing world with its evolutionary societies and ancient dinosaurs.

The stories were written in 1917 and appeared originally in one of the leading pulps of the day, *The Blue Book Magazine*, in the issues for August, October, and December 1918. By that time Burroughs had been writing for six years and both his plotting and writing had matured. For the first time he felt he was a success, after years of failure in a succession of jobs, from door-to-door salesman to peddling quack medicine, and from serving as an accountant to being a ranch hand.

He was further helped by his association with *Blue Book*'s editor, Ray Long, who went on to be editor of *Cosmopolitan* and the highest paid editor in the United States. The idea for *The Land That Time Forgot* had arisen in discussion with Long, who also provided useful advice when he read through the initial manuscript submissions. As a result Burroughs's revisions are tight yet fluid, allowing the reader to flow effortlessly through the stories with a clear vision of the strange land and peoples he is portraying.

In his six years as an author Burroughs had been remarkably prolific, having written 28 novels and short novels and a dozen short stories. All of these were pure escapist fiction with Burroughs's favoured settings of exotic locales in which humans had to rely on their basic instincts and raw power to survive. The John Carter stories had been set on a Mars that seems rather fairy tale in the light of our present-day knowledge but one that at the time had some loose relationship with scientific understanding. The Tarzan adventures were based in the heart of Africa, which whilst largely explored by Burroughs's day, had still not revealed all of its secrets. He had also written stories set in the Stone Age, on a remote South Sea island, at the center of the Earth and, in "Beyond Thirty" (1916), in a future where civilization has fallen and humans have reverted to a primitive existence.

The setting for *The Land That Time Forgot* has much in common with these other fantastic tales, but with considerable variation. We are taken to the world of Caspak, a hitherto unknown island somewhere near Antarctica which had once been a vast volcano that had long ago exploded, leaving a huge inland sea surrounded by high impenetrable cliffs. Within these cliffs, Caspak has its own microclimate so that whilst beyond the island it is freezing cold, inland it is subtropical. Dinosaurs have managed to survive here but humans took a different evolutionary course and all levels of that development remain. The opening novel partly explores the early levels of that development with hints of much more, which are revealed in the next two sections.

Burroughs may have taken the basic idea for the lost island from Arthur Conan Doyle's *The Lost World*. This had been published in 1912 and Burroughs had certainly read it. Though he claimed he did not finish it, he later remarked that he was "much impressed by the possibilities suggested by the story." Doyle's own Lost World, which is also home to dinosaurs, was set on a high plateau in South America separated from its surroundings by high, unscalable cliffs.

Burroughs had been careful not to consciously copy anything. He was alarmed while still drafting the first novel to see an announcement in *All-Story Weekly* for the forthcoming serial, "Polaris and the Goddess Glorian" by Charles B. Stilson, starting in the issue for September 15, 1917. This was also set in the Antarctic region and involves a submarine accessing an otherwise impenetrable remote world, just as Burroughs was plotting. He almost certainly revised some of his ideas to minimise any possible overlap, though the Polaris series also had much in common. It had started with "Polaris of the Snows" in *All-Story* in December 1915, and was itself an imitation Tarzan series, with the locale switched to the Antarctic world of Sardanes, which has a subtropical climate thanks to the surrounding volcanoes. Burroughs may well have seen the earlier serial and the idea of Caspak came from a mixture of Sardanes and Doyle's own Lost World.

Burroughs, however, developed the idea very differently and it is testament to his growing skills as a writer how he only gradually reveals the evolutionary mysteries of Caspak as the various explorers, separated by plot machinations, stumble in turn upon the island's dangers and its occupants.

Writing in the midst of the First World War, Burroughs cannot help but display a strong anti-German attitude. Also, by the mores of the day, the narrator of the first book has a rather condescending attitude to the chief heroine, Lys La Rue, though we soon discover she is perfectly capable of looking after herself. In fact there is much less in this book that might be termed politically incorrect than in other works by Burroughs, especially his Tarzan stories. It is just as exciting and enjoyable to read now as it was nearly a hundred years ago and, with Burroughs's depiction of human evolution, every bit as thought provoking.

MIKE ASHLEY

Mike Ashley is the author, editor and compiler of over 100 books, mostly in the fields of science fiction, fantasy, supernatural fiction and crime fiction, though he has also written biographies and reference books for children. He lives in Kent, England, with his wife, three cats and over 30,000 books and magazines.

PART I

THE LAND
THAT TIME
FORGOT

1

*It must have been a little after three o'clock in the afternoon that
it happened—the afternoon of June 3rd, 1916. It seems incredible
that all that I have passed through—all those weird and terrifying experiences—should have been encompassed within so short a
span as three brief months. Rather might I have experienced a cosmic cycle, with all its changes and evolutions for that which I have
seen with my own eyes in this brief interval of time—things that
no other mortal eye had seen before, glimpses of a world past, a
world dead, a world so long dead that even in the lowest Cambrian
stratum no trace of it remains. Fused with the melting inner crust,
it has passed forever beyond the ken of man other than in that lost
pocket of the earth whither fate has borne me and where my doom
is sealed. I am here and here I must remain.*

fter reading this far, my interest, which already
had been stimulated by the finding of the manu-
script, was approaching the boiling-point. I had
come to Greenland for the summer, on the advice
of my physician, and was slowly being bored
to extinction, as I had thoughtlessly neglected to bring sufficient
reading-matter. Being an indifferent fisherman, my enthusiasm for
this form of sport soon waned; yet in the absence of other forms of
recreation I was now risking my life in an entirely inadequate boat off
Cape Farewell at the southernmost extremity of Greenland.

Greenland! As a descriptive appellation, it is a sorry joke—but my story has nothing to do with Greenland, nothing to do with me; so I shall get through with the one and the other as rapidly as possible.

The inadequate boat finally arrived at a precarious landing, the natives, waist-deep in the surf, assisting. I was carried ashore, and while the evening meal was being prepared, I wandered to and fro along the rocky, shattered shore. Bits of surf-harried beach clove the worn granite, or whatever the rocks of Cape Farewell may be composed of, and as I followed the ebbing tide down one of these soft stretches, I saw the thing. Were one to bump into a Bengal tiger in the ravine behind the Bimini Baths, one could be no more surprised than was I to see a perfectly good quart thermos bottle turning and twisting in the surf of Cape Farewell at the southern extremity of Greenland. I rescued it, but I was soaked above the knees doing it; and then I sat down in the sand and opened it, and in the long twilight read the manuscript, neatly written and tightly folded, which was its contents.

You have read the opening paragraph, and if you are an imaginative idiot like myself, you will want to read the rest of it; so I shall give it to you here, omitting quotation marks—which are difficult of remembrance. In two minutes you will forget me.

My home is in Santa Monica. I am, or was, junior member of my father's firm. We are shipbuilders. Of recent years we have specialized on submarines, which we have built for Germany, England, France and the United States. I know a sub as a mother knows her baby's face, and have commanded a score of them on their trial runs. Yet my inclinations were all toward aviation. I graduated under Curtiss, and after a long siege with my father obtained his permission to try for the Lafayette Escadrille. As a stepping-stone I obtained an appointment in the American ambulance service and was on my way to France when three shrill whistles altered, in as many seconds, my entire scheme of life.

I was sitting on deck with some of the fellows who were going into the American ambulance service with me, my Airedale, Crown Prince Nobbler, asleep at my feet, when the first blast of the whistle shattered the peace and security of the ship. Ever since entering the U-boat zone we had been on the lookout for periscopes, and children that we were, bemoaning the unkind fate that was to see us safely into France on the morrow without a glimpse of the dread marauders. We were young; we craved thrills, and God knows we got them that day; yet by comparison with that through which I have since passed they were as tame as a Punch-and-Judy show.

I shall never forget the ashy faces of the passengers as they stampeded for their life-belts, though there was no panic. Nobs rose with a low growl. I rose, also, and over the ship's side, I saw not two hundred yards distant the periscope of a submarine, while racing toward the liner the wake of a torpedo was distinctly visible. We were aboard an American ship—which, of course, was not armed. We were entirely defenseless; yet without warning, we were being torpedoed.

I stood rigid, spellbound, watching the white wake of the torpedo. It struck us on the starboard side almost amidships. The vessel rocked as though the sea beneath it had been uptorn by a mighty volcano. We were thrown to the decks, bruised and stunned, and then above the ship, carrying with it fragments of steel and wood and dismembered human bodies, rose a column of water hundreds of feet into the air.

The silence which followed the detonation of the exploding torpedo was almost equally horrifying. It lasted for perhaps two seconds, to be followed by the screams and moans of the wounded, the cursing of the men and the hoarse commands of the ship's officers. They were splendid—they and their crew. Never before had I been so proud of my nationality as I was that moment. In all the chaos which followed the torpedoing of the liner no officer or member of the crew lost his head or showed in the slightest any degree of panic or fear.

While we were attempting to lower boats, the submarine emerged and trained guns on us. The officer in command ordered us to lower our flag, but this the captain of the liner refused to do. The ship was listing frightfully to starboard, rendering the port boats useless, while half the starboard boats had been demolished by the explosion. Even while the passengers were crowding the starboard rail and scrambling into the few boats left to us, the submarine commenced shelling the ship. I saw one shell burst in a group of women and children, and then I turned my head and covered my eyes.

When I looked again to horror was added chagrin, for with the emerging of the U-boat I had recognized her as a product of our own shipyard. I knew her to a rivet. I had superintended her construction. I had sat in that very conning-tower and directed the efforts of the sweating crew below when first her prow clove the sunny summer waters of the Pacific; and now this creature of my brain and hand had turned *Frankenstein*, bent upon pursuing me to my death.

A second shell exploded upon the deck. One of the lifeboats, frightfully overcrowded, swung at a dangerous angle from its davits. A fragment of the shell shattered the bow tackle, and I saw the women and children and the men vomited into the sea beneath, while the boat dangled stern up for a moment from its single davit, and at last with increasing momentum dived into the midst of the struggling victims screaming upon the face of the waters.

Now I saw men spring to the rail and leap into the ocean. The deck was tilting to an impossible angle. Nobs braced himself with all four feet to keep from slipping into the scuppers and looked up into my face with a questioning whine. I stooped and stroked his head.

"Come on, boy!" I cried, and running to the side of the ship, dived headforemost over the rail. When I came up, the first thing I saw was Nobs swimming about in a bewildered sort of way a few yards from me. At sight of me his ears went flat, and his lips parted in a characteristic grin.

The submarine was withdrawing toward the north, but all the time it was shelling the open boats, three of them, loaded to the gunwales with survivors. Fortunately the small boats presented a rather poor target, which, combined with the bad marksmanship of the Germans preserved their occupants from harm; and after a few minutes a blotch of smoke appeared upon the eastern horizon and the U-boat submerged and disappeared.

All the time the lifeboats has been pulling away from the danger of the sinking liner, and now, though I yelled at the top of my lungs, they either did not hear my appeals for help or else did not dare return to succor me. Nobs and I had gained some little distance from the ship when it rolled completely over and sank. We were caught in the suction only enough to be drawn backward a few yards, neither of us being carried beneath the surface. I glanced hurriedly about for something to which to cling. My eyes were directed toward the point at which the liner had disappeared when there came from the depths of the ocean the muffled reverberation of an explosion, and almost simultaneously a geyser of water in which were shattered lifeboats, human bodies, steam, coal, oil, and the flotsam of a liner's deck leaped high above the surface of the sea—a watery column momentarily marking the grave of another ship in this greatest cemetery of the seas.

When the turbulent waters had somewhat subsided and the sea had ceased to spew up wreckage, I ventured to swim back in search of something substantial enough to support my weight and that of Nobs as well. I had gotten well over the area of the wreck when not a half-dozen yards ahead of me a lifeboat shot bow foremost out of the ocean almost its entire length to flop down upon its keel with a mighty splash. It must have been carried far below, held to its mother ship by a single rope which finally parted to the enormous strain put upon it. In no other way can I account for its having leaped so far out of the water—a beneficent circumstance to which I doubtless owe my life, and that of another far dearer to me than my own. I say beneficent circumstance even in the face of the fact that a fate far more hideous confronts us than that which we escaped that day; for because of that circumstance I have met her whom otherwise I never should have known; I have met and loved her. At least I have had that great happiness in life; nor can Caspak, with all her horrors, expunge that which has been.

So for the thousandth time I thank the strange fate which sent that lifeboat hurtling upward from the green pit of destruction to which it had been dragged—sent it far up above the surface, emptying its water as it rose above the waves, and dropping it upon the surface of the sea, buoyant and safe.

It did not take me long to clamber over its side and drag Nobs in to comparative safety, and then I glanced around upon the scene of death and desolation which surrounded us. The sea was littered with wreckage among which floated the pitiful forms of women and children, buoyed up by their useless lifebelts. Some were torn and mangled; others lay rolling quietly to the motion of the sea, their countenances composed and peaceful; others were set in hideous lines of agony or horror. Close to the boat's side floated the figure of a girl. Her face was turned upward, held above the surface by her life-belt, and was framed in a floating mass of dark and waving hair. She was very beautiful. I had never looked upon such perfect features, such a divine molding which was at the same time human—intensely human. It was a face filled with character and strength and femininity—the face of one who was created to love and to be loved. The cheeks were flushed to the hue of life and health and vitality, and yet she lay there upon the bosom of the sea, dead. I felt something rise in my throat as I looked down upon that radiant vision, and I swore that I should live to avenge her murder.

And then I let my eyes drop once more to the face upon the water, and what I saw nearly tumbled me backward into the sea, for the eyes in the dead face had opened; the lips had parted; and one hand was raised toward me in a mute appeal for succor. She lived! She was not dead! I leaned over the boat's side and drew her quickly in to the comparative safety which God had given me. I removed her life-belt and my soggy coat and made a pillow for her head. I chafed her hands and arms and feet. I worked over her for an hour, and at last I was rewarded by a deep sigh, and again those great eyes opened and looked into mine.

At that I was all embarrassment. I have never been a ladies' man; at Leland-Stanford I was the butt of the class because of my hopeless imbecility in the presence of a pretty girl; but the men liked me, nevertheless. I was rubbing one of her hands when she opened her eyes, and I dropped it as though it were a red-hot rivet. Those eyes took me in slowly from head to foot; then they wandered slowly around the horizon marked by the rising and falling gunwales of the lifeboat. They looked at Nobs and softened, and then came back to me filled with questioning.

"I—I—" I stammered, moving away and stumbling over the next thwart. The vision smiled wanly.

"Aye-aye, sir!" she replied faintly, and again her lips drooped, and her long lashes swept the firm, fair texture of her skin.

"I hope that you are feeling better," I finally managed to say.

"Do you know," she said after a moment of silence, "I have been awake for a long time! But I did not dare open my eyes. I thought I must be dead, and I was afraid to look, for fear that I should see nothing but blackness about me. I am afraid to die! Tell me what happened after the ship went down. I remember all that happened before—oh, but I wish that I might forget it!" A sob broke her voice. "The beasts!" she went on after a moment. "And to think that I was to have married one of them—a lieutenant in the German navy."

9

Presently she resumed as though she had not ceased speaking. "I went down and down and down. I thought I should never cease to sink. I felt no particular distress until I suddenly started upward at ever-increasing velocity; then my lungs seemed about to burst, and I must have lost consciousness, for I remember nothing more until I opened my eyes after listening to a torrent of invective against Germany and Germans. Tell me, please, all that happened after the ship sank."

I told her, then, as well as I could, all that I had seen—the submarine shelling the open boats and all the rest of it. She thought it marvelous that we should have been spared in so providential a manner, and I had a pretty speech upon my tongue's end, but lacked the nerve to deliver it. Nobs had come over and nosed his muzzle into her lap, and she stroked his ugly face, and at last she leaned over and put her cheek against his forehead. I have always admired Nobs; but this was the first time that it had ever occurred to me that I might wish to be Nobs. I wondered how he would take it, for he is as unused to women as I. But he took to it as a duck takes to water. What I lack of being a ladies' man Nobs certainly makes up for as a ladies' dog. The old scalawag just closed his eyes and put on one of the softest "sugar-wouldn't-melt-in-my-mouth" expressions you ever saw and stood there taking it and asking for more. It made me jealous.

"You seem fond of dogs," I said.

"I am fond of this dog," she replied.

Whether she meant anything personal in that reply I did not know; but I took it as personal and it made me feel mighty good.

As we drifted about upon that vast expanse of loneliness it is not strange that we should quickly become well acquainted. Constantly we scanned the horizon for signs of smoke, venturing guesses as to our chances of rescue; but darkness settled, and the black night enveloped us without ever the sight of a speck upon the waters.

We were thirsty, hungry, uncomfortable, and cold. Our wet

garments had dried but little and I knew that the girl must be in grave danger from the exposure to a night of cold and wet upon the water in an open boat, without sufficient clothing and no food. I had managed to bail all the water out of the boat with cupped hands, ending by mopping the balance up with my handkerchief—a slow and back-breaking procedure; thus I had made a comparatively dry place for the girl to lie down low in the bottom of the boat, where the sides would protect her from the night wind, and when at last she did so, almost overcome as she was by weakness and fatigue, I threw my wet coat over her further to thwart the chill. But it was of no avail; as I sat watching her, the moonlight marking out the graceful curves of her slender young body, I saw her shiver.

"Isn't there something I can do?" I asked. "You can't lie there chilled through all night. Can't you suggest something?"

She shook her head. "We must grin and bear it," she replied after a moment.

Nobbler came and lay down on the thwart beside me, his back against my leg, and I sat staring in dumb misery at the girl, knowing in my heart of hearts that she might die before morning came, for what with the shock and the exposure, she had already gone through enough to kill almost any woman. And as I gazed down at her, so small and delicate and helpless, there was born slowly within my breast a new emotion. It had never been there before; now it will never cease to be there. It made me almost frantic in my desire to find some way to keep warm and cooling life-blood in her veins. I was cold myself, though I had almost forgotten it until Nobbler moved and I felt a new sensation of cold along my leg against which he had lain, and suddenly realized that in that one spot I had been warm. Like a great light came the understanding of a means to warm the girl. Immediately I knelt beside her to put my scheme into practice when suddenly I was overwhelmed with embarrassment. Would she permit it, even if I could muster the courage to suggest it?

Then I saw her frame convulse shudderingly, her muscles reacting to her rapidly lowering temperature, and casting prudery to the winds, I threw myself down beside her and took her in my arms, pressing her body close to mine.

She drew away suddenly, voicing a little cry of fright, and tried to push me from her.

"Forgive me," I managed to stammer. "It is the only way. You will die of exposure if you are not warmed, and Nobs and I are the only means we can command for furnishing warmth." And I held her tightly while I called Nobs and bade him lie down at her back. The girl didn't struggle any more when she learned my purpose; but she gave two or three little gasps, and then began to cry softly, burying her face on my arm, and thus she fell asleep.

2

oward morning, I must have dozed, though it seemed to me at the time that I had lain awake for days, instead of hours. When I finally opened my eyes, it was daylight, and the girl's hair was in my face, and she was breathing normally. I thanked God for that. She had turned her head during the night so that as I opened my eyes I saw her face not an inch from mine, my lips almost touching hers.

It was Nobs who finally awoke her. He got up, stretched, turned around a few times and lay down again, and the girl opened her eyes and looked into mine. Hers went very wide at first, and then slowly comprehension came to her, and she smiled.

"You have been very good to me," she said, as I helped her to rise, though if the truth were known I was more in need of assistance than she; the circulation all along my left side seeming to be paralyzed entirely. "You have been very good to me." And that was the only mention she ever made of it; yet I know that she was thankful and that only reserve prevented her from referring to what, to say the least, was an embarrassing situation, however unavoidable.

Shortly after daylight we saw smoke apparently coming straight toward us, and after a time we made out the squat lines of a tug—one of those fearless exponents of England's supremacy of the sea that tows sailing ships into French and English ports. I stood up on a thwart and waved my soggy coat above my head. Nobs stood upon another and barked. The girl sat at my feet straining her eyes toward

13

the deck of the oncoming boat. "They see us," she said at last. "There is a man answering your signal." She was right. A lump came into my throat—for her sake rather than for mine. She was saved, and none too soon. She could not have lived through another night upon the Channel; she might not have lived through the coming day.

The tug came close beside us, and a man on deck threw us a rope. Willing hands dragged us to the deck, Nobs scrambling nimbly aboard without assistance. The rough men were gentle as mothers with the girl. Plying us both with questions they hustled her to the captain's cabin and me to the boiler-room. They told the girl to take off her wet clothes and throw them outside the door that they might be dried, and then to slip into the captain's bunk and get warm. They didn't have to tell me to strip after I once got into the warmth of the boiler-room. In a jiffy, my clothes hung about where they might dry most quickly, and I myself was absorbing, through every pore, the welcome heat of the stifling compartment. They brought us hot soup and coffee, and then those who were not on duty sat around and helped me damn the Kaiser and his brood.

As soon as our clothes were dry, they bade us don them, as the chances were always more than fair in those waters that we should run into trouble with the enemy, as I was only too well aware. What with the warmth and the feeling of safety for the girl, and the knowledge that a little rest and food would quickly overcome the effects of her experiences of the past dismal hours, I was feeling more content than I had experienced since those three whistle-blasts had shattered the peace of my world the previous afternoon.

But peace upon the Channel has been but a transitory thing since August, 1914. It proved itself such that morning, for I had scarce gotten into my dry clothes and taken the girl's apparel to the captain's cabin when an order was shouted down into the engine-room for full speed ahead, and an instant later I heard the dull boom of a gun. In a moment I was up on deck to see an enemy submarine about two hundred yards off our port bow. She had signaled us to stop, and our skipper had ignored the order; but now she had her gun trained on us, and the second shot grazed the cabin, warning the belligerent tug-captain that it was time to obey. Once again an order went down to the engine-room, and the tug reduced speed. The U-boat ceased firing and ordered the tug to come about and approach. Our momentum had carried us a little beyond the enemy craft, but we were turning now on the arc of a circle that would bring us alongside her. As I stood watching the maneuver and wondering what was to become of us, I felt something touch my elbow and turned to see the girl standing at my side. She looked up into my face with a rueful expression. "They seem bent on our destruction," she said, "and it looks like the same boat that sunk us yesterday."

"It is," I replied. "I know her well. I helped design her and took her out on her first run."

The girl drew back from me with a little exclamation of surprise and disappointment. "I thought you were an American," she said. "I had no idea you were a—a——"

"Nor am I," I replied. "Americans have been building submarines for all nations for many years. I wish, though, that we had gone bankrupt, my father and I, before ever we turned out that *Frankenstein* of a thing."

We were approaching the U-boat at half speed now, and I could almost distinguish the features of the men upon her deck. A sailor stepped to my side and slipped something hard and cold into my hand. I did not have to look at it to know that it was a heavy pistol. "Tyke 'er an' use 'er," was all he said.

Our bow was pointed straight toward the U-boat now as I heard word passed to the engine for full speed ahead. I instantly grasped the brazen effrontery of the plucky English skipper—he was going to ram five hundred tons of U-boat in the face of her trained gun. I could scarce repress a cheer. At first the boches didn't seem to grasp his intention. Evidently they thought they were witnessing an exhibition of poor seamanship, and they yelled their warnings to the tug to reduce speed and throw the helm hard to port.

We were within fifty feet of them when they awakened to the intentional menace of our maneuver. Their gun crew was off its guard; but they sprang to their piece now and sent a futile shell above our heads. Nobs leaped about and barked furiously. "Let 'em have it!" commanded the tug-captain, and instantly revolvers and rifles poured bullets upon the deck of the submersible. Two of the gun-crew went down; the other trained their piece at the water-line of the oncoming tug. The balance of those on deck replied to our small-arms fire, directing their efforts toward the man at our wheel.

I hastily pushed the girl down the companionway leading to the engine-room, and then I raised my pistol and fired my first shot at a boche. What happened in the next few seconds happened so quickly that details are rather blurred in my memory. I saw the helmsman lunge forward upon the wheel, pulling the helm around so that the tug sheered off quickly from her course, and I recall realizing that all our efforts were to be in vain, because of all the men aboard, Fate had decreed that this one should fall first to an enemy bullet. I saw the depleted gun-crew on the submarine fire their piece and I felt the shock of impact and heard the loud explosion as the shell struck and exploded in our bows.

I saw and realized these things even as I was leaping into the pilot-house and grasping the wheel, standing astride the dead body of the helmsman. With all my strength I threw the helm to starboard; but it was too late to effect the purpose of our skipper. The best I did was to scrape alongside the sub. I heard some one shriek an order into the engine-room; the boat shuddered and trembled to the sudden reversing of the engines, and our speed quickly lessened. Then I saw what that madman of a skipper planned since his first scheme had gone wrong.

With a loud-yelled command, he leaped to the slippery deck of the submersible, and at his heels came his hardy crew. I sprang from the pilot-house and followed, not to be left out in the cold when it came to strafing the boches. From the engine room companionway came the engineer and stockers, and together we leaped after the balance of the crew and into the hand-to-hand fight that was covering the wet deck with red blood. Beside me came Nobs, silent now, and grim. Germans were emerging from the open hatch to take part in the battle on deck. At first the pistols cracked amidst the cursing of the men and the loud commands of the commander and his junior; but presently we were too indiscriminately mixed to make it safe to use our firearms, and the battle resolved itself into a hand-to-hand struggle for possession of the deck.

The sole aim of each of us was to hurl one of the opposing force into the sea. I shall never forget the hideous expression upon the face of the great Prussian with whom chance confronted me. He lowered his head and rushed at me, bellowing like a bull. With a quick side-step and ducking low beneath his outstretched arms, I eluded him; and as he turned to come back at me, I landed a blow upon his chin which sent him spinning toward the edge of the deck. I saw his wild endeavors to regain his equilibrium; I saw him reel drunkenly for an instant upon the brink of eternity and then, with a loud scream, slip into the sea. At the same instant a pair of giant arms encircled me from behind and lifted me entirely off my feet. Kick and squirm as I would, I could neither turn toward my antagonist nor free myself from his maniacal grasp. Relentlessly he was rushing me toward the side of the vessel and death. There was none to stay him, for each of my companions was more than occupied by from one to three of the enemy. For an instant I was fearful for myself, and then I saw that which filled me with a far greater terror for another.

My boche was bearing me toward the side of the submarine against which the tug was still pounding. That I should be ground to death between the two was lost upon me as I saw the girl standing alone upon the tug's deck, as I saw the stern high in air and the bow rapidly settling for the final dive, as I saw death from which I could not save her clutching at the skirts of the woman I now knew all too well that I loved.

I had perhaps the fraction of a second longer to live when I heard an angry growl behind us mingle with a cry of pain and rage from the giant who carried me. Instantly he went backward to the deck, and as he did so he threw his arms outwards to save himself, freeing me. I fell heavily upon him, but was upon my feet in the instant. As I arose, I cast a single glance at my opponent. Never again would he menace me or another, for Nobs' great jaws had closed upon his throat. Then I sprang toward the edge of the deck closest to the girl upon the sinking tug.

"Jump!" I cried. "Jump!" And I held out my arms to her. Instantly as though with implicit confidence in my ability to save her, she leaped over the side of the tug onto the sloping, slippery side of the U-boat. I reached far over to seize her hand. At the same instant the tug pointed its stern straight toward the sky and plunged out of sight. My hand missed the girl's by a fraction of an inch, and I saw her slip into the sea; but scarce had she touched the water when I was in after her.

The sinking tug drew us far below the surface; but I had seized her the moment I struck the water, and so we went down together, and together we came up—a few yards from the U-boat. The first thing I heard was Nobs barking furiously; evidently he had missed me and was searching. A single glance at the vessel's deck assured me that the battle was over and that we had been victorious, for I saw our survivors holding a handful of the enemy at pistol points while one by one the rest of the crew was coming out of the craft's interior and lining up on deck with the other prisoners.

As I swam toward the submarine with the girl, Nobs' persistent barking attracted the attention of some of the tug's crew, so that as soon as we reached the side there were hands to help us aboard. I asked the girl if she was hurt, but she assured me that she was none the worse for this second wetting; nor did she seem to suffer any from shock. I was to learn for myself that this slender and seemingly delicate creature possessed the heart and courage of a warrior.

As we joined our own party, I found the tug's mate checking up our survivors. There were ten of us left, not including the girl. Our brave skipper was missing, as were eight others. There had been nineteen of us in the attacking party and we had accounted in one way and another during the battle for sixteen Germans and had taken nine prisoners, including the commander. His lieutenant had been killed.

"Not a bad day's work," said Bradley, the mate, when he had completed his roll. "Only losing the skipper," he added, "was the worst. He was a fine man, a fine man."

Olson—who in spite of his name was Irish, and in spite of his not being Scotch had been the tug's engineer—was standing with Bradley and me. "Yis," he agreed, "it's a day's wor-rk we're after doin', but what are we goin' to be doin' wid it now we got it?"

"We'll run her into the nearest English port," said Bradley, "and then we'll all go ashore and get our V. C.'s," he concluded, laughing.

"How you goin' to run her?" queried Olson. "You can't trust these Dutchmen."

Bradley scratched his head. "I guess you're right," he admitted. "And I don't know the first thing about a sub."

"I do," I assured him. "I know more about this particular sub than the officer who commanded her."

Both men looked at me in astonishment, and then I had to explain all over again as I had explained to the girl. Bradley and Olson were delighted. Immediately I was put in command, and the first thing I did was to go below with Olson and inspect the craft thoroughly for hidden boches and damaged machinery. There were no Germans below, and everything was intact and in ship-shape working order. I then ordered all hands below except one man who was to act as lookout. Questioning the Germans, I found that all except the commander were willing to resume their posts and aid in bringing the vessel into an English port. I believe that they were relieved at the prospect of being detained at a comfortable English prison-camp for the duration of the war after the perils and privations through which they had passed. The officer, however, assured me that he would never be a party to the capture of his vessel.

There was, therefore, nothing to do but put the man in irons. As we were preparing to put this decision into force, the girl descended from the deck. It was the first time that she or the German officer had seen each other's faces since we had boarded the U-boat. I was assisting the girl down the ladder and still retained a hold upon her arm—possibly after such support was no longer necessary—when she turned and looked squarely into the face of the German. Each voiced a sudden exclamation of surprise and dismay.

"Lys!" he cried, and took a step toward her.

The girl's eyes went wide, and slowly filled with a great horror, as she shrank back. Then her slender figure stiffened to the erectness of a soldier, and with chin in air and without a word she turned her back upon the officer.

"Take him away," I directed the two men who guarded him, "and put him in irons."

When he had gone, the girl raised her eyes to mine. "He is the German of whom I spoke," she said. "He is Baron von Schoenvorts."

I merely inclined my head. She had loved him! I wondered if in her heart of hearts she did not love him yet. Immediately I became insanely jealous. I hated Baron Friedrich von Schoenvorts with such utter intensity that the emotion thrilled me with a species of exaltation.

But I didn't have much chance to enjoy my hatred then, for almost immediately the lookout poked his face over the hatchway and bawled down that there was smoke on the horizon, dead ahead. Immediately I went on deck to investigate, and Bradley came with me.

"If she's friendly," he said, "we'll speak her. If she's not, we'll sink her—eh, captain?"

"Yes, lieutenant," I replied, and it was his turn to smile.

We hoisted the Union Jack and remained on deck, asking Bradley to go below and assign to each member of the crew his duty, placing one Englishman with a pistol beside each German.

"Half speed ahead," I commanded.

More rapidly now we closed the distance between ourselves and the stranger, until I could plainly see the red ensign of the British merchant marine. My heart swelled with pride at the thought that presently admiring British tars would be congratulating us upon our notable capture; and just about then the merchant steamer must have sighted us, for she veered suddenly toward the north, and a moment later dense volumes of smoke issued from her funnels. Then, steering a zigzag course, she fled from us as though we had been the bubonic plague. I altered the course of the submarine and set off in chase; but the steamer was faster than we, and soon left us hopelessly astern.

With a rueful smile I directed that our original course be resumed, and once again we set off toward merry England. That was three months ago, and we haven't arrived yet; nor is there any likelihood that we ever shall.

The steamer we had just sighted must have wirelessed a warning, for it wasn't half an hour before we saw more smoke on the horizon, and this time the vessel flew the white ensign of the Royal Navy and carried guns. She didn't veer to the north or anywhere else, but bore down on us rapidly. I was just preparing to signal her, when a flame flashed from her bows, and an instant later the water in front of us was thrown high by the explosion of a shell.

Bradley had come on deck and was standing beside me. "About one more of those, and she'll have our range," he said. "She doesn't seem to take much stock in our Union Jack."

A second shell passed over us, and then I gave the command to change our direction, at the same time directing Bradley to go below and give the order to submerge. I passed Nobs down to him, and following, saw to the closing and fastening of the hatch.

It seemed to me that the diving-tanks never had filled so slowly. We heard a loud explosion apparently directly above us; the craft trembled to the shock which threw us all to the deck. I expected momentarily to feel the deluge of inrushing water, but none came. Instead we continued to submerge until the manometer registered forty feet and then I knew that we were safe. Safe! I almost smiled. I had relieved Olson, who had remained in the tower at my direction, having been a member of one of the early British submarine crews, and therefore having some knowledge of the business. Bradley was at my side. He looked at me quizzically.

"What the devil are we to do?" he asked. "The merchantman will flee us; the war-vessel will destroy us; neither will believe our colors or give us a chance to explain. We will meet even a worse reception if we go nosing around a British port—mines, nets and all of it. We can't do it."

"Let's try it again when this fellow has lost the scent," I urged. "There must come a ship that will believe us."

And try it again we did, only to be almost rammed by a huge freighter. Later we were fired upon by a destroyer, and two merchantmen turned and fled at our approach. For two days we cruised up and down the Channel trying to tell some one, who would listen, that we were friends; but no one would listen. After our encounter with the first warship I had given instructions that a wireless message be sent out explaining our predicament; but to my chagrin I discovered that both sending and receiving instruments had disappeared.

"There is only one place you can go," von Schoenvorts sent word to me, "and that is Kiel. You can't land anywhere else in these waters. If you wish, I will take you there, and I can promise that you will be treated well."

"There is another place we can go," I sent back my reply, "and we will before we'll go to Germany. That place is hell."

3

hose were anxious days, during which I had but little opportunity to associate with Lys. I had given her the commander's room, Bradley and I taking that of the deck-officer, while Olson and two of our best men occupied the room ordinarily allotted to petty officers. I made Nobs' bed down in Lys' room, for I knew she would feel less alone.

Nothing of much moment occurred for a while after we left British waters behind us. We ran steadily along upon the surface, making good time. The first two boats we sighted made off as fast as they could go; and the third, a huge freighter, fired on us, forcing us to submerge. It was after this that our troubles commenced. One of the Diesel engines broke down in the morning, and while we were working on it, the forward port diving-tank commenced to fill. I was on deck at the time and noted the gradual list. Guessing at once what was happening, I leaped for the hatch and slamming it closed above my head, dropped to the centrale. By this time the craft was going down by the head with a most unpleasant list to port, and I didn't wait to transmit orders to some one else but ran as fast as I could for the valve that let the sea into the forward port diving-tank. It was wide open. To close it and to have the pump started that would empty it were the work of but a minute; but we had had a close call.

I knew that the valve had never opened itself. Some one had opened it—some one who was willing to die himself if he might at the same time encompass the death of all of us.

After that I kept a guard pacing the length of the narrow craft. We worked upon the engine all that day and night and half the following day. Most of the time we drifted idly upon the surface, but toward noon we sighted smoke due west, and having found that only enemies inhabited the world for us, I ordered that the other engine be started so that we could move out of the path of the oncoming steamer. The moment the engine started to turn, however, there was a grinding sound of tortured steel, and when it had been stopped, we found that some one had placed a cold-chisel in one of the gears.

It was another two days before we were ready to limp along, half repaired. The night before the repairs were completed, the sentry came to my room and awoke me. He was rather an intelligent fellow of the English middle class, in whom I had much confidence.

"Well, Wilson," I asked, "what's the matter now?"

He raised his finger to his lips and came closer to me. "I think I've found out who's doin' the mischief," he whispered, and nodded his head toward the girl's room. "I seen her sneakin' from the crew's room just now," he went on. "She'd been in gassin' wit' the boche commander. Benson seen her in there las' night, too, but he never said nothin' till I goes on watch tonight. Benson's sorter slow in the head, an' he never puts two an' two together till some one else has made four out of it."

If the man had come in and struck me suddenly in the face, I could have been no more surprised.

"Say nothing of this to anyone," I ordered. "Keep your eyes and ears open and report every suspicious thing you see or hear."

The man saluted and left me; but for an hour or more I tossed, restless, upon my hard bunk in an agony of jealousy and fear. Finally I fell into a troubled sleep. It was daylight when I awoke. We were steaming along slowly upon the surface, my orders having been to proceed at half speed until we could take an observation and determine our position. The sky had been overcast all the previous day and all night; but as I stepped into the centrale that morning I was delighted to see that the sun was again shining. The spirits of the men seemed improved; everything seemed propitious. I forgot at once the cruel misgivings of the past night as I set to work to take my observations.

What a blow awaited me! The sextant and chronometer had both been broken beyond repair, and they had been broken just this very night. They had been broken upon the night that Lys had been seen talking with von Schoenvorts. I think that it was this last thought which hurt me the worst. I could look the other disaster in the face with equanimity; but the bald fact that Lys might be a traitor appalled me.

I called Bradley and Olson on deck and told them what had happened, but for the life of me I couldn't bring myself to repeat what Wilson had reported to me the previous night. In fact, as I had given the matter thought, it seemed incredible that the girl could have passed through my room, in which Bradley and I slept, and then carried on a conversation in the crew's room, in which Von Schoenvorts was kept, without having been seen by more than a single man.

Bradley shook his head. "I can't make it out," he said. "One of those boches must be pretty clever to come it over us all like this; but they haven't harmed us as much as they think; there are still the extra instruments."

It was my turn now to shake a doleful head. "There are no extra instruments," I told them. "They too have disappeared as did the wireless apparatus."

Both men looked at me in amazement. "We still have the compass and the sun," said Olson. "They may be after getting the compass some night; but they's too many of us around in the daytime fer 'em to get the sun."

It was then that one of the men stuck his head up through the hatchway and seeing me, asked permission to come on deck and get a breath of fresh air. I recognized him as Benson, the man who, Wilson had said, reported having seen Lys with von Schoenvorts two nights before. I motioned him on deck and then called him to one side, asking if he had seen anything out of the way or unusual during his trick on watch the night before. The fellow scratched his head a moment and said, "No," and then as though it was an afterthought, he told me that he had seen the girl in the crew's room about midnight talking with the German commander, but as there hadn't seemed to him to be any harm in that, he hadn't said anything about it. Telling him never to fail to report to me anything in the slightest out of the ordinary routine of the ship, I dismissed him.

Several of the other men now asked permission to come on deck, and soon all but those actually engaged in some necessary duty were standing around smoking and talking, all in the best of spirits. I took advantage of the absence of the men upon the deck to go below for my breakfast, which the cook was already preparing upon the electric stove. Lys, followed by Nobs, appeared as I entered the centrale. She met me with a pleasant "Good morning!" which I am afraid I replied to in a tone that was rather constrained and surly.

"Will you breakfast with me?" I suddenly asked the girl, determined to commence a probe of my own along the lines which duty demanded.

She nodded a sweet acceptance of my invitation, and together we sat down at the little table of the officers' mess.

"You slept well last night?" I asked.

"All night," she replied. "I am a splendid sleeper."

Her manner was so straightforward and honest that I could not bring myself to believe in her duplicity; yet—Thinking to surprise her into a betrayal of her guilt, I blurted out: "The chronometer and sextant were both destroyed last night; there is a traitor among us." But she never turned a hair by way of evidencing guilty knowledge of the catastrophe.

"Who could it have been?" she cried. "The Germans would be crazy to do it, for their lives are as much at stake as ours."

"Men are often glad to die for an ideal—an ideal of patriotism, perhaps," I replied; "and a willingness to martyr themselves includes a willingness to sacrifice others, even those who love them. Women are much the same, except that they will go even further than most men—they will sacrifice everything, even honor, for love."

I watched her face carefully as I spoke, and I thought that I detected a very faint flush mounting her cheek. Seeing an opening and an advantage, I sought to follow it up.

"Take von Schoenvorts, for instance," I continued: "he would doubtless be glad to die and take us all with him, could he prevent in no other way the falling of his vessel into enemy hands. He would sacrifice anyone, even you; and if you still love him, you might be his ready tool. Do you understand me?"

She looked at me in wide-eyed consternation for a moment, and then she went very white and rose from her seat. "I do," she replied, and turning her back upon me, she walked quickly toward her room. I started to follow, for even believing what I did, I was sorry that I had hurt her. I reached the door to the crew's room just behind her and in time to see von Schoenvorts lean forward and whisper something to her as she passed; but she must have guessed that she might be watched, for she passed on.

That afternoon it clouded over; the wind mounted to a gale, and the sea rose until the craft was wallowing and rolling frightfully. Nearly everyone aboard was sick; the air became foul and oppressive. For twenty-four hours I did not leave my post in the conning-tower, as both Olson and Bradley were sick. Finally I found that I must get a little rest, and so I looked about for some one to relieve me. Benson volunteered. He had not been sick, and assured me that he was a former R.N. man and had been detailed for submarine duty for over two years. I was glad that it was he, for I had considerable confidence in his loyalty, and so it was with a feeling of security that I went below and lay down.

I slept twelve hours straight, and when I awoke and discovered what I had done, I lost no time in getting to the conning-tower. There sat Benson as wide awake as could be, and the compass showed that we were heading straight into the west. The storm was still raging; nor did it abate its fury until the fourth day. We were all pretty well done up and looked forward to the time when we could go on deck and fill our lungs with fresh air. During the whole four days I had not seen the girl, as she evidently kept closely to her room; and during this time no untoward incident had occurred aboard the boat—a fact which seemed to strengthen the web of circumstantial evidence about her.

For six more days after the storm lessened we still had fairly rough weather; nor did the sun once show himself during all that time. For the season—it was now the middle of June—the storm was unusual; but being from southern California, I was accustomed to unusual weather. In fact, I have discovered that the world over, unusual weather prevails at all times of the year.

We kept steadily to our westward course, and as the *U-33* was one of the fastest submersibles we had ever turned out, I knew that we must be pretty close to the North American coast. What puzzled me most was the fact that for six days we had not sighted a single ship. It seemed remarkable that we could cross the Atlantic almost to the coast of the American continent without glimpsing smoke or sail, and at last I came to the conclusion that we were way off our course, but whether to the north or to the south of it I could not determine.

On the seventh day the sea lay comparatively calm at early dawn. There was a slight haze upon the ocean which had cut off our view of the stars; but conditions all pointed toward a clear morrow, and I was on deck anxiously awaiting the rising of the sun. My eyes were glued upon the impenetrable mist astern, for there in the east I should see the first glow of the rising sun that would assure me we were still upon the right course. Gradually the heavens lightened; but astern I could see no intenser glow that would indicate the rising sun behind the mist. Bradley was standing at my side. Presently he touched my arm.

"Look, captain," he said, and pointed south.

I looked and gasped, for there directly to port I saw outlined through the haze the red top of the rising sun. Hurrying to the tower, I looked at the compass. It showed that we were holding steadily upon our westward course. Either the sun was rising in the south, or the compass had been tampered with. The conclusion was obvious.

I went back to Bradley and told him what I had discovered. "And," I concluded, "we can't make another five hundred knots without oil; our provisions are running low and so is our water. God only knows how far south we have run."

"There is nothing to do," he replied, "other than to alter our course once more toward the west; we must raise land soon or we shall all be lost."

I told him to do so, and then I set to work improvising a crude sextant with which we finally took our bearings in a rough and most unsatisfactory manner; for when the work was done, we did not know how far from the truth the result might be. It showed us to be about 20° north and 30° west—nearly twenty-five hundred miles off our course. In short, if our reading was anywhere near correct, we must have been traveling due south for six days. Bradley now relieved Benson, for we had arranged our shifts so that the latter and Olson now divided the nights, while Bradley and I alternated with one another during the days.

I questioned both Olson and Benson closely in the matter of the compass; but each stoutly maintained that no one had tampered with it during his tour of duty. Benson gave me a knowing smile, as much as to say: "Well, you and I know who did this." Yet I could not believe that it was the girl.

We kept to our westerly course for several hours when the look-out's cry announced a sail. I ordered the *U-33*'s course altered, and we bore down upon the stranger, for I had come to a decision which was the result of necessity. We could not lie there in the middle of the Atlantic and starve to death if there was any way out of it. The sailing ship saw us while we were still a long way off, as was evidenced by her efforts to escape. There was scarcely any wind, however, and her case was hopeless; so when we drew near and signaled her to stop, she came into the wind and lay there with her sails flapping idly. We moved in quite close to her. She was the *Balmen* of Halmstad, Sweden, with a general cargo from Brazil for Spain.

I explained our circumstances to her skipper and asked for food, water and oil; but when he found that we were not German, he became very angry and abusive and started to draw away from us; but I was in no mood for any such business. Turning toward Bradley, who was in the conning-tower, I snapped out: "Gun-service on deck! To the diving stations!" We had no opportunity for drill; but every man had been posted as to his duties, and the German members of the crew understood that it was obedience or death for them, as each was accompanied by a man with a pistol. Most of them, though, were only too glad to obey me.

Bradley passed the order down into the ship, and a moment later the gun-crew clambered up the narrow ladder and at my direction trained their piece upon the slow-moving Swede. "Fire a shot across her bow," I instructed the gun-captain.

Accept it from me, it didn't take that Swede long to see the error of his way and get the red and white pennant signifying "I understand" to the masthead. Once again the sails flapped idly, and then I ordered him to lower a boat and come after me. With Olson and a couple of the Englishmen I boarded the ship, and from her cargo selected what we needed—oil, provisions and water. I gave the master of the *Balmen* a receipt for what we took, together with an affidavit signed by Bradley, Olson, and myself, stating briefly how we had come into possession of the *U-33* and the urgency of our need for what we took. We addressed both to any British agent with the request that the owners of the *Balmen* be reimbursed; but whether or not they were, I do not know[1].

With water, food, and oil aboard, we felt that we had obtained a new lease of life. Now, too, we knew definitely where we were, and I determined to make for Georgetown, British Guiana—but I was destined to again suffer bitter disappointment.

Six of us of the loyal crew had come on deck either to serve the gun or board the Swede during our set-to with her; and now, one by one, we descended the ladder into the centrale. I was the last to come, and when I reached the bottom, I found myself looking into the muzzle of a pistol in the hands of Baron Friedrich von Schoenvorts— I saw all my men lined up at one side with the remaining eight Germans standing guard over them.

I couldn't imagine how it had happened; but it had. Later I learned that they had first overpowered Benson, who was asleep in his bunk, and taken his pistol from him, and then had found it an easy matter to disarm the cook and the remaining two Englishmen below. After that it had been comparatively simple to stand at the foot of the ladder and arrest each individual as he descended.

The first thing von Schoenvorts did was to send for me and announce that as a pirate I was to be shot early the next morning. Then he explained that the *U-33* would cruise in these waters for

---

[1] Late in July, 1916, an item in the shipping news mentioned a Swedish sailing vessel, *Balmen*, Rio de Janeiro to Barcelona, sunk by a German raider sometime in June. A single survivor in an open boat was picked up off the Cape Verde Islands, in a dying condition. He expired without giving any details.

a time, sinking neutral and enemy shipping indiscriminately, and looking for one of the German raiders that was supposed to be in these parts.

He didn't shoot me the next morning as he had promised, and it has never been clear to me why he postponed the execution of my sentence. Instead he kept me ironed just as he had been; then he kicked Bradley out of my room and took it all to himself.

We cruised for a long time, sinking many vessels, all but one by gunfire, but we did not come across a German raider. I was surprised to note that von Schoenvorts often permitted Benson to take command; but I reconciled this by the fact that Benson appeared to know more of the duties of a submarine commander than did any of the stupid Germans.

Once or twice Lys passed me; but for the most part she kept to her room. The first time she hesitated as though she wished to speak to me; but I did not raise my head, and finally she passed on. Then one day came the word that we were about to round the Horn and that von Schoenvorts had taken it into his fool head to cruise up along the Pacific coast of North America and prey upon all sorts and conditions of merchantmen.

"I'll put the fear of God and the Kaiser into them," he said.

The very first day we entered the South Pacific we had an adventure. It turned out to be quite the most exciting adventure I had ever encountered. It fell about this way. About eight bells of the forenoon watch I heard a hail from deck, and presently the footsteps of the entire ship's company, from the amount of noise I heard at the ladder. Some one yelled back to those who had not yet reached the level of the deck: "It's the raider, the German raider *Geier!*"

I saw that we had reached the end of our rope. Below all was quiet—not a man remained. A door opened at the end of the narrow hull, and presently Nobs came trotting up to me. He licked my face and rolled over on his back, reaching for me with his big, awkward paws. Then other footsteps sounded, approaching me. I knew whose they were, and I looked straight down at the flooring. The girl was coming almost at a run—she was at my side immediately. "Here!" she cried. "Quick!" And she slipped something into my hand. It was a key—the key to my irons. At my side she also laid a pistol, and then she went on into the centrale. As she passed me, I saw that she carried another pistol for herself. It did not take me long to liberate myself, and then I was at her side. "How can I thank you?" I started; but she shut me up with a word.

"Do not thank me," she said coldly. "I do not care to hear your thanks or any other expression from you. Do not stand there looking at me. I have given you a chance to do something—now do it!" The last was a peremptory command that made me jump.

Glancing up, I saw that the tower was empty, and I lost no time in clambering up, looking about me. About a hundred yards off lay a small, swift cruiser-raider, and above her floated the German man-of-war's flag. A boat had just been lowered, and I could see it moving toward us filled with officers and men. The cruiser lay dead ahead. "My," I thought, "what a wonderful targ———"

I stopped even thinking, so surprised and shocked was I by the boldness of my imagery. The girl was just below me. I looked down on her wistfully. Could I trust her? Why had she released me at this moment? I must! I must! There was no other way. I dropped back below. "Ask Olson to step down here, please," I requested; "and don't let anyone see you ask him."

She looked at me with a puzzled expression on her face for the barest fraction of a second, and then she turned and went up the ladder. A moment later Olson returned, and the girl followed him. "Quick!" I whispered to the big Irishman, and made for the bow compartment where the torpedo-tubes are built into the boat; here, too, were the torpedoes. The girl accompanied us, and when she saw the thing I had in mind, she stepped forward and lent a hand

34

to the swinging of the great cylinder of death and destruction into the mouth of its tube. With oil and main strength we shoved the torpedo home and shut the tube; then I ran back to the conning-tower, praying in my heart of hearts that the *U-33* had not swung her bow away from the prey. No, thank God!

Never could aim have been truer. I signaled back to Olson: "Let 'er go!" The *U-33* trembled from stem to stern as the torpedo shot from its tube. I saw the white wake leap from her bow straight toward the enemy cruiser. A chorus of hoarse yells arose from the deck of our own craft; I saw the officers stand suddenly erect in the boat that was approaching us, and I heard loud cries and curses from the raider. Then I turned my attention to my own business. Most of the men on the submarine's deck were standing in paralyzed fascination, staring at the torpedo. Bradley happened to be looking toward the conning-tower and saw me. I sprang on deck and ran toward him. "Quick!" I whispered. "While they are stunned, we must overcome them."

A German was standing near Bradley—just in front of him. The Englishman struck the fellow a frantic blow upon the neck and at the same time snatched his pistol from its holster. Von Schoenvorts had recovered from his first surprise quickly and had turned toward the main hatch to investigate. I covered him with my revolver, and at the same instant the torpedo struck the raider, the terrific explosion drowning the German's command to his men.

Bradley was now running from one to another of our men, and though some of the Germans saw and heard him, they seemed too stunned for action.

Olson was below, so that there were only nine of us against eight Germans, for the man Bradley had struck still lay upon the deck. Only two of us were armed; but the heart seemed to have gone out of the boches, and they put up but half-hearted resistance. Von Schoenvorts was the worst—he was fairly frenzied with rage and chagrin, and he came charging for me like a mad bull, and as he came he discharged his pistol. If he'd stopped long enough to take aim, he might have gotten me; but his pace made him wild, so that not a shot touched me, and then we clinched and went to the deck. This left two pistols, which two of my own men were quick to appropriate. The Baron was no match for me in a hand-to-hand encounter, and I soon had him pinned to the deck and the life almost choked out of him.

A half-hour later things had quieted down, and all was much the same as before the prisoners had revolted—only we kept a much closer watch on von Schoenvorts. The *Geier* had sunk while we were still battling upon our deck, and afterward we had drawn away toward the north, leaving the survivors to the attention of the single boat which had been making its way toward us when Olson launched the torpedo. I suppose the poor devils never reached land, and if they did, they most probably perished on that cold and unhospitable shore; but I couldn't permit them aboard the *U-33*. We had all the Germans we could take care of.

That evening the girl asked permission to go on deck. She said that she felt the effects of long confinement below, and I readily granted her request. I could not understand her, and I craved an opportunity to talk with her again in an effort to fathom her and her intentions, and so I made it a point to follow her up the ladder. It was a clear, cold, beautiful night. The sea was calm except for the white water at our bows and the two long radiating swells running far off into the distance upon either hand astern, forming a great V which our propellers filled with choppy waves. Benson was in the tower, we were bound for San Diego and all looked well.

Lys stood with a heavy blanket wrapped around her slender figure, and as I approached her, she half turned toward me to see who it was. When she recognized me, she immediately turned away.

"I want to thank you," I said, "for your bravery and loyalty—you were magnificent. I am sorry that you had reason before to think that I doubted you."

"You did doubt me," she replied in a level voice. "You practically accused me of aiding Baron von Schoenvorts. I can never forgive you."

There was a great deal of finality in both her words and tone.

"I could not believe it," I said; "and yet two of my men reported having seen you in conversation with von Schoenvorts late at night upon two separate occasions—after each of which some great damage was found done us in the morning. I didn't want to doubt you; but I carried all the responsibility of the lives of these men, of the safety of the ship, of your life and mine. I had to watch you, and I had to put you on your guard against a repetition of your madness."

She was looking at me now with those great eyes of hers, very wide and round.

"Who told you that I spoke with Baron von Schoenvorts at night, or any other time?" she asked.

"I cannot tell you, Lys," I replied, "but it came to me from two different sources."

"Then two men have lied," she asserted without heat. "I have not spoken to Baron von Schoenvorts other than in your presence when first we came aboard the *U-33*. And please, when you address me, remember that to others than my intimates I am Miss La Rue."

Did you ever get slapped in the face when you least expected it? No? Well, then you do not know how I felt at that moment. I could feel the hot, red flush surging up my neck, across my cheeks, over my ears, clear to my scalp. And it made me love her all the more; it made me swear inwardly a thousand solemn oaths that I would win her.

4

or several days things went along in about the same course. I took our position every morning with my crude sextant; but the results were always most unsatisfactory. They always showed a considerable westing when I knew that we had been sailing due north. I blamed my crude instrument, and kept on. Then one afternoon the girl came to me.

"Pardon me," she said; "but were I you, I should watch this man Benson—especially when he is in charge." I asked her what she meant, thinking I could see the influence of von Schoenvorts raising a suspicion against one of my most trusted men.

"If you will note the boat's course a half-hour after Benson goes on duty," she said, "you will know what I mean, and you will understand why he prefers a night watch. Possibly, too, you will understand some other things that have taken place aboard."

Then she went back to her room, thus ending the conversation. I waited until half an hour after Benson had gone on duty, and then I went on deck, passing through the conning-tower where Benson sat, and looking at the compass. It showed that our course was north by west—that is, one point west of north, which was, for our assumed position, about right. I was greatly relieved to find that nothing was wrong, for the girl's words had caused me considerable apprehension. I was about to return to my room when a thought occurred to me that again caused me to change my mind—and, incidentally, came near proving my death-warrant.

When I had left the conning-tower little more than a half-hour since, the sea had been breaking over the port bow, and it seemed to me quite improbable that in so short a time an equally heavy sea could be deluging us from the opposite side of the ship—winds may change quickly, but not a long, heavy sea. There was only one other solution—since I left the tower, our course had been altered some eight points. Turning quickly, I climbed out upon the conning-tower. A single glance at the heavens confirmed my suspicions; the constellations which should have been dead ahead were directly starboard. We were sailing due west.

Just for an instant longer I stood there to check up my calculations—I wanted to be quite sure before I accused Benson of perfidy, and about the only thing I came near making quite sure of was death. I cannot see even now how I escaped it. I was standing on the edge of the conning-tower, when a heavy palm suddenly struck me between the shoulders and hurled me forward into space. The drop to the triangular deck forward of the conning-tower might easily have broken a leg for me, or I might have slipped off onto the deck and rolled overboard; but fate was upon my side, as I was only slightly bruised. As I came to my feet, I heard the conning-tower cover slam. There is a ladder which leads from the deck to the top of the tower. Up this I scrambled, as fast as I could go; but Benson had the cover tight before I reached it.

I stood there a moment in dumb consternation. What did the fellow intend? What was going on below? If Benson was a traitor, how could I know that there were not other traitors among us? I cursed myself for my folly in going out upon the deck, and then this thought suggested another—a hideous one: who was it that had really been responsible for my being here?

Thinking to attract attention from inside the craft, I again ran down the ladder and onto the small deck only to find that the steel covers of the conning-tower windows were shut, and then

I leaned with my back against the tower and cursed myself for a gullible idiot.

I glanced at the bow. The sea seemed to be getting heavier, for every wave now washed completely over the lower deck. I watched them for a moment, and then a sudden chill pervaded my entire being. It was not the chill of wet clothing, or the dashing spray which drenched my face; no, it was the chill of the hand of death upon my heart. In an instant I had turned the last corner of life's highway and was looking God Almighty in the face—the *U-33* was being slowly submerged!

It would be difficult, even impossible, to set down in writing my sensations at that moment. All I can particularly recall is that I laughed, though neither from a spirit of bravado nor from hysteria. And I wanted to smoke. Lord! how I did want to smoke; but that was out of the question.

I watched the water rise until the little deck I stood on was awash, and then I clambered once more to the top of the conning-tower. From the very slow submergence of the boat I knew that Benson was doing the entire trick alone—that he was merely permitting the diving-tanks to fill and that the diving-rudders were not in use. The throbbing of the engines ceased, and in its stead came the steady vibration of the electric motors. The water was halfway up the conning-tower! I had perhaps five minutes longer on the deck. I tried to decide what I should do after I was washed away. Should I swim until exhaustion claimed me, or should I give up and end the agony at the first plunge?

From below came two muffled reports. They sounded not unlike shots. Was Benson meeting with resistance? Personally it could mean little to me, for even though my men might overcome the enemy, none would know of my predicament until long after it was too late to succor me. The top of the conning-tower was now awash. I clung to the wireless mast, while the great waves surged sometimes completely over me.

I knew the end was near and, almost involuntarily, I did that which I had not done since childhood—I prayed. After that I felt better.

I clung and waited, but the water rose no higher.

Instead it receded. Now the top of the conning-tower received only the crests of the higher waves; now the little triangular deck below became visible! What had occurred within? Did Benson believe me already gone, and was he emerging because of that belief, or had he and his forces been vanquished? The suspense was more wearing than that which I had endured while waiting for dissolution. Presently the main deck came into view, and then the conning-tower opened behind me, and I turned to look into the anxious face of Bradley. An expression of relief overspread his features.

"Thank God, man!" was all he said as he reached forth and dragged me into the tower. I was cold and numb and rather all in. Another few minutes would have done for me, I am sure, but the warmth of the interior helped to revive me, aided and abetted by some brandy which Bradley poured down my throat, from which it nearly removed the membrane. That brandy would have revived a corpse.

When I got down into the centrale, I saw the Germans lined up on one side with a couple of my men with pistols standing over them. Von Schoenvorts was among them. On the floor lay Benson, moaning, and beyond him stood the girl, a revolver in one hand. I looked about, bewildered.

"What has happened down here?" I asked. "Tell me!"

Bradley replied. "You see the result, sir," he said. "It might have been a very different result but for Miss La Rue. We were all asleep. Benson had relieved the guard early in the evening; there was no one to watch him—no one but Miss La Rue. She felt the submergence of the boat and came out of her room to investigate. She was just in time to see Benson at the diving rudders. When he saw her, he raised his pistol and fired point-blank at her, but he missed and she fired—and didn't miss. The two shots awakened everyone, and as our men were armed, the result was inevitable as you see it; but it would have been very different had it not been for Miss La Rue. It was she who closed the diving-tank sea-cocks and roused Olson and me, and had the pumps started to empty them."

And there I had been thinking that through her machinations I had been lured to the deck and to my death! I could have gone on my knees to her and begged her forgiveness—or at least I could have, had I not been Anglo-Saxon. As it was, I could only remove my soggy cap and bow and mumble my appreciation. She made no reply—only turned and walked very rapidly toward her room. Could I have heard aright? Was it really a sob that came floating back to me through the narrow aisle of the *U-33*?

Benson died that night. He remained defiant almost to the last; but just before he went out, he motioned to me, and I leaned over to catch the faintly whispered words.

"I did it alone," he said. "I did it because I hate you—I hate all your kind. I was kicked out of your shipyard at Santa Monica. I was kicked out of California. I am an I. W. W. I became a German agent—not because I love them, for I hate them too—but because I wanted to injure Americans, whom I hated more. I threw the wireless apparatus overboard. I destroyed the chronometer and the sextant. I devised a scheme for varying the compass to suit my wishes. I told Wilson that I had seen the girl talking with von Schoenvorts, and I made the poor egg think he had seen her doing the same thing. I am sorry—sorry that my plans failed. I hate you."

He didn't die for a half-hour after that; nor did he speak again—aloud; but just a few seconds before he went to meet his Maker, his lips moved in a faint whisper; and as I leaned closer to catch his words, what do you suppose I heard? "Now—I—lay

42

me—down—to—sleep" That was all; Benson was dead. We threw his body overboard.

The wind of that night brought on some pretty rough weather with a lot of black clouds which persisted for several days. We didn't know what course we had been holding, and there was no way of finding out, as we could no longer trust the compass, not knowing what Benson had done to it. The long and the short of it was that we cruised about aimlessly until the sun came out again. I'll never forget that day or its surprises. We reckoned, or rather guessed, that we were somewhere off the coast of Peru. The wind, which had been blowing fitfully from the east, suddenly veered around into the south, and presently we felt a sudden chill.

"Peru!" snorted Olson. "When were yez after smellin' icebergs off Peru?"

Icebergs! "Icebergs, nothin'!" exclaimed one of the Englishmen. "Why, man, they don't come north of fourteen here in these waters."

"Then," replied Olson, "ye're sout' of fourteen, me b'y."

We thought he was crazy; but he wasn't, for that afternoon we sighted a great berg south of us, and we'd been running north, we thought, for days. I can tell you we were a discouraged lot; but we got a faint thrill of hope early the next morning when the lookout bawled down the open hatch: "Land! Land northwest by west!"

I think we were all sick for the sight of land. I know that I was; but my interest was quickly dissipated by the sudden illness of three of the Germans. Almost simultaneously they commenced vomiting. They couldn't suggest any explanation for it. I asked them what they had eaten, and found they had eaten nothing other than the food cooked for all of us. "Have you drunk anything?" I asked, for I knew that there was liquor aboard, and medicines in the same locker.

"Only water," moaned one of them. "We all drank water together this morning. We opened a new tank. Maybe it was the water."

I started an investigation which revealed a terrifying condition—some one, probably Benson, had poisoned all the running water on the ship. It would have been worse, though, had land not been in sight. The sight of land filled us with renewed hope.

Our course had been altered, and we were rapidly approaching what appeared to be a precipitous headland. Cliffs, seemingly rising perpendicularly out of the sea, faded away into the mist upon either hand as we approached. The land before us might have been a continent, so mighty appeared the shoreline; yet we knew that we must be thousands of miles from the nearest western land-mass—New Zealand or Australia.

We took our bearings with our crude and inaccurate instruments; we searched the chart; we cudgeled our brains; and at last it was Bradley who suggested a solution. He was in the tower and watching the compass, to which he called my attention. The needle was pointing straight toward the land. Bradley swung the helm hard to starboard. I could feel the *U-33* respond, and yet the arrow still clung straight and sure toward the distant cliffs.

"What do you make of it?" I asked him.

"Did you ever hear of Caproni?" he asked.

"An early Italian navigator?" I returned.

"Yes; he followed Cook about 1721. He is scarcely mentioned even by contemporaneous historians—probably because he got into political difficulties on his return to Italy. It was the fashion to scoff at his claims, but I recall reading one of his works—his only one, I believe—in which he described a new continent in the south seas, a continent made up of 'some strange metal' which attracted the compass; a rock-bound, inhospitable coast, without beach or harbor, which extended for hundreds of miles. He could make no landing; nor in the several days he cruised about it did he see sign of life. He called it Caprona and sailed away. I believe, sir, that we are looking upon the coast of Caprona, uncharted and forgotten for two hundred years."

"If you are right, it might account for much of the deviation of the compass during the past two days," I suggested. "Caprona has been luring us upon her deadly rocks. Well, we'll accept her challenge. We'll land upon Caprona. Along that long front there must be a vulnerable spot. We will find it, Bradley, for we must find it. We must find water on Caprona, or we must die."

And so we approached the coast upon which no living eyes had ever rested. Straight from the ocean's depths rose towering cliffs, shot with brown and blues and greens—withered moss and lichen and the verdigris of copper, and everywhere the rusty ocher of iron pyrites. The cliff-tops, though ragged, were of such uniform height as to suggest the boundaries of a great plateau, and now and again we caught glimpses of verdure topping the rocky escarpment, as though bush or jungle-land had pushed outward from a lush vegetation farther inland to signal to an unseeing world that Caprona lived and joyed in life beyond her austere and repellent coast.

But metaphor, however poetic, never slaked a dry throat. To enjoy Caprona's romantic suggestions we must have water, and so we came in close, always sounding, and skirted the shore. As close in as we dared cruise, we found fathomless depths, and always the same undented coast-line of bald cliff. As darkness threatened, we drew away and lay well off the coast all night. We had not as yet really commenced to suffer for lack of water; but I knew that it would not be long before we did, and so at the first streak of dawn I moved in again and once more took up the hopeless survey of the forbidding coast.

Toward noon we discovered a beach, the first we had seen. It was a narrow strip of sand at the base of a part of the cliff that seemed lower than any we had before scanned. At its foot, half buried in the sand, lay great boulders, mute evidence that in a bygone age some mighty natural force had crumpled Caprona's barrier at this point. It was Bradley who first called our attention to a strange object lying among the boulders above the surf.

"Looks like a man," he said, and passed his glasses to me.

I looked long and carefully and could have sworn that the thing I saw was the sprawled figure of a human being. Miss La Rue was on deck with us. I turned and asked her to go below. Without a word she did as I bade. Then I stripped, and as I did so, Nobs looked questioningly at me. He had been wont at home to enter the surf with me, and evidently he had not forgotten it.

"What are you going to do, sir?" asked Olson.

"I'm going to see what that thing is on shore," I replied. "If it's a man, it may mean that Caprona is inhabited, or it may merely mean that some poor devils were shipwrecked here. I ought to be able to tell from the clothing which is more near the truth."

"How about sharks?" queried Olson. "Sure, you ought to carry a knoife."

"Here you are, sir," cried one of the men.

It was a long slim blade he offered—one that I could carry between my teeth—and so I accepted it gladly.

"Keep close in," I directed Bradley, and then I dived over the side and struck out for the narrow beach. There was another splash directly behind me, and turning my head, I saw faithful old Nobs swimming valiantly in my wake.

The surf was not heavy, and there was no undertow, so we made shore easily, effecting an equally easy landing. The beach was composed largely of small stones worn smooth by the action of water. There was little sand, though from the deck of the *U-33* the beach had appeared to be all sand, and I saw no evidences of mollusca or crustacea such as are common to all beaches I have previously seen. I attribute this to the fact of the smallness of the beach, the enormous depth of surrounding water and the great distance at which Caprona lies from her nearest neighbor.

As Nobs and I approached the recumbent figure farther up the beach, I was appraised by my nose that whether man or not, the thing had once been organic and alive, but that for some time it had been dead. Nobs halted, sniffed and growled. A little later he sat down upon his haunches, raised his muzzle to the heavens and bayed forth a most dismal howl. I shied a small stone at him and bade him shut up—his uncanny noise made me nervous. When I had come quite close to the thing, I still could not say whether it had been man or beast. The carcass was badly swollen and partly decomposed. There was no sign of clothing upon or about it. A fine, brownish hair covered the chest and abdomen, and the face, the palms of the hands, the feet, the shoulders and back were practically hairless. The creature must have been about the height of a fair-sized man; its features were similar to those of a man; yet had it been a man?

I could not say, for it resembled an ape no more than it did a man. Its large toes protruded laterally as do those of the semiarboreal peoples of Borneo, the Philippines and other remote regions where low types still persist. The countenance might have been that of a cross between *Pithecanthropus*, the Java ape-man, and a daughter of the Piltdown race of prehistoric Sussex. A wooden cudgel lay beside the corpse.

Now this fact set me thinking. There was no wood of any description in sight. There was nothing about the beach to suggest a wrecked mariner. There was absolutely nothing about the body to suggest that it might possibly in life have known a maritime experience. It was the body of a low type of man or a high type of beast. In neither instance would it have been of a seafaring race. Therefore I deduced that it was native to Caprona—that it lived inland, and that it had fallen or been hurled from the cliffs above. Such being the case, Caprona was inhabitable, if not inhabited, by man; but how to reach the inhabitable interior! That was the question. A closer view of the cliffs than had been afforded me from the deck of the *U-33* only confirmed my conviction that no mortal man could scale those perpendicular heights; there was not a finger-hold, not a toe-hold, upon them. I turned away baffled.

Nobs and I met with no sharks upon our return journey to the submarine. My report filled everyone with theories and speculations, and with renewed hope and determination. They all reasoned along the same lines that I had reasoned—the conclusions were obvious, but not the water. We were now thirstier than ever.

The balance of that day we spent in continuing a minute and fruitless exploration of the monotonous coast. There was not another break in the frowning cliffs—not even another minute patch of pebbly beach. As the sun fell, so did our spirits. I had tried to make advances to the girl again; but she would have none of me, and so I was not only thirsty but otherwise sad and downhearted. I was glad when the new day broke the hideous spell of a sleepless night.

The morning's search brought us no shred of hope. Caprona was impregnable—that was the decision of all; yet we kept on. It must have been about two bells of the afternoon watch that Bradley called my attention to the branch of a tree, with leaves upon it, floating on the sea. "It may have been carried down to the ocean by a river," he suggested.

"Yes," I replied, "it may have; it may have tumbled or been thrown off the top of one of these cliffs."

Bradley's face fell. "I thought of that, too," he replied, "but I wanted to believe the other."

"Right you are!" I cried. "We must believe the other until we prove it false. We can't afford to give up heart now, when we need heart most. The branch was carried down by a river, and we are going to find that river." I smote my open palm with a clenched fist, to emphasize a determination unsupported by hope. "There!" I cried suddenly. "See that, Bradley?" And I pointed at a spot closer to shore. "See that, man!" Some flowers and grasses and another leafy branch floated toward us. We both scanned the water and the coastline. Bradley evidently discovered something, or at least thought that he had. He called down for a bucket and a rope, and when they were passed up to him, he lowered the former into the sea and drew it in filled with water. Of this he took a taste, and straightening up, looked into my eyes with an expression of elation—as much as to say "I told you so!"

"This water is warm," he announced, "and fresh!"

I grabbed the bucket and tasted its contents. The water was very warm, and it was fresh, but there was a most unpleasant taste to it.

"Did you ever taste water from a stagnant pool full of tadpoles?" Bradley asked.

"That's it," I exclaimed, "—that's just the taste exactly, though I haven't experienced it since boyhood; but how can water from a flowing stream taste thus, and what the dickens makes it so warm? It must be at least 70 or 80 Fahrenheit, possibly higher."

"Yes," agreed Bradley, "I should say higher; but where does it come from?"

"That is easily discovered now that we have found it," I answered. "It can't come from the ocean; so it must come from the land. All that we have to do is follow it, and sooner or later we shall come upon its source."

We were already rather close in; but I ordered the U-33's prow turned inshore and we crept slowly along, constantly dipping up the water and tasting it to assure ourselves that we didn't get outside the freshwater current. There was a very light off-shore wind and scarcely any breakers, so that the approach to the shore was continued with little or no danger. We sounded constantly without finding bottom; yet though we were already quite close, we saw no indication of any indention in the coast from which even a tiny brooklet might issue, and certainly no mouth of a large river such as this must necessarily be to freshen the ocean even two hundred yards from shore.

The tide was running out, and this, together with the strong flow of the freshwater current, would have prevented our going against the cliffs even had we not been under power; as it was we had to buck the combined forces in order to hold our position at all. We came up to within twenty-five feet of the sheer wall, which loomed high above us. There was no break in its forbidding face. As we watched the face of the waters and searched the cliff's face, Olson suggested that the fresh water might come from a submarine geyser. This, he said, would account for its heat; but even as he spoke a bush, covered thickly with leaves and flowers, bubbled to the surface and floated off astern.

"Flowering shrubs don't thrive in the subterranean caverns from which geysers spring," suggested Bradley.

Olson shook his head. "It beats me," he said.

"I've got it!" I exclaimed suddenly. "Look there!" And I pointed at the base of the cliff ahead of us, which the receding tide was gradually exposing to our view. They all looked, and all saw what I had seen—the top of a dark opening in the rock, through which water was pouring out into the sea. "It's the subterranean channel of an inland river," I cried. "It flows through a land covered with vegetation—and therefore a land upon which the sun shines. No subterranean caverns produce any order of plant life even remotely resembling what we have seen disgorged by this river. Beyond those cliffs lie fertile lands and fresh water—perhaps, game!"

"Yis, sir," said Olson, "behoind the cliffs! Ye spoke a true word, sir—behoind!"

Bradley laughed—a rather sorry laugh, though. "You might as well call our attention to the fact, sir," he said, "that science has indicated that there is fresh water and vegetation on Mars."

"Not at all," I rejoined. "A U-boat isn't constructed to navigate space, but it is designed to travel below the surface of the water."

"You'd be after sailin' into that blank pocket?" asked Olson.

"I would, Olson," I replied. "We haven't one chance for life in a hundred thousand if we don't find food and water upon Caprona. This water coming out of the cliff is not salt; but neither is it fit to drink, though each of us has drunk it. It is fair to assume that inland the river is fed by pure streams, that there are fruits and herbs and game. Shall we lie out here and die of thirst and starvation with a land of plenty possibly only a few hundred yards away? We have the means for navigating a subterranean river. Are we too cowardly to utilize this means?"

"Be after goin' to it," said Olson.

"I'm willing to see it through," agreed Bradley.

"Then under the bottom, wi' the best o' luck an' give 'em hell!" cried a young fellow who had been in the trenches.

"To the diving-stations!" I commanded, and in less than a minute the deck was deserted, the conning-tower covers had slammed to and the *U-33* was submerging—possibly for the last time. I know that I had this feeling, and I think that most of the others did.

As we went down, I sat in the tower with the searchlight projecting its seemingly feeble rays ahead. We submerged very slowly and without headway more than sufficient to keep her nose in the right direction, and as we went down, I saw outlined ahead of us the black opening in the great cliff. It was an opening that would have admitted a half-dozen U-boats at one and the same time, roughly cylindrical in contour—and dark as the pit of perdition.

As I gave the command which sent the *U-33* slowly ahead, I could not but feel a certain uncanny presentiment of evil. Where were we going? What lay at the end of this great sewer? Had we bidden farewell forever to the sunlight and to life, or were there before us dangers even greater than those which we now faced? I tried to keep my mind from vain imagining by calling everything which I observed to the eager ears below. I was the eyes of the whole company, and I did my best not to fail them. We had advanced a hundred yards, perhaps, when our first danger confronted us. Just ahead was a sharp right-angle turn in the tunnel. I could see the river's flotsam hurtling against the rocky wall upon the left as it was driven on by the mighty current, and I feared for the safety of the *U-33* in making so sharp a turn under such adverse conditions; but there was nothing for it but to try it. I didn't warn my fellows of the danger—it could have but caused them useless apprehension, for if we were to be smashed against the rocky wall, no power on earth could avert the quick end that would come to us. I gave the command full speed ahead and went charging toward the menace. I was forced to approach the dangerous left-hand wall in order to make the turn, and I depended upon the power of the motors to carry us through the surging waters in safety. Well, we made it; but it was a narrow squeak. As we swung around, the full force of the current caught us and drove the stern against the rocks; there was a thud which sent a tremor through the whole craft, and then a moment of nasty grinding as the steel hull scraped the rock wall. I expected momentarily the inrush of waters that would seal our doom; but presently from below came the welcome word that all was well.

In another fifty yards there was a second turn, this time toward the left! but it was more of a gentle curve, and we took it without trouble. After that it was plain sailing, though as far as I could know, there might be most anything ahead of us, and my nerves were strained to the snapping-point every instant. After the second turn the channel ran comparatively straight for between one hundred and fifty and two hundred yards. The waters grew suddenly lighter, and my spirits rose accordingly. I shouted down to those below that I saw daylight ahead, and a great shout of thanksgiving reverberated through the ship. A moment later we emerged into sunlit water, and immediately I raised the periscope and looked about me upon the strangest landscape I had ever seen.

We were in the middle of a broad and now sluggish river the

banks of which were lined by giant, arboraceous ferns, raising their mighty fronds fifty, one hundred, two hundred feet into the quiet air. Close by us something rose to the surface of the river and dashed at the periscope. I had a vision of wide, distended jaws, and then all was blotted out. A shiver ran down into the tower as the thing closed upon the periscope. A moment later it was gone, and I could see again. Above the trees there soared into my vision a huge thing on batlike wings—a creature large as a large whale, but fashioned more after the order of a lizard. Then again something charged the periscope and blotted out the mirror. I will confess that I was almost gasping for breath as I gave the commands to emerge. Into what sort of strange land had fate guided us?

The instant the deck was awash, I opened the conning-tower hatch and stepped out. In another minute the deck-hatch lifted, and those who were not on duty below streamed up the ladder, Olson bringing Nobs under one arm. For several minutes no one spoke; I think they must each have been as overcome by awe as was I. All about us was a flora and fauna as strange and wonderful to us as might have been those upon a distant planet had we suddenly been miraculously transported through ether to an unknown world. Even the grass upon the nearer bank was unearthly—lush and high it grew, and each blade bore upon its tip a brilliant flower—violet or yellow or carmine or blue—making as gorgeous a sward as human imagination might conceive. But the life! It teemed. The tall, fernlike trees were alive with monkeys, snakes, and lizards. Huge insects hummed and buzzed hither and thither. Mighty forms could be seen moving upon the ground in the thick forest, while the bosom of the river wriggled with living things, and above flapped the wings of gigantic creatures such as we are taught have been extinct throughout countless ages.

"Look!" cried Olson. "Would you look at the giraffe comin' up out o' the bottom of the say?" We looked in the direction he pointed and saw a long, glossy neck surmounted by a small head rising above the surface of the river. Presently the back of the creature was exposed, brown and glossy as the water dripped from it. It turned its eyes upon us, opened its lizardlike mouth, emitted a shrill hiss and came for us. The thing must have been sixteen or eighteen feet in length and closely resembled pictures I had seen of restored plesiosaurs of the lower Jurassic. It charged us as savagely as a mad bull, and one would have thought it intended to destroy and devour the mighty U-boat, as I verily believe it did intend.

We were moving slowly up the river as the creature bore down upon us with distended jaws. The long neck was far outstretched, and the four flippers with which it swam were working with powerful strokes, carrying it forward at a rapid pace. When it reached the craft's side, the jaws closed upon one of the stanchions of the deck rail and tore it from its socket as though it had been a toothpick stuck in putty. At this exhibition of titanic strength I think we all simultaneously stepped backward, and Bradley drew his revolver and fired. The bullet struck the thing in the neck, just above its body; but instead of disabling it, merely increased its rage. Its hissing rose to a shrill scream as it raised half its body out of water onto the sloping sides of the hull of the *U-33* and endeavored to scramble upon the deck to devour us. A dozen shots rang out as we who were armed drew our pistols and fired at the thing; but though struck several times, it showed no signs of succumbing and only floundered farther aboard the submarine.

I had noticed that the girl had come on deck and was standing not far behind me, and when I saw the danger to which we were all exposed, I turned and forced her toward the hatch. We had not spoken for some days, and we did not speak now; but she gave me a disdainful look, which was quite as eloquent as words, and broke loose from my grasp. I saw I could do nothing with her unless I exerted force, and so I turned with my back toward her that I might be in a position to shield her from the strange reptile should it really succeed in reaching the deck; and as I did so I saw the thing raise one flipper over the rail, dart its head forward and with the quickness of lightning seize upon one of the boches. I ran forward, discharging my pistol into the creature's body in an effort to force it to relinquish its prey; but I might as profitably have shot at the sun.

Shrieking and screaming, the German was dragged from the deck, and the moment the reptile was clear of the boat, it dived beneath the surface of the water with its terrified prey. I think we were all more or less shaken by the frightfulness of the tragedy—until Olson remarked that the balance of power now rested where it belonged. Following the death of Benson we had been nine and nine—nine Germans and nine "Allies," as we called ourselves; now there were but eight Germans. We never counted the girl on either side, I suppose because she was a girl, though we knew well enough now that she was ours.

And so Olson's remark helped to clear the atmosphere for the Allies at least, and then our attention was once more directed toward the river, for around us there had sprung up a perfect bedlam of screams and hisses and a seething caldron of hideous reptiles, devoid of fear and filled only with hunger and with rage. They clambered, squirmed and wriggled to the deck, forcing us steadily backward, though we emptied our pistols into them. There were all sorts and conditions of horrible things—huge, hideous, grotesque, monstrous—a veritable Mesozoic nightmare. I saw that the girl was gotten below as quickly as possible, and she took Nobs with her—poor Nobs had nearly barked his head off; and I think, too, that for the first time since his littlest puppyhood he had known fear; nor can I blame him. After the girl I sent Bradley and most of the Allies and then the Germans who were on deck—von Schoenvorts being still in irons below.

The creatures were approaching perilously close before I dropped through the hatchway and slammed down the cover. Then I went into the tower and ordered full speed ahead, hoping to distance the fearsome things; but it was useless. Not only could any of them easily outdistance the *U-33*, but the further upstream we progressed the greater the number of our besiegers, until fearful of navigating a strange river at high speed, I gave orders to reduce and moved slowly and majestically through the plunging, hissing mass. I was mighty glad that our entrance into the interior of Caprona had been inside a submarine rather than in any other form of vessel. I could readily understand how it might have been that Caprona had been invaded in the past by venturesome navigators without word of it ever reaching the outside world, for I can assure you that only by submarine could man pass up that great sluggish river, alive.

We proceeded up the river for some forty miles before darkness overtook us. I was afraid to submerge and lie on the bottom overnight for fear that the mud might be deep enough to hold us, and as we could not hold with the anchor, I ran in close to shore, and in a brief interim of attack from the reptiles we made fast to a large tree. We also dipped up some of the river water and found it, though quite warm, a little sweeter than before. We had food enough, and with the water we were all quite refreshed; but we missed fresh meat. It had been weeks, now, since we had tasted it, and the sight of the reptiles gave me an idea—that a steak or two from one of them might not be bad eating. So I went on deck with a rifle, twenty of which were aboard the *U-33*. At sight of me a huge thing charged and climbed to the deck. I retreated to the top of the conning-tower, and when it had raised its mighty bulk to the level of the little deck on which I stood, I let it have a bullet right between the eyes.

The thing stopped then and looked at me a moment as much as to say: "Why, this thing has a stinger! I must be careful." And then it reached out its long neck and opened its mighty jaws and grabbed for me; but I wasn't there. I had tumbled backward into the tower, and I mighty near killed myself doing it. When I glanced up, that little head on the end of its long neck was coming straight down on top of me, and once more I tumbled into greater safety, sprawling upon the floor of the centrale.

Olson was looking up, and seeing what was poking about in the tower, ran for an ax; nor did he hesitate a moment when he returned with one, but sprang up the ladder and commenced chopping away at that hideous face. The thing didn't have sufficient brainpan to entertain more than a single idea at once. Though chopped and hacked, and with a bullet-hole between its eyes, it still persisted madly in its attempt to get inside the tower and devour Olson, though its body was many times the diameter of the hatch; nor did it cease its efforts until after Olson had succeeded in decapitating it. Then the two men went on deck through the main hatch, and while one kept watch, the other cut a hind quarter off *Plesiosaurus Olsoni*, as Bradley dubbed the thing. Meantime Olson cut off the long neck, saying that it would make fine soup. By the time we had cleared away the blood and refuse in the tower, the cook had juicy steaks and a steaming broth upon the electric stove, and the aroma arising from P. Olsoni filled us with a hitherto unfelt admiration for him and all his kind.

5

he steaks we had that night, and they were fine; and the following morning we tasted the broth. It seemed odd to be eating a creature that should, by all the laws of paleontology, have been extinct for several million years. It gave one a feeling of newness that was almost embarrassing, although it didn't seem to embarrass our appetites. Olson ate until I thought he would burst.

The girl ate with us that night at the little officers' mess just back of the torpedo compartment. The narrow table was unfolded; the four stools were set out; and for the first time in days we sat down to eat, and for the first time in weeks we had something to eat other than the monotony of the short rations of an impoverished U-boat. Nobs sat between the girl and me and was fed with morsels of the Plesiosaurus steak, at the risk of forever contaminating his manners. He looked at me sheepishly all the time, for he knew that no well-bred dog should eat at table; but the poor fellow was so wasted from improper food that I couldn't enjoy my own meal had he been denied an immediate share in it; and anyway Lys wanted to feed him. So there you are.

Lys was coldly polite to me and sweetly gracious to Bradley and Olson. She wasn't of the gushing type, I knew; so I didn't expect much from her and was duly grateful for the few morsels of attention she threw upon the floor to me. We had a pleasant meal, with only one unfortunate occurrence—when Olson suggested that possibly the creature we were eating was the same one that ate the German.

It was some time before we could persuade the girl to continue her meal, but at last Bradley prevailed upon her, pointing out that we had come upstream nearly forty miles since the boche had been seized, and that during that time we had seen literally thousands of these denizens of the river, indicating that the chances were very remote that this was the same Plesiosaur. "And anyway," he concluded, "it was only a scheme of Mr. Olson's to get all the steaks for himself."

We discussed the future and ventured opinions as to what lay before us; but we could only theorize at best, for none of us knew. If the whole land was infested by these and similar horrid monsters, life would be impossible upon it, and we decided that we would only search long enough to find and take aboard fresh water and such meat and fruits as might be safely procurable and then retrace our way beneath the cliffs to the open sea.

And so at last we turned into our narrow bunks, hopeful, happy and at peace with ourselves, our livers and our God, to awaken the following morning refreshed and still optimistic. We had an easy time getting away—as we learned later, because the saurians do not commence to feed until late in the morning. From noon to midnight their curve of activity is at its height, while from dawn to about nine o'clock it is lowest. As a matter of fact, we didn't see one of them all the time we were getting under way, though I had the cannon raised to the deck and manned against an assault. I hoped, but I was none too sure, that shells might discourage them. The trees were full of monkeys of all sizes and shades, and once we thought we saw a man-like creature watching us from the depth of the forest.

Shortly after we resumed our course upstream, we saw the mouth of another and smaller river emptying into the main channel from the south—that is, upon our right; and almost immediately after we came upon a large island five or six miles in length; and at fifty miles there was a still larger river than the last coming in from the northwest, the course of the main stream having now changed to northeast by southwest. The water was quite free from reptiles, and the vegetation upon the banks of the river had altered to more open and parklike forest, with eucalyptus and acacia mingled with a scattering of tree ferns, as though two distinct periods of geologic time had overlapped and merged. The grass, too, was less flowering, though there were still gorgeous patches mottling the greensward; and lastly, the fauna was less multitudinous.

Six or seven miles farther, and the river widened considerably; before us opened an expanse of water to the farther horizon, and then we sailed out upon an inland sea so large that only a shore-line upon our side was visible to us. The waters all about us were alive with life. There were still a few reptiles; but there were fish by the thousands, by the millions.

The water of the inland sea was very warm, almost hot, and the atmosphere was hot and heavy above it. It seemed strange that beyond the buttressed walls of Caprona icebergs floated and the south wind was biting, for only a gentle breeze moved across the face of these living waters, and that was damp and warm. Gradually, we commenced to divest ourselves of our clothing, retaining only sufficient for modesty; but the sun was not hot. It was more the heat of a steam-room than of an oven.

We coasted up the shore of the lake in a north-westerly direction, sounding all the time. We found the lake deep and the bottom rocky and steeply shelving toward the center, and once when I moved straight out from shore to take other soundings we could find no bottom whatsoever. In open spaces along the shore we caught occasional glimpses of the distant cliffs, and here they appeared only a trifle less precipitous than those which bound Caprona on the seaward side. My theory is that in a far distant era Caprona was a mighty mountain—perhaps the world's mightiest mountain—and that in some titanic eruption volcanic action blew off the entire crest, blew thousands of feet of the mountain upward and outward and onto the surrounding continent, leaving a great crater; and then, possibly, the continent sank as ancient continents have been known to do, leaving only the summit of Caprona above the sea. The encircling walls, the central lake, the hot springs which feed the lake, all point to such a conclusion, and the fauna and the flora bear indisputable evidence that Caprona was once part of some great land-mass.

As we cruised up along the coast, the landscape continued a more or less open forest, with here and there a small plain where we saw animals grazing. With my glass I could make out a species of large red deer, some antelope and what appeared to be a species of horse; and once I saw the shaggy form of what might have been a monstrous bison. Here was game a plenty! There seemed little danger of starving upon Caprona. The game, however, seemed wary; for the instant the animals discovered us, they threw up their heads and tails and went cavorting off, those farther inland following the example of the others until all were lost in the mazes of the distant forest. Only the great, shaggy ox stood his ground. With lowered head he watched us until we had passed, and then continued feeding.

About twenty miles up the coast from the mouth of the river we encountered low cliffs of sandstone, broken and tortured evidence of the great upheaval which had torn Caprona asunder in the past, intermingling upon a common level the rock formations of widely separated eras, fusing some and leaving others untouched.

We ran along beside them for a matter of ten miles, arriving off a broad cleft which led into what appeared to be another lake. As we were in search of pure water, we did not wish to overlook any portion of the coast, and so after sounding and finding that we had ample depth, I ran the *U-33* between head-lands into as pretty a landlocked harbor as sailormen could care to see, with good water right up to within a few yards of the shore. As we cruised slowly along, two of the boches again saw what they believed to be a man, or manlike creature, watching us from a fringe of trees a hundred yards inland,

and shortly after we discovered the mouth of a small stream empty-ing into the bay: It was the first stream we had found since leaving the river, and I at once made preparations to test its water. To land, it would be necessary to run the *U-33* close in to the shore, at least as close as we could, for even these waters were infested, though, not so thickly, by savage reptiles. I ordered sufficient water let into the diving-tanks to lower us about a foot, and then I ran the bow slowly toward the shore, confident that should we run aground, we still had sufficient lifting force to free us when the water should be pumped out of the tanks; but the bow nosed its way gently into the reeds and touched the shore with the keel still clear.

My men were all armed now with both rifles and pistols, each having plenty of ammunition. I ordered one of the Germans ashore with a line, and sent two of my own men to guard him, for from what little we had seen of Caprona, or Caspak as we learned later to call the interior, we realized that any instant some new and terrible danger might confront us. The line was made fast to a small tree, and at the same time I had the stern anchor dropped.

As soon as the boche and his guard were aboard again, I called all hands on deck, including von Schoenvorts, and there I explained to them that the time had come for us to enter into some sort of an agreement among ourselves that would relieve us of the annoyance and embarrassment of being divided into two antagonistic parts—prisoners and captors. I told them that it was obvious our very exis-tence depended upon our unity of action, that we were to all intent and purpose entering a new world as far from the seat and causes of our own world-war as if millions of miles of space and eons of time separated us from our past lives and habitations.

"There is no reason why we should carry our racial and politi-cal hatreds into Caprona," I insisted. "The Germans among us might kill all the English, or the English might kill the last German, with-out affecting in the slightest degree either the outcome of even the smallest skirmish upon the western front or the opinion of a single individual in any belligerent or neutral country. I therefore put the issue squarely to you all: shall we bury our animosities and work together with and for one another while we remain upon Caprona, or must we continue thus divided and but half armed, possibly until death has claimed the last of us? And let me tell you, if you have not already realized it, the chances are a thousand to one that not one of us ever will see the outside world again. We are safe now in the matter of food and water; we could provision the *U-33* for a long cruise; but we are practically out of fuel, and without fuel we cannot hope to reach the ocean, as only a submarine can pass through the barrier cliffs. What is your answer?" I turned toward von Schoenvorts.

He eyed me in that disagreeable way of his and demanded to know, in case they accepted my suggestion, what their status would be in event of our finding a way to escape with the *U-33*. I replied that I felt that if we had all worked loyally together we should leave Caprona upon a common footing, and to that end I suggested that should the remote possibility of our escape in the submarine develop into reality, we should then immediately make for the nearest neutral port and give ourselves into the hands of the authorities, when we should all probably be interned for the duration of the war. To my surprise he agreed that this was fair and told me that they would accept my conditions and that I could depend upon their loyalty to the common cause.

I thanked him and then addressed each one of his men individually, and each gave me his word that he would abide by all that I had outlined. It was further understood that we were to act as a military organization under military rules and discipline—I as commander, with Bradley as my first lieutenant and Olson as my second, in command of the Englishmen; while von Schoenvorts was to act as an additional second lieutenant and have charge of his own men. The four of us were to constitute a military court under which men might be tried and sentenced to punishment for infraction of military rules and discipline, even to the passing of the death-sentence.

I then had arms and ammunition issued to the Germans, and leaving Bradley and five men to guard the U-33, the balance of us went ashore. The first thing we did was to taste the water of the little stream—which, to our delight, we found sweet, pure and cold. This stream was entirely free from dangerous reptiles, because, as I later discovered, they become immediately dormant when subjected to a much lower temperature than 70 degrees Fahrenheit. They dislike cold water and keep as far away from it as possible. There were count-less brook-trout here, and deep holes that invited us to bathe, and along the bank of the stream were trees bearing a close resemblance to ash and beech and oak, their characteristics evidently induced by the lower temperature of the air above the cold water and by the fact that their roots were watered by the water from the stream rather than from the warm springs which we afterward found in such abundance elsewhere.

Our first concern was to fill the water tanks of the U-33 with fresh water, and that having been accomplished, we set out to hunt for game and explore inland for a short distance. Olson, von Schoenvorts, two Englishmen and two Germans accompanied me, leaving ten to guard the ship and the girl. I had intended leaving Nobs behind, but he got away and joined me and was so happy over it that I hadn't the heart to send him back. We followed the stream upward through a beautiful country for about five miles, and then came upon its source in a little boulder-strewn clearing. From among the rocks bubbled fully twenty ice-cold springs. North of the clearing rose sandstone cliffs to a height of some fifty to seventy-five feet, with tall trees growing at their base and almost concealing them from our view. To the west the country was flat and sparsely wooded, and here it was that we saw our first game—a large red deer. It was grazing away from us and had not seen us when one of my men called my attention to it. Motioning for silence and having the rest of the party lie down, I crept toward the quarry, accompanied only by Whitely. We got within a hundred yards of the deer when he suddenly raised his antlered head and pricked up his great ears. We both fired at once and had the satisfaction of seeing the buck drop; then we ran forward to finish him with our knives. The deer lay in a small open space close to a clump of acacias, and we had advanced to within several yards of our kill when we both halted suddenly and simultaneously. Whitely looked at me, and I looked at Whitely, and then we both looked back in the direction of the deer.

"Blime!" he said. "Wot is hit, sir?"

"It looks to me, Whitely, like an error," I said; "some assistant god who had been creating elephants must have been temporarily transferred to the lizard-department."

"Hi wouldn't s'y that, sir," said Whitely; "it sounds blasphemous."

"It is more blasphemous than that thing which is swiping our meat," I replied, for whatever the thing was, it had leaped upon our deer and was devouring it in great mouthfuls which it swallowed without mastication. The creature appeared to be a great lizard at least ten feet high, with a huge, powerful tail as long as its torso, mighty hind legs and short forelegs. When it had advanced from the wood, it hopped much after the fashion of a kangaroo, using its hind feet and tail to propel it, and when it stood erect, it sat upon its tail. Its head was long and thick, with a blunt muzzle, and the opening of the jaws ran back to a point behind the eyes, and the jaws were armed with long sharp teeth. The scaly body was covered with black and yellow spots about a foot in diameter and irregular in contour. These spots were outlined in red with edgings about an inch wide. The underside of the chest, body and tail were a greenish white.

"Wot s'y we pot the bloomin' bird, sir?" suggested Whitely.

I told him to wait until I gave the word; then we would fire simultaneously, he at the heart and I at the spine.

"Hat the 'eart, sir—yes, sir," he replied, and raised his piece to his shoulder.

Our shots rang out together. The thing raised its head and looked about until its eyes rested upon us; then it gave vent to a most appalling hiss that rose to the crescendo of a terrific shriek and came for us.

"Beat it, Whitely!" I cried as I turned to run.

We were about a quarter of a mile from the rest of our party, and in full sight of them as they lay in the tall grass watching us. That they saw all that had happened was evidenced by the fact that they now rose and ran toward us, and at their head leaped Nobs. The creature in our rear was gaining on us rapidly when Nobs flew past me like a meteor and rushed straight for the frightful reptile. I tried to recall him, but he would pay no attention to me, and as I couldn't see him sacrificed, I, too, stopped and faced the monster. The creature appeared to be more impressed with Nobs than by us and our firearms, for it stopped as the Airedale dashed at it growling, and struck at him viciously with its powerful jaws.

Nobs, though, was lightning by comparison with the slow-thinking beast and dodged his opponent's thrust with ease. Then he raced to the rear of the tremendous thing and seized it by the tail. There Nobs made the error of his life. Within that mottled organ were the muscles of a Titan, the force of a dozen mighty catapults, and the owner of the tail was fully aware of the possibilities which it contained. With a single fillip of the tip it sent poor Nobs sailing through the air a hundred feet above the ground, straight back into the clump of acacias from which the beast had leaped upon our kill—and then the grotesque thing sank lifeless to the ground.

Olson and von Schoenvorts came up a minute later with their men; then we all cautiously approached the still form upon the ground. The creature was quite dead, and an examination resulted in disclosing the fact that Whitely's bullet had pierced its heart, and mine had severed the spinal cord.

"But why didn't it die instantly?" I exclaimed.

"Because," said von Schoenvorts in his disagreeable way, "the beast is so large, and its nervous organization of so low a caliber, that it took all this time for the intelligence of death to reach and be impressed upon the minute brain. The thing was dead when your bullets struck it; but it did not know it for several seconds—possibly a minute. If I am not mistaken, it is an Allosaurus of the Upper Jurassic, remains of which have been found in Central Wyoming, in the suburbs of New York."

An Irishman by the name of Brady grinned. I afterward learned that he had served three years on the traffic-squad of the Chicago police force.

I had been calling Nobs in the meantime and was about to set out in search of him, fearing, to tell the truth, to do so lest I find him mangled and dead among the trees of the acacia grove, when he suddenly emerged from among the boles, his ears flattened, his tail between his legs and his body screwed into a suppliant S. He was unharmed except for minor bruises; but he was the most chastened dog I have ever seen.

We gathered up what was left of the red deer after skinning and cleaning it, and set out upon our return journey toward the U-boat. On the way Olson, von Schoenvorts, and I discussed the needs of our immediate future, and we were unanimous in placing foremost the necessity of a permanent camp on shore. The interior of a U-boat is about as impossible and uncomfortable an abiding-place as one can well imagine, and in this warm climate, and in warm water, it was almost unendurable. So we decided to construct a palisaded camp.

s we strolled slowly back toward the boat, planning and discussing this, we were suddenly startled by a loud and unmistakable detonation.

"A shell from the *U-33*!" exclaimed von Schoenvorts.

"What can be after signifyin'?" queried Olson.

"They are in trouble," I answered for all, "and it's up to us to get back to them. Drop that carcass," I directed the men carrying the meat, "and follow me!" I set off at a rapid run in the direction of the harbor.

We ran for the better part of a mile without hearing anything more from the direction of the harbor, and then I reduced the speed to a walk, for the exercise was telling on us who had been cooped up for so long in the confined interior of the *U-33*. Puffing and panting, we plodded on until within about a mile of the harbor we came upon a sight that brought us all up standing. We had been passing through a little heavier timber than was usual to this part of the country, when we suddenly emerged into an open space in the center of which was such a band as might have caused the most courageous to pause. It consisted of upward of five hundred individuals representing several species closely allied to man. There were anthropoid apes and gorillas—these I had no difficulty in recognizing; but there were other forms which I had never before seen, and I was hard put to it to say whether they were ape or man. Some of them resembled the corpse we had found upon the narrow beach against Caprona's sea-wall, while others were of a still lower type, more nearly resembling the apes, and yet others were uncannily manlike, standing almost erect, being less hairy and possessing better shaped heads.

There was one among the lot, evidently the leader of them, who bore a close resemblance to the so-called Neanderthal man of La Chapelle-aux-Saints. There was the same short, stocky trunk upon which rested an enormous head habitually bent forward into the same curvature as the back, the arms shorter than the legs, and the lower leg considerably shorter than that of modern man, the knees bent forward and never straightened. This creature and one or two others who appeared to be of a lower order than he, yet higher than that of the apes, carried heavy clubs; the others were armed only with giant muscles and fighting fangs—nature's weapons. All were males, and all were entirely naked; nor was there upon even the highest among them a sign of ornamentation.

At sight of us they turned with bared fangs and low growls to confront us. I did not wish to fire among them unless it became absolutely necessary, and so I started to lead my party around them; but the instant that the Neanderthal man guessed my intention, he evidently attributed it to cowardice upon our part, and with a wild cry he leaped toward us, waving his cudgel above his head. The others followed him, and in a minute we should have been overwhelmed. I gave the order to fire, and at the first volley six of them went down, including the Neanderthal man. The others hesitated a moment and then broke for the trees, some running nimbly among the branches, while others lost themselves to us between the boles. Both von Schoenvorts and I noticed that at least two of the higher, manlike types took to the trees quite as nimbly as the apes, while others that more nearly approached man in carriage and appearance sought safety upon the ground with the gorillas.

An examination disclosed that five of our erstwhile opponents were dead and the sixth, the Neanderthal man, was but slightly wounded, a bullet having glanced from his thick skull, stunning him. We decided to take him with us to camp, and by means of belts we managed to secure his hands behind his back and place a leash around his neck before he regained consciousness. We then retraced our steps for our meat, being convinced by our own experience that those aboard the U-33 had been able to frighten off this party with a single shell—but when we came to where we had left the deer it had disappeared.

On the return journey Whitely and I preceded the rest of the party by about a hundred yards in the hope of getting another shot at something edible, for we were all greatly disgusted and disappointed by the loss of our venison. Whitely and I advanced very cautiously, and not having the whole party with us, we fared better than on the journey out, bagging two large antelope not a half-mile from the harbor; so with our game and our prisoner we made a cheerful return to the boat, where we found that all were safe. On the shore a little north of where we lay there were the corpses of twenty of the wild creatures who had attacked Bradley and his party in our absence, and the rest of whom we had met and scattered a few minutes later.

We felt that we had taught these wild ape-men a lesson and that because of it we would be safer in the future—at least safer from them; but we decided not to abate our carefulness one whit; feeling that this new world was filled with terrors still unknown to us; nor were we wrong.

The following morning we commenced work upon our camp, Bradley, Olson, von Schoenvorts, Miss La Rue, and I having sat up half the night discussing the matter and drawing plans. We set the men at work felling trees, selecting for the purpose jarrah, a hard, weather-resisting timber which grew in profusion near by. Half the men labored while the other half stood guard, alternating each hour with an hour off at noon. Olson directed this work. Bradley, von Schoenvorts and I, with Miss La Rue's help, staked out the various buildings and the outer wall. When the day was done, we had quite an array of logs nicely notched and ready for our building operations on the morrow, and we were all tired, for after the buildings had been staked out we all fell in and helped with the logging—all but von Schoenvorts. He, being a Prussian and a gentleman, couldn't stoop to such menial labor in the presence of his men, and I didn't see fit to ask it of him, as the work was purely voluntary upon our part. He spent the afternoon shaping a swagger-stick from the branch of jarrah and talking with Miss La Rue, who had sufficiently unbent toward him to notice his existence.

We saw nothing of the wild men of the previous day, and only once were we menaced by any of the strange denizens of Caprona, when some frightful nightmare of the sky swooped down upon us, only to be driven off by a fusillade of bullets. The thing appeared to be some variety of pterodactyl, and what with its enormous size and ferocious aspect was most awe-inspiring. There was another incident, too, which to me at least was far more unpleasant than the sudden onslaught of the prehistoric reptile. Two of the men, both Germans, were stripping a felled tree of its branches. Von Schoenvorts had completed his swagger-stick, and he and I were passing close to where the two worked.

One of them threw to his rear a small branch that he had just chopped off, and as misfortune would have it, it struck von Schoenvorts across the face. It couldn't have hurt him, for it didn't leave a mark; but he flew into a terrific rage, shouting: "Attention!" in a loud voice. The sailor immediately straightened up, faced his officer, clicked his heels together and saluted. "Pig!" roared the Baron, and struck the fellow across the face, breaking his nose. I grabbed von Schoenvorts' arm and jerked him away before he could strike again, if such had been his intention, and then he raised his little stick to strike me; but before it descended the muzzle of my pistol was against his belly and he must have seen in my eyes that nothing would suit me better than an excuse to pull the trigger. Like all his kind and all other bullies, von Schoenvorts was a coward at heart, and so he dropped his hand to his side and started to turn away; but I pulled him back, and there before his men I told him that such a thing must never again occur—that no man was to be struck or otherwise punished other than in due process of the laws that we had made and the court that we had established. All the time the sailor stood rigidly at attention, nor could I tell from his expression whether he most resented the blow his officer had struck him or my interference in the gospel of the Kaiser-breed. Nor did he move until I said to him: "Plesser, you may return to your quarters and dress your wound." Then he saluted and marched stiffly off toward the *U-33*.

Just before dusk we moved out into the bay a hundred yards from shore and dropped anchor, for I felt that we should be safer there than elsewhere. I also detailed men to stand watch during the night and appointed Olson officer of the watch for the entire night, telling him to bring his blankets on deck and get what rest he could. At dinner we tasted our first roast Caprona antelope, and we had a mess of greens that the cook had found growing along the stream. All during the meal von Schoenvorts was silent and surly.

After dinner we all went on deck and watched the unfamiliar scenes of a Capronian night—that is, all but von Schoenvorts. There was less to see than to hear. From the great inland lake behind us came the hissing and the screaming of countless saurians. Above us we heard the flap of giant wings, while from the shore rose the multitudinous voices of a tropical jungle—of a warm, damp atmosphere such as must have enveloped the entire earth during the Palezoic and Mesozoic eras. But here were intermingled the voices of later eras—the scream of the panther, the roar of the lion, the baying of wolves and a thunderous growling which we could attribute to nothing earthly but which one day we were to connect with the most fearsome of ancient creatures.

One by one the others went to their rooms, until the girl and I were left alone together, for I had permitted the watch to go below for a few minutes, knowing that I would be on deck. Miss La Rue was very quiet, though she replied graciously enough to whatever I had to say that required reply. I asked her if she did not feel well.

"Yes," she said, "but I am depressed by the awfulness of it all. I feel of so little consequence—so small and helpless in the face of all these myriad manifestations of life stripped to the bone of its savagery and brutality. I realize as never before how cheap and valueless a thing is life. Life seems a joke, a cruel, grim joke. You are a laughable incident or a terrifying one as you happen to be less powerful or more powerful than some other form of life which crosses your path; but as a rule you are of no moment whatsoever to anything but yourself. You are a comic little figure, hopping from the cradle to the grave. Yes, that is our trouble—we take ourselves too seriously; but Caprona should be a sure cure for that." She paused and laughed.

"You have evolved a beautiful philosophy," I said. "It fills such a longing in the human breast. It is full, it is satisfying, it is ennobling. What wonderous strides toward perfection the human race might have made if the first man had evolved it and it had persisted until now as the creed of humanity."

"I don't like irony," she said; "it indicates a small soul."

"What other sort of soul, then, would you expect from 'a comic little figure hopping from the cradle to the grave'?" I inquired. "And what difference does it make, anyway, what you like and what you don't like? You are here for but an instant, and you mustn't take yourself too seriously."

She looked up at me with a smile. "I imagine that I am frightened and blue," she said, "and I know that I am very, very homesick and lonely." There was almost a sob in her voice as she concluded. It was the first time that she had spoken thus to me. Involuntarily, I laid my hand upon hers where it rested on the rail.

"I know how difficult your position is," I said; "but don't feel that you are alone. There is—is one here who—who would do anything in the world for you," I ended lamely. She did not withdraw her hand, and she looked up into my face with tears on her cheeks and I read in her eyes the thanks her lips could not voice. Then she looked away across the weird moonlit landscape and sighed. Evidently her new-found philosophy had tumbled about her ears, for she was seemingly taking herself seriously. I wanted to take her in my arms and tell her how I loved her, and had taken her hand from the rail and started to draw her toward me when Olson came blundering up on deck with his bedding.

The following morning we started building-operations in earnest, and things progressed finely. The Neanderthal man was something of a care, for we had to keep him in irons all the time, and he was mighty savage when approached; but after a time he became more docile, and then we tried to discover if he had a language. Lys spent a great deal of time talking to him and trying to draw him out; but for a long while she was unsuccessful. It took us three weeks to build all the houses, which we constructed close by a cold spring some two miles from the harbor.

We changed our plans a trifle when it came to building the palisade, for we found a rotted cliff near by where we could get all the flat building-stone we needed, and so we constructed a stone wall entirely around the buildings. It was in the form of a square, with bastions and towers at each corner which would permit an enfilading fire along any side of the fort, and was about one hundred and thirty-five feet square on the outside, with walls three feet thick at the bottom and about a foot and a half wide at the top, and fifteen feet high. It took a long time to build that wall, and we all turned in and helped except von Schoenvorts, who, by the way, had not spoken to me except in the line of official business since our encounter—a condition of armed neutrality which suited me to a T. We have just finished it, the last touches being put on today. I quit about a week ago and commenced working on this chronicle for our strange adventures, which will account for any minor errors in chronology which may have crept in; there was so much material that I may have made some mistakes, but I think they are but minor and few.

I see in reading over the last few pages that I neglected to state that Lys finally discovered that the Neanderthal man possessed a language. It is very meagre, but still it is a spoken language. She had learned to speak it, and so have I, to some extent. It was he—his name he says is Am, or Ahm—who told us that this country is called Caspak. When we asked him how far it extended, he waved both arms about his head in an all-including gesture which took in, apparently, the entire universe. He is more tractable now, and we are going to release him, for he has assured us that he will not permit his fellows to harm us. He calls us Galus and says that in a short time he will be a Galu. It is not quite clear to us what he means. He says that there are many Galus north of us, and that as soon as he becomes one he will go and live with them.

Ahm went out to hunt with us yesterday and was much impressed by the ease with which our rifles brought down antelopes and deer. We have been living upon the fat of the land, Ahm having shown us the edible fruits, tubers and herbs, and twice a week we go out after fresh meat. A certain proportion of this we dry and store away, for we do not know what may come. Our drying process is really smoking. We have also dried a large quantity of two varieties of cereal which grow wild a few miles south of us. One of these is a giant Indian maize—a lofty perennial often fifty and sixty feet in height, with ears the size off a man's body and kernels as large as your fist. We have had to construct a second store house for the great quantity of this that we have gathered.

September 3, 1916: Three months ago today the torpedo from the *U-33* started me from the peaceful deck of the American liner upon the strange voyage which has ended here in Caspak. We have settled down to an acceptance of our fate, for all are convinced that none of us will ever see the outer world again. Ahm's repeated assertions that there are human beings like ourselves in Caspak have roused the men to a keen desire for exploration. I sent out one party last week under Bradley. Ahm, who is now free to go and come as he wishes, accompanied them. They marched about twenty-five miles due west, encountering many terrible beasts and reptiles and not a few man-like creatures whom Ahm sent away. Here is Bradley's report of the expedition:

Marched fifteen miles the first day, camping on the bank of a large stream which runs southward. Game was plentiful and we saw several varieties which we had not before encountered in Caspak. Just before making camp we were charged by an enormous woolly rhinoceros, which Plesser dropped with a perfect shot. We had rhinoceros-steaks for supper. Ahm called the thing "Atis." It was almost a continuous battle from the time we left the fort until we arrived at camp. The mind of man can scarce conceive the plethora of carnivorous life in this lost world; and their prey, of course, is even more abundant.

The second day we marched about ten miles to the foot of the cliffs. Passed through dense forests close to the base of the cliffs. Saw manlike creatures and a low order of ape in one band, and some of the men swore that there was a white man among them. They were inclined to attack us at first; but a volley from our rifles caused them to change their minds. We scaled the cliffs as far as we could; but near the top they are absolutely perpendicular without any sufficient cleft or protuberance to give hand or foot-hold. All were disappointed, for we hungered for a view of the ocean and the outside world. We even had a hope that we might see and attract the attention of a passing ship. Our exploration has determined one thing which will probably be of little value to us and never heard of beyond Caprona's walls—this crater was once entirely filled with water. Indisputable evidence of this is on the face of the cliffs.

Our return journey occupied two days and was as filled with adventure as usual. We are all becoming accustomed to adventure. It is beginning to pall on us. We suffered no casualties and there was no illness.

I had to smile as I read Bradley's report. In those four days he had doubtless passed through more adventures than an African big-game hunter experiences in a lifetime, and yet he covered it all in a few lines. Yes, we are becoming accustomed to adventure. Not a day passes that one or more of us does not face death at least once. Ahm taught us a few things that have proved profitable and saved us much ammunition, which it is useless to expend except for food or in the last recourse of self-preservation. Now when we are attacked by large flying reptiles we run beneath spreading trees; when land carnivora threaten us, we climb into trees, and we have learned not to fire at any of the dinosaurs unless we can keep out of their reach for at least two minutes after hitting them in the brain or spine, or five minutes after puncturing their hearts—it takes them so long to die. To hit them elsewhere is worse than useless, for they do not seem to notice it, and we had discovered that such shots do not kill or even disable them.

September 7, 1916: Much has happened since I last wrote. Bradley is away again on another exploration expedition to the cliffs. He expects to be gone several weeks and to follow along their base in search of a point where they may be scaled. He took Sinclair, Brady, James, and Tippet with him. Ahm has disappeared. He has been gone about three days; but the most startling thing I have on record is that von Schoenvorts and Olson while out hunting the other day discovered oil about fifteen miles north of us beyond the sandstone cliffs. Olson says there is a geyser of oil there, and von Schoenvorts is making preparations to refine it. If he succeeds, we shall have the means for leaving Caspak and returning to our own world. I can scarce believe the truth of it. We are all elated to the seventh heaven of bliss. Pray God we shall not be disappointed.

I have tried on several occasions to broach the subject of my love to Lys; but she will not listen.

7

ctober 8, 1916: This is the last entry I shall make upon my manuscript. When this is done, I shall be through. Though I may pray that it reaches the haunts of civilized man, my better judgment tells me that it will never be perused by other eyes than mine, and that even though it should, it would be too late to avail me. I am alone upon the summit of the great cliff overlooking the broad Pacific. A chill south wind bites at my marrow, while far below me I can see the tropic foliage of Caspak on the one hand and huge icebergs from the near Antarctic upon the other. Presently I shall stuff my folded manuscript into the thermos bottle I have carried with me for the purpose since I left the fort—Fort Dinosaur we named it—and hurl it far outward over the cliff-top into the Pacific. What current washes the shore of Caprona I know not; whither my bottle will be borne I cannot even guess; but I have done all that mortal man may do to notify the world of my whereabouts and the dangers that threaten those of us who remain alive in Caspak—if there be any other than myself.

About the 8th of September I accompanied Olson and von Schoenvorts to the oil-geyser. Lys came with us, and we took a number of things which von Schoenvorts wanted for the purpose of erecting a crude refinery. We went up the coast some ten or twelve miles in the *U-33*, tying up to shore near the mouth of a small stream which emptied great volumes of crude oil into the sea—I find it difficult to call this great lake by any other name. Then we disembarked and went inland about five miles, where we came upon a small lake entirely filled with oil, from the center of which a geyser of oil spouted.

On the edge of the lake we helped von Schoenvorts build his primitive refinery. We worked with him for two days until he got things fairly well started, and then we returned to Fort Dinosaur, as I feared that Bradley might return and be worried by our absence. The *U-33* merely landed those of us that were to return to the fort and then retraced its course toward the oil-well. Olson, Whitely, Wilson, Miss La Rue, and myself disembarked, while von Schoenvorts and his German crew returned to refine the oil. The next day Plesser and two other Germans came down overland for ammunition. Plesser said they had been attacked by wild men and had exhausted a great deal of ammunition. He also asked permission to get some dried meat and maize, saying that they were so busy with the work of refining that they had no time to hunt. I let him have everything he asked for, and never once did a suspicion of their intentions enter my mind. They returned to the oil-well the same day, while we continued with the multitudinous duties of camp life.

For three days nothing of moment occurred. Bradley did not return; nor did we have any word from von Schoenvorts. In the evening Lys and I went up into one of the bastion towers and listened to the grim and terrible night-life of the frightful ages of the past. Once a saber-tooth screamed almost beneath us, and the girl shrank close against me. As I felt her body against mine, all the pent love of these three long months shattered the bonds of timidity and conviction, and I swept her up into my arms and covered her face and lips with kisses. She did not struggle to free herself; but instead her dear arms crept up about my neck and drew my own face even closer to hers.

"You love me, Lys?" I cried.

I felt her head nod an affirmative against my breast. "Tell me, Lys," I begged, "tell me in words how much you love me."

Low and sweet and tender came the answer: "I love you beyond all conception."

My heart filled with rapture then, and it fills now as it has each of the countless times I have recalled those dear words, as it shall fill always until death has claimed me. I may never see her again; she may not know how I love her—she may question, she may doubt; but always true and steady and warm with the fires of love my heart beats for the girl who said that night: "I love you beyond all conception."

For a long time we sat there upon the little bench constructed for the sentry that we had not as yet thought it necessary to post in more than one of the four towers. We learned to know one another better in those two brief hours than we had in all the months that had intervened since we had been thrown together. She told me that she had loved me from the first, and that she never had loved von Schoenvorts, their engagement having been arranged by her aunt for social reasons.

That was the happiest evening of my life; nor ever do I expect to experience its like; but at last, as is the way of happiness, it terminated. We descended to the compound, and I walked with Lys to the door of her quarters. There again she kissed me and bade me good night, and then she went in and closed the door.

I went to my own room, and there I sat by the light of one of the crude candles we had made from the tallow of the beasts we had killed, and lived over the events of the evening. At last I turned in and fell asleep, dreaming happy dreams and planning for the future, for even in savage Caspak I was bound to make my girl safe and happy. It was daylight when I awoke. Wilson, who was acting as cook, was up and astir at his duties in the cook-house. The others slept; but I arose and followed by Nobs went down to the stream for a plunge. As was our custom, I went armed with both rifle and revolver; but I stripped and had my swim without further disturbance than the approach of a large hyena, a number of which occupied caves in the sandstone cliffs north of the camp. These brutes are enormous and exceedingly ferocious. I imagine they correspond with the cave-hyena of prehistoric times. This fellow charged Nobs, whose Capronian experiences had taught him that discretion is the better part of valor—with the result that he dived head foremost into the stream beside me after giving vent to a series of ferocious growls which had no more effect upon *Hyaena spelaeus* than might a sweet smile upon an enraged tusker. Afterward I shot the beast, and Nobs had a feast while I dressed, for he had become quite a raw-meat eater during our numerous hunting expeditions, upon which we always gave him a portion of the kill.

Whitely and Olson were up and dressed when we returned, and we all sat down to a good breakfast. I could not but wonder at Lys' absence from the table, for she had always been one of the earliest risers in camp; so about nine o'clock, becoming apprehensive lest she might be indisposed, I went to the door of her room and knocked. I received no response, though I finally pounded with all my strength; then I turned the knob and entered, only to find that she was not there. Her bed had been occupied, and her clothing lay where she had placed it the previous night upon retiring; but Lys was gone. To say that I was distracted with terror would be to put it mildly. Though I knew she could not be in camp, I searched every square inch of the compound and all the buildings, yet without avail.

It was Whitely who discovered the first clue—a huge human-like footprint in the soft earth beside the spring, and indications of a struggle in the mud. Then I found a tiny handkerchief close to the outer wall. Lys had been stolen! It was all too plain. Some hideous member of the ape-man tribe had entered the fort and carried her off. While I stood stunned and horrified at the frightful evidence before me, there came from the direction of the great lake an increasing sound that rose to the volume of a shriek. We all looked up as the noise approached apparently just above us, and a moment later there followed a terrific explosion which hurled us to the ground. When we clambered to our feet, we saw a large section of the west wall torn and shattered. It was Olson who first recovered from his daze sufficiently to guess the explanation of the phenomenon.

"A shell!" he cried. "And there ain't no shells in Caspak besides what's on the *U-33*. The dirty boches are shellin' the fort. Come on!" And he grasped his rifle and started on a run toward the lake. It was over two miles, but we did not pause until the harbor was in view, and still we could not see the lake because of the sandstone cliffs which intervened. We ran as fast as we could around the lower end of the harbor, scrambled up the cliffs and at last stood upon their summit in full view of the lake. Far away down the coast, toward the river through which we had come to reach the lake, we saw upon the surface the outline of the *U-33*, black smoke vomiting from her funnel.

Von Schoenvorts had succeeded in refining the oil! The cur had broken his every pledge and was leaving us there to our fates. He had even shelled the fort as a parting compliment; nor could anything have been more truly Prussian than this leave-taking of the Baron Friedrich von Schoenvorts.

Olson, Whitely, Wilson, and I stood for a moment looking at one another. It seemed incredible that man could be so perfidious— that we had really seen with our own eyes the thing that we had seen; but when we returned to the fort, the shattered wall gave us ample evidence that there was no mistake.

Then we began to speculate as to whether it had been an ape-man or a Prussian that had abducted Lys. From what we knew of von Schoenvorts, we would not have been surprised at anything from him; but the footprints by the spring seemed indisputable evidence that one of Caprona's undeveloped men had borne off the girl I loved.

As soon as I had assured myself that such was the case, I made my preparations to follow and rescue her. Olson, Whitely, and Wilson each wished to accompany me; but I told them that they were needed here, since with Bradley's party still absent and the Germans gone it was necessary that we conserve our force as far as might be possible.

8

t was a sad leave-taking as in silence I shook hands with each of the three remaining men. Even poor Nobs appeared dejected as we quit the compound and set out upon the well-marked spoor of the abductor. Not once did I turn my eyes backward toward Fort Dinosaur. I have not looked upon it since—nor in all likelihood shall I ever look upon it again. The trail led northwest until it reached the western end of the sandstone cliffs to the north of the fort; there it ran into a well-defined path which wound northward into a country we had not as yet explored. It was a beautiful, gently rolling country, broken by occasional outcroppings of sandstone and by patches of dense forest relieved by open, parklike stretches and broad meadows whereon grazed countless herbivorous animals—red deer, aurochs, and infinite variety of antelope and at least three distinct species of horse, the latter ranging in size from a creature about as large as Nobs to a magnificent animal fourteen to sixteen hands high. These creatures fed together in perfect amity; nor did they show any great indications of terror when Nobs and I approached. They moved out of our way and kept their eyes upon us until we had passed; then they resumed their feeding.

The path led straight across the clearing into another forest, lying upon the verge of which I saw a bit of white. It appeared to stand out in marked contrast and incongruity to all its surroundings, and when I stopped to examine it, I found that it was a small strip of muslin—part of the hem of a garment. At once I was all excitement, for I knew that it was a sign left by Lys that she had been carried this way; it was a tiny bit torn from the hem of the undergarment that she wore in lieu of the night-robes she had lost with the sinking of the liner. Crushing the bit of fabric to my lips, I pressed on even more rapidly than before, because I now knew that I was upon the right trail and that up to this, point at least, Lys still had lived.

I made over twenty miles that day, for I was now hardened to fatigue and accustomed to long hikes, having spent considerable time hunting and exploring in the immediate vicinity of camp. A dozen times that day was my life threatened by fearsome creatures of the earth or sky, though I could not but note that the farther north I traveled, the fewer were the great dinosaurs, though they still persisted in lesser numbers. On the other hand the quantity of ruminants and the variety and frequency of carnivorous animals increased. Each square mile of Caspak harbored its terrors.

At intervals along the way I found bits of muslin, and often they reassured me when otherwise I should have been doubtful of the trail to take where two crossed or where there were forks, as occurred at several points. And so, as night was drawing on, I came to the southern end of a line of cliffs loftier than any I had seen before, and as I approached them, there was wafted to my nostrils the pungent aroma of wood-smoke. What could it mean? There could, to my mind, be but a single solution: man abided close by, a higher order of man than we had as yet seen, other than Ahm, the Neanderthal man. I wondered again as I had so many times that day if it had not been Ahm who stole Lys.

Cautiously I approached the flank of the cliffs, where they terminated in an abrupt escarpment as though some all-powerful hand had broken off a great section of rock and set it upon the surface of the earth. It was now quite dark, and as I crept around the edge of the cliff, I saw at a little distance a great fire around which were many figures—apparently human figures. Cautioning Nobs to silence, and he had learned many lessons in the value of obedience since we had entered Caspak, I slunk forward, taking advantage of whatever cover I could find, until from behind a bush I could distinctly see the creatures assembled by the fire. They were human and yet not human. I should say that they were a little higher in the scale of evolution than Ahm, possibly occupying a place of evolution between that of the Neanderthal man and what is known as the Grimaldi race. Their features were distinctly negroid, though their skins were white. A considerable portion of both torso and limbs was covered with short hair, and their physical proportions were in many aspects apelike, though not so much so as were Ahm's. They carried themselves in a more erect position, although their arms were considerably longer than those of the Neanderthal man. As I watched them, I saw that they possessed a language, that they had knowledge of fire and that they carried besides the wooden club of Ahm a thing which resembled a crude stone hatchet. Evidently they were very low in the scale of humanity, but they were a step upward from those I had previously seen in Caspak.

But what interested me most was the slender figure of a dainty girl, clad only in a thin bit of muslin which scarce covered her knees— a bit of muslin torn and ragged about the lower hem. It was Lys, and she was alive and so far as I could see, unharmed. A huge brute with thick lips and prognathous jaw stood at her shoulder. He was talking loudly and gesticulating wildly. I was close enough to hear his words, which were similar to the language of Ahm, though much fuller, for there were many words I could not understand. However I caught the gist of what he was saying—which in effect was that he had found and captured this Galu, that she was his and that he defied anyone to question his right of possession. It appeared to me, as I afterward learned was the fact, that I was witnessing the most primitive of marriage ceremonies. The assembled members of the tribe looked on and listened in a sort of dull and perfunctory apathy, for the speaker was by far the mightiest of the clan. There seemed no one to dispute his claims when he said, or rather shouted, in stentorian tones: "I am Tsa. This is my she. Who wishes her more than Tsa?"

"I do," I said in the language of Ahm, and I stepped out into the firelight before them. Lys gave a little cry of joy and started toward me, but Tsa grasped her arm and dragged her back.

"Who are you?" shrieked Tsa. "I kill! I kill! I kill!"

"The she is mine," I replied, "and I have come to claim her. I kill if you do not let her come to me." And I raised my pistol to a level with his heart. Of course the creature had no conception of the purpose of the strange little implement which I was poking toward him. With a sound that was half human and half the growl of a wild beast, he sprang toward me. I aimed at his heart and fired, and as he sprawled headlong to the ground, the others of his tribe, overcome by fright at the report of the pistol, scattered toward the cliffs—while Lys, with outstretched arms, ran toward me.

As I crushed her to me, there rose from the black night behind us and then to our right and to our left a series of frightful screams and shrieks, bellowings, roars and growls. It was the night-life of this jungle world coming into its own—the huge, carnivorous nocturnal beasts which make the nights of Caspak hideous. A shuddering sob ran through Lys' figure. "O God," she cried, "give me the strength to endure, for his sake!" I saw that she was upon the verge of a break-down, after all that she must have passed through of fear and horror that day, and I tried to quiet and reassure her as best I might; but even to me the future looked most unpromising, for what chance of life had we against the frightful hunters of the night who even now were prowling closer to us?

Now I turned to see what had become of the tribe, and in the fit-ful glare of the fire I perceived that the face of the cliff was pitted with large holes into which the man-things were clambering. "Come," I said to Lys, "we must follow them. We cannot last a half-hour out here. We must find a cave." Already we could see the blazing green eyes of the hungry carnivora. I seized a brand from the fire and hurled it out into the night, and there came back an answering chorus of savage and rageful protest; but the eyes vanished for a short time. Selecting a burning branch for each of us, we advanced toward the cliffs, where we were met by angry threats.

"They will kill us," said Lys. "We may as well keep on in search of another refuge."

"They will not kill us so surely as will those others out there," I replied. "I am going to seek shelter in one of these caves; nor will the man-things prevent." And I kept on in the direction of the cliff's base. A huge creature stood upon a ledge and brandished his stone hatchet. "Come and I will kill you and take the she," he boasted.

"You saw how Tsa fared when he would have kept my she," I replied in his own tongue. "Thus will you fare and all your fellows if you do not permit us to come in peace among you out of the dangers of the night."

"Go north," he screamed. "Go north among the Galus, and we will not harm you. Some day will we be Galus; but now we are not. You do not belong among us. Go away or we will kill you. The she may remain if she is afraid, and we will keep her; but the he must depart."

"The he won't depart," I replied, and approached still nearer. Rough and narrow ledges formed by nature gave access to the upper caves. A man might scale them if unhampered and unhindered, but to clamber upward in the face of a belligerent tribe of half-men and with a girl to assist was beyond my capability.

"I do not fear you," screamed the creature. "You were close to Tsa; but I am far above you. You cannot harm me as you harmed Tsa. Go away!"

I placed a foot upon the lowest ledge and clambered upward, reaching down and pulling Lys to my side. Already I felt safer. Soon we would be out of danger of the beasts again closing in upon us. The man above us raised his stone hatchet above his head and leaped lightly down to meet us. His position above me gave him a great advantage, or at least so he probably thought, for he came with every show of confidence. I hated to do it, but there seemed no other way, and so I shot him down as I had shot down Tsa.

"You see," I cried to his fellows, "that I can kill you wherever you may be. A long way off I can kill you as well as I can kill you near by. Let us come among you in peace. I will not harm you if you do not harm us. We will take a cave high up. Speak!"

"Come, then," said one. "If you will not harm us, you may come. Take Tsa's hole, which lies above you."

The creature showed us the mouth of a black cave, but he kept at a distance while he did it, and Lys followed me as I crawled in to explore. I had matches with me, and in the light of one I found a small cavern with a flat roof and floor which followed the cleavage of the strata. Pieces of the roof had fallen at some long-distant date, as was evidenced by the depth of the filth and rubble in which they were embedded. Even a superficial examination revealed the fact that nothing had ever been attempted that might have improved the livability of the cavern; nor, should I judge, had it ever been cleaned out. With considerable difficulty I loosened some of the larger pieces of broken rock which littered the floor and placed them as a barrier before the doorway. It was too dark to do more than this. I then gave Lys a piece of dried meat, and sitting inside the entrance, we dined as must have some of our ancient forbears at the dawning of the age of man, while from below the open diapason of the savage night rose weird and horrifying to our ears. In the light of the great fire still burning we could see huge, skulking forms, and in the blacker background countless flaming eyes.

Lys shuddered, and I put my arm around her and drew her to me; and thus we sat throughout the hot night. She told me of her abduction and of the fright she had undergone, and together we thanked God that she had come through unharmed, because the great brute had dared not pause along the danger-infested way. She said that they had but just reached the cliffs when I arrived, for on several occasions her captor had been forced to take to the trees with her to escape the clutches of some hungry cave-lion or saber-toothed tiger, and that twice they had been obliged to remain for considerable periods before the beasts had retired.

Nobs, by dint of much scrambling and one or two narrow escapes from death, had managed to follow us up the cliff and was now curled between me and the doorway, having devoured a piece of the dried meat, which he seemed to relish immensely. He was the first to fall asleep; but I imagine we must have followed suit soon, for we were both tired. I had laid aside my ammunition-belt and rifle, though both were close beside me; but my pistol I kept in my lap beneath my hand. However, we were not disturbed during the night, and when I awoke, the sun was shining on the tree-tops in the distance. Lys' head had drooped to my breast, and my arm was still about her.

Shortly afterward Lys awoke, and for a moment she could not seem to comprehend her situation. She looked at me and then turned and glanced at my arm about her, and then she seemed quite suddenly to realize the scantiness of her apparel and drew away, covering her face with her palms and blushing furiously. I drew her back toward me and kissed her, and then she threw her arms about my neck and wept softly in mute surrender to the inevitable.

It was an hour later before the tribe began to stir about. We watched them from our "apartment," as Lys called it. Neither men nor women wore any sort of clothing or ornaments, and they all seemed to be about of an age; nor were there any babies or children among them. This was, to us, the strangest and most inexplicable of facts, but it recalled to us that though we had seen many of the lesser developed wild people of Caspak, we had never yet seen a child or an old man or woman.

After a while they became less suspicious of us and then quite friendly in their brutish way. They picked at the fabric of our clothing, which seemed to interest them, and examined my rifle and pistol and the ammunition in the belt around my waist. I showed them the thermos-bottle, and when I poured a little water from it, they were delighted, thinking that it was a spring which I carried about with me—a never-failing source of water supply.

One thing we both noticed among their other characteristics: they never laughed nor smiled; and then we remembered that Ahm had never done so, either. I asked them if they knew Ahm; but they said they did not.

One of them said: "Back there we may have known him." And he jerked his head to the south.

"You came from back there?" I asked. He looked at me in surprise.

"We all come from there," he said. "After a while we go there." And this time he jerked his head toward the north. "Be Galus," he concluded.

Many times now had we heard this reference to becoming Galus. Ahm had spoken of it many times. Lys and I decided that it was a sort of original religious conviction, as much a part of them as their instinct for self-preservation—a primal acceptance of a hereafter and a holier state. It was a brilliant theory, but it was all wrong. I know it now, and how far we were from guessing the wonderful, the miraculous, the gigantic truth which even yet I may only guess at—the thing that sets Caspak apart from all the rest of the world far more definitely than her isolated geographical position or her impregnable barrier of giant cliffs. If I could live to return to civilization, I should have meat for the clergy and the layman to chew upon for years—and for the evolutionists, too.

After breakfast the men set out to hunt, while the women went to a large pool of warm water covered with a green scum and filled with billions of tadpoles. They waded in to where the water was about a foot deep and lay down in the mud. They remained there from one to two hours and then returned to the cliff. While we were with them, we saw this same thing repeated every morning; but though we asked them why they did it we could get no reply which was intelligible to us. All they vouchsafed in way of explanation was the single word *Ata*. They tried to get Lys to go in with them and could not understand why she refused. After the first day I went hunting with the men, leaving my pistol and Nobs with Lys, but she never had to use them, for no reptile or beast ever approached the pool while the women were there—nor, so far as we know, at other times. There was no spoor of wild beast in the soft mud along the banks, and the water certainly didn't look fit to drink.

This tribe lived largely upon the smaller animals which they bowled over with their stone hatchets after making a wide circle about their quarry and driving it so that it had to pass close to one of their number. The little horses and the smaller antelope they secured in sufficient numbers to support life, and they also ate numerous varieties of fruits and vegetables. They never brought in more than sufficient food for their immediate needs; but why bother? The food problem of Caspak is not one to cause worry to her inhabitants.

The fourth day Lys told me that she thought she felt equal to attempting the return journey on the morrow, and so I set out for the hunt in high spirits, for I was anxious to return to the fort and learn if Bradley and his party had returned and what had been the result of his expedition. I also wanted to relieve their minds as to Lys and myself, as I knew that they must already have given us up for dead. It was a cloudy day, though warm, as it always is in Caspak. It seemed odd to realize that just a few miles away winter lay upon the storm-tossed ocean, and that snow might be falling all about Caprona;

but no snow could ever penetrate the damp, hot atmosphere of the great crater.

We had to go quite a bit farther than usual before we could surround a little bunch of antelope, and as I was helping drive them, I saw a fine red deer a couple of hundred yards behind me. He must have been asleep in the long grass, for I saw him rise and look about him in a bewildered way, and then I raised my gun and let him have it. He dropped, and I ran forward to finish him with the long thin knife, which one of the men had given me; but just as I reached him, he staggered to his feet and ran on for another two hundred yards—when I dropped him again. Once more was this repeated before I was able to reach him and cut his throat; then I looked around for my companions, as I wanted them to come and carry the meat home; but I could see nothing of them. I called a few times and waited, but there was no response and no one came. At last I became disgusted, and cutting off all the meat that I could conveniently carry, I set off in the direction of the cliffs. I must have gone about a mile before the truth dawn upon me—I was lost, hopelessly lost.

The entire sky was still completely blotted out by dense clouds; nor was there any landmark visible by which I might have taken my bearings. I went on in the direction I thought was south but which I now imagine must have been about due north, without detecting a single familiar object. In a dense wood I suddenly stumbled upon a thing which at first filled me with hope and later with the most utter despair and dejection. It was a little mound of new-turned earth sprinkled with flowers long since withered, and at one end was a flat slab of sandstone stuck in the ground. It was a grave, and it meant for me that I had at last stumbled into a country inhabited by human beings. I would find them; they would direct me to the cliffs; perhaps they would accompany me and take us back with them to their abodes—to the abodes of men and women like ourselves. My hopes and my imagination ran riot in the few yards I had to cover to reach that lonely grave and stoop that I might read the rude characters scratched upon the simple headstone. This is what I read:

**HERE LIES JOHN TIPPET
ENGLISHMAN
KILLED BY TYRANNOSAURUS
10 SEPT., A.D. 1916
R. I. P.**

Tippet! It seemed incredible. Tippet lying here in this gloomy wood! Tippet dead! He had been a good man, but the personal loss was not what affected me. It was the fact that this silent grave gave evidence that Bradley had come this far upon his expedition and that he too probably was lost, for it was not our intention that he should be long gone. If I had stumbled upon the grave of one of the party, was it not within reason to believe that the bones of the others lay scattered somewhere near?

9

s I stood looking down upon that sad and lonely mound, wrapped in the most dismal of reflections and premonitions, I was suddenly seized from behind and thrown to earth. As I fell, a warm body fell on top of me, and hands grasped my arms and legs. When I could look up, I saw a number of giant fingers pinioning me down, while others stood about surveying me. Here again was a new type of man—a higher type than the primitive tribe I had just quitted. They were a taller people, too, with better-shaped skulls and more intelligent faces. There were less of the ape characteristics about their features, and less of the negroid, too. They carried weapons, stone-shod spears, stone knives, and hatchets—and they wore ornaments and breech-cloths—the former of feathers worn in their hair and the latter made of a single snake-skin cured with the head on, the head depending to their knees.

Of course I did not take in all these details upon the instant of my capture, for I was busy with other matters. Three of the warriors were sitting upon me, trying to hold me down by main strength and awkwardness, and they were having their hands full in the doing, I can tell you. I don't like to appear conceited, but I may as well admit that I am proud of my strength and the science that I have acquired and developed in the directing of it—that and my horsemanship I always have been proud of. And now, that day, all the long hours that I had put into careful study, practice and training brought me in two or three minutes a full return upon my investment. Californians, as a rule, are familiar with ju-jutsu, and I especially had made a study of it for several years, both at school and in the gym of the Los Angeles Athletic Club, while recently I had had, in my employ, a Jap who was a wonder at the art.

It took me just about thirty seconds to break the elbow of one of my assailants, trip another and send him stumbling backward among his fellows, and throw the third completely over my head in such a way that when he fell his neck was broken. In the instant that the others of the party stood in mute and inactive surprise, I unslung my rifle—which, carelessly, I had been carrying across my back; and when they charged, as I felt they would, I put a bullet in the forehead of one of them. This stopped them all temporarily—not the death of their fellow, but the report of the rifle, the first they had ever heard. Before they were ready to attack me again, one of them spoke in a commanding tone to his fellows, and in a language similar but still more comprehensive than that of the tribe to the south, as theirs was more complete than Ahm's. He commanded them to stand back and then he advanced and addressed me.

He asked me who I was, from whence I came and what my intentions were. I replied that I was a stranger in Caspak, that I was lost and that my only desire was to find my way back to my companions. He asked where they were and I told him toward the south somewhere, using the Caspakian phrase which, literally translated, means "toward the beginning." His surprise showed upon his face before he voiced it in words. "There are no Galus there," he said. "You have lied. The Galus have turned you out."

"I tell you," I said angrily, "that I am from another country, far from Caspak, far beyond the high cliffs. I do not know who the Galus may be; I have never seen them. This is the farthest north I have been. Look at me—look at my clothing and my weapons. Have you ever seen a Galu or any other creature in Caspak who possessed such things?"

He had to admit that he had not, and also that he was much interested in me, my rifle and the way I had handled his three warriors. Finally he became half convinced that I was telling him the truth and offered to aid me if I would show him how I had thrown the man over my head and also make him a present of the "bang-spear," as he called it. I refused to give him my rifle, but promised to show him the trick he wished to learn if he would guide me in the right direction. He told me that he would do so tomorrow, that it was too late today and that I might come to their village and spend the night with them. I was loath to lose so much time; but the fellow was obdurate, and so I accompanied them. The two dead men they left where they had fallen, nor gave them a second glance—thus cheap is life upon Caspak.

These people also were cave-dwellers, but their caves showed the result of a higher intelligence that brought them a step nearer to civilized man than the tribe next "toward the beginning." The interiors of their caverns were cleared of rubbish, though still far from clean, and they had pallets of dried grasses covered with the skins of leopard, lynx, and bear, while before the entrances were barriers of stone and small, rudely circular stone ovens. The walls of the cavern to which I was conducted were covered with drawings scratched upon the sandstone. There were the outlines of the giant red deer, of mammoths, of tigers and other beasts. Here, as in the last tribe, there were no children or any old people. The men of this tribe had two names, or rather names of two syllables, and their language contained words of two syllables; whereas in the tribe of Tsa the words were all of a single syllable, with the exception of a very few like *Atis* and *Galus*. The chief's name was To-jo, and his household consisted of seven females and himself. These women were much more comely, or rather less hideous than those of Tsa's people; one of them, even, was almost pretty, being less hairy and having a rather nice skin, with high coloring.

They were all much interested in me and examined my clothing and equipment carefully, handling and feeling and smelling of each article. I learned from them that their people were known as Band-lu, or spear-men; Tsa's race was called Sto-lu—hatchet-men. Below these in the scale of evolution came the Bo-lu, or club-men, and then the Alus, who had no weapons and no language. In that word I recognized what to me seemed the most remarkable discovery I had made upon Caprona, for unless it were mere coincidence, I had come upon a word that had been handed down from the beginning of spoken language upon earth, been handed down for millions of years, perhaps, with little change. It was the sole remaining thread of the ancient woof of a dawning culture which had been woven when Caprona was a fiery mount upon a great land-mass teeming with life. It linked the unfathomable then to the eternal now. And yet it may have been pure coincidence; my better judgment tells me that it is coincidence that in Caspak the term for speechless man is *Alus*, and in the outer world of our own day it is *Alalus*.

The comely woman of whom I spoke was called So-ta, and she took such a lively interest in me that To-jo finally objected to her attentions, emphasizing his displeasure by knocking her down and kicking her into a corner of the cavern. I leaped between them while he was still kicking her, and obtaining a quick hold upon him, dragged him screaming with pain from the cave. Then I made him promise not to hurt the she again, upon pain of worse punishment. So-ta gave me a grateful look; but To-jo and the balance of his women were sullen and ominous.

Later in the evening So-ta confided to me that she was soon to leave the tribe.

"So-ta soon to be Kro-lu," she confided in a low whisper. I asked her what a Kro-lu might be, and she tried to explain, but I do not yet know if I understood her. From her gestures I deduced that the Kro-lus were a people who were armed with bows and arrows, had vessels in which to cook their food and huts of some sort in which they lived, and were accompanied by animals. It was all very fragmentary and vague, but the idea seemed to be that the Kro-lus were a more advanced people than the Band-lus. I pondered a long time upon all that I had heard, before sleep came to me. I tried to find some connection between these various races that would explain the universal hope which each of them harbored that some day they would become Galus. So-ta had given me a suggestion; but the resulting idea was so weird that I could scarce even entertain it; yet it coincided with Ahm's expressed hope, with the various steps in evolution I had noted in the several tribes I had encountered and with the range of type represented in each tribe. For example, among the Band-lu were such types as So-ta, who seemed to me to be the highest in the scale of evolution, and To-jo, who was just a shade nearer the ape, while there were others who had flatter noses, more prognathous faces and hairier bodies. The question puzzled me. Possibly in the outer world the answer to it is locked in the bosom of the Sphinx. Who knows? I do not.

Thinking the thoughts of a lunatic or a dope-fiend, I fell asleep; and when I awoke, my hands and feet were securely tied and my weapons had been taken from me. How they did it without awakening me I cannot tell you. It was humiliating, but it was true. To-jo stood above me. The early light of morning was dimly filtering into the cave.

"Tell me," he demanded, "how to throw a man over my head and break his neck, for I am going to kill you, and I wish to know this thing before you die."

Of all the ingenuous declarations I have ever heard, this one copped the proverbial bun. It struck me as so funny that, even in the face of death, I laughed. Death, I may remark here, had, however, lost much of his terror for me. I had become a disciple of Lys' fleeting philosophy of the valuelessness of human life. I realized that she was quite right—that we were but comic figures hopping from the cradle to the grave, of interest to practically no other created thing than ourselves and our few intimates.

Behind To-jo stood So-ta. She raised one hand with the palm toward me—the Caspakian equivalent of a negative shake of the head.

"Let me think about it," I parried, and To-jo said that he would wait until night. He would give me a day to think it over; then he left, and the women left—the men for the hunt, and the women, as I later learned from So-ta, for the warm pool where they immersed their bodies as did the shes of the Sto-lu. "Ata," explained So-ta, when I questioned her as to the purpose of this matutinal rite; but that was later.

I must have lain there bound and uncomfortable for two or three hours when at last So-ta entered the cave. She carried a sharp knife—mine, in fact, and with it she cut my bonds.

"Come!" she said. "So-ta will go with you back to the Galus. It is time that So-ta left the Band-lu. Together we will go to the Kro-lu, and after that the Galus. To-jo will kill you tonight. He will kill So-ta if he knows that So-ta aided you. We will go together."

"I will go with you to the Kro-lu," I replied, "but then I must return to my own people 'toward the beginning.'"

"You cannot go back," she said. "It is forbidden. They would kill you. Thus far have you come—there is no returning."

"But I must return," I insisted. "My people are there. I must return and lead them in this direction."

She insisted, and I insisted; but at last we compromised. I was to escort her as far as the country of the Kro-lu and then I was to go back after my own people and lead them north into a land where the dangers were fewer and the people less murderous. She brought me all my belongings that had been filched from me—rifle, ammunition, knife, and thermos bottle, and then hand in hand we descended the cliff and set off toward the north.

For three days we continued upon our way, until we arrived outside a village of thatched huts just at dusk. So-ta said that she would enter alone; I must not be seen if I did not intend to remain, as it was forbidden that one should return and live after having advanced this far. So she left me. She was a dear girl and a stanch and true comrade—more like a man than a woman. In her simple barbaric way she was both refined and chaste. She had been the wife of To-jo. Among the Kro-lu she would find another mate after the manner of the strange Caspakian world; but she told me very frankly that whenever I returned, she would leave her mate and come to me, as she preferred me above all others. I was becoming a ladies' man after a lifetime of bashfulness!

At the outskirts of the village I left her without even seeing the sort of people who inhabited it, and set off through the growing darkness toward the south. On the third day I made a detour westward to avoid the country of the Band-lu, as I did not care to be detained by a meeting with To-jo. On the sixth day I came to the cliffs of the Sto-lu, and my heart beat fast as I approached them, for here was Lys. Soon I would hold her tight in my arms again; soon her warm lips would merge with mine. I felt sure that she was still safe among the hatchet people, and I was already picturing the joy and the love-light in her eyes when she should see me once more as I emerged from the last clump of trees and almost ran toward the cliffs.

It was late in the morning. The women must have returned from the pool; yet as I drew near, I saw no sign of life whatever. "They have remained longer," I thought; but when I was quite close to the base of the cliffs, I saw that which dashed my hopes and my happiness to earth. Strewn along the ground were a score of mute and horrible suggestions of what had taken place during my absence—bones picked clean of flesh, the bones of manlike creatures, the bones of many of the tribe of Sto-lu; nor in any cave was there sign of life.

Closely I examined the ghastly remains fearful each instant that I should find the dainty skull that would shatter my happiness for life; but though I searched diligently, picking up every one of the twenty-odd skulls, I found none that was the skull of a creature but slightly removed from the ape. Hope, then, still lived. For another three days I searched north and south, east and west for the hatchetmen of Caspak; but never a trace of them did I find. It was raining most of the time now, and the weather was as near cold as it ever seems to get on Caprona.

At last I gave up the search and set off toward Fort Dinosaur. For a week—a week filled with the terrors and dangers of a primeval world—I pushed on in the direction I thought was south. The sun never shone; the rain scarcely ever ceased falling. The beasts I met with were fewer in number but infinitely more terrible in temper; yet I lived on until there came to me the realization that I was hopelessly lost, that a year of sunshine would not again give me my bearings; and while I was cast down by this terrifying knowledge, the knowledge that I never again could find Lys, I stumbled upon another grave—the grave of William James, with its little crude headstone and its scrawled characters recording that he had died upon the 13th of September—killed by a saber-tooth tiger.

I think that I almost gave up then. Never in my life have I felt more hopeless or helpless or alone. I was lost. I could not find my friends. I did not even know that they still lived; in fact, I could not bring myself to believe that they did. I was sure that Lys was dead. I wanted myself to die, and yet I clung to life—useless and hopeless and harrowing a thing as it had become. I clung to life because some ancient, reptilian forbear had clung to life and transmitted to me through the ages the most powerful motive that guided his minute brain—the motive of self-preservation.

At last I came to the great barrier-cliffs; and after three days of mad effort—of maniacal effort—I scaled them. I built crude ladders;

I wedged sticks in narrow fissures; I chopped toe-holds and finger-holds with my long knife; but at last I scaled them. Near the summit I came upon a huge cavern. It is the abode of some mighty winged creature of the Triassic—or rather it was. Now it is mine. I slew the thing and took its abode. I reached the summit and looked out upon the broad gray terrible Pacific of the far-southern winter. It was cold up there. It is cold here today; yet here I sit watching, watching, watching for the thing I know will never come—for a sail.

10

nce a day I descend to the base of the cliff and hunt, and fill my stomach with water from a clear cold spring. I have three gourds which I fill with water and take back to my cave against the long nights. I have fashioned a spear and a bow and arrow, that I may conserve my ammunition, which is running low. My clothes are worn to shreds. Tomorrow I shall discard them for leopard-skins which I have tanned and sewn into a garment strong and warm. It is cold up here. I have a fire burning and I sit bent over it while I write; but I am safe here. No other living creature ventures to the chill summit of the barrier cliffs. I am safe, and I am alone with my sorrows and my remembered joys—but without hope. It is said that hope springs eternal in the human breast; but there is none in mine.

I am about done. Presently I shall fold these pages and push them into my thermos bottle. I shall cork it and screw the cap tight, and then I shall hurl it as far out into the sea as my strength will permit. The wind is off-shore; the tide is running out; perhaps it will be carried into one of those numerous ocean-currents which sweep perpetually from pole to pole and from continent to continent, to be deposited at last upon some inhabited shore. If fate is kind and this does happen, then, *for God's sake, come and get me!*

It was a week ago that I wrote the preceding paragraph, which I thought would end the written record of my life upon Caprona. I had paused to put a new point on my quill and stir the crude ink (which I made by crushing a black variety of berry and mixing it with water) before attaching my signature, when faintly from the valley far below came an unmistakable sound which brought me to my feet, trembling with excitement, to peer eagerly downward from my dizzy ledge. How full of meaning that sound was to me you may guess when I tell you that it was the report of a firearm! For a moment my gaze traversed the landscape beneath until it was caught and held by four figures near the base of the cliff—a human figure held at bay by three hyaenodons, those ferocious and blood-thirsty wild dogs of the Eocene. A fourth beast lay dead or dying near by.

I couldn't be sure, looking down from above as I was; but yet I trembled like a leaf in the intuitive belief that it was Lys, and my judgment served to confirm my wild desire, for whoever it was carried only a pistol, and thus had Lys been armed. The first wave of sudden joy which surged through me was short-lived in the face of the swift-following conviction that the one who fought below was already doomed. Luck and only luck it must have been which had permitted that first shot to lay low one of the savage creatures, for even such a heavy weapon as my pistol is entirely inadequate against even the lesser carnivora of Caspak. In a moment the three would charge! A futile shot would but tend more greatly to enrage the one it chanced to hit; and then the three would drag down the little human figure and tear it to pieces.

And maybe it was Lys! My heart stood still at the thought, but mind and muscle responded to the quick decision I was forced to make. There was but a single hope—a single chance—and I took it. I raised my rifle to my shoulder and took careful aim. It was a long shot, a dangerous shot, for unless one is accustomed to it, shooting from a considerable altitude is most deceptive work. There is, though, something about marksmanship which is quite beyond all scientific laws.

Upon no other theory can I explain my marksmanship of that moment. Three times my rifle spoke—three quick, short syllables of death. I did not take conscious aim; and yet at each report a beast crumpled in its tracks!

From my ledge to the base of the cliff is a matter of several thousand feet of dangerous climbing; yet I venture to say that the first ape from whose loins my line has descended never could have equaled the speed with which I literally dropped down the face of that rugged escarpment. The last two hundred feet is over a steep incline of loose rubble to the valley bottom, and I had just reached the top of this when there arose to my ears an agonized cry—"Bowen! Bowen! Quick, my love, quick!"

I had been too much occupied with the dangers of the descent to glance down toward the valley; but that cry which told me that it was indeed Lys, and that she was again in danger, brought my eyes quickly upon her in time to see a hairy, burly brute seize her and start off at a run toward the near-by wood. From rock to rock, chamoislike, I leaped downward toward the valley, in pursuit of Lys and her hideous abductor.

He was heavier than I by many pounds, and so weighted by the burden he carried that I easily overtook him; and at last he turned, snarling, to face me. It was Kho of the tribe of Tsa, the hatchet-men. He recognized me, and with a low growl he threw Lys aside and came for me. "The she is mine," he cried. "I kill! I kill!"

I had had to discard my rifle before I commenced the rapid descent of the cliff, so that now I was armed only with a hunting knife, and this I whipped from its scabbard as Kho leaped toward me. He was a mighty beast, mightily muscled, and the urge that has made males fight since the dawn of life on earth filled him with the blood-lust and the thirst to slay; but not one whit less did it fill me with the same primal passions. Two abysmal beasts sprang at each other's throats that day beneath the shadow of earth's oldest cliffs—the man of now and the man-thing of the earliest, forgotten then, imbued by the same deathless passion that has come down unchanged through all the epochs, periods and eras of time from the beginning, and which shall continue to the incalculable end—woman, the imperishable Alpha and Omega of life.

Kho closed and sought my jugular with his teeth. He seemed to forget the hatchet dangling by its aurochs-hide thong at his hip, as I forgot, for the moment, the dagger in my hand. And I doubt not but that Kho would easily have bested me in an encounter of that sort had not Lys' voice awakened within my momentarily reverted brain the skill and cunning of reasoning man. "Bowen!" she cried. "Your knife! Your knife!"

It was enough. It recalled me from the forgotten eon to which my brain had flown and left me once again a modern man battling with a clumsy, unskilled brute. No longer did my jaws snap at the hairy throat before me; but instead my knife sought and found a space between two ribs over the savage heart. Kho voiced a single horrid scream, stiffened spasmodically and sank to the earth. And Lys threw herself into my arms. All the fears and sorrows of the past were wiped away, and once again I was the happiest of men.

With some misgivings I shortly afterward cast my eyes upward toward the precarious ledge which ran before my cave, for it seemed to me quite beyond all reason to expect a dainty modern belle to essay the perils of that frightful climb. I asked her if she thought she could brave the ascent, and she laughed gayly in my face.

"Watch!" she cried, and ran eagerly toward the base of the cliff. Like a squirrel she clambered swiftly aloft, so that I was forced to exert myself to keep pace with her. At first she frightened me; but presently I was aware that she was quite as safe here as was I. When we finally came to my ledge and I again held her in my arms, she recalled to my mind that for several weeks she had been living the life of a cave-girl with the tribe of hatchet-men. They had been driven from their former caves by another tribe which had slain many and carried off quite half the females, and the new cliffs to which they had flown had proven far higher and more precipitous, so that she had become, through necessity, a most practiced climber.

She told me of Kho's desire for her, since all his females had been stolen and of how her life had been a constant nightmare of terror as she sought by night and by day to elude the great brute. For a time Nobs had been all the protection she required; but one day he disappeared—nor has she seen him since. She believes that he was deliberately made away with; and so do I, for we both are sure that he never would have deserted her. With her means of protection gone, Lys was now at the mercy of the hatchet-man; nor was it many hours before he had caught her at the base of the cliff and seized her; but as he bore her triumphantly aloft toward his cave, she had managed to break loose and escape him.

"For three days he has pursued me," she said, "through this horrible world. How I have passed through in safety I cannot guess, nor how I have always managed to outdistance him; yet I have done it, until just as you discovered me. Fate was kind to us, Bowen."

I nodded my head in assent and crushed her to me. And then we talked and planned as I cooked antelope-steaks over my fire, and we came to the conclusion that there was no hope of rescue, that she and I were doomed to live and die upon Caprona. Well, it might be worse! I would rather live here always with Lys than to live elsewhere without her; and she, dear girl, says the same of me; but I am afraid of this life for her. It is a hard, fierce, dangerous life, and I shall pray always that we shall be rescued from it—for her sake.

That night the clouds broke, and the moon shone down upon our little ledge; and there, hand in hand, we turned our faces toward heaven and plighted our troth beneath the eyes of God. No human agency could have married us more sacredly than we are wed. We are man and wife, and we are content. If God wills it, we shall live out our lives here. If He wills otherwise, then this manuscript which I shall now consign to the inscrutable forces of the sea shall fall into friendly hands. However, we are each without hope. And so we say good-bye in this, our last message to the world beyond the barrier cliffs.

(Signed) Bowen J. Tyler, Jr.

Lys La R. Tyler.

PART II

THE PEOPLE
THAT TIME
FORGOT

The Adventures of Thomas Billings

1

I am forced to admit that even though I had traveled a long distance to place Bowen Tyler's manuscript in the hands of his father, I was still a trifle skeptical as to its sincerity, since I could not but recall that it had not been many years since Bowen had been one of the most notorious practical jokers of his alma mater. The truth was that as I sat in the Tyler library at Santa Monica I commenced to feel a trifle foolish and to wish that I had merely forwarded the manuscript by express instead of bearing it personally, for I confess that I do not enjoy being laughed at. I have a well-developed sense of humor—when the joke is not on me.

Mr. Tyler, Sr., was expected almost hourly. The last steamer in from Honolulu had brought information of the date of the expected sailing of his yacht *Toreador*, which was now twenty-four hours overdue. Mr. Tyler's assistant secretary, who had been left at home, assured me that there was no doubt but that the *Toreador* had sailed as promised, since he knew his employer well enough to be positive that nothing short of an act of God would prevent his doing what he had planned to do. I was also aware of the fact that the sending apparatus of the *Toreador's* wireless equipment was sealed, and that it would only be used in event of dire necessity. There was, therefore, nothing to do but wait, and we waited.

We discussed the manuscript and hazarded guesses concerning it and the strange events it narrated. The torpedoing of the liner upon which Bowen J. Tyler, Jr., had taken passage for France to join the

113

American Ambulance was a well-known fact, and I had further sub-
stantiated by wire to the New York office of the owners, that a Miss
La Rue had been booked for passage. Further, neither she nor Bowen
had been mentioned among the list of survivors; nor had the body of
either of them been recovered.

Their rescue by the English tug was entirely probable; the capture of the enemy *U-33* by the tug's crew was not beyond the range
of possibility; and their adventures during the perilous cruise which
the treachery and deceit of Benson extended until they found themselves in the waters of the far South Pacific with depleted stores and
poisoned water-casks, while bordering upon the fantastic, appeared
logical enough as narrated, event by event, in the manuscript.

Caprona has always been considered a more or less mythical
land, though it is vouched for by an eminent navigator of the eigh-
teenth century; but Bowen's narrative made it seem very real, however many miles of trackless ocean lay between us and it. Yes, the
narrative had us guessing. We were agreed that it was most improbable; but neither of us could say that anything which it contained was
beyond the range of possibility. The weird flora and fauna of Caspak
were as possible under the thick, warm atmospheric conditions of
the superheated crater as they were in the Mesozoic era under almost
exactly similar conditions, which were then probably world-wide.
The assistant secretary had heard of Caproni and his discoveries, but
admitted that he never had taken much stock in the one nor the other.
We were agreed that the one statement most difficult of explanation
was that which reported the entire absence of human young among
the various tribes which Tyler had had intercourse. This was the one
irreconcilable statement of the manuscript. A world of adults! It was
impossible.

We speculated upon the probable fate of Bradley and his party of
English sailors. Tyler had found the graves of two of them; how many
more might have perished! And Miss La Rue—could a young girl

long have survived the horrors of Caspak after having been separated from all of her own kind? The assistant secretary wondered if Nobs still was with her, and then we both smiled at this tacit acceptance of the truth of the whole uncanny tale.

"I suppose I'm a fool," remarked the assistant secretary; "but by George, I can't help believing it, and I can see that girl now, with the big Airedale at her side protecting her from the terrors of a million years ago. I can visualize the entire scene—the apelike Grimaldi men huddled in their filthy caves; the huge pterodactyls soaring through the heavy air upon their batlike wings; the mighty dinosaurs moving their clumsy hulks beneath the dark shadows of pre-glacial forests—the dragons which we considered myths until science taught us that they were the true recollections of the first man, handed down through countless ages by word of mouth from father to son out of the unrecorded dawn of humanity."

"It is stupendous—if true," I replied. "And to think that possibly they are still there—Tyler and Miss La Rue—surrounded by hideous dangers, and that possibly Bradley still lives, and some of his party! I can't help hoping all the time that Bowen and the girl have found the others; the last Bowen knew of them, there were six left, all told—the mate Bradley, the engineer Olson, and Wilson, Whitely, Brady and Sinclair. There might be some hope for them if they could join forces; but separated, I'm afraid they couldn't last long."

"If only they hadn't let the German prisoners capture the U-33! Bowen should have had better judgment than to have trusted them at all. The chances are von Schoenvorts succeeded in getting safely back to Kiel and is strutting around with an Iron Cross this very minute. With a large supply of oil from the wells they discovered in Caspak, with plenty of water and ample provisions, there is no reason why they couldn't have negotiated the submerged tunnel beneath the barrier cliffs and made good their escape."

"I don't like 'em," said the assistant secretary; "but sometimes you got to hand it to 'em."

"Yes," I growled, "and there's nothing I'd enjoy more than *handing it to them!*" And then the telephone-bell rang.

The assistant secretary answered, and as I watched him, I saw his jaw drop and his face go white. "My God!" he exclaimed as he hung up the receiver as one in a trance. "It can't be!"

"What?" I asked.

"Mr. Tyler is dead," he answered in a dull voice. "He died at sea, suddenly, yesterday."

The next ten days were occupied in burying Mr. Bowen J. Tyler, Sr., and arranging plans for the succor of his son. Mr. Tom Billings, the late Mr. Tyler's secretary, did it all. He is force, energy, initiative and good judgment combined and personified. I never have beheld a more dynamic young man. He handled lawyers, courts and executors as a sculptor handles his modeling clay. He formed, fashioned and forced them to his will. He had been a classmate of Bowen Tyler at college, and a fraternity brother, and before, that he had been an impoverished and improvident cow-puncher on one of the great Tyler ranches. Tyler, Sr., had picked him out of thousands of employees and made him; or rather Tyler had given him the opportunity, and then Billings had made himself. Tyler, Jr., as good a judge of men as his father, had taken him into his friendship, and between the two of them they had turned out a man who would have died for a Tyler as quickly as he would have for his flag. Yet there was none of the sycophant or fawner in Billings; ordinarily I do not wax enthusiastic about men, but this man Billings comes as close to my conception of what a regular man should be as any I have ever met. I venture to say that before Bowen J. Tyler sent him to college he had never heard the word *ethics*, and yet I am equally sure that in all his life he never has transgressed a single tenet of the code of ethics of an American gentleman.

Ten days after they brought Mr. Tyler's body off the *Toreador*, we steamed out into the Pacific in search of Caprona. There were forty in the party, including the master and crew of the *Toreador*; and Billings the indomitable was in command. We had a long and uninteresting search for Caprona, for the old map upon which the assistant secretary had finally located it was most inaccurate. When its grim walls finally rose out of the ocean's mists before us, we were so far south that it was a question as to whether we were in the South Pacific or the Antarctic. Bergs were numerous, and it was very cold.

All during the trip Billings had steadfastly evaded questions as to how we were to enter Caspak after we had found Caprona. Bowen Tyler's manuscript had made it perfectly evident to all that the subterranean outlet of the Caspakian River was the only means of ingress or egress to the crater world beyond the impregnable cliffs. Tyler's party had been able to navigate this channel because their craft had been a submarine; but the *Toreador* could as easily have flown over the cliffs as sailed under them. Jimmy Hollis and Colin Short whiled away many an hour inventing schemes for surmounting the obstacle presented by the barrier cliffs, and making ridiculous wagers as to which one Tom Billings had in mind; but immediately we were all assured that we had raised Caprona, Billings called us together.

"There was no use in talking about these things," he said, "until we found the island. At best it can be but conjecture on our part until we have been able to scrutinize the coast closely. Each of us has formed a mental picture of the Capronian seacoast from Bowen's manuscript, and it is not likely that any two of these pictures resemble each other, or that any of them resemble the coast as we shall presently find it. I have in view three plans for scaling the cliffs, and the means for carrying out each is in the hold. There is an electric drill with plenty of waterproof cable to reach from the ship's dynamos to the cliff-top when the *Toreador* is anchored at a safe distance from shore, and there is sufficient half-inch iron rod to build a ladder from the base to the top of the cliff. It would be a long, arduous and dangerous work to bore the holes and insert the rungs of the ladder from the bottom upward; yet it can be done.

"I also have a life-saving mortar with which we might be able to throw a line over the summit of the cliffs; but this plan would necessitate one of us climbing to the top with the chances more than even that the line would cut at the summit, or the hooks at the upper end would slip.

"My third plan seems to me the most feasible. You all saw a number of large, heavy boxes lowered into the hold before we sailed. I know you did, because you asked me what they contained and commented upon the large letter 'H' which was painted upon each box. These boxes contain the various parts of a hydro-aeroplane. I purpose assembling this upon the strip of beach described in Bowen's manuscript—the beach where he found the dead body of the apelike man—provided there is sufficient space above high water; otherwise we shall have to assemble it on deck and lower it over the side. After it is assembled, I shall carry tackle and ropes to the cliff-top, and then it will be comparatively simple to hoist the search-party and its supplies in safety. Or I can make a sufficient number of trips to land the entire party in the valley beyond the barrier; all will depend, of course, upon what my first reconnaissance reveals."

That afternoon we steamed slowly along the face of Caprona's towering barrier.

"You see now," remarked Billings as we craned our necks to scan the summit thousands of feet above us, "how futile it would have been to waste our time in working out details of a plan to surmount those." And he jerked his thumb toward the cliffs. "It would take weeks, possibly months, to construct a ladder to the top. I had no conception of their formidable height. Our mortar would not carry a line halfway to the crest of the lowest point. There is no use discussing any plan other than the hydro-aeroplane. We'll find the beach and get busy."

Late the following morning the lookout announced that he could discern surf about a mile ahead; and as we approached, we all saw the line of breakers broken by a long sweep of rolling surf upon a narrow beach. The launch was lowered, and five of us made a landing, getting a good ducking in the ice-cold waters in the doing of it; but we were rewarded by the finding of the clean-picked bones of what might have been the skeleton of a high order of ape or a very low order of man, lying close to the base of the cliff. Billings was satisfied, as were the rest of us, that this was the beach mentioned by Bowen, and we further found that there was ample room to assemble the seaplane.

Billings, having arrived at a decision, lost no time in acting, with the result that before mid-afternoon we had landed all the large boxes marked "*H*" upon the beach, and were busily engaged in opening them. Two days later the plane was assembled and tuned. We loaded tackles and ropes, water, food and ammunition in it, and then we each implored Billings to let us be the one to accompany him. But he would take no one. That was Billings; if there was any especially difficult or dangerous work to be done, that one man could do, Billings always did it himself. If he needed assistance, he never called for volunteers—just selected the man or men he considered best qualified for the duty. He said that he considered the principles underlying all volunteer service fundamentally wrong, and that it seemed to him that calling for volunteers reflected upon the courage and loyalty of the entire command.

We rolled the plane down to the water's edge, and Billings mounted the pilot's seat. There was a moment's delay as he assured himself that he had everything necessary. Jimmy Hollis went over his armament and ammunition to see that nothing had been omitted. Besides pistol and rifle, there was the machine-gun mounted in front of him on the plane, and ammunition for all three. Bowen's account of the terrors of Caspak had impressed us all with the necessity for proper means of defense.

At last all was ready. The motor was started, and we pushed the plane out into the surf. A moment later, and she was skimming seaward. Gently she rose from the surface of the water, executed a wide spiral as she mounted rapidly, circled once far above us and then disappeared over the crest of the cliffs. We all stood silent and expectant, our eyes glued upon the towering summit above us. Hollis, who was now in command, consulted his wrist-watch at frequent intervals.

"Gad," exclaimed Short, "we ought to be hearing from him pretty soon!"

Hollis laughed nervously. "He's been gone only ten minutes," he announced.

"Seems like an hour," snapped Short. "What's that? Did you hear that? He's firing! It's the machine-gun! Oh, Lord; and here we are as helpless as a lot of old ladies ten thousand miles away! We can't do a thing. We don't know what's happening. Why didn't he let one of us go with him?"

Yes, it was the machine-gun. We would hear it distinctly for at least a minute. Then came silence. That was two weeks ago. We have had no sign nor signal from Tom Billings since.

2

'll never forget my first impressions of Caspak as I circled in, high over the surrounding cliffs. From the plane I looked down through a mist upon the blurred landscape beneath me. The hot, humid atmosphere of Caspak condenses as it is fanned by the cold Antarctic air-currents which sweep across the crater's top, sending a tenuous ribbon of vapor far out across the Pacific. Through this the picture gave one the suggestion of a colossal impressionistic canvas in greens and browns and scarlets and yellows surrounding the deep blue of the inland sea—just blobs of color taking form through the tumbling mist.

I dived close to the cliffs and skirted them for several miles without finding the least indication of a suitable landing-place; and then I swung back at a lower level, looking for a clearing close to the bottom of the mighty escarpment; but I could find none of sufficient area to insure safety. I was flying pretty low by this time, not only looking for landing places but watching the myriad life beneath me. I was down pretty well toward the south end of the island, where an arm of the lake reaches far inland, and I could see the surface of the water literally black with creatures of some sort. I was too far up to recognize individuals, but the general impression was of a vast army of amphibious monsters. The land was almost equally alive with crawling, leaping, running, flying things. It was one of the latter which nearly did for me while my attention was fixed upon the weird scene below.

The first intimation I had of it was the sudden blotting out of the sunlight from above, and as I glanced quickly up, I saw a most terrific creature swooping down upon me. It must have been fully eighty feet long from the end of its long, hideous beak to the tip of its thick, short tail, with an equal spread of wings. It was coming straight for me and hissing frightfully—I could hear it above the whir of the propeller. It was coming straight down toward the muzzle of the machine-gun and I let it have it right in the breast; but still it came for me, so that I had to dive and turn, though I was dangerously close to earth.

The thing didn't miss me by a dozen feet, and when I rose, it wheeled and followed me, but only to the cooler air close to the level of the cliff-tops; there it turned again and dropped. Something— man's natural love of battle and the chase, I presume—impelled me to pursue it, and so I too circled and dived. The moment I came down into the warm atmosphere of Caspak, the creature came for me again, rising above me so that it might swoop down upon me. Nothing could better have suited my armament, since my machine-gun was pointed upward at an angle of about 45° and could not be either depressed or elevated by the pilot. If I had brought someone along with me, we could have raked the great reptile from almost any position, but as the creature's mode of attack was always from above, he always found me ready with a hail of bullets. The battle must have lasted a minute or more before the thing suddenly turned completely over in the air and fell to the ground.

Bowen and I roomed together at college, and I learned a lot from him outside my regular course. He was a pretty good scholar despite his love of fun, and his particular hobby was paleontology. He used to tell me about the various forms of animal and vegetable life which had covered the globe during former eras, and so I was pretty well acquainted with the fishes, amphibians, reptiles, and mammals of paleolithic times. I knew that the thing that had attacked me was some sort of pterodactyl which should have been extinct millions of years ago. It was all that I needed to realize that Bowen had exaggerated nothing in his manuscript.

Having disposed of my first foe, I set myself once more to search for a landing-place near to the base of the cliffs beyond which my party awaited me. I knew how anxious they would be for word from me, and I was equally anxious to relieve their minds and also to get them and our supplies well within Caspak, so that we might set off about our business of finding and rescuing Bowen Tyler; but the pterodactyl's carcass had scarcely fallen before I was surrounded by at least a dozen of the hideous things, some large, some small, but all bent upon my destruction. I could not cope with them all, and so I rose rapidly from among them to the cooler strata wherein they dared not follow; and then I recalled that Bowen's narrative distinctly indicated that the farther north one traveled in Caspak, the fewer were the terrible reptiles which rendered human life impossible at the southern end of the island.

There seemed nothing now but to search out a more northerly landing-place and then return to the *Toreador* and transport my companions, two by two, over the cliffs and deposit them at the rendezvous. As I flew north, the temptation to explore overcame me. I knew that I could easily cover Caspak and return to the beach with less petrol than I had in my tanks; and there was the hope, too, that I might find Bowen or some of his party. The broad expanse of the inland sea lured me out over its waters, and as I crossed, I saw at either extremity of the great body of water an island—one to the south and one to the north; but I did not alter my course to examine either closely, leaving that to a later time.

The further shore of the sea revealed a much narrower strip of land between the cliffs and the water than upon the western side; but it was a hillier and more open country. There were splendid landing-places, and in the distance, toward the north, I thought I descried a village; but of that I was not positive. However, as I approached the land, I saw a number of human figures apparently pursuing one who fled across a broad expanse of meadow. As I dropped lower to have a better look at these people, they caught the whirring of my propellers and looked aloft. They paused an instant—pursuers and pursued; and then they broke and raced for the shelter of the nearest wood. Almost instantaneously a huge bulk swooped down upon me, and as I looked up, I realized that there were flying reptiles even in this part of Caspak. The creature dived for my right wing so quickly that nothing but a sheer drop could have saved me. I was already close to the ground, so that my maneuver was extremely dangerous; but I was in a fair way of making it successfully when I saw that I was too closely approaching a large tree. My effort to dodge the tree and the pterodactyl at the same time resulted disastrously. One wing touched an upper branch; the plane tipped and swung around, and then, out of control, dashed into the branches of the tree, where it came to rest, battered and torn, forty feet above the ground.

Hissing loudly, the huge reptile swept close above the tree in which my plane had lodged, circled twice over me and then flapped away toward the south. As I guessed then and was to learn later, forests are the surest sanctuary from these hideous creatures, which, with their enormous spread of wing and their great weight, are as much out of place among trees as is a seaplane.

For a minute or so I clung there to my battered flyer, now useless beyond redemption, my brain numbed by the frightful catastrophe that had befallen me. All my plans for the succor of Bowen and Miss La Rue had depended upon this craft, and in a few brief minutes my own selfish love of adventure had wrecked their hopes and mine. And what effect it might have upon the future of the balance of the rescuing expedition I could not even guess. Their lives, too, might be sacrificed to my suicidal foolishness. That I was doomed seemed inevitable; but I can honestly say that the fate of my friends concerned me more greatly than did my own.

Beyond the barrier cliffs my party was even now nervously awaiting my return. Presently apprehension and fear would claim them—and they would never know! They would attempt to scale the cliffs—of that I was sure; but I was not so positive that they would succeed; and after a while they would turn back, what there were left of them, and go sadly and mournfully upon their return-journey to home. Home! I set my jaws and tried to forget the word, for I knew that I should never again see home.

And what of Bowen and his girl? I had doomed them too. They would never even know that an attempt had been made to rescue them. If they still lived, they might some day come upon the ruined remnants of this great plane hanging in its lofty sepulcher and hazard vain guesses and be filled with wonder; but they would never know; and I could not but be glad that they would not know that Tom Billings had sealed their death-warrants by his criminal selfishness.

All these useless regrets were getting me in a bad way; but at last I shook myself and tried to put such things out of my mind and take hold of conditions as they existed and do my level best to wrest victory from defeat. I was badly shaken up and bruised, but considered myself mighty lucky to escape with my life. The plane hung at a precarious angle, so that it was with difficulty and considerable danger that I climbed from it into the tree and then to the ground.

My predicament was grave. Between me and my friends lay an inland sea fully sixty miles wide at this point and an estimated land-distance of some three hundred miles around the northern end of the sea, through such hideous dangers as I am perfectly free to admit had me pretty well buffaloed. I had seen quite enough of Caspak this day to assure me that Bowen had in no way exaggerated its perils. As a matter of fact, I am inclined to believe that he had become so accustomed to them before he started upon his manuscript that he rather slighted them. As I stood there beneath that tree—a tree which should have been part of a coal-bed countless ages since—and

125

looked out across a sea teeming with frightful life—life which should have been fossil before God conceived of Adam—I would not have given a minim of stale beer for my chances of ever seeing my friends or the outside world again; yet then and there I swore to fight my way as far through this hideous land as circumstances would permit. I had plenty of ammunition, an automatic pistol and a heavy rifle— the latter one of twenty added to our equipment on the strength of Bowen's description of the huge beasts of prey which ravaged Caspak. My greatest danger lay in the hideous reptilia whose low nervous organizations permitted their carnivorous instincts to function for several minutes after they had ceased to live.

But to these things I gave less thought than to the sudden frustration of all our plans. With the bitterest of thoughts I condemned myself for the foolish weakness that had permitted me to be drawn from the main object of my flight into premature and useless exploration. It seemed to me then that I must be totally eliminated from further search for Bowen, since, as I estimated it, the three hundred miles of Caspakian territory I must traverse to reach the base of the cliffs beyond which my party awaited me were practically impassable for a single individual unaccustomed to Caspakian life and ignorant of all that lay before him. Yet I could not give up hope entirely. My duty lay clear before me; I must follow it while life remained to me, and so I set forth toward the north.

The country through which I took my way was as lovely as it was unusual—I had almost said unearthly, for the plants, the trees, the blooms were not of the earth that I knew. They were larger, the colors more brilliant and the shapes startling, some almost to grotesqueness, though even such added to the charm and romance of the landscape as the giant cacti render weirdly beautiful the waste spots of the sad Mohave. And over all the sun shone huge and round and red, a monster sun above a monstrous world, its light dispersed by the humid air of Caspak—the warm, moist air which lies sluggish upon the breast of this great mother of life, Nature's mightiest incubator.

All about me, in every direction, was life. It moved through the tree-tops and among the boles; it displayed itself in widening and intermingling circles upon the bosom of the sea; it leaped from the depths; I could hear it in a dense wood at my right, the murmur of it rising and falling in ceaseless volumes of sound, riven at intervals by a horrid scream or a thunderous roar which shook the earth; and always I was haunted by that inexplicable sensation that unseen eyes were watching me, that soundless feet dogged my trail. I am neither nervous nor highstrung; but the burden of responsibility upon me weighed heavily, so that I was more cautious than is my wont. I turned often to right and left and rear lest I be surprised, and I carried my rifle at the ready in my hand. Once I could have sworn that among the many creatures dimly perceived amidst the shadows of the wood I saw a human figure dart from one cover to another, but I could not be sure.

For the most part I skirted the wood, making occasional detours rather than enter those forbidding depths of gloom, though many times I was forced to pass through arms of the forest which extended to the very shore of the inland sea. There was so sinister a suggestion in the uncouth sounds and the vague glimpses of moving things within the forest, of the menace of strange beasts and possibly still stranger men, that I always breathed more freely when I had passed once more into open country.

I had traveled northward for perhaps an hour, still haunted by the conviction that I was being stalked by some creature which kept always hidden among the trees and shrubbery to my right and a little to my rear, when for the hundredth time I was attracted by a sound from that direction, and turning, saw some animal running rapidly through the forest toward me. There was no longer any effort on its part at concealment; it came on through the underbrush swiftly, and I was confident that whatever it was, it had finally gathered the courage to charge me boldly. Before it finally broke into plain view, I became aware that it was not alone, for a few yards in its rear a second thing thrashed through the leafy jungle. Evidently I was to be attacked in force by a pair of hunting beasts or men.

And then through the last clump of waving ferns broke the figure of the foremost creature, which came leaping toward me on light feet as I stood with my rifle to my shoulder covering the point at which I had expected it would emerge. I must have looked foolish indeed if my surprise and consternation were in any way reflected upon my countenance as I lowered my rifle and gazed incredulous at the lithe figure of the girl speeding swiftly in my direction. But I did not have long to stand thus with lowered weapon, for as she came, I saw her cast an affrighted glance over her shoulder, and at the same moment there broke from the jungle at the same spot at which I had seen her, the hugest cat I had ever looked upon.

At first I took the beast for a saber-tooth tiger, as it was quite the most fearsome-appearing beast one could imagine; but it was not that dread monster of the past, though quite formidable enough to satisfy the most fastidious thrill-hunter. On it came, grim and terrible, its baleful eyes glaring above its distended jaws, its lips curled in a frightful snarl which exposed a whole mouthful of formidable teeth. At sight of me it had abandoned its impetuous rush and was now sneaking slowly toward us; while the girl, a long knife in her hand, took her stand bravely at my left and a little to my rear. She had called something to me in a strange tongue as she raced toward me, and now she spoke again; but what she said I could not then, of course, know—only that her tones were sweet, well modulated and free from any suggestion of panic.

Facing the huge cat, which I now saw was an enormous panther, I waited until I could place a shot where I felt it would do the most good, for at best a frontal shot at any of the large carnivora is a ticklish matter. I had some advantage in that the beast was not charging; its head was held low and its back exposed; and so at forty yards I took careful aim at its spine at the junction of neck and shoulders. But at the same instant, as though sensing my intention, the great creature lifted its head and leaped forward in full charge. To fire at that sloping forehead I knew would be worse than useless, and so I quickly shifted my aim and pulled the trigger, hoping against hope that the soft-nosed bullet and the heavy charge of powder would have sufficient stopping effect to give me time to place a second shot.

In answer to the report of the rifle I had the satisfaction of seeing the brute spring into the air, turning a complete somersault; but it was up again almost instantly, though in the brief second that it took it to scramble to its feet and get its bearings, it exposed its left side fully toward me, and a second bullet went crashing through its heart. Down it went for the second time—and then up and at me. The vitality of these creatures of Caspak is one of the marvelous features of this strange world and bespeaks the low nervous organization of the old paleolithic life which has been so long extinct in other portions of the world.

I put a third bullet into the beast at three paces, and then I thought that I was done for; but it rolled over and stopped at my feet, stone dead. I found that my second bullet had torn its heart almost completely away, and yet it had lived to charge ferociously upon me, and but for my third shot would doubtless have slain me before it finally expired—or as Bowen Tyler so quaintly puts it, before it knew that it was dead.

With the panther quite evidently conscious of the fact that dissolution had overtaken it, I turned toward the girl, who was regarding me with evident admiration and not a little awe, though I must admit that my rifle claimed quite as much of her attention as did I. She was quite the most wonderful animal that I have ever looked upon, and what few of her charms her apparel hid, it quite effectively succeeded in accentuating. A bit of soft, undressed leather was caught over her left shoulder and beneath her right breast, falling upon her left side to her hip and upon the right to a metal band which encircled her leg above the knee and to which the lowest point of the hide was attached. About her waist was a loose leather belt, to the center of which was attached the scabbard belonging to her knife. There was a single armlet between her right shoulder and elbow, and a series of them covered her left forearm from elbow to wrist. These, I learned later, answered the purpose of a shield against knife attack when the left arm is raised in guard across the breast or face.

Her masses of heavy hair were held in place by a broad metal band which bore a large triangular ornament directly in the center of her forehead. This ornament appeared to be a huge turquoise, while the metal of all her ornaments was beaten, virgin gold, inlaid in intricate design with bits of mother-of-pearl and tiny pieces of stone of various colors. From the left shoulder depended a leopard's tail, while her feet were shod with sturdy little sandals. The knife was her only weapon. Its blade was of iron, the grip was wound with hide and protected by a guard of three out-bowing strips of flat iron, and upon the top of the hilt was a knob of gold.

I took in much of this in the few seconds during which we stood facing each other, and I also observed another salient feature of her appearance: she was frightfully dirty! Her face and limbs and garment were streaked with mud and perspiration, and yet even so, I felt that I had never looked upon so perfect and beautiful a creature as she. Her figure beggars description, and equally so, her face. Were I one of these writer-fellows, I should probably say that her features were Grecian, but being neither a writer nor a poet I can do her greater justice by saying that she combined all of the finest lines that one sees in the typical American girl's face rather than the pronounced sheep-like physiognomy of the Greek goddess. No, even the dirt couldn't hide that fact; she was beautiful beyond compare.

As we stood looking at each other, a slow smile came to her face, parting her symmetrical lips and disclosing a row of strong white teeth.

"*Galu?*" she asked with rising inflection.

And remembering that I read in Bowen's manuscript that Galu seemed to indicate a higher type of man, I answered by pointing to myself and repeating the word. Then she started off on a regular catechism, if I could judge by her inflection, for I certainly understood no word of what she said. All the time the girl kept glancing toward the forest, and at last she touched my arm and pointed in that direction.

Turning, I saw a hairy figure of a manlike thing standing watching us, and presently another and another emerged from the jungle and joined the leader until there must have been at least twenty of them. They were entirely naked. Their bodies were covered with hair, and though they stood upon their feet without touching their hands to the ground, they had a very ape-like appearance, since they stooped forward and had very long arms and quite apish features. They were not pretty to look upon with their close-set eyes, flat noses, long upper lips and protruding yellow fangs.

"*Alus!*" said the girl.

I had reread Bowen's adventures so often that I knew them almost by heart, and so now I knew that I was looking upon the last remnant of that ancient man-race—the Alus of a forgotten period— the speechless man of antiquity.

"*Kazor!*" cried the girl, and at the same moment the Alus came jabbering toward us. They made strange growling, barking noises, as with much baring of fangs they advanced upon us. They were armed only with nature's weapons—powerful muscles and giant fangs; yet I knew that these were quite sufficient to overcome us had we nothing better to offer in defense, and so I drew my pistol and fired at the leader. He dropped like a stone, and the others turned and fled. Once again the girl smiled her slow smile and stepping closer, caressed the barrel of my automatic. As she did so, her fingers came in contact with mine, and a sudden thrill ran through me, which I attributed to the fact that it had been so long since I had seen a woman of any sort or kind.

She said something to me in her low, liquid tones; but I could not understand her, and then she pointed toward the north and started away. I followed her, for my way was north too; but had it been south I still should have followed, so hungry was I for human companionship in this world of beasts and reptiles and half-men.

We walked along, the girl talking a great deal and seeming mystified that I could not understand her. Her silvery laugh rang merrily when I in turn essayed to speak to her, as though my language was the quaintest thing she ever had heard. Often after fruitless attempts to make me understand she would hold her palm toward me, saying, "*Galu!*" and then touch my breast or arm and cry, "*Alu, alu!*" I knew what she meant, for I had learned from Bowen's narrative the negative gesture and the two words which she repeated. She meant that I was no Galu, as I claimed, but an Alu, or speechless one. Yet every time she said this she laughed again, and so infectious were her tones that I could only join her. It was only natural, too, that she should be mystified by my inability to comprehend her or to make her comprehend me, for from the club-men, the lowest human type in Caspak to have speech, to the golden race of Galus, the tongues of the various tribes are identical—except for amplifications in the rising scale of evolution. She, who is a Galu, can understand one of the Bo-lu and make herself understood to him, or to a hatchet-man, a spear-man or an archer. The Ho-lus, or apes, the Alus and myself were the only creatures of human semblance with which she could hold no converse; yet it was evident that her intelligence told her that I was neither Ho-lu nor Alu, neither anthropoid ape nor speechless man.

Yet she did not despair, but set out to teach me her language; and had it not been that I worried so greatly over the fate of Bowen and my companions of the *Toreador*, I could have wished the period of instruction prolonged.

I never have been what one might call a ladies' man, though I like their company immensely, and during my college days and since have made various friends among the sex. I think that I rather appeal to a certain type of girl for the reason that I never make love to them; I leave that to the numerous others who do it infinitely better than I could hope to, and take my pleasure out of girls' society in what seem to be more rational ways—dancing, golfing, boating, riding, tennis, and the like. Yet in the company of this half-naked little savage I found a new pleasure that was entirely distinct from any that I ever had experienced. When she touched me, I thrilled as I had never before thrilled in contact with another woman. I could not quite understand it, for I am sufficiently sophisticated to know that this is a symptom of love and I certainly did not love this filthy little barbarian with her broken, unkempt nails and her skin so besmeared with mud and the green of crushed foliage that it was difficult to say what color it originally had been. But if she was outwardly uncouth, her clear eyes and strong white, even teeth, her silvery laugh and her queenly carriage, bespoke an innate fineness which dirt could not quite successfully conceal.

The sun was low in the heavens when we came upon a little river which emptied into a large bay at the foot of low cliffs. Our journey so far had been beset with constant danger, as is every journey in this frightful land. I have not bored you with a recital of the wearying successions of attacks by the multitude of creatures which were constantly crossing our path or deliberately stalking us. We were always upon the alert; for here, to paraphrase, eternal vigilance is indeed the price of life.

I had managed to progress a little in the acquisition of a knowledge of her tongue, so that I knew many of the animals and reptiles by their Caspakian names, and trees and ferns and grasses. I knew the words for *sea* and *river* and *cliff*, for *sky* and *sun* and *cloud*. Yes, I was getting along finely, and then it occurred to me that I didn't know my companion's name; so I pointed to myself and said, "Tom," and to her and raised my eyebrows in interrogation. The girl ran her fingers into that mass of hair and looked puzzled. I repeated the action a dozen times.

"Tom," she said finally in that clear, sweet, liquid voice. "Tom!"

I had never thought much of my name before; but when she spoke it, it sounded to me for the first time in my life like a mighty nice name, and then she brightened suddenly and tapped her own breast and said: "Ajor!"

"Ajor!" I repeated, and she laughed and struck her palms together.

Well, we knew each other's names now, and that was some satisfaction. I rather liked hers—Ajor! And she seemed to like mine, for she repeated it.

So we came to the cliffs beside the little river where it empties into the bay with the great inland sea beyond. The cliffs were weather-worn and rotted, and in one place a deep hollow ran back beneath the overhanging stone for several feet, suggesting shelter for the night. There were loose rocks strewn all about with which I might build a barricade across the entrance to the cave, and so I halted there and pointed out the place to Ajor, trying to make her understand that we would spend the night there.

As soon as she grasped my meaning, she assented with the Caspakian equivalent of an affirmative nod, and then touching my rifle, motioned me to follow her to the river. At the bank she paused, removed her belt and dagger, dropping them to the ground at her side; then unfastening the lower edge of her garment from the metal leg-band to which it was attached, slipped it off her left shoulder and let it drop to the ground around her feet. It was done so naturally, so simply and so quickly that it left me gasping like a fish out of water. Turning, she flashed a smile at me and then dived into the river, and there she bathed while I stood guard over her. For five or ten minutes she splashed about, and when she emerged her glistening skin was smooth and white and beautiful. Without means of drying herself, she simply ignored what to me would have seemed a necessity, and in a moment was arrayed in her simple though effective costume.

It was now within an hour of darkness, and as I was nearly famished, I led the way back about a quarter of a mile to a low meadow where we had seen antelope and small horses a short time before. Here I brought down a young buck, the report of my rifle sending the balance of the herd scampering for the woods, where they were met by a chorus of hideous roars as the carnivora took advantage of their panic and leaped among them.

With my hunting-knife I removed a hind-quarter, and then we returned to camp. Here I gathered a great quantity of wood from fallen trees, Ajor helping me; but before I built a fire, I also gathered sufficient loose rock to build my barricade against the frightful terrors of the night to come.

I shall never forget the expression upon Ajor's face as she saw me strike a match and light the kindling beneath our camp-fire. It was such an expression as might transform a mortal face with awe as its owner beheld the mysterious workings of divinity. It was evident that Ajor was quite unfamiliar with modern methods of fire-making. She had thought my rifle and pistol wonderful; but these tiny slivers of wood which from a magic rub brought flame to the camp hearth were indeed miracles to her.

As the meat roasted above the fire, Ajor and I tried once again to talk; but though copiously filled with incentive, gestures and sounds, the conversation did not flourish notably. And then Ajor took up in earnest the task of teaching me her language. She commenced, as I later learned, with the simplest form of speech known to Caspak or for that matter to the world—that employed by the Bo-lu. I found it far from difficult, and even though it was a great handicap upon my instructor that she could not speak my language, she did remarkably well and demonstrated that she possessed ingenuity and intelligence of a high order.

After we had eaten, I added to the pile of firewood so that I could replenish the fire before the entrance to our barricade, believing this as good a protection against the carnivora as we could have; and then Ajor and I sat down before it, and the lesson proceeded, while from all about us came the weird and awesome noises of the Caspakian night—the moaning and the coughing and roaring of the tigers, the panthers and the lions, the barking and the dismal howling of a wolf, jackal and hyaenadon, the shrill shrieks of stricken prey and the hissing of the great reptiles; the voice of man alone was silent.

But though the voice of this choir-terrible rose and fell from far and near in all directions, reaching at time such a tremendous volume of sound that the earth shook to it, yet so engrossed was I in my lesson and in my teacher that often I was deaf to what at another time would have filled me with awe. The face and voice of the beautiful girl who leaned so eagerly toward me as she tried to explain the meaning of some word or correct my pronunciation of another quite entirely occupied my every faculty of perception. The firelight shone upon her animated features and sparkling eyes; it accentuated the graceful motions of her gesturing arms and hands; it sparkled from her white teeth and from her golden ornaments, and glistened on the smooth firmness of her perfect skin. I am afraid that often I was more occupied with admiration of this beautiful animal than with a desire for knowledge; but be that as it may, I nevertheless learned much that evening, though part of what I learned had naught to do with any new language.

Ajor seemed determined that I should speak Caspakian as quickly as possible, and I thought I saw in her desire a little of that all-feminine trait which has come down through all the ages from the first lady of the world—curiosity. Ajor desired that I should speak her tongue in order that she might satisfy a curiosity concerning me that was filling her to a point where she was in danger of bursting; of that I was positive. She was a regular little animated question-mark. She bubbled over with interrogations which were never to be satisfied unless I learned to speak her tongue. Her eyes sparkled with excitement; her hand flew in expressive gestures; her little tongue raced with time; yet all to no avail. I could say *man* and *tree* and *cliff* and *lion* and a number of other words in perfect Caspakian; but such a vocabulary was only tantalizing; it did not lend itself well to a very general conversation, and the result was that Ajor would wax so wroth that she would clench her little fists and beat me on the breast as hard as ever she could, and then she would sink back laughing as the humor of the situation captured her.

She was trying to teach me some verbs by going through the actions herself as she repeated the proper word. We were very much engrossed—so much so that we were giving no heed to what went on beyond our cave—when Ajor stopped very suddenly, crying: "*Kazor!*" Now she had been trying to teach me that *ju* meant *stop*; so when she cried *Kazor* and at the same time stopped, I thought for a moment that this was part of my lesson—for the moment I forgot that *kazor* means *beware*. I therefore repeated the word after her; but when I saw the expression in her eyes as they were directed past me and saw her point toward the entrance to the cave, I turned quickly—to see a hideous face at the small aperture leading out into the night. It was the fierce and snarling countenance of a gigantic bear. I have hunted silver-tips in the White Mountains of Arizona and thought them quite the largest and most formidable of big game; but from the appearance of the head of this awful creature I judged that the largest grizzly I had ever seen would shrink by comparison to the dimensions of a Newfoundland dog.

Our fire was just within the cave, the smoke rising through the apertures between the rocks that I had piled in such a way that they arched inward toward the cliff at the top. The opening by means of which we were to reach the outside was barricaded with a few large fragments which did not by any means close it entirely; but through the apertures thus left no large animal could gain ingress. I had depended most, however, upon our fire, feeling that none of the dangerous nocturnal beasts of prey would venture close to the flames. In this, however, I was quite evidently in error, for the great bear stood with his nose not a foot from the blaze, which was now low, owing to the fact that I had been so occupied with my lesson and my teacher that I had neglected to replenish it.

Ajor whipped out her futile little knife and pointed to my rifle. At the same time she spoke in a quite level voice entirely devoid of nervousness or any evidence of fear or panic. I knew she was exhorting me to fire upon the beast; but this I did not wish to do other than as a last resort, for I was quite sure that even my heavy bullets would not more than further enrage him—in which case he might easily force an entrance to our cave.

Instead of firing, I piled some more wood upon the fire, and as the smoke and blaze arose in the beast's face, it backed away, growling most frightfully; but I still could see two ugly points of light blazing in the outer darkness and hear its growls rumbling terrifically without. For some time the creature stood there watching the entrance to our frail sanctuary while I racked my brains in futile endeavor to plan some method of defense or escape. I knew full well that should the bear make a determined effort to get at us, the rocks I had piled as a barrier would come tumbling down about his giant shoulders like a house of cards, and that he would walk directly in upon us.

Ajor, having less knowledge of the effectiveness of firearms than I, and therefore greater confidence in them, entreated me to shoot the beast; but I knew that the chance that I could stop it with a single shot was most remote, while that I should but infuriate it was real and present; and so I waited for what seemed an eternity, watching those devilish points of fire glaring balefully at us, and listening to the ever-increasing volume of those seismic growls which seemed to rumble upward from the bowels of the earth, shaking the very cliffs beneath which we cowered, until at last I saw that the brute was again approaching the aperture. It availed me nothing that I piled the blaze high with firewood, until Ajor and I were near to roasting; on came that mighty engine of destruction until once again the hideous face yawned its fanged yawn directly within the barrier's opening. It stood thus a moment, and then the head was withdrawn. I breathed a sigh of relief, the thing had altered its intention and was going on in search of other and more easily procurable prey; the fire had been too much for it.

But my joy was short-lived, and my heart sank once again as a moment later I saw a mighty paw insinuated into the opening—a paw as large around as a large dish-pan. Very gently the paw toyed with the great rock that partly closed the entrance, pushed and pulled upon it and then very deliberately drew it outward and to one side. Again came the head, and this time much farther into the cavern; but still the great shoulders would not pass through the opening. Ajor moved closer to me until her shoulder touched my side, and I thought I felt a slight tremor run through her body, but otherwise she gave no indication of fear. Involuntarily I threw my left arm about her and drew her to me for an instant. It was an act of reassurance rather than a caress, though I must admit that again and even in the face of death I thrilled at the contact with her; and then I released her and threw my rifle to my shoulder, for at last I had reached the conclusion that nothing more could be gained by waiting. My only hope was to get as many shots into the creature as I could before it was upon me. Already it had torn away a second rock and was in the very act of forcing its huge bulk through the opening it had now made.

So now I took careful aim between its eyes; my right fingers closed firmly and evenly upon the small of the stock, drawing back my trigger-finger by the muscular action of the hand. The bullet could not fail to hit its mark! I held my breath lest I swerve the muzzle a hair by my breathing. I was as steady and cool as I ever had been upon a target-range, and I had the full consciousness of a perfect hit in anticipation; I knew that I could not miss. And then, as the bear surged forward toward me, the hammer fell—futilely, upon an imperfect cartridge.

Almost simultaneously I heard from without a perfectly hellish roar; the bear gave voice to a series of growls far transcending in volume and ferocity anything that he had yet essayed and at the same time backed quickly from the cave. For an instant I couldn't understand what had happened to cause this sudden retreat when his prey was practically within his clutches. The idea that the harmless clicking of the hammer had frightened him was too ridiculous to entertain. However, we had not long to wait before we could at least guess at the cause of the diversion, for from without came mingled growls and roars and the sound of great bodies thrashing about until the earth shook. The bear had been attacked in the rear by some other mighty beast, and the two were now locked in a titanic struggle for supremacy. With brief respites, during which we could hear the labored breathing of the contestants, the battle continued for the better part of an hour until the sounds of combat grew gradually less and finally ceased entirely.

At Ajor's suggestion, made by signs and a few of the words we knew in common, I moved the fire directly to the entrance to the cave so that a beast would have to pass directly through the flames to reach us, and then we sat and waited for the victor of the battle to come and claim his reward; but though we sat for a long time with our eyes glued to the opening, we saw no sign of any beast.

At last I signed to Ajor to lie down, for I knew that she must have sleep, and I sat on guard until nearly morning, when the girl awoke and insisted that I take some rest; nor would she be denied, but dragged me down as she laughingly menaced me with her knife.

3

hen I awoke, it was daylight, and I found Ajor squatting before a fine bed of coals roasting a large piece of antelope-meat. Believe me, the sight of the new day and the delicious odor of the cooking meat filled me with renewed happiness and hope that had been all but expunged by the experience of the previous night; and perhaps the slender figure of the bright-faced girl proved also a potent restorative. She looked up and smiled at me, showing those perfect teeth, and dimpling with evident happiness—the most adorable picture that I had ever seen. I recall that it was then I first regretted that she was only a little untutored savage and so far beneath me in the scale of evolution.

Her first act was to beckon me to follow her outside, and there she pointed to the explanation of our rescue from the bear—a huge saber-tooth tiger, its fine coat and its flesh torn to ribbons, lying dead a few paces from our cave, and beside it, equally mangled, and disemboweled, was the carcass of a huge cave-bear. To have had one's life saved by a saber-tooth tiger, and in the twentieth century into the bargain, was an experience that was to say the least unique; but it had happened—I had the proof of it before my eyes.

So enormous are the great carnivora of Caspak that they must feed perpetually to support their giant thews, and the result is that they will eat the meat of any other creature and will attack anything that comes within their ken, no matter how formidable the quarry. From later observation—I mention this as worthy the attention of paleontologists and naturalists—I came to the conclusion that such creatures as the cave-bear, the cave-lion and the saber-tooth tiger, as well as the larger carnivorous reptiles make, ordinarily, two kills a day—one in the morning and one after nightfall. They immediately devour the entire carcass, after which they lie up and sleep for a few hours. Fortunately their numbers are comparatively few; otherwise there would be no other life within Caspak. It is their very voracity that keeps their numbers down to a point which permits other forms of life to persist, for even in the season of love the great males often turn upon their own mates and devour them, while both males and females occasionally devour their young. How the human and semihuman races have managed to survive during all the countless ages that these conditions must have existed here is quite beyond me.

After breakfast Ajor and I set out once more upon our northward journey. We had gone but a little distance when we were attacked by a number of apelike creatures armed with clubs. They seemed a little higher in the scale than the Alus. Ajor told me they were Bo-lu, or club-men. A revolver-shot killed one and scattered the others; but several times later during the day we were menaced by them, until we had left their country and entered that of the Sto-lu, or hatchet-men. These people were less hairy and more man-like; nor did they appear so anxious to destroy us. Rather they were curious, and followed us for some distance examining us most closely. They called out to us, and Ajor answered them; but her replies did not seem to satisfy them, for they gradually became threatening, and I think they were preparing to attack us when a small deer that had been hiding in some low brush suddenly broke cover and dashed across our front. We needed meat, for it was near one o'clock and I was getting hungry; so I drew my pistol and with a single shot dropped the creature in its tracks. The effect upon the Bo-lu was electrical. Immediately they abandoned all thoughts of war, and turning, scampered for the forest which fringed our path.

That night we spent beside a little stream in the Sto-lu country. We found a tiny cave in the rock bank, so hidden away that only chance could direct a beast of prey to it, and after we had eaten of the deer-meat and some fruit which Ajor gathered, we crawled into the little hole, and with sticks and stones which I had gathered for the purpose I erected a strong barricade inside the entrance. Nothing could reach us without swimming and wading through the stream, and I felt quite secure from attack. Our quarters were rather cramped. The ceiling was so low that we could not stand up, and the floor so narrow that it was with difficulty that we both wedged into it together; but we were very tired, and so we made the most of it; and so great was the feeling of security that I am sure I fell asleep as soon as I had stretched myself beside Ajor.

During the three days which followed, our progress was exasperatingly slow. I doubt if we made ten miles in the entire three days. The country was hideously savage, so that we were forced to spend hours at a time in hiding from one or another of the great beasts which menaced us continually. There were fewer reptiles; but the quantity of carnivora seemed to have increased, and the reptiles that we did see were perfectly gigantic. I shall never forget one enormous specimen which we came upon browsing upon water-reeds at the edge of the great sea. It stood well over twelve feet high at the rump, its highest point, and with its enormously long tail and neck it was somewhere between seventy-five and a hundred feet in length. Its head was ridiculously small; its body was unarmored, but its great bulk gave it a most formidable appearance. My experience of Caspakian life led me to believe that the gigantic creature would but have to see us to attack us, and so I raised my rifle and at the same time drew away toward some brush which offered concealment; but Ajor only laughed, and picking up a stick, ran toward the great thing, shouting. The little head was raised high upon the long neck as the animal stupidly looked here and there in search of the author of the disturbance. At last its eyes discovered tiny little Ajor, and then she hurled the stick at the diminutive head. With a cry that sounded not unlike the bleat of a sheep, the colossal creature shuffled into the water and was soon submerged.

As I slowly recalled my collegiate studies and paleontological readings in Bowen's text-books, I realized that I had looked upon nothing less than a diplodocus of the Upper Jurassic; but how infinitely different was the true, live thing from the crude restorations of Hatcher and Holland! I had had the idea that the diplodocus was a land-animal, but evidently it is partially amphibious. I have seen several since my first encounter, and in each case the creature took to the sea for concealment as soon as it was disturbed. With the exception of its gigantic tail, it has no weapon of defense; but with this appendage it can lash so terrific a blow as to lay low even a giant cave-bear, stunned and broken. It is a stupid, simple, gentle beast—one of the few within Caspak which such a description might even remotely fit.

For three nights we slept in trees, finding no caves or other places of concealment. Here we were free from the attacks of the large land carnivora; but the smaller flying reptiles, the snakes, leopards, and panthers were a constant menace, though by no means as much to be feared as the huge beasts that roamed the surface of the earth.

At the close of the third day Ajor and I were able to converse with considerable fluency, and it was a great relief to both of us, especially to Ajor. She now did nothing but ask questions whenever I would let her, which could not be all the time, as our preservation depended largely upon the rapidity with which I could gain knowledge of the geography and customs of Caspak, and accordingly I had to ask numerous questions myself.

I enjoyed immensely hearing and answering her, so naive were many of her queries and so filled with wonder was she at the things I told her of the world beyond the lofty barriers of Caspak; not once did she seem to doubt me, however marvelous my statements must have seemed; and doubtless they were the cause of marvel to Ajor, who before had never dreamed that any life existed beyond Caspak and the life she knew.

Artless though many of her questions were, they evidenced a keen intellect and a shrewdness which seemed far beyond her years of her experience. Altogether I was finding my little savage a mighty interesting and companionable person, and I often thanked the kind fate that directed the crossing of our paths. From her I learned much of Caspak, but there still remained the mystery that had proved so baffling to Bowen Tyler—the total absence of young among the ape, the semihuman and the human races with which both he and I had come in contact upon opposite shores of the inland sea. Ajor tried to explain the matter to me, though it was apparent that she could not conceive how so natural a condition should demand explanation. She told me that among the Galus there were a few babies, that she had once been a baby but that most of her people "came up," as he put it, "*cor sva jo*," or literally, "from the beginning"; and as they all did when they used that phrase, she would wave a broad gesture toward the south.

"For long," she explained, leaning very close to me and whispering the words into my ear while she cast apprehensive glances about and mostly skyward, "for long my mother kept me hidden lest the Wieroo, passing through the air by night, should come and take me away to Oo-oh." And the child shuddered as she voiced the word. I tried to get her to tell me more; but her terror was so real when she spoke of the Wieroo and the land of Oo-oh where they dwell that I at last desisted, though I did learn that the Wieroo carried off only female babes and occasionally women of the Galus who had "come up from the beginning." It was all very mysterious and unfathomable, but I got the idea that the Wieroo were creatures of imagination—the demons or gods of her race, omniscient and omnipresent. This led me to assume that the Galus had a religious sense, and further questioning brought out the fact that such was the case. Ajor spoke in tones of reverence of Luata, the god of heat and life. The word is derived from two others: *Lua*, meaning *sun*, and *ata*, meaning variously *eggs*, *life*, *young*, and *reproduction*. She told me that they worshiped Luata in several forms, as fire, the sun, eggs and other material objects which suggested heat and reproduction.

I had noticed that whenever I built a fire, Ajor outlined in the air before her with a forefinger an isosceles triangle, and that she did the same in the morning when she first viewed the sun. At first I had not connected her act with anything in particular, but after we learned to converse and she had explained a little of her religious superstitions, I realized that she was making the sign of the triangle as a Roman Catholic makes the sign of the cross. Always the short side of the triangle was uppermost. As she explained all this to me, she pointed to the decorations on her golden armlets, upon the knob of her dagger-hilt and upon the band which encircled her right leg above the knee—always was the design partly made up of isosceles triangles, and when she explained the significance of this particular geometric figure, I at once grasped its appropriateness.

We were now in the country of the Band-lu, the spear-men of Caspak. Bowen had remarked in his narrative that these people were analogous to the so-called Cro-Magnon race of the Upper Paleolithic, and I was therefore very anxious to see them. Nor was I to be disappointed; I saw them, all right! We had left the Sto-lu country and literally fought our way through cordons of wild beasts for two days when we decided to make camp a little earlier than usual, owing to the fact that we had reached a line of cliffs running east and west in which were numerous likely cave-lodgings. We were both very tired, and the sight of these caverns, several of which could be easily barricaded, decided us to halt until the following morning. It took but a few minutes' exploration to discover one particular cavern high up the face of the cliff which seemed ideal for our purpose. It opened upon a narrow ledge where we could build our cook-fire; the opening was so small that we had to lie flat and wriggle through it to gain ingress, while the interior was high-ceiled and spacious. I lighted a faggot and looked about; but as far as I could see, the chamber ran back into the cliff.

Laying aside my rifle, pistol and heavy ammunition-belt, I left Ajor in the cave while I went down to gather firewood. We already had meat and fruits which we had gathered just before reaching the cliffs, and my canteen was filled with fresh water. Therefore, all we required was fuel, and as I always saved Ajor's strength when I could, I would not permit her to accompany me. The poor girl was very tired; but she would have gone with me until she dropped, I know, so loyal was she. She was the best comrade in the world, and sometimes I regretted and sometimes I was glad that she was not of my own caste, for had she been, I should unquestionably have fallen in love with her. As it was, we traveled together like two boys, with huge respect for each other but no softer sentiment.

There was little timber close to the base of the cliffs, and so I was forced to enter the wood some two hundred yards distant. I realize now how foolhardy was my act in such a land as Caspak, teeming with danger and with death; but there is a certain amount of fool in every man; and whatever proportion of it I own must have been in the ascendant that day, for the truth of the matter is that I went down into those woods absolutely defenseless; and I paid the price, as people usually do for their indiscretions. As I searched around in the brush for likely pieces of firewood, my head bowed and my eyes upon the ground, I suddenly felt a great weight hurl itself upon me. I struggled to my knees and seized my assailant, a huge, naked man—naked except for a breechcloth of snake-skin, the head hanging down to the knees. The fellow was armed with a stone-shod spear, a stone knife and a hatchet. In his black hair were several gay-colored feathers. As we struggled to and fro, I was slowly gaining advantage of him, when a score of his fellows came running up and overpowered me.

They bound my hands behind me with long rawhide thongs and then surveyed me critically. I found them fine-looking specimens of manhood, for the most part. There were some among them who bore a resemblance to the Sto-lu and were hairy; but the majority had massive heads and not unlovely features. There was little about them to suggest the ape, as in the Sto-lu, Bo-lu and Alus. I expected them to kill me at once, but they did not. Instead they questioned me; but it was evident that they did not believe my story, for they scoffed and laughed.

"The Galus have turned you out," they cried. "If you go back to them, you will die. If you remain here, you will die. We shall kill you; but first we shall have a dance and you shall dance with us—the dance of death."

It sounded quite reassuring! But I knew that I was not to be killed immediately, and so I took heart. They led me toward the cliffs, and as we approached them, I glanced up and was sure that I saw Ajor's bright eyes peering down upon us from our lofty cave; but she gave no sign if she saw me; and we passed on, rounded the end of the cliffs and proceeded along the opposite face of them until we came to a section literally honeycombed with caves. All about, upon the ground and swarming the ledges before the entrances, were hundreds of members of the tribe. There were many women but no babes or children, though I noticed that the females had better developed breasts than any that I had seen among the hatchet-men, the club-men, the Alus or the apes. In fact, among the lower orders of Caspakian man the female breast is but a rudimentary organ, barely suggested in the apes and Alus, and only a little more defined in the Bo-lu and Sto-lu, though always increasingly so until it is found about half developed in the females of the spear-men; yet never was there an indication that the females had suckled young; nor were there any young among them. Some of the Band-lu women were quite comely. The figures of all, both men and women, were symmetrical though heavy, and though there were some who verged strongly upon the Sto-lu type, there were others who were positively handsome and whose bodies were quite hairless. The Alus are all bearded, but among the Bo-lu the beard disappears in the women. The Sto-lu men show a sparse beard, the Band-lu none; and there is little hair upon the bodies of their women.

The members of the tribe showed great interest in me, especially in my clothing, the like of which, of course, they never had seen. They pulled and hauled upon me, and some of them struck me; but for the most part they were not inclined to brutality. It was only the hairier ones, who most closely resembled the Sto-lu, who maltreated me. At last my captors led me into a great cave in the mouth of which a fire was burning. The floor was littered with filth, including the bones of many animals, and the atmosphere reeked with the stench of human bodies and putrefying flesh. Here they fed me, releasing my arms, and I ate of half-cooked aurochs steak and a stew which may have been made of snakes, for many of the long, round pieces of meat suggested them most nauseatingly.

The meal completed, they led me well within the cavern, which they lighted with torches stuck in various crevices in the light of which I saw, to my astonishment, that the walls were covered with paintings and etchings. There were aurochs, red deer, saber-tooth tiger, cave-bear, hyaenadon and many other examples of the fauna of Caspak done in colors, usually of four shades of brown, or scratched upon the surface of the rock. Often they were super-imposed upon each other until it required careful examination to trace out the various outlines. But they all showed a rather remarkable aptitude for delineation which further fortified Bowen's comparisons between these people and the extinct Cro-Magnons whose ancient art is still preserved in the caverns of Niaux and Le Portel. The Band-lu, however, did not have the bow and arrow, and in this respect they differ from their extinct progenitors, or descendants, of Western Europe.

Should any of my friends chance to read the story of my adventures upon Caprona, I hope they will not be bored by these diversions, and if they are, I can only say that I am writing my memoirs for my own edification and therefore setting down those things which interested me particularly at the time. I have no desire that the general public should ever have access to these pages; but it is possible that my friends may, and also certain savants who are interested; and to them, while I do not apologize for my philosophizing, I humbly explain that they are witnessing the groupings of a finite mind after the infinite, the search for explanations of the inexplicable.

In a far recess of the cavern my captors bade me halt. Again my hands were secured, and this time my feet as well. During the operation they questioned me, and I was mighty glad that the marked similarity between the various tribal tongues of Caspak enabled us to understand each other perfectly, even though they were unable to believe or even to comprehend the truth of my origin and the circumstances of my advent in Caspak; and finally they left me saying that they would come for me before the dance of death upon the morrow. Before they departed with their torches, I saw that I had not been conducted to the farthest extremity of the cavern, for a dark and gloomy corridor led beyond my prison room into the heart of the cliff.

I could not but marvel at the immensity of this great underground grotto. Already I had traversed several hundred yards of it, from many points of which other corridors diverged. The whole cliff must be honeycombed with apartments and passages of which this community occupied but a comparatively small part, so that the possibility of the more remote passages being the lair of savage beasts that have other means of ingress and egress than that used by the Band-lu filled me with dire forebodings.

I believe that I am not ordinarily hysterically apprehensive; yet I must confess that under the conditions with which I was confronted, I felt my nerves to be somewhat shaken. On the morrow I was to die some sort of nameless death for the diversion of a savage horde, but the morrow held fewer terrors for me than the present, and I submit to any fair-minded man if it is not a terrifying thing to lie bound hand and foot in the Stygian blackness of an immense cave peopled by unknown dangers in a land overrun by hideous beasts and reptiles of the greatest ferocity. At any moment, perhaps at this very moment, some silent-footed beast of prey might catch my scent where it laired in some contiguous passage, and might creep stealthily upon me. I craned my neck about, and stared through the inky darkness for the twin spots of blazing hate which I knew would herald the coming of my executioner. So real were the imaginings of my overwrought brain that I broke into a cold sweat in absolute conviction that some beast was close before me; yet the hours dragged, and no sound broke the gravelike stillness of the cavern.

During that period of eternity many events of my life passed before my mental vision, a vast parade of friends and occurrences which would be blotted out forever on the morrow. I cursed myself for the foolish act which had taken me from the search-party that so depended upon me, and I wondered what progress, if any, they had made. Were they still beyond the barrier cliffs, awaiting my return? Or had they found a way into Caspak? I felt that the latter would be the truth, for the party was not made up of men easily turned from a purpose. Quite probable it was that they were already searching for me; but that they would ever find a trace of me I doubted. Long since, had I come to the conclusion that it was beyond human prowess to circle the shores of the inland sea of Caspak in the face of the myriad menaces which lurked in every shadow by day and by night. Long since, had I given up any hope of reaching the point where I had made my entry into the country, and so I was now equally convinced that our entire expedition had been worse than futile before ever it was conceived, since Bowen J. Tyler and his wife could not by any possibility have survived during all these long months; no more could Bradley and his party of seamen be yet in existence. If the superior force and equipment of my party enabled them to circle the north end of the sea, they might some day come upon the broken wreck of my plane hanging in the great tree to the south; but long before that, my bones would be added to the litter upon the floor of this mighty cavern.

And through all my thoughts, real and fanciful, moved the image of a perfect girl, clear-eyed and strong and straight and beautiful, with the carriage of a queen and the supple, undulating grace of a leopard. Though I loved my friends, their fate seemed of less importance to me than the fate of this little barbarian stranger for whom, I had convinced myself many a time, I felt no greater sentiment than passing friendship for a fellow-wayfarer in this land of horrors. Yet I so worried and fretted about her and her future that at last I quite forgot my own predicament, though I still struggled intermittently with bonds in vain endeavor to free myself; as much, however, that I might hasten to her protection as that I might escape the fate which had been planned for me. And while I was thus engaged and had for the moment forgotten my apprehensions concerning prowling beasts, I was startled into tense silence by a distinct and unmistakable sound coming from the dark corridor farther toward the heart of the cliff— the sound of padded feet moving stealthily in my direction.

I believe that never before in all my life, even amidst the terrors of childhood nights, have I suffered such a sensation of extreme horror as I did that moment in which I realized that I must lie bound and helpless while some horrid beast of prey crept upon me to devour me in that utter darkness of the Bandlu pits of Caspak. I reeked with cold sweat, and my flesh crawled—I could feel it crawl. If ever I came nearer to abject cowardice, I do not recall the instance; and yet it was not that I was afraid to die, for I had long since given myself up as lost—a few days of Caspak must impress anyone with the utter nothingness of life. The waters, the land, the air teem with it, and always it is being devoured by some other form of life. Life is the cheapest thing in Caspak, as it is the cheapest thing on earth and, doubtless, the cheapest cosmic production. No, I was not afraid to die; in fact, I prayed for death, that I might be relieved of the frightfulness of the interval of life which remained to me—the waiting, the awful waiting, for that fearsome beast to reach me and to strike.

Presently it was so close that I could hear its breathing, and then it touched me and leaped quickly back as though it had come upon me unexpectedly. For long moments no sound broke the sepulchral silence of the cave. Then I heard a movement on the part of the creature near me, and again it touched me, and I felt something like a hairless hand pass over my face and down until it touched the collar of my flannel shirt. And then, subdued, but filled with pent emotion, a voice cried: "Tom!"

I think I nearly fainted, so great was the reaction. "Ajor!" I managed to say. "Ajor, my girl, can it be you?"

"Oh, Tom!" she cried again in a trembly little voice and flung herself upon me, sobbing softly. I had not known that Ajor could cry.

As she cut away my bonds, she told me that from the entrance to our cave she had seen the Band-lu coming out of the forest with me, and she had followed until they took me into the cave, which she had seen was upon the opposite side of the cliff in which ours was located; and then, knowing that she could do nothing for me until after the Band-lu slept, she had hastened to return to our cave. With difficulty she had reached it, after having been stalked by a cave-lion and almost seized. I trembled at the risk she had run.

It had been her intention to wait until after midnight, when most of the carnivora would have made their kills, and then attempt to reach the cave in which I was imprisoned and rescue me. She explained that with my rifle and pistol—both of which she assured

153

me she could use, having watched me so many times—she planned upon frightening the Band-lu and forcing them to give me up. Brave little girl! She would have risked her life willingly to save me. But some time after she reached our cave she heard voices from the far recesses within, and immediately concluded that we had but found another entrance to the caves which the Band-lu occupied upon the other face of the cliff. Then she had set out through those winding passages and in total darkness had groped her way, guided solely by a marvelous sense of direction, to where I lay. She had had to proceed with utmost caution lest she fall into some abyss in the darkness and in truth she had thrice come upon sheer drops and had been forced to take the most frightful risks to pass them. I shudder even now as I contemplate what this girl passed through for my sake and how she enhanced her peril in loading herself down with the weight of my arms and ammunition and the awkwardness of the long rifle which she was unaccustomed to bearing.

I could have knelt and kissed her hand in reverence and gratitude; nor am I ashamed to say that that is precisely what I did after I had been freed from my bonds and heard the story of her trials. Brave little Ajor! Wonder-girl out of the dim, unthinkable past! Never before had she been kissed; but she seemed to sense something of the meaning of the new caress, for she leaned forward in the dark and pressed her own lips to my forehead. A sudden urge surged through me to seize her and strain her to my bosom and cover her hot young lips with the kisses of a real love, but I did not do so, for I knew that I did not love her; and to have kissed her thus, with passion, would have been to inflict a great wrong upon her who had offered her life for mine.

No, Ajor should be as safe with me as with her own mother, if she had one, which I was inclined to doubt, even though she told me that she had once been a babe and hidden by her mother. I had come to doubt if there was such a thing as a mother in Caspak, a mother such as we know. From the Bo-lu to the Kro-lu there is no word which corresponds with our word *mother*. They speak of *ata* and *cor sva jo*, meaning *reproduction* and *from the beginning*, and point toward the south; but no one has a mother.

After considerable difficulty we gained what we thought was our cave, only to find that it was not, and then we realized that we were lost in the labyrinthine mazes of the great cavern. We retraced our steps and sought the point from which we had started, but only succeeded in losing ourselves the more. Ajor was aghast—not so much from fear of our predicament; but that she should have failed in the functioning of that wonderful sense she possessed in common with most other creatures Caspakian, which makes it possible for them to move unerringly from place to place without compass or guide.

Hand in hand we crept along, searching for an opening into the outer world, yet realizing that at each step we might be burrowing more deeply into the heart of the great cliff, or circling futilely in the vague wandering that could end only in death. And the darkness! It was almost palpable, and utterly depressing. I had matches, and in some of the more difficult places I struck one; but we couldn't afford to waste them, and so we groped our way slowly along, doing the best we could to keep to one general direction in the hope that it would eventually lead us to an opening into the outer world. When I struck matches, I noticed that the walls bore no paintings; nor was there other sign that man had penetrated this far within the cliff, nor any spoor of animals of other kinds.

It would be difficult to guess at the time we spent wandering through those black corridors, climbing steep ascents, feeling our way along the edges of bottomless pits, never knowing at what moment we might be plunged into some abyss and always haunted by the ever-present terror of death by starvation and thirst. As difficult as it was, I still realized that it might have been infinitely worse had I had another companion than Ajor—courageous, uncomplaining, loyal little Ajor! She was tired and hungry and thirsty, and she must have been discouraged; but she never faltered in her cheerfulness. I asked her if she was afraid, and she replied that here the Wieroo could not get her, and that if she died of hunger, she would at least die with me and she was quite content that such should be her end. At the time I attributed her attitude to something akin to a doglike devotion to a new master who had been kind to her. I can take oath to the fact that I did not think it was anything more.

Whether we had been imprisoned in the cliff for a day or a week I could not say; nor even now do I know. We became very tired and hungry; the hours dragged; we slept at least twice, and then we rose and stumbled on, always weaker and weaker. There were ages during which the trend of the corridors was always upward. It was heartbreaking work for people in the state of exhaustion in which we then were, but we clung tenaciously to it. We stumbled and fell; we sank through pure physical inability to retain our feet; but always we managed to rise at last and go on. At first, wherever it had been possible, we had walked hand in hand lest we become separated, and later, when I saw that Ajor was weakening rapidly, we went side by side, I supporting her with an arm about her waist. I still retained the heavy burden of my armament; but with the rifle slung to my back, my hands were free. When I too showed indisputable evidences of exhaustion, Ajor suggested that I lay aside my arms and ammunition; but I told her that as it would mean certain death for me to traverse Caspak without them, I might as well take the chance of dying here in the cave with them, for there was the other chance that we might find our way to liberty.

There came a time when Ajor could no longer walk, and then it was that I picked her up in my arms and carried her. She begged me to leave her, saying that after I found an exit, I could come back and get her; but she knew, and she knew that I knew, that if ever I did leave her, I could never find her again. Yet she insisted. Barely had I sufficient strength to take a score of steps at a time; then I would have to sink down and rest for five to ten minutes. I don't know what force urged me on and kept me going in the face of an absolute conviction that my efforts were utterly futile. I counted us already as good as dead; but still I dragged myself along until the time came that I could no longer rise, but could only crawl along a few inches at a time, dragging Ajor beside me. Her sweet voice, now almost inaudible from weakness, implored me to abandon her and save myself—she seemed to think only of me. Of course I couldn't have left her there alone, no matter how much I might have desired to do so; but the fact of the matter was that I didn't desire to leave her. What I said to her then came very simply and naturally to my lips. It couldn't very well have been otherwise, I imagine, for with death so close, I doubt if people are much inclined to heroics. "I would rather not get out at all, Ajor," I said to her, "than to get out without you." We were resting against a rocky wall, and Ajor was leaning against me, her head on my breast. I could feel her press closer to me, and one hand stroked my arm in a weak caress; but she didn't say anything, nor were words necessary.

After a few minutes' more rest, we started on again upon our utterly hopeless way; but I soon realized that I was weakening rapidly, and presently I was forced to admit that I was through. "It's no use, Ajor," I said, "I've come as far as I can. It may be that if I sleep, I can go on again after," but I knew that that was not true, and that the end was near. "Yes, sleep," said Ajor. "We will sleep together—forever."

She crept close to me as I lay on the hard floor and pillowed her head upon my arm. With the little strength which remained to me, I drew her up until our lips touched, and, then I whispered: "Goodbye!" I must have lost consciousness almost immediately, for I recall nothing more until I suddenly awoke out of a troubled sleep, during which I dreamed that I was drowning, to find the cave lighted by what appeared to be diffused daylight, and a tiny trickle of water running down the corridor and forming a puddle in the little depression in which it chanced that Ajor and I lay. I turned my eyes quickly upon Ajor, fearful for what the light might disclose; but she still breathed, though very faintly. Then I searched about for an explanation of the light, and soon discovered that it came from about a bend in the corridor just ahead of us and at the top of a steep incline; and instantly I realized that Ajor and I had stumbled by night almost to the portal of salvation. Had chance taken us a few yards further, up either of the corridors which diverged from ours just ahead of us, we might have been irrevocably lost; we might still be lost; but at least we could die in the light of day, out of the horrid blackness of this terrible cave.

I tried to rise, and found that sleep had given me back a portion of my strength; and then I tasted the water and was further refreshed. I shook Ajor gently by the shoulder; but she did not open her eyes, and then I gathered a few drops of water in my cupped palm and let them trickle between her lips. This revived her so that she raised her lids, and when she saw me, she smiled.

"What happened?" she asked. "Where are we?"

"We are at the end of the corridor," I replied, "and daylight is coming in from the outside world just ahead. We are saved, Ajor!"

She sat up then and looked about, and then, quite womanlike, she burst into tears. It was the reaction, of course; and then too, she was very weak. I took her in my arms and quieted her as best I could, and finally, with my help, she got to her feet; for she, as well as I, had found some slight recuperation in sleep. Together we staggered upward toward the light, and at the first turn we saw an opening a few yards ahead of us and a leaden sky beyond—a leaden sky from which was falling a drizzling rain, the author of our little, trickling stream which had given us drink when we were most in need of it.

The cave had been damp and cold; but as we crawled through the aperture, the muggy warmth of the Caspakian air caressed and confronted us; even the rain was warmer than the atmosphere of those dark corridors. We had water now, and warmth, and I was sure that Caspak would soon offer us meat or fruit; but as we came to where we could look about, we saw that we were upon the summit of the cliffs, where there seemed little reason to expect game. However, there were trees, and among them we soon descried edible fruits with which we broke our long fast.

4

e spent two days upon the cliff-top, resting and recuperating. There was some small game which gave us meat, and the little pools of rainwater were sufficient to quench our thirst. The sun came out a few hours after we emerged from the cave, and in its warmth we soon cast off the gloom which our recent experiences had saddled upon us.

Upon the morning of the third day we set out to search for a path down to the valley. Below us, to the north, we saw a large pool lying at the foot of the cliffs, and in it we could discern the women of the Band-lu lying in the shallow waters, while beyond and close to the base of the mighty barrier-cliffs there was a large party of Band-lu warriors going north to hunt. We had a splendid view from our lofty cliff-top. Dimly, to the west, we could see the farther shore of the inland sea, and southwest the large southern island loomed distinctly before us. A little east of north was the northern island, which Ajor, shuddering, whispered was the home of the Wieroo—the land of Oo-oh. It lay at the far end of the lake and was barely visible to us, being fully sixty miles away.

From our elevation, and in a clearer atmosphere, it would have stood out distinctly; but the air of Caspak is heavy with moisture, with the result that distant objects are blurred and indistinct. Ajor also told me that the mainland east of Oo-oh was her land—the land of the Galu. She pointed out the cliffs at its southern boundary, which mark the frontier, south of which lies the country of Kro-lu—the archers. We now had but to pass through the balance of the Band-lu territory and that of the Kro-lu to be within the confines of her own land; but that meant traversing thirty-five miles of hostile country filled with every imaginable terror, and possibly many beyond the powers of imagination. I would certainly have given a lot for my plane at that moment, for with it, twenty minutes would have landed us within the confines of Ajor's country.

We finally found a place where we could slip over the edge of the cliff onto a narrow ledge which seemed to give evidence of being something of a game-path to the valley, though it apparently had not been used for some time. I lowered Ajor at the end of my rifle and then slid over myself, and I am free to admit that my hair stood on end during the process, for the drop was considerable and the ledge appallingly narrow, with a frightful drop sheer below down to the rocks at the base of the cliff; but with Ajor there to catch and steady me, I made it all right, and then we set off down the trail toward the valley. There were two or three more bad places, but for the most part it was an easy descent, and we came to the highest of the Band-lu caves without further trouble. Here we went more slowly, lest we should be set upon by some member of the tribe.

We must have passed about half the Band-lu cave-levels before we were accosted, and then a huge fellow stepped out in front of me, barring our further progress.

"Who are you?" he asked; and he recognized me and I him, for he had been one of those who had led me back into the cave and bound me the night that I had been captured. From me his gaze went to Ajor. He was a fine-looking man with clear, intelligent eyes, a good forehead and superb physique—by far the highest type of Caspakian I had yet seen, barring Ajor, of course.

"You are a true Galu," he said to Ajor, "but this man is of a different mold. He has the face of a Galu, but his weapons and the strange skins he wears upon his body are not of the Galus nor of Caspak. Who is he?"

"He is Tom," replied Ajor succinctly.

"There is no such people," asserted the Band-lu quite truthfully, toying with his spear in a most suggestive manner.

"My name is Tom," I explained, "and I am from a country beyond Caspak." I thought it best to propitiate him if possible, because of the necessity of conserving ammunition as well as to avoid the loud alarm of a shot which might bring other Band-lu warriors upon us. "I am from America, a land of which you never heard, and I am seeking others of my countrymen who are in Caspak and from whom I am lost. I have no quarrel with you or your people. Let us go our way in peace."

"You are going there?" he asked, and pointed toward the north.

"I am," I replied.

He was silent for several minutes, apparently weighing some thought in his mind. At last he spoke. "What is that?" he asked. "And what is that?" He pointed first at my rifle and then to my pistol.

"They are weapons," I replied, "weapons which kill at a great distance." I pointed to the women in the pool beneath us. "With this," I said, tapping my pistol, "I could kill as many of those women as I cared to, without moving a step from where we now stand."

He looked his incredulity, but I went on. "And with this"—I weighed my rifle at the balance in the palm of my right hand— "I could slay one of those distant warriors." And I waved my left hand toward the tiny figures of the hunters far to the north.

The fellow laughed. "Do it," he cried derisively, "and then it may be that I shall believe the balance of your strange story."

"But I do not wish to kill any of them," I replied. "Why should I?"

"Why not?" he insisted. "They would have killed you when they had you prisoner. They would kill you now if they could get their hands on you, and they would eat you into the bargain. But I know why you do not try it—it is because you have spoken lies; your weapon will not kill at a great distance. It is only a queerly wrought club. For all I know, you are nothing more than a lowly Bo-lu."

"Why should you wish me to kill your own people?" I asked.

"They are no longer my people," he replied proudly. "Last night, in the very middle of the night, the call came to me. Like that it came into my head"—and he struck his hands together smartly once—"that I had risen. I have been waiting for it and expecting it for a long time; today I am a Kro-lu. Today I go into the *coslupak*" (unpeopled country, or literally, no man's land) "between the Band-lu and the Kro-lu, and there I fashion my bow and my arrows and my shield; there I hunt the red deer for the leathern jerkin which is the badge of my new estate. When these things are done, I can go to the chief of the Kro-lu, and he dare not refuse me. That is why you may kill those low Band-lu if you wish to live, for I am in a hurry."

"But why do you wish to kill me?" I asked.

He looked puzzled and finally gave it up. "I do not know," he admitted. "It is the way in Caspak. If we do not kill, we shall be killed, therefore it is wise to kill first whomever does not belong to one's own people. This morning I hid in my cave till the others were gone upon the hunt, for I knew that they would know at once that I had become a Kro-lu and would kill me. They will kill me if they find me in the *coslupak*; so will the Kro-lu if they come upon me before I have won my Kro-lu weapons and jerkin. You would kill me if you could, and that is the reason I know that you speak lies when you say that your weapons will kill at a great distance. Would they, you would long since have killed me. Come! I have no more time to waste in words. I will spare the woman and take her with me to the Kro-lu, for she is comely." And with that he advanced upon me with raised spear.

My rifle was at my hip at the ready. He was so close that I did not need to raise it to my shoulder, having but to pull the trigger to send him into Kingdom Come whenever I chose; but yet I hesitated.

It was difficult to bring myself to take a human life. I could feel no enmity toward this savage barbarian who acted almost as wholly upon instinct as might a wild beast, and to the last moment I was determined to seek some way to avoid what now seemed inevitable. Ajor stood at my shoulder, her knife ready in her hand and a sneer on her lips at his suggestion that he would take her with him.

Just as I thought I should have to fire, a chorus of screams broke from the women beneath us. I saw the man halt and glance downward, and following his example my eyes took in the panic and its cause. The women had, evidently, been quitting the pool and slowly returning toward the caves, when they were confronted by a monstrous cave-lion which stood directly between them and their cliffs in the center of the narrow path that led down to the pool among the tumbled rocks. Screaming, the women were rushing madly back to the pool.

"It will do them no good," remarked the man, a trace of excitement in his voice. "It will do them no good, for the lion will wait until they come out and take as many as he can carry away; and there is one there," he added, a trace of sadness in his tone, "whom I hoped would soon follow me to the Kro-lu. Together have we come up from the beginning." He raised his spear above his head and poised it ready to hurl downward at the lion. "She is nearest to him," he muttered. "He will get her and she will never come to me among the Kro-lu, or ever thereafter. It is useless! No warrior lives who could hurl a weapon so great a distance."

But even as he spoke, I was leveling my rifle upon the great brute below; and as he ceased speaking, I squeezed the trigger. My bullet must have struck to a hair the point at which I had aimed, for it smashed the brute's spine back of his shoulders and tore on through his heart, dropping him dead in his tracks. For a moment the women were as terrified by the report of the rifle as they had been by the menace of the lion; but when they saw that the loud noise had evidently destroyed their enemy, they came creeping cautiously back to examine the carcass.

The man, toward whom I had immediately turned after firing, lest he should pursue his threatened attack, stood staring at me in amazement and admiration.

"Why," he asked, "if you could do that, did you not kill me long before?"

"I told you," I replied, "that I had no quarrel with you. I do not care to kill men with whom I have no quarrel."

But he could not seem to get the idea through his head. "I can believe now that you are not of Caspak," he admitted, "for no Caspakian would have permitted such an opportunity to escape him." This, however, I found later to be an exaggeration, as the tribes of the west coast and even the Kro-lu of the east coast are far less bloodthirsty than he would have had me believe. "And your weapon!" he continued. "You spoke true words when I thought you spoke lies." And then, suddenly: "Let us be friends!"

I turned to Ajor. "Can I trust him?" I asked.

"Yes," she replied. "Why not? Has he not asked to be friends?"

I was not at the time well enough acquainted with Caspakian ways to know that truthfulness and loyalty are two of the strongest characteristics of these primitive people. They are not sufficiently cultured to have become adept in hypocrisy, treason and dissimulation. There are, of course, a few exceptions.

"We can go north together," continued the warrior. "I will fight for you, and you can fight for me. Until death will I serve you, for you have saved So-al, whom I had given up as dead." He threw down his spear and covered both his eyes with the palms of his two hands. I looked inquiringly toward Ajor, who explained as best she could that this was the form of the Caspakian oath of allegiance. "You need never fear him after this," she concluded.

"What should I do?" I asked.

"Take his hands down from before his eyes and return his spear to him," she explained.

I did as she bade, and the man seemed very pleased. I then asked what I should have done had I not wished to accept his friendship. They told me that had I walked away, the moment that I was out of sight of the warrior we would have become deadly enemies again. "But I could so easily have killed him as he stood there defenseless!" I exclaimed.

"Yes," replied the warrior, "but no man with good sense blinds his eyes before one whom he does not trust."

It was rather a decent compliment, and it taught me just how much I might rely on the loyalty of my new friend. I was glad to have him with us, for he knew the country and was evidently a fearless warrior. I wished that I might have recruited a battalion like him.

As the women were now approaching the cliffs, To-mar the warrior suggested that we make our way to the valley before they could intercept us, as they might attempt to detain us and were almost certain to set upon Ajor. So we hastened down the narrow path, reaching the foot of the cliffs but a short distance ahead of the women. They called after us to stop; but we kept on at a rapid walk, not wishing to have any trouble with them, which could only result in the death of some of them.

We had proceeded about a mile when we heard some one behind us calling To-mar by name, and when we stopped and looked around, we saw a woman running rapidly toward us. As she approached nearer I could see that she was a very comely creature, and like all her sex that I had seen in Caspak, apparently young.

"It is So-al!" exclaimed To-mar. "Is she mad that she follows me thus?"

In another moment the young woman stopped, panting, before us. She paid not the slightest attention to Ajor or me; but devouring To-mar with her sparkling eyes, she cried: "I have risen! I have risen!"

"So-al!" was all that the man could say.

"Yes," she went on, "the call came to me just before I quit the pool; but I did not know that it had come to you. I can see it in your eyes, To-mar, my To-mar! We shall go on together!" And she threw herself into his arms.

It was a very affecting sight, for it was evident that these two had been mates for a long time and that they had each thought that they were about to be separated by that strange law of evolution which holds good in Caspak and which was slowly unfolding before my incredulous mind. I did not then comprehend even a tithe of the wondrous process, which goes on eternally within the confines of Caprona's barrier cliffs nor am I any too sure that I do even now.

To-mar explained to So-al that it was I who had killed the cave-lion and saved her life, and that Ajor was my woman and thus entitled to the same loyalty which was my due.

At first Ajor and So-al were like a couple of stranger cats on a back fence but soon they began to accept each other under something of an armed truce, and later became fast friends. So-al was a mighty fine-looking girl, built like a tigress as to strength and sinuosity, but withal sweet and womanly. Ajor and I came to be very fond of her, and she was, I think, equally fond of us. To-mar was very much of a man—a savage, if you will, but none the less a man.

Finding that traveling in company with To-mar made our journey both easier and safer, Ajor and I did not continue on our way alone while the novitiates delayed their approach to the Kro-lu country in order that they might properly fit themselves in the matter of arms and apparel, but remained with them. Thus we became well acquainted—to such an extent that we looked forward with regret to the day when they took their places among their new comrades and we should be forced to continue upon our way alone. It was a matter of much concern to To-mar that the Kro-lu would undoubtedly not receive Ajor and me in a friendly manner, and that consequently we should have to avoid these people.

It would have been very helpful to us could we have made friends with them, as their country abutted directly upon that of the Galus. Their friendship would have meant that Ajor's dangers were practically passed, and that I had accomplished fully one-half of my long journey. In view of what I had passed through, I often wondered what chance I had to complete that journey in search of my friends. The further south I should travel on the west side of the island, the more frightful would the dangers become as I neared the stamping-grounds of the more hideous reptilia and the haunts of the Alus and the Ho-lu, all of which were at the southern half of the island; and then if I should not find the members of my party, what was to become of me? I could not live for long in any portion of Caspak with which I was familiar; the moment my ammunition was exhausted, I should be as good as dead.

There was a chance that the Galus would receive me; but even Ajor could not say definitely whether they would or not, and even provided that they would, could I retrace my steps from *the beginning*, after failing to find my own people, and return to the far northern land of Galus? I doubted it. However, I was learning from Ajor, who was more or less of a fatalist, a philosophy which was as necessary in Caspak to peace of mind as is faith to the devout Christian of the outer world.

5

e were sitting before a little fire inside a safe grotto one night shortly after we had quit the cliff-dwellings of the Band-lu, when So-al raised a question which it had never occurred to me to propound to Ajor. She asked her why she had left her own people and how she had come so far south as the country of the Alus, where I had found her.

At first Ajor hesitated to explain; but at last she consented, and for the first time I heard the complete story of her origin and experiences. For my benefit she entered into greater detail of explanation than would have been necessary had I been a native Caspakian.

"I am a *cos-ata-lo*," commenced Ajor, and then she turned toward me. "A *cos-ata-lo*, my Tom, is a woman" *(lo)* "who did not come from an egg and thus on up *from the beginning*" *(cor sva jo)*. "I was a babe at my mother's breast. Only among the Galus are such, and then but infrequently. The Wieroo get most of us; but my mother hid me until I had attained such size that the Wieroo could not readily distinguish me from one who had come up from the beginning. I knew both my mother and my father, as only such as I may. My father is high chief among the Galus. His name is Jor, and both he and my mother came up from the beginning; but one of them, probably my mother, had completed the seven cycles" (approximately seven hundred years), "with the result that their offspring might be *cos-ata-lo*, or born as are all the children of your race, my Tom, as you tell me is the fact. I was therefore apart from my fellows in that my children would probably

169

be as I, of a higher state of evolution, and so I was sought by the men of my people; but none of them appealed to me. I cared for none. The most persistent was Du-seen, a huge warrior of whom my father stood in considerable fear, since it was quite possible that Du-seen could wrest from him his chieftainship of the Galus. He has a large following of the newer Galus, those most recently come up from the Kro-lu, and as this class is usually much more powerful numerically than the older Galus, and as Du-seen's ambition knows no bounds, we have for a long time been expecting him to find some excuse for a break with Jor the High Chief, my father.

"A further complication lay in the fact that Du-seen wanted me, while I would have none of him, and then came evidence to my father's ears that he was in league with the Wieroo; a hunter, returning late at night, came trembling to my father, saying that he had seen Du-seen talking with a Wieroo in a lonely spot far from the village, and that plainly he had heard the words: 'If you will help me, I will help you—I will deliver into your hands all *cos-ata-lo* among the Galus, now and hereafter; but for that service you must slay Jor the High Chief and bring terror and confusion to his followers.'

"Now, when my father heard this, he was angry; but he was also afraid—afraid for me, who am *cos-ata-lo*. He called me to him and told me what he had heard, pointing out two ways in which we might frustrate Du-seen. The first was that I go to Du-seen as his mate, after which he would be loath to give me into the hands of the Wieroo or to further abide by the wicked compact he had made—a compact which would doom his own offspring, who would doubtless be as am I, their mother. The alternative was flight until Du-seen should have been overcome and punished. I chose the latter and fled toward the south. Beyond the confines of the Galu country is little danger from the Wieroo, who seek ordinarily only Galus of the highest orders. There are two excellent reasons for this: One is that from the beginning of time jealousy had existed between the Wieroo and the Galus as to which would eventually dominate the world. It seems generally conceded that that race which first reaches a point of evolution which permits them to produce young of their own species and of both sexes must dominate all other creatures. The Wieroo first began to produce their own kind—after which evolution from Galu to Wieroo ceased gradually until now it is unknown; but the Wieroo produce only males—which is why they steal our female young, and by stealing *cos-ata-lo* they increase their own chances of eventually reproducing both sexes and at the same time lessen ours. Already the Galus produce both male and female; but so carefully do the Wieroo watch us that few of the males ever grow to manhood, while even fewer are the females that are not stolen away. It is indeed a strange condition, for while our greatest enemies hate and fear us, they dare not exterminate us, knowing that they too would become extinct but for us.

"Ah, but could we once get a start, I am sure that when all were true *cos-ata-lo* there would have been evolved at last the true dominant race before which all the world would be forced to bow."

Ajor always spoke of the world as though nothing existed beyond Caspak. She could not seem to grasp the truth of my origin or the fact that there were countless other peoples outside her stern barrier-cliffs. She apparently felt that I came from an entirely different world. Where it was and how I came to Caspak from it were matters quite beyond her with which she refused to trouble her pretty head.

"Well," she continued, "and so I ran away to hide, intending to pass the cliffs to the south of Galu and find a retreat in the Kro-lu country. It would be dangerous, but there seemed no other way.

"The third night I took refuge in a large cave in the cliffs at the edge of my own country; upon the following day I would cross over into the Kro-lu country, where I felt that I should be reasonably safe from the Wieroo, though menaced by countless other dangers. However, to a *cos-ata-lo* any fate is preferable to that of falling into the clutches of the frightful Wieroo, from whose land none returns.

"I had been sleeping peacefully for several hours when I was awakened by a slight noise within the cavern. The moon was shining brightly, illumining the entrance, against which I saw silhouetted the dread figure of a Wieroo. There was no escape. The cave was shallow, the entrance narrow. I lay very still, hoping against hope, that the creature had but paused here to rest and might soon depart without discovering me; yet all the while I knew that he came seeking me.

"I waited, scarce breathing, watching the thing creep stealthily toward me, its great eyes luminous in the darkness of the cave's interior, and at last I knew that those eyes were directed upon me, for the Wieroo can see in the darkness better than even the lion or the tiger. But a few feet separated us when I sprang to my feet and dashed madly toward my menacer in a vain effort to dodge past him and reach the outside world. It was madness of course, for even had I succeeded temporarily, the Wieroo would have but followed and swooped down upon me from above. As it was, he reached forth and seized me, and though I struggled, he overpowered me. In the duel his long, white robe was nearly torn from him, and he became very angry, so that he trembled and beat his wings together in his rage.

"He asked me my name; but I would not answer him, and that angered him still more. At last he dragged me to the entrance of the cave, lifted me in his arms, spread his great wings and leaping into the air, flapped dismally through the night. I saw the moonlit landscape sliding away beneath me, and then we were out above the sea and on our way to Oo-oh, the country of the Wieroo.

"The dim outlines of Oo-oh were unfolding below us when there came from above a loud whirring of giant wings. The Wieroo and I glanced up simultaneously, to see a pair of huge *jo-oos*" (flying reptiles—pterodactyls) "swooping down upon us. The Wieroo wheeled and dropped almost to sea-level, and then raced southward in an effort to outdistance our pursuers. The great creatures, notwithstanding their enormous weight, are swift on their wings; but the Wieroo are swifter. Even with my added weight, the creature that bore me maintained his lead, though he could not increase it. Faster than the fastest wind we raced through the night, southward along the coast. Sometimes we rose to great heights, where the air was chill and the world below but a blur of dim outlines; but always the jo-oos stuck behind us.

"I knew that we had covered a great distance, for the rush of the wind by my face attested the speed of our progress, but I had no idea where we were when at last I realized that the Wieroo was weakening. One of the jo-oos gained on us and succeeded in heading us, so that my captor had to turn in toward the coast. Further and further they forced him to the left; lower and lower he sank. More labored was his breathing, and weaker the stroke of his once powerful wings. We were not ten feet above the ground when they overtook us, and at the edge of a forest. One of them seized the Wieroo by his right wing, and in an effort to free himself, he loosed his grasp upon me, dropping me to earth. Like a frightened *ecca* I leaped to my feet and raced for the sheltering sanctuary of the forest, where I knew neither could follow or seize me. Then I turned and looked back to see two great reptiles tear my abductor asunder and devour him on the spot.

"I was saved; yet I felt that I was lost. How far I was from the country of the Galus I could not guess; nor did it seem probable that I ever could make my way in safety to my native land.

"Day was breaking; soon the carnivora would stalk forth for their first kill; I was armed only with my knife. About me was a strange landscape—the flowers, the trees, the grasses, even, were different from those of my northern world, and presently there appeared before me a creature fully as hideous as the Wieroo—a hairy man-thing that barely walked erect. I shuddered, and then I fled. Through the hideous dangers that my forebears had endured in the earlier stages of their human evolution I fled; and always pursuing was the hairy monster that had discovered me. Later he was joined by others of his kind. They were the speechless men, the Alus, from whom you rescued me, my Tom. From then on, you know the story of my adventures, and from the first, I would endure them all again because they led me to you!"

It was very nice of her to say that, and I appreciated it. I felt that she was a mighty nice little girl whose friendship anyone might be glad to have; but I wished that when she touched me, those peculiar thrills would not run through me. It was most discomforting, because it reminded me of love; and I knew that I never could love this half-baked little barbarian. I was very much interested in her account of the Wieroo, which up to this time I had considered a purely mythological creature; but Ajor shuddered so at even the veriest mention of the name that I was loath to press the subject upon her, and so the Wieroo still remained a mystery to me.

While the Wieroo interested me greatly, I had little time to think about them, as our waking hours were filled with the necessities of existence—the constant battle for survival which is the chief occupation of Caspakians. To-mar and So-al were now about fitted for their advent into Kro-lu society and must therefore leave us, as we could not accompany them without incurring great danger ourselves and running the chance of endangering them; but each swore to be always our friend and assured us that should we need their aid at any time we had but to ask it; nor could I doubt their sincerity, since we had been so instrumental in bringing them safely upon their journey toward the Kro-lu village.

This was our last day together. In the afternoon we should separate, To-mar and So-al going directly to the Kro-lu village, while Ajor and I made a detour to avoid a conflict with the archers. The former both showed evidence of nervous apprehension as the time approached for them to make their entry into the village of their new people, and yet both were very proud and happy. They told us that they would be well received as additions to a tribe always are welcomed, and the more so as the distance from the beginning increased, the higher tribes or races being far weaker numerically than the lower. The southern end of the island fairly swarms with the Ho-lu, or apes; next above these are the Alus, who are slightly fewer in number than the Ho-lu; and again there are fewer Bo-lu than Alus, and fewer Sto-lu than Bo-lu. Thus it goes until the Kro-lu are fewer in number than any of the others; and here the law reverses, for the Galus outnumber the Kro-lu. As Ajor explained it to me, the reason for this is that as evolution practically ceases with the Galus, there is no less among them on this score, for even the *cos-ata-lo* are still considered Galus and remain with them. And Galus come up both from the west and east coasts. There are, too, fewer carnivorous reptiles at the north end of the island, and not so many of the great and ferocious members of the cat family as take their hideous toll of life among the races further south.

By now I was obtaining some idea of the Caspakian scheme of evolution, which partly accounted for the lack of young among the races I had so far seen. Coming up from the beginning, the Caspakian passes, during a single existence, through the various stages of evolution, or at least many of them, through which the human race has passed during the countless ages since life first stirred upon a new world; but the question which continued to puzzle me was: What creates life at the beginning, *cor sva jo?*

I had noticed that as we traveled northward from the Alus' country the land had gradually risen until we were now several hundred feet above the level of the inland sea. Ajor told me that the Galus country was still higher and considerably colder, which accounted for the scarcity of reptiles. The change in form and kinds of the lower animals was even more marked than the evolutionary stages of man. The diminutive *ecca*, or small horse, became a rough-coated and sturdy little pony in the Kro-lu country. I saw a greater number of small lions and tigers, though many of the huge ones still persisted, while the woolly mammoth was more in evidence, as were several varieties of the Labyrinthadonta. These creatures, from which God save me, I should have expected to find further south; but for some unaccountable reason they gain their greatest bulk in the Kro-lu and Galu countries, though fortunately they are rare. I rather imagine that they are a very early life which is rapidly nearing extinction in Caspak, though wherever they are found, they constitute a menace to all forms of life.

It was mid-afternoon when To-mar and So-al bade us good-bye. We were not far from the Kro-lu village; in fact, we had approached it much closer than we had intended, and now Ajor and I were to make a detour toward the sea while our companions went directly in search of the Kro-lu chief.

Ajor and I had gone perhaps a mile or two and were just about to emerge from a dense wood when I saw that ahead of us which caused me to draw back into concealment, at the same time pushing Ajor behind me. What I saw was a party of Band-lu warriors—large, fierce-appearing men. From the direction of their march I saw that they were returning to their caves, and that if we remained where we were, they would pass without discovering us.

Presently Ajor nudged me. "They have a prisoner," she whispered. "He is a Kro-lu."

And then I saw him, the first fully developed Kro-lu I had seen. He was a fine-looking savage, tall and straight with a regal carriage. To-mar was a handsome fellow; but this Kro-lu showed plainly in his every physical attribute a higher plane of evolution. While To-mar was just entering the Kro-lu sphere, this man, it seemed to me, must be close indeed to the next stage of his development, which would see him an envied Galu.

"They will kill him?" I whispered to Ajor.

"The dance of death," she replied, and I shuddered, so recently had I escaped the same fate. It seemed cruel that one who must have passed safely up through all the frightful stages of human evolution within Caspak, should die at the very foot of his goal. I raised my rifle to my shoulder and took careful aim at one of the Band-lu. If I hit him, I would hit two, for another was directly behind the first.

Ajor touched my arm. "What would you do?" she asked. "They are all our enemies."

"I am going to save him from the dance of death," I replied, "enemy or no enemy," and I squeezed the trigger. At the report, the two Band-lu lunged forward upon their faces. I handed my rifle to Ajor, and drawing my pistol, stepped out in full view of the startled party. The Band-lu did not run away as had some of the lower orders of Caspakians at the sound of the rifle. Instead, the moment they saw me, they let out a series of demoniac war-cries, and raising their spears above their heads, charged me.

The Kro-lu stood silent and statuesque, watching the proceedings. He made no attempt to escape, though his feet were not bound and none of the warriors remained to guard him. There were ten of the Band-lu coming for me. I dropped three of them with my pistol as rapidly as a man might count by three, and then my rifle spoke close to my left shoulder, and another of them stumbled and rolled over and over upon the ground. Plucky little Ajor! She had never fired a shot before in all her life, though I had taught her to sight and aim and how to squeeze the trigger instead of pulling it. She had practiced these new accomplishments often, but little had I thought they would make a marksman of her so quickly.

With six of their fellows put out of the fight so easily, the remaining six sought cover behind some low bushes and commenced a council of war. I wished that they would go away, as I had no ammunition to waste, and I was fearful that should they institute another charge, some of them would reach us, for they were already quite close. Suddenly one of them rose and launched his spear. It was the most marvelous exhibition of speed I have ever witnessed. It seemed to me that he had scarce gained an upright position when the weapon was halfway upon its journey, speeding like an arrow toward Ajor. And then it was, with that little life in danger, that I made the best shot I have ever made in my life! I took no conscious aim; it was as though my subconscious mind, impelled by a stronger power even than that of self-preservation, directed my hand. Ajor was in danger! Simultaneously with the thought my pistol flew to position, a streak of incandescent powder marked the path of the bullet from its muzzle; and the spear, its point shattered, was deflected from its path. With a howl of dismay the six Band-lu rose from their shelter and raced away toward the south.

I turned toward Ajor. She was very white and wide-eyed, for the clutching fingers of death had all but seized her; but a little smile came to her lips and an expression of great pride to her eyes. "My Tom!" she said, and took my hand in hers. That was all—"My Tom!" and a pressure of the hand. Her Tom! Something stirred within my bosom. Was it exaltation or was it consternation? Impossible! I turned away almost brusquely.

"Come!" I said, and strode off toward the Kro-lu prisoner.

The Kro-lu stood watching us with stolid indifference. I presume that he expected to be killed; but if he did, he showed no outward sign of fear. His eyes, indicating his greatest interest, were fixed upon my pistol or the rifle which Ajor still carried. I cut his bonds with my knife. As I did so, an expression of surprise tinged and animated the haughty reserve of his countenance. He eyed me quizzically.

"What are you going to do with me?" he asked.

"You are free," I replied. "Go home, if you wish."

"Why don't you kill me?" he inquired. "I am defenseless."

"Why should I kill you? I have risked my life and that of this young lady to save your life. Why, therefore should I now take it?" Of course, I didn't say "young lady" as there is no Caspakian equivalent for that term; but I have to allow myself considerable latitude in the translation of Caspakian conversations. To speak always of a beautiful young girl as a "she" may be literal; but it seems far from gallant.

The Kro-lu concentrated his steady, level gaze upon me for at least a full minute. Then he spoke again.

"Who are you, man of strange skins?" he asked. "Your she is Galu; but you are neither Galu nor Kro-lu nor Band-lu, nor any other sort of man which I have seen before. Tell me from whence comes so mighty a warrior and so generous a foe."

"It is a long story," I replied, "but suffice it to say that I am not of Caspak. I am a stranger here, and—let this sink in—I am not a foe. I have no wish to be an enemy of any man in Caspak, with the possible exception of the Galu warrior Du-seen."

"Du-seen!" he exclaimed. "You are an enemy of Du-seen? And why?"

"Because he would harm Ajor," I replied. "You know him?"

"He cannot know him," said Ajor. "Du-seen rose from the Kro-lu long ago, taking a new name, as all do when they enter a new sphere. He cannot know him, as there is no intercourse between the Kro-lu and the Galu."

The warrior smiled. "Du-seen rose not so long ago," he said, "that I do not recall him well, and recently he has taken it upon himself to abrogate the ancient laws of Caspak; he had had intercourse with the Kro-lu. Du-seen would be chief of the Galus, and he has come to the Kro-lu for help."

Ajor was aghast. The thing was incredible. Never had Kro-lu and Galu had friendly relations; by the savage laws of Caspak they were deadly enemies, for only so can the several races maintain their individuality.

"Will the Kro-lu join him?" asked Ajor. "Will they invade the country of Jor my father?"

"The younger Kro-lu favor the plan," replied the warrior, "since they believe they will thus become Galus immediately. They hope to span the long years of change through which they must pass in the ordinary course of events and at a single stride become Galus. We of the older Kro-lu tell them that though they occupy the land of the Galu and wear the skins and ornaments of the golden people, still they will not be Galus till the time arrives that they are ripe to rise. We also tell them that even then they will never become a true Galu race, since there will still be those among them who can never rise. It is all right to raid the Galu country occasionally for plunder, as our people do; but to attempt to conquer it and hold it is madness. For my part, I have been content to wait until the call came to me. I feel that it cannot now be long."

"What is your name?" asked Ajor.

"Chal-az," replied the man.

"You are chief of the Kro-lu?" Ajor continued.

"No, it is Al-tan who is chief of the Kro-lu of the east," answered Chal-az.

"And he is against this plan to invade my father's country?"

"Unfortunately he is rather in favor of it," replied the man, "since he has about come to the conclusion that he is *batu*. He has been chief ever since, before I came up from the Band-lu, and I can see no change in him in all those years. In fact, he still appears to be more Band-lu than Kro-lu. However, he is a good chief and a mighty warrior, and if Du-seen persuades him to his cause, the Galus may find themselves under a Kro-lu chieftain before long—Du-seen as well as the others, for Al-tan would never consent to occupy a subordinate position, and once he plants a victorious foot in Galu, he will not withdraw it without a struggle."

I asked them what *batu* meant, as I had not before heard the word. Literally translated, it is equivalent to *through, finished, done-for*, as applied to an individual's evolutionary progress in Caspak, and with this information was developed the interesting fact that not every individual is capable of rising through every stage to that of Galu. Some never progress beyond the Alu stage; others stop as Bo-lu, as Sto-lu, as Band-lu or as Kro-lu. The Ho-lu of the first generation may rise to become Alus; the Alus of the second generation may become Bo-lu, while it requires three generations of Bo-lu to become Band-lu, and so on until Kro-lu's parent on one side must be of the sixth generation.

It was not entirely plain to me even with this explanation, since I couldn't understand how there could be different generations of peoples who apparently had no offspring. Yet I was commencing to get a slight glimmer of the strange laws which govern propagation and evolution in this weird land. Already I knew that the warm pools which always lie close to every tribal abiding-place were closely linked with the Caspakian scheme of evolution, and that the daily immersion of the females in the greenish slimy water was in response to some natural law, since neither pleasure nor cleanliness could be derived from what seemed almost a religious rite. Yet I was still at sea; nor, seemingly, could Ajor enlighten me, since she was compelled to use words which I could not understand and which it was impossible for her to explain the meanings of.

As we stood talking, we were suddenly startled by a commotion in the bushes and among the boles of the trees surrounding us, and simultaneously a hundred Kro-lu warriors appeared in a rough circle about us. They greeted Chal-az with a volley of questions as they approached slowly from all sides, their heavy bows fitted with long, sharp arrows. Upon Ajor and me they looked with covetousness in the one instance and suspicion in the other; but after they had heard Chal-az's story, their attitude was more friendly. A huge savage did all the talking. He was a mountain of a man, yet perfectly proportioned.

"This is Al-tan the chief," said Chal-az by way of introduction. Then he told something of my story, and Al-tan asked me many questions of the land from which I came. The warriors crowded around close to hear my replies, and there were many expressions of incredulity as I spoke of what was to them another world, of the yacht which had brought me over vast waters, and of the plane that had borne me Jo-oo-like over the summit of the barrier-cliffs. It was the mention of the hydro-aeroplane which precipitated the first outspoken skepticism, and then Ajor came to my defense.

"I saw it with my own eyes!" she exclaimed. "I saw him flying through the air in battle with a Jo-oo. The Alus were chasing me, and they saw and ran away."

"Whose is this she?" demanded Al-tan suddenly, his eyes fixed fiercely upon Ajor.

For a moment there was silence. Ajor looked up at me, a hurt and questioning expression on her face. "Whose she is this?" repeated Al-tan.

"She is mine," I replied, though what force it was that impelled me to say it I could not have told; but an instant later I was glad that I had spoken the words, for the reward of Ajor's proud and happy face was reward indeed.

Al-tan eyed her for several minutes and then turned to me. "Can you keep her?" he asked, just the tinge of a sneer upon his face.

I laid my palm upon the grip of my pistol and answered that I could. He saw the move, glanced at the butt of the automatic where it protruded from its holster, and smiled. Then he turned and raising his great bow, fitted an arrow and drew the shaft far back. His warriors, supercilious smiles upon their faces, stood silently watching him. His bow was the longest and the heaviest among them all. A mighty man indeed must he be to bend it; yet Al-tan drew the shaft back until the stone point touched his left forefinger, and he did it with consummate ease. Then he raised the shaft to the level of his right eye, held it there for an instant and released it. When the arrow stopped, half its length protruded from the opposite side of a six-inch tree fifty feet away. Al-tan and his warriors turned toward me with expressions of immense satisfaction upon their faces, and then, apparently for Ajor's benefit, the chieftain swaggered to and fro a couple of times, swinging his great arms and his bulky shoulders for all the world like a drunken prize-fighter at a beach dance-hall.

I saw that some reply was necessary, and so in a single motion, I drew my gun, dropped it on the still quivering arrow and pulled the trigger. At the sound of the report, the Kro-lu leaped back and raised their weapons; but as I was smiling, they took heart and lowered them again, following my eyes to the tree; the shaft of their chief was gone, and through the bole was a little round hole marking the path of my bullet. It was a good shot if I do say it myself, "as shouldn't;" but necessity must have guided that bullet; I simply *had* to make a good shot, that I might immediately establish my position among those savage and warlike Caspakians of the sixth sphere. That it had its effect was immediately noticeable, but I am none too sure that it helped my cause with Al-tan. Whereas he might have condescended to tolerate me as a harmless and interesting curiosity, he now, by the change in his expression, appeared to consider me in a new and unfavorable light. Nor can I wonder, knowing this type as I did, for had I not made him ridiculous in the eyes of his warriors, beating him at his own game? What king, savage or civilized, could condone such impudence? Seeing his black scowls, I deemed it expedient, especially on Ajor's account, to terminate the interview and continue upon our way; but when I would have done so, Al-tan detained us with a gesture, and his warriors pressed around us.

"What is the meaning of this?" I demanded, and before Al-tan could reply, Chal-az raised his voice in our behalf.

"Is this the gratitude of a Kro-lu chieftain, Al-tan," he asked, "to one who has served you by saving one of your warriors from the enemy—saving him from the death dance of the Band-lu?"

Al-tan was silent for a moment, and then his brow cleared, and the faint imitation of a pleasant expression struggled for existence as he said: "The stranger will not be harmed. I wished only to detain him that he may be feasted tonight in the village of Al-tan the Kro-lu. In the morning he may go his way. Al-tan will not hinder him."

I was not entirely reassured; but I wanted to see the interior of the Kro-lu village, and anyway I knew that if Al-tan intended treachery I would be no more in his power in the morning than I now was—in fact, during the night I might find opportunity to escape with Ajor, while at the instant neither of us could hope to escape unscathed from the encircling warriors. Therefore, in order to disarm him of any thought that I might entertain suspicion as to his sincerity, I promptly and courteously accepted his invitation. His satisfaction was evident, and as we set off toward his village, he walked beside me, asking many questions as to the country from which I came, its peoples and their customs. He seemed much mystified by the fact that we could walk abroad by day or night without fear of being devoured by wild beasts or savage reptiles, and when I told him of the great armies which we maintained, his simple mind could not grasp the fact that they existed solely for the slaughtering of human beings.

"I am glad," he said, "that I do not dwell in your country among such savage peoples. Here, in Caspak, men fight with men when they meet—men of different races—but their weapons are first for the slaying of beasts in the chase and in defense. We do not fashion weapons solely for the killing of man as do your peoples. Your country must indeed be a savage country, from which you are fortunate to have escaped to the peace and security of Caspak."

Here was a new and refreshing viewpoint; nor could I take exception to it after what I had told Al-tan of the great war which had been raging in Europe for over two years before I left home.

On the march to the Kro-lu village we were continually stalked by innumerable beasts of prey, and three times we were attacked by frightful creatures; but Al-tan took it all as a matter of course, rushing forward with raised spear or sending a heavy shaft into the body of the attacker and then returning to our conversation as though no interruption had occurred. Twice were members of his band mauled, and one was killed by a huge and bellicose rhinoceros; but the instant the action was over, it was as though it never had occurred. The dead man was stripped of his belongings and left where he had died; the carnivora would take care of his burial. The trophies that these Kro-lu left to the meat-eaters would have turned an English big-game hunter green with envy. They did, it is true, cut all the edible parts from the rhino and carry them home; but already they were pretty well weighted down with the spoils of the chase, and only the fact that they are particularly fond of rhino-meat caused them to do so.

They left the hide on the pieces they selected, as they use it for sandals, shield-covers, the hilts of their knives and various other purposes where tough hide is desirable. I was much interested in their shields, especially after I saw one used in defense against the attack of a saber-tooth tiger. The huge creature had charged us without warning from a clump of dense bushes where it was lying up after eating. It was met with an avalanche of spears, some of which passed entirely through its body, with such force were they hurled. The charge was from a very short distance, requiring the use of the spear rather than the bow and arrow; but after the launching of the spears, the men not directly in the path of the charge sent bolt after bolt into the great carcass with almost incredible rapidity. The beast, screaming with pain and rage, bore down upon Chal-az while I stood helpless with my rifle for fear of hitting one of the warriors who were closing in upon it. But Chal-az was ready. Throwing aside his bow, he crouched behind his large oval shield, in the center of which was a hole about six inches in diameter. The shield was held by tight loops to his left arm, while in his right hand he grasped his heavy knife. Bristling with spears and arrows, the great cat hurled itself upon the shield, and down went Chal-az upon his back with the shield entirely covering him. The tiger clawed and bit at the heavy rhinoceros hide with which the shield was faced, while Chal-az, through the round hole in the shield's center, plunged his blade repeatedly into the vitals of the savage animal. Doubtless the battle would have gone to Chal-az even though I had not interfered; but the moment that I saw a clean opening, with no Kro-lu beyond, I raised my rifle and killed the beast.

When Chal-az arose, he glanced at the sky and remarked that it looked like rain. The others already had resumed the march toward the village. The incident was closed. For some unaccountable reason the whole thing reminded me of a friend who once shot a cat in his backyard. For three weeks he talked of nothing else.

It was almost dark when we reached the village—a large palisaded enclosure of several hundred leaf-thatched huts set in groups of from two to seven. The huts were hexagonal in form, and where grouped were joined so that they resembled the cells of a bee-hive. One hut meant a warrior and his mate, and each additional hut in a group indicated an additional female. The palisade which surrounded the village was of logs set close together and woven into a solid wall with tough creepers which were planted at their base and trained to weave in and out to bind the logs together. The logs slanted outward at an angle of about thirty degrees, in which position they were held by shorter logs embedded in the ground at right angles to them and with their upper ends supporting the longer pieces a trifle above their centers of equilibrium. Along the top of the palisade sharpened stakes had been driven at all sorts of angles.

The only opening into the inclosure was through a small aperture three feet wide and three feet high, which was closed from the inside by logs about six feet long laid horizontally, one upon another, between the inside face of the palisade and two other braced logs which paralleled the face of the wall upon the inside.

As we entered the village, we were greeted by a not unfriendly crowd of curious warriors and women, to whom Chal-az generously explained the service we had rendered him, whereupon they showered us with the most well-meant attentions, for Chal-az, it seemed, was a most popular member of the tribe. Necklaces of lion and tiger-teeth, bits of dried meat, finely tanned hides and earthen pots, beautifully decorated, they thrust upon us until we were loaded down, and all the while Al-tan glared balefully upon us, seemingly jealous of the attentions heaped upon us because we had served Chal-az.

At last we reached a hut that they set apart for us, and there we cooked our meat and some vegetables the women brought us, and had milk from cows—the first I had had in Caspak—and cheese from the milk of wild goats, with honey and thin bread made from wheat flour of their own grinding, and grapes and the fermented juice of grapes. It was quite the most wonderful meal I had eaten since I quit the *Toreador* and Bowen J. Tyler's colored chef, who could make pork-chops taste like chicken, and chicken taste like heaven.

6

fter dinner I rolled a cigaret and stretched myself at ease upon a pile of furs before the doorway, with Ajor's head pillowed in my lap and a feeling of great content pervading me. It was the first time since my plane had topped the barrier-cliffs of Caspak that I had felt any sense of peace or security. My hand wandered to the velvet cheek of the girl I had claimed as mine, and to her luxuriant hair and the golden fillet which bound it close to her shapely head. Her slender fingers groping upward sought mine and drew them to her lips, and then I gathered her in my arms and crushed her to me, smothering her mouth with a long, long kiss. It was the first time that passion had tinged my intercourse with Ajor. We were alone, and the hut was ours until morning.

But now from beyond the palisade in the direction of the main gate came the hallooing of men and the answering calls and queries of the guard. We listened. Returning hunters, no doubt. We heard them enter the village amidst the barking dogs. I have forgotten to mention the dogs of Kro-lu. The village swarmed with them, gaunt, wolflike creatures that guarded the herd by day when it grazed without the palisade, ten dogs to a cow. By night the cows were herded in an outer inclosure roofed against the onslaughts of the carnivorous cats; and the dogs, with the exception of a few, were brought into the village; these few well-tested brutes remained with the herd. During the day they fed plentifully upon the beasts of prey which they killed in protection of the herd, so that their keep amounted to nothing at all.

Part II: The People That Time Forgot

Shortly after the commotion at the gate had subsided, Ajor and I arose to enter the hut, and at the same time a warrior appeared from one of the twisted alleys which, lying between the irregularly placed huts and groups of huts, form the streets of the Kro-lu village. The fellow halted before us and addressed me, saying that Al-tan desired my presence at his hut. The wording of the invitation and the manner of the messenger threw me entirely off my guard, so cordial was the one and respectful the other, and the result was that I went willingly, telling Ajor that I would return presently. I had laid my arms and ammunition aside as soon as we had taken over the hut, and I left them with Ajor now, as I had noticed that aside from their hunting-knives the men of Kro-lu bore no weapons about the village streets. There was an atmosphere of peace and security within that village that I had not hoped to experience within Caspak, and after what I had passed through, it must have cast a numbing spell over my faculties of judgment and reason. I had eaten of the lotus-flower of safety; dangers no longer threatened for they had ceased to be.

The messenger led me through the labyrinthine alleys to an open plaza near the center of the village. At one end of this plaza was a long hut, much the largest that I had yet seen, before the door of which were many warriors. I could see that the interior was lighted and that a great number of men were gathered within. The dogs about the plaza were as thick as fleas, and those I approached closely evinced a strong desire to devour me, their noses evidently apprising them of the fact that I was of an alien race, since they paid no attention whatever to my companion. Once inside the council-hut, for such it appeared to be, I found a large concourse of warriors seated, or rather squatted, around the floor. At one end of the oval space which the warriors left down the center of the room stood Al-tan and another warrior whom I immediately recognized as a Galu, and then I saw that there were many Galus present. About the walls were a number of flaming torches stuck in holes in a clay plaster which evidently

189

served the purpose of preventing the inflammable wood and grasses of which the hut was composed from being ignited by the flames. Lying about among the warriors or wandering restlessly to and fro were a number of savage dogs.

The warriors eyed me curiously as I entered, especially the Galus, and then I was conducted into the center of the group and led forward toward Al-tan. As I advanced I felt one of the dogs sniffing at my heels, and of a sudden a great brute leaped upon my back. As I turned to thrust it aside before its fangs found a hold upon me, I beheld a huge Airedale leaping frantically about me. The grinning jaws, the half-closed eyes, the back-laid ears spoke to me louder than might the words of man that here was no savage enemy but a joyous friend, and then I recognized him, and fell to one knee and put my arms about his neck while he whined and cried with joy. It was Nobs, dear old Nobs. Bowen Tyler's Nobs, who had loved me next to his master.

"Where is the master of this dog?" I asked, turning toward Al-tan.

The chieftain inclined his head toward the Galu standing at his side. "He belongs to Du-seen the Galu," he replied.

"He belongs to Bowen J. Tyler, Jr., of Santa Monica," I retorted, "and I want to know where his master is."

The Galu shrugged. "The dog is mine," he said. "He came to me cor-sva-jo, and he is unlike any dog in Caspak, being kind and docile and yet a killer when aroused. I would not part with him. I do not know the man of whom you speak."

So this was Du-seen! This was the man from whom Ajor had fled. I wondered if he knew that she was here. I wondered if they had sent for me because of her; but after they had commenced to question me, my mind was relieved; they did not mention Ajor. Their interest seemed centered upon the strange world from which I had come, my journey to Caspak and my intentions now that I had arrived. I answered them frankly as I had nothing to conceal and assured them that my only wish was to find my friends and return to my own country. In the Galu Du-seen and his warriors I saw something of the explanation of the term "golden race" which is applied to them, for their ornaments and weapons were either wholly of beaten gold or heavily decorated with the precious metal. They were a very imposing set of men—tall and straight and handsome. About their heads were bands of gold like that which Ajor wore, and from their left shoulders depended the leopard-tails of the Galus. In addition to the deer-skin tunic which constituted the major portion of their apparel, each carried a light blanket of barbaric yet beautiful design—the first evidence of weaving I had seen in Caspak. Ajor had had no blanket, having lost it during her flight from the attentions of Du-seen; nor was she so heavily incrusted with gold as these male members of her tribe.

The audience must have lasted fully an hour when Al-tan signified that I might return to my hut. All the time Nobs had lain quietly at my feet; but the instant that I turned to leave, he was up and after me. Du-seen called to him; but the terrier never even so much as looked in his direction. I had almost reached the doorway leading from the council-hall when Al-tan rose and called after me. "Stop!" he shouted. "Stop, stranger! The beast of Du-seen the Galu follows you."

"The dog is not Du-seen's," I replied. "He belongs to my friend, as I told you, and he prefers to stay with me until his master is found." And I turned again to resume my way. I had taken but a few steps when I heard a commotion behind me, and at the same moment a man leaned close and whispered "*Kazar!*" close to my ear—*kazar*, the Caspakian equivalent of *beware*. It was To-mar. As he spoke, he turned quickly away as though loath to have others see that he knew me, and at the same instant I wheeled to discover Du-seen striding rapidly after me. Al-tan followed him, and it was evident that both were angry.

Du-seen, a weapon half drawn, approached truculently. "The beast is mine," he reiterated. "Would you steal him?"

"He is not yours nor mine," I replied, "and I am not stealing him. If he wishes to follow you, he may; I will not interfere; but if he wishes to follow me, he shall; nor shall you prevent." I turned to Al-tan. "Is not that fair?" I demanded. "Let the dog choose his master."

Du-seen, without waiting for Al-tan's reply, reached for Nobs and grasped him by the scruff of the neck. I did not interfere, for I guessed what would happen; and it did. With a savage growl Nobs turned like lightning upon the Galu, wrenched loose from his hold and leaped for his throat. The man stepped back and warded off the first attack with a heavy blow of his fist, immediately drawing his knife with which to meet the Airedale's return. And Nobs would have returned, all right, had not I spoken to him. In a low voice I called him to heel. For just an instant he hesitated, standing there trembling and with bared fangs, glaring at his foe; but he was well trained and had been out with me quite as much as he had with Bowen—in fact, I had had most to do with his early training; then he walked slowly and very stiff-legged to his place behind me.

Du-seen, red with rage, would have had it out with the two of us had not Al-tan drawn him to one side and whispered in his ear—upon which, with a grunt, the Galu walked straight back to the opposite end of the hall, while Nobs and I continued upon our way toward the hut and Ajor. As we passed out into the village plaza, I saw Chal-az—we were so close to one another that I could have reached out and touched him—and our eyes met; but though I greeted him pleasantly and paused to speak to him, he brushed past me without a sign of recognition. I was puzzled at his behavior, and then I recalled that To-mar, though he had warned me, had appeared not to wish to seem friendly with me. I could not understand their attitude, and was trying to puzzle out some sort of explanation, when the matter was suddenly driven from my mind by the report of a firearm. Instantly

I broke into a run, my brain in a whirl of forebodings, for the only firearms in the Kro-lu country were those I had left in the hut with Ajor.

That she was in danger I could not but fear, as she was now something of an adept in the handling of both the pistol and rifle, a fact which largely eliminated the chance that the shot had come from an accidentally discharged firearm. When I left the hut, I had felt that she and I were safe among friends; no thought of danger was in my mind; but since my audience with Al-tan, the presence and bearing of Du-seen and the strange attitude of both To-mar and Chal-az had each contributed toward arousing my suspicions, and now I ran along the narrow, winding alleys of the Kro-lu village with my heart fairly in my mouth.

I am endowed with an excellent sense of direction, which has been greatly perfected by the years I have spent in the mountains and upon the plains and deserts of my native state, so that it was with little or no difficulty that I found my way back to the hut in which I had left Ajor. As I entered the doorway, I called her name aloud. There was no response. I drew a box of matches from my pocket and struck a light and as the flame flared up, a half-dozen brawny warriors leaped upon me from as many directions; but even in the brief instant that the flare lasted, I saw that Ajor was not within the hut, and that my arms and ammunition had been removed.

As the six men leaped upon me, an angry growl burst from behind them. I had forgotten Nobs. Like a demon of hate he sprang among those Kro-lu fighting-men, tearing, rending, ripping with his long tusks and his mighty jaws. They had me down in an instant, and it goes without saying that the six of them could have kept me there had it not been for Nobs; but while I was struggling to throw them off, Nobs was springing first upon one and then upon another of them until they were so put to it to preserve their hides and their lives from him that they could give me only a small part of their attention. One of them was assiduously attempting to strike me on the head with his stone hatchet; but I caught his arm and at the same time turned over upon my belly, after which it took but an instant to get my feet under me and rise suddenly.

As I did so, I kept a grip upon the man's arm, carrying it over one shoulder. Then I leaned suddenly forward and hurled my antagonist over my head to a hasty fall at the opposite side of the hut. In the dim light of the interior I saw that Nobs had already accounted for one of the others—one who lay very quiet upon the floor—while the four remaining upon their feet were striking at him with knives and hatchets.

Running to one side of the man I had just put out of the fighting, I seized his hatchet and knife, and in another moment was in the thick of the argument. I was no match for these savage warriors with their own weapons and would soon have gone down to ignominious defeat and death had it not been for Nobs, who alone was a match for the four of them. I never saw any creature so quick upon its feet as was that great Airedale, nor such frightful ferocity as he manifested in his attacks. It was as much the latter as the former which contributed to the undoing of our enemies, who, accustomed though they were to the ferocity of terrible creatures, seemed awed by the sight of this strange beast from another world battling at the side of his equally strange master. Yet they were no cowards, and only by teamwork did Nobs and I overcome them at last. We would rush for a man, simultaneously, and as Nobs leaped for him upon one side, I would strike at his head with the stone hatchet from the other.

As the last man went down, I heard the running of many feet approaching us from the direction of the plaza. To be captured now would mean death; yet I could not attempt to leave the village without first ascertaining the whereabouts of Ajor and releasing her if she were held a captive. That I could escape the village I was not at all sure; but of one thing I was positive; that it would do neither Ajor nor myself any service to remain where I was and be captured; so with Nobs, bloody but happy, following at heel, I turned down the first alley and slunk away in the direction of the northern end of the village.

Friendless and alone, hunted through the dark labyrinths of this savage community, I seldom have felt more helpless than at that moment; yet far transcending any fear which I may have felt for my own safety was my concern for that of Ajor. What fate had befallen her? Where was she, and in whose power? That I should live to learn the answers to these queries I doubted; but that I should face death gladly in the attempt—of that I was certain. And why? With all my concern for the welfare of my friends who had accompanied me to Caprona, and of my best friend of all, Bowen J. Tyler, Jr., I never yet had experienced the almost paralyzing fear for the safety of any other creature which now threw me alternately into a fever of despair and into a cold sweat of apprehension as my mind dwelt upon the fate on one bit of half-savage femininity of whose very existence even I had not dreamed a few short weeks before.

What was this hold she had upon me? Was I bewitched, that my mind refused to function sanely, and that judgment and reason were dethroned by some mad sentiment which I steadfastly refused to believe was love? I had never been in love. I was not in love now— the very thought was preposterous. How could I, Thomas Billings, the right-hand man of the late Bowen J. Tyler, Sr., one of America's foremost captains of industry and the greatest man in California, be in love with a—a—the word stuck in my throat; yet by my own American standards Ajor could be nothing else; at home, for all her beauty, for all her delicately tinted skin, little Ajor by her apparel, by the habits and customs and manners of her people, by her life, would have been classed a *squaw*. Tom Billings in love with a squaw! I shuddered at the thought.

And then there came to my mind, in a sudden, brilliant flash upon the screen of recollection the picture of Ajor as I had last seen her, and I lived again the delicious moment in which we had clung to one another, lips smothering lips, as I left her to go to the council hall of Al-tan; and I could have kicked myself for the snob and the cad that my thoughts had proven me—me, who had always prided myself that I was neither the one nor the other!

These things ran through my mind as Nobs and I made our way through the dark village, the voices and footsteps of those who sought us still in our ears. These and many other things, nor could I escape the incontrovertible fact that the little figure round which my recollections and my hopes entwined themselves was that of Ajor—beloved barbarian! My reveries were broken in upon by a hoarse whisper from the black interior of a hut past which we were making our way. My name was called in a low voice, and a man stepped out beside me as I halted with raised knife. It was Chal-az.

"Quick!" he warned. "In here! It is my hut, and they will not search it."

I hesitated, recalled his attitude of a few minutes before; and as though he had read my thoughts, he said quickly: "I could not speak to you in the plaza without danger of arousing suspicions which would prevent me aiding you later, for word had gone out that Al-tan had turned against you and would destroy you—this was after Du-seen the Galu arrived."

I followed him into the hut, and with Nobs at our heels we passed through several chambers into a remote and windowless apartment where a small lamp sputtered in its unequal battle with the inky darkness. A hole in the roof permitted the smoke from burning oil egress; yet the atmosphere was far from lucid. Here Chal-az motioned me to a seat upon a furry hide spread upon the earthen floor.

"I am your friend," he said. "You saved my life; and I am no ingrate as is the *batu* Al-tan. I will serve you, and there are others here who will serve you against Al-tan and this renegade Galu, Du-seen."

"But where is Ajor?" I asked, for I cared little for my own safety while she was in danger.

"Ajor is safe, too," he answered. "We learned the designs of Al-tan and Du-seen. The latter, learning that Ajor was here, demanded her; and Al-tan promised that he should have her; but when the warriors went to get her, To-mar went with them. Ajor tried to defend herself. She killed one of the warriors, and then To-mar picked her up in his arms when the others had taken her weapons from her. He told the others to look after the wounded man, who was really already dead, and to seize you upon your return, and that he, To-mar, would bear Ajor to Al-tan; but instead of bearing her to Al-tan, he took her to his own hut, where she now is with So-al, To-mar's she. It all happened very quickly. To-mar and I were in the council-hut when Du-seen attempted to take the dog from you. I was seeking To-mar for this work. He ran out immediately and accompanied the warriors to your hut while I remained to watch what went on within the council-hut and to aid you if you needed aid. What has happened since you know."

I thanked him for his loyalty and then asked him to take me to Ajor; but he said that it could not be done, as the village streets were filled with searchers. In fact, we could hear them passing to and fro among the huts, making inquiries, and at last Chal-az thought it best to go to the doorway of his dwelling, which consisted of many huts joined together, lest they enter and search.

Chal-az was absent for a long time—several hours which seemed an eternity to me. All sounds of pursuit had long since ceased, and I was becoming uneasy because of his protracted absence when I heard him returning through the other apartments of his dwelling. He was perturbed when he entered that in which I awaited him, and I saw a worried expression upon his face.

"What is wrong?" I asked. "Have they found Ajor?"

"No," he replied; "but Ajor has gone. She learned that you had escaped them and was told that you had left the village, believing that she had escaped too. So-al could not detain her. She made her way out over the top of the palisade, armed with only her knife."

"Then I must go," I said, rising. Nobs rose and shook himself. He had been dead asleep when I spoke.

"Yes," agreed Chal-az, "you must go at once. It is almost dawn. Du-seen leaves at daylight to search for her." He leaned close to my ear and whispered: "There are many to follow and help you. Al-tan has agreed to aid Du-seen against the Galus of Jor; but there are many of us who have combined to rise against Al-tan and prevent this ruthless desecration of the laws and customs of the Kro-lu and of Caspak. We will rise as Luata has ordained that we shall rise, and only thus. No *batu* may win to the estate of a Galu by treachery and force of arms while Chal-az lives and may wield a heavy blow and a sharp spear with true Kro-lus at his back!"

"I hope that I may live to aid you," I replied. "If I had my weapons and my ammunition, I could do much. Do you know where they are?" "No," he said, "they have disappeared." And then: "Wait! You cannot go forth half armed, and garbed as you are. You are going into the Galu country, and you must go as a Galu. Come!" And without waiting for a reply, he led me into another apartment, or to be more explicit, another of the several huts which formed his cellular dwelling.

Here was a pile of skins, weapons, and ornaments. "Remove your strange apparel," said Chal-az, "and I will fit you out as a true Galu. I have slain several of them in the raids of my early days as a Kro-lu, and here are their trappings."

I saw the wisdom of his suggestion, and as my clothes were by now so ragged as to but half conceal my nakedness, I had no regrets in laying them aside. Stripped to the skin, I donned the red-deerskin tunic, the leopard-tail, the golden fillet, armlets and leg-ornaments of a Galu, with the belt, scabbard and knife, the shield, spear, bow and arrow and the long rope which I learned now for the first time is the distinctive weapon of the Galu warrior. It is a rawhide rope, not dissimilar to those of the Western plains and cow-camps of my youth. The *honda* is a golden oval and accurate weight for the throwing of the noose. This heavy *honda*, Chal-az explained, is used as a weapon, being thrown with great force and accuracy at an enemy and then coiled in for another cast. In hunting and in battle, they use both the noose and the *honda*. If several warriors surround a single foeman or quarry, they rope it with the noose from several sides; but a single warrior against a lone antagonist will attempt to brain his foe with the metal oval.

I could not have been more pleased with any weapon, short of a rifle, which he could have found for me, since I have been adept with the rope from early childhood; but I must confess that I was less favorably inclined toward my apparel. In so far as the sensation was concerned, I might as well have been entirely naked, so short and light was the tunic. When I asked Chal-az for the Caspakian name for rope, he told me *ga*, and for the first time I understood the derivation of the word *Galu*, which means ropeman.

Entirely outfitted I would not have known myself, so strange was my garb and my armament. Upon my back were slung my bow, arrows, shield, and short spear; from the center of my girdle depended my knife; at my right hip was my stone hatchet; and at my left hung the coils of my long rope. By reaching my right hand over my left shoulder, I could seize the spear or arrows; my left hand could find my bow over my right shoulder, while a veritable contortionist-act was necessary to place my shield in front of me and upon my left arm. The shield, long and oval, is utilized more as back-armor than as a defense against frontal attack, for the close-set armlets of gold upon the left forearm are principally depended upon to ward off knife, spear, hatchet, or arrow from in front; but against the greater carnivora and the attacks of several human antagonists, the shield is utilized to its best advantage and carried by loops upon the left arm.

Fully equipped, except for a blanket, I followed Chal-az from his domicile into the dark and deserted alleys of Kro-lu. Silently we crept along, Nobs silent at heel, toward the nearest portion of the palisade. Here Chal-az bade me farewell, telling me that he hoped to see me soon among the Galus, as he felt that "the call soon would come" to him. I thanked him for his loyal assistance and promised that whether I reached the Galu country or not, I should always stand ready to repay his kindness to me, and that he could count on me in the revolution against Al-tan.

7

o run up the inclined surface of the palisade and drop to the ground outside was the work of but a moment, or would have been but for Nobs. I had to put my rope about him after we reached the top, lift him over the sharpened stakes and lower him upon the outside. To find Ajor in the unknown country to the north seemed rather hopeless; yet I could do no less than try, praying in the meanwhile that she would come through unscathed and in safety to her father.

As Nobs and I swung along in the growing light of the coming day, I was impressed by the lessening numbers of savage beasts the farther north I traveled. With the decrease among the carnivora, the herbivora increased in quantity, though anywhere in Caspak they are sufficiently plentiful to furnish ample food for the meat-eaters of each locality. The wild cattle, antelope, deer, and horses I passed showed changes in evolution from their cousins farther south. The kine were smaller and less shaggy, the horses larger. North of the Kro-lu village I saw a small band of the latter of about the size of those of our old Western plains—such as the Indians bred in former days and to a lesser extent even now. They were fat and sleek, and I looked upon them with covetous eyes and with thoughts that any old cow-puncher may well imagine I might entertain after having hoofed it for weeks; but they were wary, scarce permitting me to approach within bow-and-arrow range, much less within roping-distance; yet I still had hopes which I never discarded.

Twice before noon we were stalked and charged by man-eaters; but even though I was without firearms, I still had ample protection in Nobs, who evidently had learned something of Caspakian hunt rules under the tutelage of Du-seen or some other Galu, and of course a great deal more by experience. He always was on the alert for dangerous foes, invariably warning me by low growls of the approach of a large carnivorous animal long before I could either see or hear it, and then when the thing appeared, he would run snapping at its heels, drawing the charge away from me until I found safety in some tree; yet never did the wily Nobs take an unnecessary chance of a mauling. He would dart in and away so quickly that not even the lightning-like movements of the great cats could reach him. I have seen him tantalize them thus until they fairly screamed in rage.

The greatest inconvenience the hunters caused me was the delay, for they have a nasty habit of keeping one treed for an hour or more if balked in their designs; but at last we came in sight of a line of cliffs running east and west across our path as far as the eye could see in either direction, and I knew that we reached the natural boundary which marks the line between the Kro-lu and Galu countries. The southern face of these cliffs loomed high and forbidding, rising to an altitude of some two hundred feet, sheer and precipitous, without a break that the eye could perceive. How I was to find a crossing I could not guess. Whether to search to the east toward the still loftier barrier-cliffs fronting upon the ocean, or westward in the direction of the inland sea was a question which baffled me. Were there many passes or only one? I had no way of knowing. I could but trust to chance. It never occurred to me that Nobs had made the crossing at least once, possibly a greater number of times, and that he might lead me to the pass; and so it was with no idea of assistance that I appealed to him as a man alone with a dumb brute so often does.

"Nobs," I said, "how the devil are we going to cross those cliffs?"

I do not say that he understood me, even though I realize that an

Airedale is a mighty intelligent dog; but I do swear that he seemed to understand me, for he wheeled about, barking joyously and trotted off toward the west; and when I didn't follow him, he ran back to me barking furiously, and at last taking hold of the calf of my leg in an effort to pull me along in the direction he wished me to go. Now, as my legs were naked and Nobs' jaws are much more powerful than he realizes, I gave in and followed him, for I knew that I might as well go west as east, as far as any knowledge I had of the correct direction went.

We followed the base of the cliffs for a considerable distance. The ground was rolling and tree-dotted and covered with grazing animals, alone, in pairs and in herds—a motley aggregation of the modern and extinct herbivore of the world. A huge woolly mastodon stood swaying to and fro in the shade of a giant fern—a mighty bull with enormous upcurving tusks. Near him grazed an aurochs bull with a cow and a calf, close beside a lone rhinoceros asleep in a dust-hole. Deer, antelope, bison, horses, sheep, and goats were all in sight at the same time, and at a little distance a great megatherium reared up on its huge tail and massive hind feet to tear the leaves from a tall tree. The forgotten past rubbed flanks with the present—while Tom Billings, modern of the moderns, passed in the garb of pre-Glacial man, and before him trotted a creature of a breed scarce sixty years old. Nobs was a parvenu; but it failed to worry him.

As we neared the inland sea we saw more flying reptiles and several great amphibians, but none of them attacked us. As we were topping a rise in the middle of the afternoon, I saw something that brought me to a sudden stop. Calling Nobs in a whisper, I cautioned him to silence and kept him at heel while I threw myself flat and watched, from behind a sheltering shrub, a body of warriors approaching the cliff from the south. I could see that they were Galus, and I guessed that Du-seen led them. They had taken a shorter route to the pass and so had overhauled me. I could see them plainly, for they were no great distance away, and saw with relief that Ajor was not with them.

The cliffs before them were broken and ragged, those coming from the east overlapping the cliffs from the west. Into the defile formed by this overlapping the party filed. I could see them climbing upward for a few minutes, and then they disappeared from view. When the last of them had passed from sight, I rose and bent my steps in the direction of the pass—the same pass toward which Nobs had evidently been leading me. I went warily as I approached it, for fear the party might have halted to rest. If they hadn't halted, I had no fear of being discovered, for I had seen that the Galus marched without point, flankers or rear guard; and when I reached the pass and saw a narrow, one-man trail leading upward at a stiff angle, I wished that I were chief of the Galus for a few weeks. A dozen men could hold off forever in that narrow pass all the hordes which might be brought up from the south; yet there it lay entirely unguarded.

The Galus might be a great people in Caspak; but they were pitifully inefficient in even the simpler forms of military tactics. I was surprised that even a man of the Stone Age should be so lacking in military perspicacity. Du-seen dropped far below par in my estimation as I saw the slovenly formation of his troop as it passed through an enemy country and entered the domain of the chief against whom he had risen in revolt; but Du-seen must have known Jor the chief and known that Jor would not be waiting for him at the pass. Nevertheless he took unwarranted chances. With one squad of a home-guard company I could have conquered Caspak.

Nobs and I followed to the summit of the pass, and there we saw the party defiling into the Galu country, the level of which was not, on an average, over fifty feet below the summit of the cliffs and about a hundred and fifty feet above the adjacent Kro-lu domain. Immediately the landscape changed. The trees, the flowers and the shrubs were of a hardier type, and I realized that at night the Galu blanket might be almost a necessity. Acacia and eucalyptus predominated among the trees; yet there were ash and oak and even pine and fir and hemlock. The tree-life was riotous. The forests were dense and peopled by enormous trees. From the summit of the cliff I could see forests rising hundreds of feet above the level upon which I stood, and even at the distance they were from me I realized that the boles were of gigantic size.

At last I had come to the Galu country. Though not conceived in Caspak, I had indeed come up *cor-sva jo*—from the beginning I had come up through the hideous horrors of the lower Caspakian spheres of evolution, and I could not but feel something of the elation and pride which had filled To-mar and So-al when they realized that the call had come to them and they were about to rise from the estate of Band-lus to that of Kro-lus. I was glad that I was not *batu*.

But where was Ajor? Though my eyes searched the wide land-scape before me, I saw nothing other than the warriors of Du-seen and the beasts of the fields and the forests. Surrounded by forests, I could see wide plains dotting the country as far as the eye could reach; but nowhere was a sign of a small Galu she—the beloved she whom I would have given my right hand to see.

Nobs and I were hungry; we had not eaten since the preceding night, and below us was game—deer, sheep, anything that a hungry hunter might crave; so down the steep trail we made our way, and then upon my belly with Nobs crouching low behind me, I crawled toward a small herd of red deer feeding at the edge of a plain close beside a forest. There was ample cover, what with solitary trees and dotting bushes so that I found no difficulty in stalking up wind to within fifty feet of my quarry—a large, sleek doe unaccompanied by a fawn. Greatly then did I regret my rifle. Never in my life had I shot an arrow, but I knew how it was done, and fitting the shaft to my string, I aimed carefully and let drive. At the same instant I called to Nobs and leaped to my feet.

The arrow caught the doe full in the side, and in the same

moment Nobs was after her. She turned to flee with the two of us pursuing her, Nobs with his great fangs bared and I with my short spear poised for a cast. The balance of the herd sprang quickly away; but the hurt doe lagged, and in a moment Nobs was beside her and had leaped at her throat. He had her down when I came up, and I finished her with my spear. It didn't take me long to have a fire going and a steak broiling, and while I was preparing for my own feast, Nobs was filling himself with raw venison. Never have I enjoyed a meal so heartily.

For two days I searched fruitlessly back and forth from the inland sea almost to the barrier cliffs for some trace of Ajor, and always I trended northward; but I saw no sign of any human being, not even the band of Galu warriors under Du-seen; and then I commenced to have misgivings. Had Chal-az spoken the truth to me when he said that Ajor had quit the village of the Kro-lu? Might he not have been acting upon the orders of Al-tan, in whose savage bosom might have lurked some small spark of shame that he had attempted to do to death one who had befriended a Kro-lu warrior—a guest who had brought no harm upon the Kro-lu race—and thus have sent me out upon a fruitless mission in the hope that the wild beasts would do what Al-tan hesitated to do? I did not know; but the more I thought upon it, the more convinced I became that Ajor had not quitted the Kro-lu village; but if not, what had brought Du-seen forth without her? There was a puzzler, and once again I was all at sea.

On the second day of my experience of the Galu country I came upon a bunch of as magnificent horses as it has ever been my lot to see. They were dark bays with blazed faces and perfect surcingles of white about their barrels. Their forelegs were white to the knees. In height they stood almost sixteen hands, the mares being a trifle smaller than the stallions, of which there were three or four in this band of a hundred, which comprised many colts and half-grown horses. Their markings were almost identical, indicating a purity of strain that might have persisted since long ages ago. If I had coveted one of the little ponies of the Kro-lu country, imagine my state of mind when I came upon these magnificent creatures! No sooner had I espied them than I determined to possess one of them; nor did it take me long to select a beautiful young stallion—a four-year-old, I guessed him.

The horses were grazing close to the edge of the forest in which Nobs and I were concealed, while the ground between us and them was dotted with clumps of flowering brush which offered perfect concealment. The stallion of my choice grazed with a filly and two yearlings a little apart from the balance of the herd and nearest to the forest and to me. At my whispered "Charge!" Nobs flattened himself to the ground, and I knew that he would not again move until I called him, unless danger threatened me from the rear. Carefully I crept forward toward my unsuspecting quarry, coming undetected to the concealment of a bush not more than twenty feet from him. Here I quietly arranged my noose, spreading it flat and open upon the ground.

To step to one side of the bush and throw directly from the ground, which is the style I am best in, would take but an instant, and in that instant the stallion would doubtless be under way at top speed in the opposite direction. Then he would have to wheel about when I surprised him, and in doing so, he would most certainly rise slightly upon his hind feet and throw up his head, presenting a perfect target for my noose as he pivoted.

Yes, I had it beautifully worked out, and I waited until he should turn in my direction. At last it became evident that he was doing so, when apparently without cause, the filly raised her head, neighed and started off at a trot in the opposite direction, immediately followed, of course, by the colts and my stallion. It looked for a moment as though my last hope was blasted; but presently their fright, if fright it was, passed, and they resumed grazing again a hundred yards farther on. This time there was no bush within fifty feet of them, and I was at a loss as to how to get within safe roping-distance. Anywhere under forty feet I am an excellent roper, at fifty feet I am fair; but over that I knew it would be a matter of luck if I succeeded in getting my noose about that beautiful arched neck.

As I stood debating the question in my mind, I was almost upon the point of making the attempt at the long throw. I had plenty of rope, this Galu weapon being fully sixty feet long. How I wished for the collies from the ranch! At a word they would have circled this little bunch and driven it straight down to me; and then it flashed into my mind that Nobs had run with those collies all one summer, that he had gone down to the pasture with them after the cows every evening and done his part in driving them back to the milking-barn, and had done it intelligently; but Nobs had never done the thing alone, and it had been a year since he had done it at all. However, the chances were more in favor of my foozling the long throw than that Nobs would fall down in his part if I gave him the chance.

Having come to a decision, I had to creep back to Nobs and get him, and then with him at my heels return to a large bush near the four horses. Here we could see directly through the bush, and pointing the animals out to Nobs I whispered: "Fetch 'em, boy!"

In an instant he was gone, circling wide toward the rear of the quarry. They caught sight of him almost immediately and broke into a trot away from him; but when they saw that he was apparently giving them a wide berth they stopped again, though they stood watching him, with high-held heads and quivering nostrils. It was a beautiful sight. And then Nobs turned in behind them and trotted slowly back toward me. He did not bark, nor come rushing down upon them, and when he had come closer to them, he proceeded at a walk. The splendid creatures seemed more curious than fearful, making no effort to escape until Nobs was quite close to them; then they trotted slowly away, but at right angles.

And now the fun and trouble commenced. Nobs, of course, attempted to turn them, and he seemed to have selected the stallion to work upon, for he paid no attention to the others, having intelligence enough to know that a lone dog could run his legs off before he could round up four horses that didn't wish to be rounded up. The stallion, however, had notions of his own about being headed, and the result was as pretty a race as one would care to see. Gad, how that horse could run! He seemed to flatten out and shoot through the air with the very minimum of exertion, and at his forefoot ran Nobs, doing his best to turn him. He was barking now, and twice he leaped high against the stallion's flank; but this cost too much effort and always lost him ground, as each time he was hurled heels over head by the impact; yet before they disappeared over a rise in the ground I was sure that Nob's persistence was bearing fruit; it seemed to me that the horse was giving way a trifle to the right. Nobs was between him and the main herd, to which the yearling and filly had already fled.

As I stood waiting for Nobs' return, I could not but speculate upon my chances should I be attacked by some formidable beast. I was some distance from the forest and armed with weapons in the use of which I was quite untrained, though I had practiced some with the spear since leaving the Kro-lu country. I must admit that my thoughts were not pleasant ones, verging almost upon cowardice, until I chanced to think of little Ajor alone in this same land and armed only with a knife! I was immediately filled with shame; but in thinking the matter over since, I have come to the conclusion that my state of mind was influenced largely by my approximate nakedness. If you have never wandered about in broad daylight garbed in a bit of red-deer skin in inadequate length, you can have no conception of the sensation of futility that overwhelms one. Clothes, to a man accustomed to wearing clothes, impart a certain self-confidence; lack of them induces panic.

But no beast attacked me, though I saw several menacing forms passing through the dark aisles of the forest. At last I commenced to worry over Nobs' protracted absence and to fear that something had befallen him. I was coiling my rope to start out in search of him, when I saw the stallion leap into view at almost the same spot behind which he had disappeared, and at his heels ran Nobs. Neither was running so fast or furiously as when last I had seen them.

The horse, as he approached me, I could see was laboring hard; yet he kept gamely to his task, and Nobs, too. The splendid fellow was driving the quarry straight toward me. I crouched behind my bush and laid my noose in readiness to throw. As the two approached my hiding-place, Nobs reduced his speed, and the stallion, evidently only too glad of the respite, dropped into a trot. It was at this gait that he passed me; my rope-hand flew forward; the *honda*, well down, held the noose open, and the beautiful bay fairly ran his head into it.

Instantly he wheeled to dash off at right angles. I braced myself with the rope around my hip and brought him to a sudden stand. Rearing and struggling, he fought for his liberty while Nobs, panting and with lolling tongue, came and threw himself down near me. He seemed to know that his work was done and that he had earned his rest. The stallion was pretty well spent, and after a few minutes of struggling he stood with feet far spread, nostrils dilated and eyes wide, watching me as I edged toward him, taking in the slack of the rope as I advanced. A dozen times he reared and tried to break away; but always I spoke soothingly to him and after an hour of effort I succeeded in reaching his head and stroking his muzzle. Then I gathered a handful of grass and offered it to him, and always I talked to him in a quiet and reassuring voice.

I had expected a battle royal; but on the contrary I found his taming a matter of comparative ease. Though wild, he was gentle to a degree, and of such remarkable intelligence that he soon discovered that I had no intention of harming him. After that, all was easy.

Before that day was done, I had taught him to lead and to stand while I stroked his head and flanks, and to eat from my hand, and had the satisfaction of seeing the light of fear die in his large, intelligent eyes.

The following day I fashioned a hackamore from a piece which I cut from the end of my long Galu rope, and then I mounted him fully prepared for a struggle of titanic proportions in which I was none too sure that he would not come off victor; but he never made the slightest effort to unseat me, and from then on his education was rapid. No horse ever learned more quickly the meaning of the rein and the pressure of the knees. I think he soon learned to love me, and I know that I loved him; while he and Nobs were the best of pals. I called him Ace. I had a friend who was once in the French flying-corps, and when Ace let himself out, he certainly flew.

I cannot explain to you, nor can you understand, unless you too are a horseman, the exhilarating feeling of well-being which pervaded me from the moment that I commenced riding Ace. I was a new man, imbued with a sense of superiority that led me to feel that I could go forth and conquer all Caspak single-handed. Now, when I needed meat, I ran it down on Ace and roped it, and when some great beast with which we could not cope threatened us, we galloped away to safety; but for the most part the creatures we met looked upon us in terror, for Ace and I in combination presented a new and unusual beast beyond their experience and ken.

For five days I rode back and forth across the southern end of the Galu country without seeing a human being; yet all the time I was working slowly toward the north, for I had determined to comb the territory thoroughly in search of Ajor; but on the fifth day as I emerged from a forest, I saw some distance ahead of me a single small figure pursued by many others. Instantly I recognized the quarry as Ajor. The entire party was fully a mile away from me, and they were crossing my path at right angles. Ajor a few hundred yards in advance of those who followed her. One of her pursuers was far in advance of the others, and was gaining upon her rapidly. With a word and a pressure of the knees I sent Ace leaping out into the open, and with Nobs running close alongside, we raced toward her.

At first none of them saw us; but as we neared Ajor, the pack behind the foremost pursuer discovered us and set up such a howl as I never before have heard. They were all Galus, and I soon recognized the foremost as Du-seen. He was almost upon Ajor now, and with a sense of terror such as I had never before experienced, I saw that he ran with his knife in his hand, and that his intention was to slay rather than capture. I could not understand it, but I could only urge Ace to greater speed, and most nobly did the wondrous creature respond to my demands. If ever a four-footed creature approximated flying, it was Ace that day.

Du-seen, intent upon his brutal design, had as yet not noticed us. He was within a pace of Ajor when Ace and I dashed between them, and I, leaning down to the left, swept my little barbarian into the hollow of an arm and up on the withers of my glorious Ace. We had snatched her from the very clutches of Du-seen, who halted, mystified and raging. Ajor, too, was mystified, as we had come up from diagonally behind her so that she had no idea that we were near until she was swung to Ace's back. The little savage turned with drawn knife to stab me, thinking that I was some new enemy, when her eyes found my face and she recognized me. With a little sob she threw her arms about my neck, gasping: "My Tom! My Tom!"

And then Ace sank suddenly into thick mud to his belly, and Ajor and I were thrown far over his head. He had run into one of those numerous springs which cover Caspak. Sometimes they are little lakes, again but tiny pools, and often mere quagmires of mud, as was this one overgrown with lush grasses which effectually hid its treacherous identity. It is a wonder that Ace did not break a leg, so fast he was going when he fell; but he didn't, though with four good legs he was unable to wallow from the mire. Ajor and I had sprawled face down in the covering grasses and so had not sunk deeply; but when we tried to rise, we found that there was not footing, and presently we saw that Du-seen and his followers were coming down upon us. There was no escape. It was evident that we were doomed.

"Slay me!" begged Ajor. "Let me die at thy loved hands rather than beneath the knife of this hateful thing, for he will kill me. He has sworn to kill me. Last night he captured me, and when later he would have his way with me, I struck him with my fists and with my knife I stabbed him, and then I escaped, leaving him raging in pain and thwarted desire. Today they searched for me and found me; and as I fled, Du-seen ran after me crying that he would slay me. Kill me, my Tom, and then fall upon thine own spear, for they will kill you horribly if they take you alive."

I couldn't kill her—not at least until the last moment; and I told her so, and that I loved her, and that until death came, I would live and fight for her.

Nobs had followed us into the bog and had done fairly well at first, but when he neared us he too sank to his belly and could only flounder about. We were in this predicament when Du-seen and his followers approached the edge of the horrible swamp. I saw that Al-tan was with him and many other Kro-lu warriors. The alliance against Jor the chief had, therefore, been consummated, and this horde was already marching upon the Galu city. I sighed as I thought how close I had been to saving not only Ajor but her father and his people from defeat and death.

Beyond the swamp was a dense wood. Could we have reached this, we would have been safe; but it might as well have been a hundred miles away as a hundred yards across that hidden lake of sticky mud. Upon the edge of the swamp Du-seen and his horde halted to revile us. They could not reach us with their hands; but at a command from Du-seen they fitted arrows to their bows, and I saw that the end had come. Ajor huddled close to me, and I took her in my arms.

"I love you, Tom," she said, "only you." Tears came to my eyes then, not tears of self-pity for my predicament, but tears from a heart filled with a great love—a heart that sees the sun of its life and its love setting even as it rises.

The renegade Galus and their Kro-lu allies stood waiting for the word from Du-seen that would launch that barbed avalanche of death upon us, when there broke from the wood beyond the swamp the sweetest music that ever fell upon the ears of man—the sharp staccato of at least two score rifles fired rapidly at will. Down went the Galu and Kro-lu warriors like tenpins before that deadly fusillade.

What could it mean? To me it meant but one thing, and that was that Hollis and Short and the others had scaled the cliffs and made their way north to the Galu country upon the opposite side of the island in time to save Ajor and me from almost certain death. I didn't have to have an introduction to them to know that the men who held those rifles were the men of my own party; and when, a few minutes later, they came forth from their concealment, my eyes verified my hopes. There they were, every man-jack of them; and with them were a thousand straight, sleek warriors of the Galu race; and ahead of the others came two men in the garb of Galus. Each was tall and straight and wonderfully muscled; yet they differed as Ace might differ from a perfect specimen of another species. As they approached the mire, Ajor held forth her arms and cried, "Jor, my chief! My father!" and the elder of the two rushed in knee-deep to rescue her, and then the other came close and looked into my face, and his eyes went wide, and mine too, and I cried: "Bowen! For heaven's sake, Bowen Tyler!"

It was he. My search was ended. Around me were all my company and the man we had searched a new world to find. They cut saplings from the forest and laid a road into the swamp before they could get us all out, and then we marched back to the city of Jor the Galu chief, and there was great rejoicing when Ajor came home again mounted upon the glossy back of the stallion Ace.

Tyler and Hollis and Short and all the rest of us Americans nearly worked our jaws loose on the march back to the village, and for days afterward we kept it up. They told me how they had crossed the barrier cliffs in five days, working twenty-four hours a day in three eight-hour shifts with two reliefs to each shift alternating half-hourly. Two men with electric drills driven from the dynamos aboard the *Toreador* drilled two holes four feet apart in the face of the cliff and in the same horizontal plane. The holes slanted slightly downward. Into these holes the iron rods brought as a part of our equipment and for just this purpose were inserted, extending about a foot beyond the face of the rock, across these two rods a plank was laid, and then the next shift, mounting to the new level, bored two more holes five feet above the new platform, and so on.

During the nights the searchlights from the *Toreador* were kept playing upon the cliff at the point where the drills were working, and at the rate of ten feet an hour the summit was reached upon the fifth day. Ropes were lowered, blocks lashed to trees at the top, and crude elevators rigged, so that by the night of the fifth day the entire party, with the exception of the few men needed to man the *Toreador*, were within Caspak with an abundance of arms, ammunition and equipment.

From then on, they fought their way north in search of me, after a vain and perilous effort to enter the hideous reptile-infested country to the south. Owing to the number of guns among them, they had not lost a man; but their path was strewn with the dead creatures they had been forced to slay to win their way to the north end of the island, where they had found Bowen and his bride among the Galus of Jor.

The reunion between Bowen and Nobs was marked by a frantic display upon Nobs' part, which almost stripped Bowen of the scanty attire that the Galu custom had vouchsafed him. When we arrived at the Galu city, Lys La Rue was waiting to welcome us. She was

Mrs. Tyler now, as the master of the *Toreador* had married them the very day that the search-party had found them, though neither Lys nor Bowen would admit that any civil or religious ceremony could have rendered more sacred the bonds with which God had united them.

Neither Bowen nor the party from the *Toreador* had seen any sign of Bradley and his party. They had been so long lost now that any hopes for them must be definitely abandoned. The Galus had heard rumors of them, as had the Western Kro-lu and Band-lu; but none had seen aught of them since they had left Fort Dinosaur months since.

We rested in Jor's village for a fortnight while we prepared for the southward journey to the point where the *Toreador* was to lie off shore in wait for us. During these two weeks Chal-az came up from the Krolu country, now a full-fledged Galu. He told us that the remnants of Al-tan's party had been slain when they attempted to re-enter Kro-lu. Chal-az had been made chief, and when he rose, had left the tribe under a new leader whom all respected.

Nobs stuck close to Bowen; but Ace and Ajor and I went out upon many long rides through the beautiful north Galu country. Chal-az had brought my arms and ammunition up from Kro-lu with him; but my clothes were gone; nor did I miss them once I became accustomed to the free attire of the Galu.

At last came the time for our departure; upon the following morning we were to set out toward the south and the *Toreador* and dear old California. I had asked Ajor to go with us; but Jor her father had refused to listen to the suggestion. No pleas could swerve him from his decision: Ajor, the *cos-ata-lo*, from whom might spring a new and greater Caspakian race, could not be spared. I might have any other she among the Galus; but Ajor—no!

The poor child was heartbroken; and as for me, I was slowly realizing the hold that Ajor had upon my heart and wondered how I should get along without her. As I held her in my arms that last night, I tried to imagine what life would be like without her, for at last there had come to me the realization that I loved her—loved my little barbarian; and as I finally tore myself away and went to my own hut to snatch a few hours' sleep before we set off upon our long journey on the morrow, I consoled myself with the thought that time would heal the wound and that back in my native land I should find a mate who would be all and more to me than little Ajor could ever be—a woman of my own race and my own culture.

Morning came more quickly than I could have wished. I rose and breakfasted, but saw nothing of Ajor. It was best, I thought, that I go thus without the harrowing pangs of a last farewell. The party formed for the march, an escort of Galu warriors ready to accompany us. I could not even bear to go to Ace's corral and bid him farewell. The night before, I had given him to Ajor, and now in my mind the two seemed inseparable.

And so we marched away, down the street flanked with its stone houses and out through the wide gateway in the stone wall which surrounds the city and on across the clearing toward the forest through which we must pass to reach the northern boundary of Galu, beyond which we would turn south. At the edge of the forest I cast a backward glance at the city which held my heart, and beside the massive gateway I saw that which brought me to a sudden halt. It was a little figure leaning against one of the great upright posts upon which the gates swing—a crumpled little figure; and even at this distance I could see its shoulders heave to the sobs that racked it. It was the last straw.

Bowen was near me. "Good-bye old man," I said. "I'm going back."

He looked at me in surprise. "Good-bye, old man," he said, and grasped my hand. "I thought you'd do it in the end."

And then I went back and took Ajor in my arms and kissed the tears from her eyes and a smile to her lips while together we watched the last of the Americans disappear into the forest.

PART III

OUT OF TIME'S ABYSS

The Tale of Bradley

1

his is the tale of Bradley after he left Fort Dinosaur upon the west coast of the great lake that is in the center of the island.

Upon the fourth day of September, 1916, he set out with four companions, Sinclair, Brady, James, and Tippet, to search along the base of the barrier cliffs for a point at which they might be scaled.

Through the heavy Caspakian air, beneath the swollen sun, the five men marched northwest from Fort Dinosaur, now waist-deep in lush, jungle grasses starred with myriad gorgeous blooms, now across open meadow-land and parklike expanses and again plunging into dense forests of eucalyptus and acacia and giant arboreous ferns with feathered fronds waving gently a hundred feet above their heads.

About them upon the ground, among the trees and in the air over them moved and swung and soared the countless forms of Caspak's teeming life. Always were they menaced by some frightful thing and seldom were their rifles cool, yet even in the brief time they had dwelt upon Caprona they had become callous to danger, so that they swung along laughing and chatting like soldiers on a summer hike.

"This reminds me of South Clark Street," remarked Brady, who had once served on the traffic squad in Chicago; and as no one asked him why, he volunteered that it was "because it's no place for an Irishman."

"South Clark Street and heaven have something in common, then," suggested Sinclair. James and Tippet laughed, and then a hideous growl broke from a dense thicket ahead and diverted their attention to other matters.

"One of them behemoths of 'Oly Writ," muttered Tippet as they came to a halt and with guns ready awaited the almost inevitable charge.

"Hungry lot o' beggars, these," said Bradley; "always trying to eat everything they see."

For a moment no further sound came from the thicket. "He may be feeding now," suggested Bradley. "We'll try to go around him. Can't waste ammunition. Won't last forever. Follow me." And he set off at right angles to their former course, hoping to avert a charge. They had taken a dozen steps, perhaps, when the thicket moved to the advance of the thing within it, the leafy branches parted, and the hideous head of a gigantic bear emerged.

"Pick your trees," whispered Bradley. "Can't waste ammunition."

The men looked about them. The bear took a couple of steps forward, still growling menacingly. He was exposed to the shoulders now. Tippet took one look at the monster and bolted for the nearest tree; and then the bear charged. He charged straight for Tippet. The other men scattered for the various trees they had selected—all except Bradley. He stood watching Tippet and the bear. The man had a good start and the tree was not far away; but the speed of the enormous creature behind him was something to marvel at, yet Tippet was in a fair way to make his sanctuary when his foot caught in a tangle of roots and down he went, his rifle flying from his hand and falling several yards away. Instantly Bradley's piece was at his shoulder, there was a sharp report answered by a roar of mingled rage and pain from the carnivore. Tippet attempted to scramble to his feet.

"Lie still!" shouted Bradley. "Can't waste ammunition."

The bear halted in its tracks, wheeled toward Bradley and then back again toward Tippet. Again the former's rifle spit angrily, and the bear turned again in his direction. Bradley shouted loudly. "Come on, you behemoth of Holy Writ!" he cried. "Come on, you duffer! Can't waste ammunition." And as he saw the bear apparently upon the verge of deciding to charge him, he encouraged the idea by backing rapidly away, knowing that an angry beast will more often charge one who moves than one who lies still.

And the bear did charge. Like a bolt of lightning he flashed down upon the Englishman. "Now run!" Bradley called to Tippet and himself turned in flight toward a near-by tree. The other men, now safely ensconced upon various branches, watched the race with breathless interest. Would Bradley make it? It seemed scarce possible. And if he didn't! James gasped at the thought. Six feet at the shoulder stood the frightful mountain of blood-mad flesh and bone and sinew that was bearing down with the speed of an express train upon the seemingly slow-moving man.

It all happened in a few seconds; but they were seconds that seemed like hours to the men who watched. They saw Tippet leap to his feet at Bradley's shouted warning. They saw him run, stooping to recover his rifle as he passed the spot where it had fallen. They saw him glance back toward Bradley, and then they saw him stop short of the tree that might have given him safety and turn back in the direction of the bear. Firing as he ran, Tippet raced after the great cave bear—the monstrous thing that should have been extinct ages before—ran for it and fired even as the beast was almost upon Bradley. The men in the trees scarcely breathed. It seemed to them such a futile thing for Tippet to do, and Tippet of all men! They had never looked upon Tippet as a coward—there seemed to be no cowards among that strangely assorted company that Fate had gathered together from the four corners of the

223

earth—but Tippet was considered a cautious man. Overcautious, some thought him. How futile he and his little pop-gun appeared as he dashed after that living engine of destruction! But, oh, how glorious! It was some such thought as this that ran through Brady's mind, though articulated it might have been expressed otherwise, albeit more forcefully.

Just then it occurred to Brady to fire and he, too, opened upon the bear, but at the same instant the animal stumbled and fell forward, though still growling most fearsomely. Tippet never stopped running or firing until he stood within a foot of the brute, which lay almost touching Bradley and was already struggling to regain its feet. Placing the muzzle of his gun against the bear's ear, Tippet pulled the trigger. The creature sank limply to the ground and Bradley scrambled to his feet.

"Good work, Tippet," he said. "Mightily obliged to you—awful waste of ammunition, really."

And then they resumed the march and in fifteen minutes the encounter had ceased even to be a topic of conversation.

For two days they continued upon their perilous way. Already the cliffs loomed high and forbidding close ahead without sign of break to encourage hope that somewhere they might be scaled. Late in the afternoon the party crossed a small stream of warm water upon the sluggishly moving surface of which floated countless millions of tiny green eggs surrounded by a light scum of the same color, though of a darker shade. Their past experience of Caspak had taught them that they might expect to come upon a stagnant pool of warm water if they followed the stream to its source; but there they were almost certain to find some of Caspak's grotesque, manlike creatures. Already since they had disembarked from the *U-33* after its perilous trip through the subterranean channel beneath the barrier cliffs had brought them into the inland sea of Caspak, had they encountered what had appeared to be three distinct types of these creatures. There had been the pure apes—huge, gorillalike beasts—and those who walked, a trifle more erect and had features with just a shade more of the human cast about them. Then there were men like Ahm, whom they had captured and confined at the fort—Ahm, the club-man. "Well-known club-man," Tyler had called him. Ahm and his people had knowledge of a speech. They had a language, in which they were unlike the race just inferior to them, and they walked much more erect and were less hairy: but it was principally the fact that they possessed a spoken language and carried a weapon that differentiated them from the others.

All of these peoples had proven belligerent in the extreme. In common with the rest of the fauna of Caprona the first law of nature as they seemed to understand it was to kill—kill—kill. And so it was that Bradley had no desire to follow up the little stream toward the pool near which were sure to be the caves of some savage tribe, but fortune played him an unkind trick, for the pool was much closer than he imagined, its southern end reaching fully a mile south of the point at which they crossed the stream, and so it was that after forcing their way through a tangle of jungle vegetation they came out upon the edge of the pool which they had wished to avoid.

Almost simultaneously there appeared south of them a party of naked men armed with clubs and hatchets. Both parties halted as they caught sight of one another. The men from the fort saw before them a hunting party evidently returning to its caves or village laden with meat. They were large men with features closely resembling those of the African Negro though their skins were white. Short hair grew upon a large portion of their limbs and bodies, which still retained a considerable trace of apish progenitors. They were, however, a distinctly higher type than the Bo-lu, or club-men.

Bradley would have been glad to have averted a meeting; but as he desired to lead his party south around the end of the pool, and as it was hemmed in by the jungle on one side and the water on the other, there seemed no escape from an encounter.

On the chance that he might avoid a clash, Bradley stepped forward with upraised hand. "We are friends," he called in the tongue of Ahm, the Bo-lu, who had been held a prisoner at the fort; "permit us to pass in peace. We will not harm you."

At this the hatchet-men set up a great jabbering with much laughter, loud and boisterous. "No," shouted one, "you will not harm us, for we shall kill you. Come! We kill! We kill!" And with hideous shouts they charged down upon the Europeans.

"Sinclair, you may fire," said Bradley quietly. "Pick off the leader. Can't waste ammunition."

The Englishman raised his piece to his shoulder and took quick aim at the breast of the yelling savage leaping toward them. Directly behind the leader came another hatchet-man, and with the report of Sinclair's rifle both warriors lunged forward in the tall grass, pierced by the same bullet. The effect upon the rest of the band was electrical. As one man they came to a sudden halt, wheeled to the east and dashed into the jungle, where the men could hear them forcing their way in an effort to put as much distance as possible between themselves and the authors of this new and frightful noise that killed warriors at a great distance.

Both the savages were dead when Bradley approached to examine them, and as the Europeans gathered around, other eyes were bent upon them with greater curiosity than they displayed for the victim of Sinclair's bullet. When the party again took up the march around the southern end of the pool the owner of the eyes followed them—large, round eyes, almost expressionless except for a certain cold cruelty which glinted malignly from under their pale gray irises.

All unconscious of the stalker, the men came, late in the afternoon, to a spot which seemed favorable as a campsite. A cold spring bubbled from the base of a rocky formation which overhung and partially encircled a small inclosure. At Bradley's command, the men took up the duties assigned them—gathering wood, building a cook-fire and preparing the evening meal. It was while they were thus engaged that Brady's attention was attracted by the dismal flapping of huge wings. He glanced up, expecting to see one of the great flying reptiles of a bygone age, his rifle ready in his hand. Brady was a brave man. He had groped his way up narrow tenement stairs and taken an armed maniac from a dark room without turning a hair; but now as he looked up, he went white and staggered back.

"Gawd!" he almost screamed. "What is it?"

Attracted by Brady's cry the others seized their rifles as they followed his wide-eyed, frozen gaze, nor was there one of them that was not moved by some species of terror or awe. Then Brady spoke again in an almost inaudible voice. "Holy Mother protect us—it's a banshee!"

Bradley, always cool almost to indifference in the face of danger, felt a strange, creeping sensation run over his flesh, as slowly, not a hundred feet above them, the thing flapped itself across the sky, its huge, round eyes glaring down upon them. And until it disappeared over the tops of the trees of a near-by wood the five men stood as though paralyzed, their eyes never leaving the weird shape; nor never one of them appearing to recall that he grasped a loaded rifle in his hands.

With the passing of the thing, came the reaction. Tippet sank to the ground and buried his face in his hands. "Oh, Gord," he moaned. "Tyke me away from this orful plice." Brady, recovered from the first shock, swore loud and luridly. He called upon all the saints to witness that he was unafraid and that anybody with half an eye could have seen that the creature was nothing more than "one av thim flyin' alligators" that they all were familiar with.

"Yes," said Sinclair with fine sarcasm, "we've saw so many of them with white shrouds on 'em."

"Shut up, you fool!" growled Brady. "If you know so much, tell us what it was after bein' then."

Then he turned toward Bradley. "What was it, sor, do you think?" he asked.

Bradley shook his head. "I don't know," he said. "It looked like a winged human being clothed in a flowing white robe. Its face was more human than otherwise. That is the way it looked to me; but what it really was I can't even guess, for such a creature is as far beyond my experience or knowledge as it is beyond yours. All that I am sure of is that whatever else it may have been, it was quite material—it was no ghost; rather just another of the strange forms of life which we have met here and with which we should be accustomed by this time."

Tippet looked up. His face was still ashy. "Yer cawn't tell me," he cried. "Hi seen hit. Blime, Hi seen hit. Hit was ha dead man flyin' through the hair. Didn't Hi see 'is heyes? Oh, Gord! Didn't Hi see 'em?"

"It didn't look like any beast or reptile to me," spoke up Sinclair. "It was lookin' right down at me when I looked up and I saw its face plain as I see yours. It had big round eyes that looked all cold and dead, and its cheeks were sunken in deep, and I could see its yellow teeth behind thin, tight-drawn lips—like a man who had been dead a long while, sir," he added, turning toward Bradley.

"Yes!" James had not spoken since the apparition had passed over them, and now it was scarce speech which he uttered—rather a series of articulate gasps. "Yes—dead—a—long—while. It—means something. It—come—for some—one. For one—of us. One—of—us is—goin'—to die. I'm goin' to die!" he ended in a wail.

"Come! Come!" snapped Bradley. "Won't do. Won't do at all. Get to work, all of you. Waste of time. Can't waste time."

His authoritative tones brought them all up standing, and presently each was occupied with his own duties; but each worked in silence and there was no singing and no bantering such as had marked the making of previous camps. Not until they had eaten and to each had been issued the little ration of smoking tobacco allowed after each evening meal did any sign of a relaxation of taut nerves appear. It was Brady who showed the first signs of returning good spirits. He commenced humming "It's a Long Way to Tipperary" and presently to voice the words, but he was well into his third song before anyone joined him, and even then there seemed a dismal note in even the gayest of tunes.

A huge fire blazed in the opening of their rocky shelter that the prowling carnivora might be kept at bay; and always one man stood on guard, watchfully alert against a sudden rush by some maddened beast of the jungle. Beyond the fire, yellow-green spots of flame appeared, moved restlessly about, disappeared and reappeared, accompanied by a hideous chorus of screams and growls and roars as the hungry meat-eaters hunting through the night were attracted by the light or the scent of possible prey.

But to such sights and sounds as these the five men had become callous. They sang or talked as unconcernedly as they might have done in the bar-room of some public-house at home.

Sinclair was standing guard. The others were listening to Brady's description of traffic congestion at the Rush Street bridge during the rush hour at night. The fire crackled cheerily. The owners of the yellow-green eyes raised their frightful chorus to the heavens. Conditions seemed again to have returned to normal. And then, as though the hand of Death had reached out and touched them all, the five men tensed into sudden rigidity.

Above the nocturnal diapason of the teeming jungle sounded a dismal flapping of wings and over head, through the thick night, a shadowy form passed across the diffused light of the flaring campfire. Sinclair raised his rifle and fired. An eerie wail floated down from above and the apparition, whatever it might have been, was swallowed by the darkness. For several seconds the listening men heard the sound of those dismally flapping wings lessening in the distance until they could no longer be heard.

Bradley was the first to speak. "Shouldn't have fired, Sinclair," he said; "can't waste ammunition." But there was no note of censure in his tone. It was as though he understood the nervous reaction that had compelled the other's act.

"I couldn't help it, sir," said Sinclair. "Lord, it would take an iron man to keep from shootin' at that awful thing. Do you believe in ghosts, sir?"

"No," replied Bradley. "No such things."

"I don't know about that," said Brady. "There was a woman murdered over on the prairie near Brighton—her throat was cut from ear to ear, and——"

"Shut up," snapped Bradley.

"My gran'daddy used to live down Coppington wy," said Tippet. "They were a hold ruined castle on a 'ill near by, hand at midnight they used to see pale blue lights through the windows an 'ear——"

"Will you close your hatch!" demanded Bradley. "You fools will have yourselves scared to death in a minute. Now go to sleep."

But there was little sleep in camp that night until utter exhaustion overtook the harassed men toward morning; nor was there any return of the weird creature that had set the nerves of each of them on edge.

The following forenoon the party reached the base of the barrier cliffs and for two days marched northward in an effort to discover a break in the frowning abutment that raised its rocky face almost perpendicularly above them, yet nowhere was there the slightest indication that the cliffs were scalable.

Disheartened, Bradley determined to turn back toward the fort, as he already had exceeded the time decided upon by Bowen Tyler and himself for the expedition. The cliffs for many miles had been trending in a northeasterly direction, indicating to Bradley that they were approaching the northern extremity of the island. According to past two days to have brought them to a point almost directly north of Fort Dinosaur and as nothing could be gained by retracing their steps along the base of the cliffs he decided to strike due south through the unexplored country between them and the fort.

That night (September 9, 1916), they made camp a short distance from the cliffs beside one of the numerous cool springs that are to be found within Caspak, oftentimes close beside the still more numerous warm and hot springs which feed the many pools. After supper the men lay smoking and chatting among themselves. Tippet was on guard. Fewer night prowlers threatened them, and the men were commenting upon the fact that the farther north they had traveled the smaller the number of all species of animals became, though it was still present in what would have seemed appalling plenitude in any other part of the world. The diminution in reptilian life was the most noticeable change in the fauna of northern Caspak. Here, however, were forms they had not met elsewhere, several of which were of gigantic proportions.

According to their custom all, with the exception of the man on guard, sought sleep early, nor, once disposed upon the ground for slumber, were they long in finding it. It seemed to Bradley that he had scarcely closed his eyes when he was brought to his feet, wide awake, by a piercing scream which was punctuated by the sharp report of a rifle from the direction of the fire where Tippet stood guard. As he ran toward the man, Bradley heard above him the same uncanny wail that had set every nerve on edge several nights before, and the dismal flapping of huge wings. He did not need to look up at the white-shrouded figure winging slowly away into the night to know that their grim visitor had returned.

The muscles of his arm, reacting to the sight and sound of the menacing form, carried his hand to the butt of his pistol; but after he had drawn the weapon, he immediately returned it to its holster with a shrug.

"What for?" he muttered. "Can't waste ammunition." Then he walked quickly to where Tippet lay sprawled upon his face. By this time James, Brady and Sinclair were at his heels, each with his rifle in readiness.

"Is he dead, sir?" whispered James as Bradley kneeled beside the prostrate form.

Bradley turned Tippet over on his back and pressed an ear close to the other's heart. In a moment he raised his head. "Fainted," he announced. "Get water. Hurry!" Then he loosened Tippet's shirt at the throat and when the water was brought, threw a cupful in the man's face. Slowly Tippet regained consciousness and sat up. At first he looked curiously into the faces of the men about him; then an expression of terror overspread his features. He shot a startled glance up into the black void above and then burying his face in his arms began to sob like a child.

"What's wrong, man?" demanded Bradley. "Buck up! Can't play cry-baby. Waste of energy. What happened?"

"Wot 'appened, sir!" wailed Tippet. "Oh, Gord, sir! Hit came back. Hit came for me, sir. Right hit did, sir; strite hat me, sir; hand with long w'ite 'ands it clawed for me. Oh, Gord! Hit almost caught me, sir. Hi'm has good as dead; Hi'm a marked man; that's wot Hi ham. Hit was a-goin' for to carry me horf, sir."

"Stuff and nonsense," snapped Bradley. "Did you get a good look at it?"

Tippet said that he did—a much better look than he wanted. The thing had almost clutched him, and he had looked straight into its eyes—"dead heyes in a dead face," he had described them.

"Wot was it after bein', do you think?" inquired Brady.

"Hit was Death," moaned Tippet, shuddering, and again a pall of gloom fell upon the little party.

The following day Tippet walked as one in a trance. He never spoke except in reply to a direct question, which more often than not had to be repeated before it could attract his attention. He insisted that he was already a dead man, for if the thing didn't come for him during the day he would never live through another night of agonized apprehension, waiting for the frightful end that he was positive was in store for him. "I'll see to that," he said, and they all knew that Tippet meant to take his own life before darkness set in.

Bradley tried to reason with him, in his short, crisp way, but soon saw the futility of it; nor could he take the man's weapons from him without subjecting him to almost certain death from any of the numberless dangers that beset their way.

The entire party was moody and glum. There was none of the bantering that had marked their intercourse before, even in the face of blighting hardships and hideous danger. This was a new menace that threatened them, something that they couldn't explain; and so, naturally, it aroused within them superstitious fear which Tippet's attitude only tended to augment. To add further to their gloom, their way led through a dense forest, where, on account of the underbrush, it was difficult to make even a mile an hour. Constant watchfulness was required to avoid the many snakes of various degrees of repulsiveness and enormity that infested the wood; and the only ray of hope they had to cling to was that the forest would, like the majority of Caspakian forests, prove to be of no considerable extent.

Bradley was in the lead when he came suddenly upon a grotesque creature of Titanic proportions. Crouching among the trees, which here commenced to thin out slightly, Bradley saw what appeared to be an enormous dragon devouring the carcass of a mammoth. From frightful jaws to the tip of its long tail it was fully forty feet in length. Its body was covered with plates of thick skin which bore a striking resemblance to armor-plate. The creature saw Bradley almost at the same instant that he saw it and reared up on its enormous hind legs until its head towered a full twenty-five feet above the ground. From the cavernous jaws issued a hissing sound of a volume equal to the escaping steam from the safety-valves of half a dozen locomotives, and then the creature came for the man.

"Scatter!" shouted Bradley to those behind him; and all but Tippet heeded the warning. The man stood as though dazed, and when Bradley saw the other's danger, he too stopped and wheeling about sent a bullet into the massive body forcing its way through the trees toward him. The shot struck the creature in the belly where there was no protecting armor, eliciting a new note which rose in a shrill whistle and ended in a wail. It was then that Tippet appeared to come out of his trance, for with a cry of terror he turned and fled to the left. Bradley, seeing that he had as good an opportunity as the others to escape, now turned his attention to extricating himself; and as the woods seemed dense on the right, he ran in that direction, hoping that the close-set boles would prevent pursuit on the part of the great reptile. The dragon paid no further attention to him, however, for Tippet's sudden break for liberty had attracted its attention; and after Tippet it went, bowling over small trees, uprooting underbrush and leaving a wake behind it like that of a small tornado.

Bradley, the moment he had discovered the thing was pursuing Tippet, had followed it. He was afraid to fire for fear of hitting the man, and so it was that he came upon them at the very moment that the monster lunged its great weight forward upon the doomed man. The sharp, three-toed talons of the forelimbs seized poor Tippet, and Bradley saw the unfortunate fellow lifted high above the ground as the creature again reared up on its hind legs, immediately transferring Tippet's body to its gaping jaws, which closed with a sickening, crunching sound as Tippet's bones cracked beneath the great teeth.

Bradley half raised his rifle to fire again and then lowered it with a shake of his head. Tippet was beyond succor—why waste a bullet that Caspak could never replace? If he could now escape the further notice of the monster it would be a wiser act than to throw his life away in futile revenge. He saw that the reptile was not looking in his direction, and so he slipped noiselessly behind the bole of a large tree and thence quietly faded away in the direction he believed the others to have taken. At what he considered a safe distance he halted and looked back. Half hidden by the intervening trees he still could see the huge head and the massive jaws from which protrude the limp legs of the dead man. Then, as though struck by the hammer of Thor, the creature collapsed and crumpled to the ground. Bradley's single bullet, penetrating the body through the soft skin of the belly, had slain the Titan.

A few minutes later, Bradley found the others of the party. The four returned cautiously to the spot where the creature lay and after convincing themselves that it was quite dead, came close to it. It was an arduous and gruesome job extricating Tippet's mangled remains from the powerful jaws, the men working for the most part silently.

"It was the work of the banshee all right," muttered Brady. "It warned poor Tippet, it did."

"Hit killed him, that's wot hit did, hand hit'll kill some more of us," said James, his lower lip trembling.

"If it was a ghost," interjected Sinclair, "and I don't say as it was; but if it was, why, it could take on any form it wanted to. It might have turned itself into this thing, which ain't no natural thing at all, just to get poor Tippet. If it had of been a lion or something else humanlike it wouldn't look so strange; but this here thing ain't humanlike. There ain't no such thing an' never was."

"Bullets don't kill ghosts," said Bradley, "so this couldn't have been a ghost. Furthermore, there are no such things. I've been trying to place this creature. Just succeeded. It's a tyrannosaurus. Saw picture of skeleton in magazine. There's one in New York Natural History Museum. Seems to me it said it was found in place called Hell Creek somewhere in western North America. Supposed to have lived about six million years ago."

"Hell Creek's in Montana," said Sinclair. "I used to punch cows in Wyoming, an' I've heard of Hell Creek. Do you s'pose that there thing's six million years old?" His tone was skeptical.

"No," replied Bradley; "but it would indicate that the island of Caprona has stood almost without change for more than six million years."

The conversation and Bradley's assurance that the creature was not of supernatural origin helped to raise a trifle the spirits of the men; and then came another diversion in the form of ravenous meat-eaters attracted to the spot by the uncanny sense of smell which had apprised them of the presence of flesh, killed and ready for the eating.

It was a constant battle while they dug a grave and consigned all that was mortal of John Tippet to his last, lonely resting-place. Nor would they leave then; but remained to fashion a rude headstone from a crumbling out-cropping of sandstone and to gather a mass of the gorgeous flowers growing in such great profusion around them and heap the new-made grave with bright blooms. Upon the headstone Sinclair scratched in rude characters the words:

HERE LIES JOHN TIPPET
ENGLISHMAN
KILLED BY TYRANNOSAURUS
10 SEPT. A.D. 1916
R.I.P.

and Bradley repeated a short prayer before they left their comrade forever.

For three days the party marched due south through forests and meadow-land and great park-like areas where countless herbivorous animals grazed—deer and antelope and bos and the little *ecca*, the smallest species of Caspakian horse, about the size of a rabbit. There

were other horses, too; but all were small, the largest being not above
eight hands in height. Preying continually upon the herbivora were
the meat-eaters, large and small—wolves, hyaenadons, panthers,
lions, tigers, and bear as well as several large and ferocious species of
reptilian life.

On September twelfth the party scaled a line of sandstone cliffs
which crossed their route toward the south; but they crossed them
only after an encounter with the tribe that inhabited the numerous
caves which pitted the face of the escarpment. That night they camped
upon a rocky plateau which was sparsely wooded with jarrah, and
here once again they were visited by the weird, nocturnal apparition
that had already filled them with a nameless terror.

As on the night of September ninth the first warning came from
the sentinel standing guard over his sleeping companions. A terror-
stricken cry punctuated by the crack of a rifle brought Bradley,
Sinclair and Brady to their feet in time to see James, with clubbed
rifle, battling with a white-robed figure that hovered on widespread
wings on a level with the Englishman's head. As they ran, shouting,
forward, it was obvious to them that the weird and terrible apparition
was attempting to seize James; but when it saw the others coming to
his rescue, it desisted, flapping rapidly upward and away, its long,
ragged wings giving forth the peculiarly dismal notes which always
characterized the sound of its flying.

Bradley fired at the vanishing menacer of their peace and safety;
but whether he scored a hit or not, none could tell, though, following
the shot, there was wafted back to them the same piercing wail that
had on other occasions frozen their marrow.

Then they turned toward James, who lay face downward upon
the ground, trembling as with ague. For a time he could not even
speak, but at last regained sufficient composure to tell them how the
thing must have swooped silently upon him from above and behind as
the first premonition of danger he had received was when the long,

clawlike fingers had clutched him beneath either arm. In the melee
his rifle had been discharged and he had broken away at the same
instant and turned to defend himself with the butt. The rest they had
seen.

From that instant James was an absolutely broken man. He maintained with shaking lips that his doom was sealed, that the thing had
marked him for its own, and that he was as good as dead, nor could
any amount of argument or raillery convince him to the contrary. He
had seen Tippet marked and claimed and now he had been marked.
Nor were his constant reiterations of this belief without effect upon
the rest of the party. Even Bradley felt depressed, though for the sake
of the others he managed to hide it beneath a show of confidence he
was far from feeling.

And on the following day William James was killed by a saber-
tooth tiger—September 13, 1916. Beneath a jarrah tree on the stony
plateau on the northern edge of the Sto-lu country in the land that
Time forgot, he lies in a lonely grave marked by a rough headstone.

Southward from his grave marched three grim and silent men.
To the best of Bradley's reckoning they were some twenty-five miles
north of Fort Dinosaur, and that they might reach the fort on the
following day, they plodded on until darkness overtook them. With
comparative safety fifteen miles away, they made camp at last; but
there was no singing now and no joking. In the bottom of his heart
each prayed that they might come safely through just this night,
for they knew that during the morrow they would make the final
stretch, yet the nerves of each were taut with strained anticipation of
what gruesome thing might flap down upon them from the black sky,
marking another for its own. Who would be the next?

As was their custom, they took turns at guard, each man doing
two hours and then arousing the next. Brady had gone on from eight
to ten, followed by Sinclair from ten to twelve, then Bradley had been
awakened. Brady would stand the last guard from two to four, as they

had determined to start the moment that it became light enough to insure comparative safety upon the trail.

The snapping of a twig aroused Brady out of a dead sleep, and as he opened his eyes, he saw that it was broad daylight and that at twenty paces from him stood a huge lion. As the man sprang to his feet, his rifle ready in his hand, Sinclair awoke and took in the scene in a single swift glance. The fire was out and Bradley was nowhere in sight. For a long moment the lion and the men eyed one another. The latter had no mind to fire if the beast minded its own affairs—they were only too glad to let it go its way if it would; but the lion was of a different mind.

Suddenly the long tail snapped stiffly erect, and as though it had been attached to two trigger fingers the two rifles spoke in unison, for both men knew this signal only too well—the immediate fore-runner of a deadly charge. As the brute's head had been raised, his spine had not been visible; and so they did what they had learned by long experience was best to do. Each covered a front leg, and as the tail snapped aloft, fired. With a hideous roar the mighty flesh-eater lurched forward to the ground with both front legs broken. It was an easy accomplishment in the instant before the beast charged—after, it would have been well-nigh an impossible feat. Brady stepped close in and finished him with a shot in the base of the brain lest his terrific roarings should attract his mate or others of their kind.

Then the two men turned and looked at one another. "Where is Lieutenant Bradley?" asked Sinclair. They walked to the fire. Only a few smoking embers remained. A few feet away lay Bradley's rifle. There was no evidence of a struggle. The two men circled about the camp twice and on the last lap Brady stooped and picked up an object which had lain about ten yards beyond the fire—it was Bradley's cap. Again the two looked questioningly at one another, and then, simultaneously, both pairs of eyes swung upward and searched the sky. A moment later Brady was examining the ground about the spot where Bradley's cap had lain. It was one of those little barren, sandy stretches that they had found only upon this stony plateau. Brady's own footsteps showed as plainly as black ink upon white paper; but his was the only foot that had marred the smooth, windswept surface—there was no sign that Bradley had crossed the spot *upon the surface of the ground*, and yet his cap lay well toward the center of it.

Breakfastless and with shaken nerves the two survivors plunged madly into the long day's march. Both were strong, courageous, resourceful men; but each had reached the limit of human nerve endurance and each felt that he would rather die than spend another night in the hideous open of that frightful land. Vivid in the mind of each was a picture of Bradley's end, for though neither had witnessed the tragedy, both could imagine almost precisely what had occurred. They did not discuss it—they did not even mention it—yet all day long the thing was uppermost in the mind of each and mingled with it a similar picture with himself as victim should they fail to make Fort Dinosaur before dark.

And so they plunged forward at reckless speed, their clothes, their hands, their faces torn by the retarding underbrush that reached forth to hinder them. Again and again they fell; but be it to their credit that the one always waited and helped the other and that into the mind of neither entered the thought or the temptation to desert his companion—they would reach the fort together if both survived, or neither would reach it.

They encountered the usual number of savage beasts and reptiles; but they met them with a courageous recklessness born of desperation, and by virtue of the very madness of the chances they took, they came through unscathed and with the minimum of delay.

Shortly after noon they reached the end of the plateau. Before them was a drop of two hundred feet to the valley beneath. To the left, in the distance, they could see the waters of the great inland sea that covers a considerable portion of the area of the crater island of

Caprona and at a little lesser distance to the south of the cliffs they saw a thin spiral of smoke arising above the tree-tops.

The landscape was familiar—each recognized it immediately and knew that that smoky column marked the spot where Dinosaur had stood. Was the fort still there, or did the smoke arise from the smoldering embers of the building they had helped to fashion for the housing of their party? Who could say!

Thirty precious minutes that seemed as many hours to the impatient men were consumed in locating a precarious way from the summit to the base of the cliffs that bounded the plateau upon the south, and then once again they struck off upon level ground toward their goal. The closer they approached the fort the greater became their apprehension that all would not be well. They pictured the barracks deserted or the small company massacred and the buildings in ashes. It was almost in a frenzy of fear that they broke through the final fringe of jungle and stood at last upon the verge of the open meadow a half-mile from Fort Dinosaur.

"Lord!" ejaculated Sinclair. "They are still there!" And he fell to his knees, sobbing.

Brady trembled like a leaf as he crossed himself and gave silent thanks, for there before them stood the sturdy ramparts of Dinosaur and from inside the inclosure rose a thin spiral of smoke that marked the location of the cook-house. All was well, then, and their comrades were preparing the evening meal!

Across the clearing they raced as though they had not already covered in a single day a trackless, primeval country that might easily have required two days by fresh and untired men. Within hailing distance they set up such a loud shouting that presently heads appeared above the top of the parapet and soon answering shouts were rising from within Fort Dinosaur. A moment later three men issued from the inclosure and came forward to meet the survivors and listen to the hurried story of the eleven eventful days since they had set out upon their expedition to the barrier cliffs. They heard of the deaths of Tippet and James and of the disappearance of Lieutenant Bradley, and a new terror settled upon Dinosaur.

Olson, the Irish engineer, with Whitely and Wilson constituted the remnants of Dinosaur's defenders, and to Brady and Sinclair they narrated the salient events that had transpired since Bradley and his party had marched away on September 4th. They told them of the infamous act of Baron Friedrich von Schoenvorts and his German crew who had stolen the *U-33*, breaking their parole, and steaming away toward the subterranean opening through the barrier cliffs that carried the waters of the inland sea into the open Pacific beyond; and of the cowardly shelling of the fort.

They told of the disappearance of Miss La Rue in the night of September 11th, and of the departure of Bowen Tyler in search of her, accompanied only by his Airedale, Nobs. Thus of the original party of eleven Allies and nine Germans that had constituted the company of the *U-33* when she left English waters after her capture by the crew of the English tug there were but five now to be accounted for at Fort Dinosaur. Benson, Tippet, James, and one of the Germans were known to be dead. It was assumed that Bradley, Tyler and the girl had already succumbed to some of the savage denizens of Caspak, while the fate of the Germans was equally unknown, though it might readily be believed that they had made good their escape. They had had ample time to provision the ship and the refining of the crude oil they had discovered north of the fort could have insured them an ample supply to carry them back to Germany.

2

When Bradley went on guard at midnight, September 14th, his thoughts were largely occupied with rejoicing that the night was almost spent without serious mishap and that the morrow would doubtless see them all safely returned to Fort Dinosaur. The hopefulness of his mood was tinged with sorrow by recollection of the two members of his party who lay back there in the savage wilderness and for whom there would never again be a homecoming.

No premonition of impending ill cast gloom over his anticipations for the coming day, for Bradley was a man who, while taking every precaution against possible danger, permitted no gloomy forebodings to weigh down his spirit. When danger threatened, he was prepared; but he was not forever courting disaster, and so it was that when about one o'clock in the morning of the fifteenth, he heard the dismal flapping of giant wings overhead, he was neither surprised nor frightened but idly prepared for an attack he had known might reasonably be expected.

The sound seemed to come from the south, and presently, low above the trees in that direction, the man made out a dim, shadowy form circling slowly about. Bradley was a brave man, yet so keen was the feeling of revulsion engendered by the sight and sound of that grim, uncanny shape that he distinctly felt the gooseflesh rise over the surface of his body, and it was with difficulty that he refrained from following an instinctive urge to fire upon the nocturnal intruder. Better, far better would it have been had he given in to the insistent demand of his subconscious mentor; but his almost fanatical obsession to save ammunition proved now his undoing, for while his attention was riveted upon the thing circling before him and while his ears were filled with the beating of its wings, there swooped silently out of the black night behind him another weird and ghostly shape. With its huge wings partly closed for the dive and its white robe fluttering in its wake, the apparition swooped down upon the Englishman.

So great was the force of the impact when the thing struck Bradley between the shoulders that the man was half stunned. His rifle flew from his grasp; he felt clawlike talons of great strength seize him beneath his arms and sweep him off his feet; and then the thing rose swiftly with him, so swiftly that his cap was blown from his head by the rush of air as he was borne rapidly upward into the inky sky and the cry of warning to his companions was forced back into his lungs.

The creature wheeled immediately toward the east and was at once joined by its fellow, who circled them once and then fell in behind them. Bradley now realized the strategy that the pair had used to capture him and at once concluded that he was in the power of reasoning beings closely related to the human race if not actually of it.

Past experience suggested that the great wings were a part of some ingenious mechanical device, for the limitations of the human mind, which is always loath to accept aught beyond its own little experience, would not permit him to entertain the idea that the creatures might be naturally winged and at the same time of human origin. From his position Bradley could not see the wings of his captor, nor in the darkness had he been able to examine those of the second creature closely when it circled before him. He listened for the puff of a motor or some other telltale sound that would prove the correctness of his theory. However, he was rewarded with nothing more than the constant *flap-flap*.

Presently, far below and ahead, he saw the waters of the inland sea, and a moment later he was borne over them. Then his captor did that which proved beyond doubt to Bradley that he was in the hands of human beings who had devised an almost perfect scheme of duplicating, mechanically, the wings of a bird—the thing spoke to its companion and in a language that Bradley partially understood, since he recognized words that he had learned from the savage races of Caspak. From this he judged that they were human, and being human, he knew that they could have no natural wings—for who had ever seen a human being so adorned! Therefore their wings must be mechanical. Thus Bradley reasoned—thus most of us reason; not by what might be possible; but by what has fallen within the range of our experience.

What he heard them say was to the effect that having covered half the distance the burden would now be transferred from one to the other. Bradley wondered how the exchange was to be accomplished. He knew that those giant wings would not permit the creatures to approach one another closely enough to effect the transfer in this manner; but he was soon to discover that they had other means of doing it.

He felt the thing that carried him rise to a greater altitude, and below he glimpsed momentarily the second white-robed figure; then the creature above sounded a low call, it was answered from below, and instantly Bradley felt the clutching talons release him; gasping for breath, he hurtled downward through space.

For a terrifying instant, pregnant with horror, Bradley fell; then something swooped for him from behind, another pair of talons clutched him beneath the arms, his downward rush was checked, within another hundred feet, and close to the surface of the sea he was again borne upward. As a hawk dives for a songbird on the wing, so this great, human bird dived for Bradley. It was a harrowing experience, but soon over, and once again the captive was being carried swiftly toward the east and what fate he could not even guess.

It was immediately following his transfer in mid-air that Bradley made out the shadowy form of a large island far ahead, and not long after, he realized that this must be the intended destination of his captors. Nor was he mistaken. Three quarters of an hour from the time of his seizure his captors dropped gently to earth in the strangest city that human eye had ever rested upon. Just a brief glimpse of his immediate surroundings vouchsafed Bradley before he was whisked into the interior of one of the buildings; but in that momentary glance he saw strange piles of stone and wood and mud fashioned into buildings of all conceivable sizes and shapes, sometimes piled high on top of one another, sometimes standing alone in an open courtway, but usually crowded and jammed together, so that there were no streets or alleys between them other than a few which ended almost as soon as they began. The principal doorways appeared to be in the roofs, and it was through one of these that Bradley was inducted into the dark interior of a low-ceiled room. Here he was pushed roughly into a corner where he tripped over a thick mat, and there his captors left him. He heard them moving about in the darkness for a moment, and several times he saw their large luminous eyes glowing in the dark. Finally, these disappeared and silence reigned, broken only by the breathing of the creature which indicated to the Englishman that they were sleeping somewhere in the same apartment.

It was now evident that the mat upon the floor was intended for sleeping purposes and that the rough shove that had sent him to it had been a rude invitation to repose. After taking stock of himself and finding that he still had his pistol and ammunition, some matches, a little tobacco, a canteen full of water and a razor, Bradley made himself comfortable upon the mat and was soon asleep, knowing that an attempted escape in the darkness without knowledge of his surroundings would be predoomed to failure.

When he awoke, it was broad daylight, and the sight that met his eyes made him rub them again and again to assure himself that they were really open and that he was not dreaming. A broad shaft of morning light poured through the open doorway in the ceiling of the room which was about thirty feet square, or roughly square, being irregular in shape, one side curving outward, another being indented by what might have been the corner of another building jutting into it, another alcoved by three sides of an octagon, while the fourth was serpentine in contour. Two windows let in more daylight, while two doors evidently gave ingress to other rooms. The walls were partially ceiled with thin strips of wood, nicely fitted and finished, partially plastered and the rest covered with a fine, woven cloth. Figures of reptiles and beasts were painted without regard to any uniform scheme here and there upon the walls. A striking feature of the decorations consisted of several engaged columns set into the walls at no regular intervals, the capitals of each supporting a human skull the cranium of which touched the ceiling, as though the latter was supported by these grim reminders either of departed relatives or of some hideous tribal rite—Bradley could not but wonder which.

Yet it was none of these things that filled him with greatest wonder—no, it was the figures of the two creatures that had captured him and brought him hither. At one end of the room a stout pole about two inches in diameter ran horizontally from wall to wall some six or seven feet from the floor, its ends securely set in two of the columns. Hanging by their knees from this perch, their heads downward and their bodies wrapped in their huge wings, slept the creatures of the night before—like two great, horrid bats they hung, asleep.

As Bradley gazed upon them in wide-eyed astonishment, he saw plainly that all his intelligence, all his acquired knowledge through years of observation and experience were set at naught by the simple evidence of the fact that stood out glaringly before his eyes—the creatures' wings were not mechanical devices but as natural appendages, growing from their shoulderblades, as were their arms and legs.

He saw, too, that except for their wings the pair bore a strong resemblance to human beings, though fashioned in a most grotesque mold.

As he sat gazing at them, one of the two awoke, separated his wings to release his arms that had been folded across his breast, placed his hands upon the floor, dropped his feet and stood erect. For a moment he stretched his great wings slowly, solemnly blinking his large round eyes. Then his gaze fell upon Bradley. The thin lips drew back tightly against yellow teeth in a grimace that was nothing but hideous. It could not have been termed a smile, and what emotion it registered the Englishman was at a loss to guess. No expression whatever altered the steady gaze of those large, round eyes; there was no color upon the pasty, sunken cheeks. A death's head grimaced as though a man long dead raised his parchment-covered skull from an old grave.

The creature stood about the height of an average man but appeared much taller from the fact that the joints of his long wings rose fully a foot above his hairless head. The bare arms were long and sinewy, ending in strong, bony hands with clawlike fingers—almost talonlike in their suggestiveness. The white robe was separated in front, revealing skinny legs and the further fact that the thing wore but the single garment, which was of fine, woven cloth. From crown to sole the portions of the body exposed were entirely hairless, and as he noted this, Bradley also noted for the first time the cause of much of the seeming expressionlessness of the creature's countenance—it had neither eye-brows or lashes. The ears were small and rested flat against the skull, which was noticeably round, though the face was quite flat. The creature had small feet, beautifully arched and plump, but so out of keeping with every other physical attribute it possessed as to appear ridiculous.

After eyeing Bradley for a moment the thing approached him. "Where from?" it asked.

"England," replied Bradley, as briefly.

"Where is England and what?" pursued the questioner.

"It is a country far from here," answered the Englishman.

"Are your people *cor-sva-jo* or *cos-ata-lu?*"

"I do not understand you," said Bradley; "and now suppose you answer a few questions. Who are you? What country is this? Why did you bring me here?"

Again the sepulchral grimace. "We are Wieroos. Luata is our father. Caspak is ours. This, our country, is called Oo-oh. We brought you here for (literally) Him Who Speaks for Luata to gaze upon and question. He would know from whence you came and why; but principally if you be *cos-ata-lu.*"

"And if I am not *cos*—whatever you call the bloomin' beast—what of it?"

The Wieroo raised his wings in a very human shrug and waved his bony claws toward the human skulls supporting the ceiling. His gesture was eloquent; but he embellished it by remarking, "And possibly if you are."

"I'm hungry," snapped Bradley.

The Wieroo motioned him to one of the doors which he threw open, permitting Bradley to pass out onto another roof on a level lower than that upon which they had landed earlier in the morning. By daylight the city appeared even more remarkable than in the moonlight, though less weird and unreal. The houses of all shapes and sizes were piled about as a child might pile blocks of various forms and colors. He saw now that there were what might be called streets or alleys, but they ran in baffling turns and twists, nor ever reached a destination, always ending in a dead wall where some Wieroo had built a house across them.

Upon each house was a slender column supporting a human skull. Sometimes the columns were at one corner of the roof, sometimes at another, or again they rose from the center or near the center, and the columns were of varying heights, from that of a man to those which rose twenty feet above their roofs. The skulls were, as a rule, painted—blue or white, or in combinations of both colors. The most effective were painted blue with the teeth white and the eye-sockets rimmed with white.

There were other skulls—thousands of them—tens, hundreds of thousands. They rimmed the eaves of every house, they were set in the plaster of the outer walls and at no great distance from where Bradley stood rose a round tower built entirely of human skulls. And the city extended in every direction as far as the Englishman could see.

All about him Wieroos were moving across the roofs or winging through the air. The sad sound of their flapping wings rose and fell like a solemn dirge. Most of them were appareled all in white, like his captors; but others had markings of red or blue or yellow slashed across the front of their robes.

His guide pointed toward a doorway in an alley below them. "Go there and eat," he commanded, "and then come back. You cannot escape. If any question you, say that you belong to Fosh-bal-soj. There is the way." And this time he pointed to the top of a ladder which protruded above the eaves of the roof near-by. Then he turned and reentered the house.

Bradley looked about him. No, he could not escape—that seemed evident. The city appeared interminable, and beyond the city, if not a savage wilderness filled with wild beasts, there was the broad inland sea infested with horrid monsters. No wonder his captor felt safe in turning him loose in Oo-oh—he wondered if that was the name of the country or the city and if there were other cities like this upon the island.

Slowly he descended the ladder to the seemingly deserted alley which was paved with what appeared to be large, round cobble-stones. He looked again at the smooth, worn pavement, and a rueful grin crossed his features—the alley was paved with skulls.

"The City of Human Skulls," mused Bradley. "They must have been collectin' 'em since Adam," he thought, and then he crossed and entered the building through the doorway that had been pointed out to him.

Inside he found a large room in which were many Wieroos seated before pedestals the tops of which were hollowed out so that they resembled the ordinary bird drinking- and bathing-fonts so commonly seen on suburban lawns. A seat protruded from each of the four sides of the pedestals—just a flat board with a support running from its outer end diagonally to the base of the pedestal.

As Bradley entered, some of the Wieroos espied him, and a dismal wail arose. Whether it was a greeting or a threat, Bradley did not know. Suddenly from a dark alcove another Wieroo rushed out toward him. "Who are you?" he cried. "What do you want?"

"Fosh-bal-soj sent me here to eat," replied Bradley.

"Do you belong to Fosh-bal-soj?" asked the other.

"That appears to be what he thinks," answered the Englishman.

"Are you *cos-ata-lu*?" demanded the Wieroo.

"Give me something to eat or I'll be all of that," replied Bradley.

The Wieroo looked puzzled. "Sit here, *jaal-lu*," he snapped, and Bradley sat down unconscious of the fact that he had been insulted by being called a hyena-man, an appellation of contempt in Caspak.

The Wieroo had seated him at a pedestal by himself, and as he sat waiting for what was next to transpire, he looked about him at the Wieroo in his immediate vicinity. He saw that in each font was a quantity of food, and that each Wieroo was armed with a wooden skewer, sharpened at one end; with which they carried solid portions of food to their mouths. At the other end of the skewer was fastened a small clam-shell. This was used to scoop up the smaller and softer portions of the repast into which all four of the occupants of each table dipped impartially. The Wieroo leaned far over their food, scooping it up rapidly and with much noise, and so great was their haste that a part of each mouthful always fell back into the common dish; and when they choked, by reason of the rapidity with which they attempted to bolt their food, they often lost it all. Bradley was glad that he had a pedestal all to himself.

Soon the keeper of the place returned with a wooden bowl filled with food. This he dumped into Bradley's "trough," as he already thought of it. The Englishman was glad that he could not see into the dark alcove or know what were all the ingredients that constituted the mess before him, for he was very hungry.

After the first mouthful he cared even less to investigate the antecedents of the dish, for he found it peculiarly palatable. It seemed to consist of a combination of meat, fruits, vegetables, small fish and other undistinguishable articles of food all seasoned to produce a gastronomic effect that was at once baffling and delicious.

When he had finished, his trough was empty, and then he commenced to wonder who was to settle for his meal. As he waited for the proprietor to return, he fell to examining the dish from which he had eaten and the pedestal upon which it rested. The font was of stone worn smooth by long-continued use, the four outer edges hollowed and polished by the contact of the countless Wieroo bodies that had leaned against them for how long a period of time Bradley could not even guess. Everything about the place carried the impression of hoary age. The carved pedestals were black with use, the wooden seats were worn hollow, the floor of stone slabs was polished by the contact of possibly millions of naked feet and worn away in the aisles between the pedestals so that the latter rested upon little mounds of stone several inches above the general level of the floor.

Finally, seeing that no one came to collect, Bradley arose and started for the doorway. He had covered half the distance when he heard the voice of mine host calling to him: "Come back, *jaallu*," screamed the Wieroo; and Bradley did as he was bid. As he approached the creature which stood now behind a large, flat-topped pedestal beside the alcove, he saw lying upon the smooth surface something that almost elicited a gasp of astonishment from him—a simple, common thing it was, or would have been almost anywhere in the world but Caspak—a square bit of paper!

And on it, in a fine hand, written compactly, were many strange hieroglyphics! These remarkable creatures, then, had a written as well as a spoken language and besides the art of weaving cloth possessed that of paper-making. Could it be that such grotesque beings represented the high culture of the human race within the boundaries of Caspak? Had natural selection produced during the countless ages of Caspakian life a winged monstrosity that represented the earthly pinnacle of man's evolution?

Bradley had noted something of the obvious indications of a gradual evolution from ape to spear-man as exemplified by the several overlapping races of Alalus, club-men and hatchet-men that formed the connecting links between the two extremes with which he had come in contact. He had heard of the Kro-lus and the Galus—reputed to be still higher in the plane of evolution—and now he had indisputable evidence of a race possessing refinements of civilization eons in advance of the spear-men. The conjectures awakened by even a momentary consideration of the possibilities involved became at once as wildly bizarre as the insane imagings of a drug addict.

As these thoughts flashed through his mind, the Wieroo held out a pen of bone fixed to a wooden holder and at the same time made a sign that Bradley was to write upon the paper. It was difficult to judge from the expressionless features of the Wieroo what was passing in the creature's mind, but Bradley could not but feel that the thing cast a supercilious glance upon him as much as to say, "Of course you do not know how to write, you poor, low creature; but you can make your mark."

Bradley seized the pen and in a clear, bold hand wrote: "John Bradley, England." The Wieroo showed evidences of consternation as it seized the piece of paper and examined the writing with every mark of incredulity and surprise. Of course it could make nothing of the strange characters; but it evidently accepted them as proof that Bradley possessed knowledge of a written language of his own, for following the Englishman's entry it made a few characters of its own.

"You will come here again just before Lua hides his face behind the great cliff," announced the creature, "unless before that you are summoned by Him Who Speaks for Luata, in which case you will not have to eat any more."

"Reassuring cuss," thought Bradley as he turned and left the building.

Outside were several Wieroos that had been eating at the pedestals within. They immediately surrounded him, asking all sorts of questions, plucking at his garments, his ammunition-belt and his pistol. Their demeanor was entirely different from what it had been within the eating-place and Bradley was to learn that a house of food was sanctuary for him, since the stern laws of the Wieroos forbade altercations within such walls. Now they were rough and threatening, as with wings half spread they hovered about him in menacing attitudes, barring his way to the ladder leading to the roof from whence he had descended; but the Englishman was not one to brook interference for long. He attempted at first to push his way past them, and then when one seized his arm and jerked him roughly back, Bradley swung upon the creature and with a heavy blow to the jaw felled it.

Instantly pandemonium reigned. Loud wails arose, great wings opened and closed with a loud, beating noise and many clawlike hands reached forth to clutch him. Bradley struck to right and left. He dared not use his pistol for fear that once they discovered its power he would be overcome by weight of numbers and relieved of possession of what he considered his trump card, to be reserved until the last moment that it might be used to aid in his escape, for already the Englishman was planning, though almost hopelessly, such an attempt.

254

A few blows convinced Bradley that the Wieroos were arrant cowards and that they bore no weapons, for after two or three had fallen beneath his fists the others formed a circle about him, but at a safe distance and contented themselves with threatening and blustering, while those whom he had felled lay upon the pavement without trying to arise, the while they moaned and wailed in lugubrious chorus.

Again Bradley strode toward the ladder, and this time the circle parted before him; but no sooner had he ascended a few rungs than he was seized by one foot and an effort made to drag him down. With a quick backward glance the Englishman, clinging firmly to the ladder with both hands, drew up his free foot and with all the strength of a powerful leg, planted a heavy shoe squarely in the flat face of the Wieroo that held him. Shrieking horribly, the creature clapped both hands to its face and sank to the ground while Bradley clambered quickly the remaining distance to the roof, though no sooner did he reach the top of the ladder than a great flapping of wings beneath him warned him that the Wieroos were rising after him. A moment later they swarmed about his head as he ran for the apartment in which he had spent the early hours of the morning after his arrival.

It was but a short distance from the top of the ladder to the doorway, and Bradley had almost reached his goal when the door flew open and Fosh-bal-soj stepped out. Immediately the pursuing Wieroos demanded punishment of the *jaal-lu* who had so grievously maltreated them. Fosh-bal-soj listened to their complaints and then with a sudden sweep of his right hand seized Bradley by the scruff of the neck and hurled him sprawling through the doorway upon the floor of the chamber.

So sudden was the assault and so surprising the strength of the Wieroo that the Englishman was taken completely off his guard. When he arose, the door was closed, and Fosh-bal-soj was standing over him, his hideous face contorted into an expression of rage and hatred.

"Hyena, snake, lizard!" he screamed. "You would dare lay your low, vile, profaning hands upon even the lowliest of the Wieroos—the sacred chosen of Luata!"

Bradley was mad, and so he spoke in a very low, calm voice while a half-smile played across his lips but his cold, gray eyes were unsmiling.

"What you did to me just now," he said, "—I am going to kill you for that," and even as he spoke, he launched himself at the throat of Fosh-bal-soj. The other Wieroo that had been asleep when Bradley left the chamber had departed, and the two were alone. Fosh-bal-soj displayed little of the cowardice of those that had attacked Bradley in the alleyway, but that may have been because he had so slight opportunity, for Bradley had him by the throat before he could utter a cry and with his right hand struck him heavily and repeatedly upon his face and over his heart—ugly, smashing, short-arm jabs of the sort that take the fight out of a man in quick time.

But Fosh-bal-soj was of no mind to die passively. He clawed and struck at Bradley while with his great wings he attempted to shield himself from the merciless rain of blows, at the same time searching for a hold upon his antagonist's throat. Presently he succeeded in tripping the Englishman, and together the two fell heavily to the floor, Bradley underneath, and at the same instant the Wieroo fastened his long talons about the other's windpipe.

Fosh-bal-soj was possessed of enormous strength and he was fighting for his life. The Englishman soon realized that the battle was going against him. Already his lungs were pounding painfully for air as he reached for his pistol. It was with difficulty that he drew it from its holster, and even then, with death staring him in the face, he thought of his precious ammunition. "Can't waste it," he thought; and slipping his fingers to the barrel he raised the weapon and struck

Fosh-bal-soj a terrific blow between the eyes. Instantly the clawlike fingers released their hold, and the creature sank limply to the floor beside Bradley, who lay for several minutes gasping painfully in an effort to regain his breath.

When he was able, he rose, and leaned close over the Wieroo, lying silent and motionless, his wings dropping limply and his great, round eyes staring blankly toward the ceiling. A brief examination convinced Bradley that the thing was dead, and with the conviction came an overwhelming sense of the dangers which must now confront him; but how was he to escape?

His first thought was to find some means for concealing the evidence of his deed and then to make a bold effort to escape. Stepping to the second door he pushed it gently open and peered in upon what seemed to be a store room. In it was a litter of cloth such as the Wieroos' robes were fashioned from, a number of chests painted blue and white, with white hieroglyphics painted in bold strokes upon the blue and blue hieroglyphics upon the white. In one corner was a pile of human skulls reaching almost to the ceiling and in another a stack of dried Wieroo wings. The chamber was as irregularly shaped as the other and had but a single window and a second door at the further end, but was without the exit through the roof and, most important of all, there was no creature of any sort in it.

As quickly as possible Bradley dragged the dead Wieroo through the doorway and closed the door; then he looked about for a place to conceal the corpse. One of the chests was large enough to hold the body if the knees were bent well up, and with this idea in view Bradley approached the chest to open it. The lid was made in two pieces, each being hinged at an opposite end of the chest and joining nicely where they met in the center of the chest, making a snug, well-fitting joint. There was no lock. Bradley raised one half the cover and looked in. With a smothered "By Jove!" he bent closer to examine the contents—the chest was about half filled with an assortment of golden trinkets. There were what appeared to be bracelets, anklets and brooches of virgin gold.

Realizing that there was no room in the chest for the body of the Wieroo, Bradley turned to seek another means of concealing the evidence of his crime. There was a space between the chests and the wall, and into this he forced the corpse, piling the discarded robes upon it until it was entirely hidden from sight; but now how was he to make good his escape in the bright glare of that early Spring day?

He walked to the door at the far end of the apartment and cautiously opened it an inch. Before him and about two feet away was the blank wall of another building. Bradley opened the door a little farther and looked in both directions. There was no one in sight to the left over a considerable expanse of roof-top, and to the right another building shut off his line of vision at about twenty feet. Slipping out, he turned to the right and in a few steps found a narrow passageway between two buildings. Turning into this he passed about half its length when he saw a Wieroo appear at the opposite end and halt. The creature was not looking down the passageway; but at any moment it might turn its eyes toward him, when he would be immediately discovered.

To Bradley's left was a triangular niche in the wall of one of the houses and into this he dodged, thus concealing himself from the sight of the Wieroo. Beside him was a door painted a vivid yellow and constructed after the same fashion as the other Wieroo doors he had seen, being made up of countless narrow strips of wood from four to six inches in length laid on in patches of about the same width, the strips in adjacent patches never running in the same direction. The result bore some resemblance to a crazy patchwork quilt, which was heightened when, as in one of the doors he had seen, contiguous patches were painted different colors. The strips appeared to have been bound together and to the underlying framework of the door with gut or fiber and also glued, after which a thick coating of paint had been applied. One edge of the door was formed of a straight, round pole about two inches in diameter that protruded at top and bottom, the projections setting in round holes in both lintel and sill forming the axis upon which the door swung. An eccentric disk upon the inside face of the door engaged a slot in the frame when it was desired to secure the door against intruders.

As Bradley stood flattened against the wall waiting for the Wieroo to move on, he heard the creature's wings brushing against the sides of the buildings as it made its way down the narrow passage in his direction. As the yellow door offered the only means of escape without detection, the Englishman decided to risk whatever might lie beyond it, and so, boldly pushing it in, he crossed the threshold and entered a small apartment.

As he did so, he heard a muffled ejaculation of surprise, and turning his eyes in the direction from whence the sound had come, he beheld a wide-eyed girl standing flattened against the opposite wall, an expression of incredulity upon her face. At a glance he saw that she was of no race of humans that he had come in contact with since his arrival upon Caprona—there was no trace about her form or features of any relationship to those low orders of men, nor was she appareled as they—or, rather, she did not entirely lack apparel as did most of them.

A soft hide fell from her left shoulder to just below her left hip on one side and almost to her right knee on the other, a loose girdle was about her waist, and golden ornaments such as he had seen in the blue-and-white chest encircled her arms and legs, while a golden fillet with a triangular diadem bound her heavy hair above her brows. Her skin was white as from long confinement within doors; but it was clear and fine. Her figure, but partially concealed by the soft deerskin, was all curves of symmetry and youthful grace, while her features might easily have been the envy of the most feted of Continental beauties.

If the girl was surprised by the sudden appearance of Bradley, the latter was absolutely astounded to discover so wondrous a creature among the hideous inhabitants of the City of Human Skulls. For a moment the two looked at one another in unconcealed consternation, and then Bradley spoke, using to the best of his poor ability, the common tongue of Caspak.

"Who are you," he asked, "and from where do you come? Do not tell me that you are a Wieroo."

"No," she replied, "I am no Wieroo." And she shuddered slightly as she pronounced the word. "I am a Galu; but who and what are you? I am sure that you are no Galu, from your garments; but you are like the Galus in other respects. I know that you are not of this frightful city, for I have been here for almost ten moons, and never have I seen a male Galu brought hither before, nor are there such as you and I, other than prisoners in the land of Oo-oh, and these are all females. Are you a prisoner, then?"

He told her briefly who and what he was, though he doubted if she understood, and from her he learned that she had been a prisoner there for many months; but for what purpose he did not then learn, as in the midst of their conversation the yellow door swung open and a Wieroo with a robe slashed with yellow entered.

At sight of Bradley the creature became furious. "Whence came this reptile?" it demanded of the girl. "How long has it been here with you?"

"It came through the doorway just ahead of you," Bradley answered for the girl.

The Wieroo looked relieved. "It is well for the girl that this is so," it said, "for now only you will have to die." And stepping to the door the creature raised its voice in one of those uncanny, depressing wails.

The Englishman looked toward the girl. "Shall I kill it?" he asked, half drawing his pistol. "What is best to do?—I do not wish to endanger you."

The Wieroo backed toward the door. "Defiler!" it screamed. "You dare to threaten one of the sacred chosen of Luata!"

"Do not kill him," cried the girl, "for then there could be no hope for you. That you are here, alive, shows that they may not intend to kill you at all, and so there is a chance for you if you do not anger them; but touch him in violence and your bleached skull will top the loftiest pedestal of Oo-oh."

"And what of you?" asked Bradley.

"I am already doomed," replied the girl; "I am *cos-ata-lo.*"

"*Cos-ata-lo! Cos-ata-lu!*" What did these phrases mean that they were so oft repeated by the denizens of Oo-oh? *Lu* and *lo*, Bradley knew to mean man and *woman*; *ata* was employed variously to indicate life, eggs, young, reproduction and kindred subject; *cos* was a negative; but in combination they were meaningless to the European.

"Do you mean they will kill you?" asked Bradley.

"I but wish that they would," replied the girl. "My fate is to be worse than death—in just a few nights more, with the coming of the new moon."

"Poor she-snake!" snapped the Wieroo. "You are to become sacred above all other shes. He Who Speaks for Luata has chosen you for himself. Today you go to his temple—" the Wieroo used a phrase meaning literally High Place—"where you will receive the sacred commands."

The girl shuddered and cast a sorrowful glance toward Bradley. "Ah," she sighed, "if I could but see my beloved country once again!"

The man stepped suddenly close to her side before the Wieroo could interpose and in a low voice asked her if there was no way by which he might encompass her escape. She shook her head sorrowfully. "Even if we escaped the city," she replied, "there is the big water between the island of Oo-oh and the Galu shore."

"And what is beyond the city, if we could leave it?" pursued Bradley.

261

"I may only guess from what I have heard since I was brought here," she answered; "but by reports and chance remarks I take it to be a beautiful land in which there are but few wild beasts and no men, for only the Wieroos live upon this island and they dwell always in cities of which there are three, this being the largest. The others are at the far end of the island, which is about three marches from end to end and at its widest point about one march."

From his own experience and from what the natives on the mainland had told him, Bradley knew that ten miles was a good day's march in Caspak, owing to the fact that at most points it was a track-less wilderness and at all times travelers were beset by hideous beasts and reptiles that greatly impeded rapid progress.

The two had spoken rapidly but were now interrupted by the advent through the opening in the roof of several Wieroos who had come in answer to the alarm it of the yellow slashing had uttered.

"This *jaal-lu*," cried the offended one, "has threatened me. Take its hatchet from it and make it fast where it can do no harm until He Who Speaks for Luata has said what shall be done with it. It is one of those strange creatures that Fosh-bal-soj discovered first above the Band-lu country and followed back toward the beginning. He Who Speaks for Luata sent Fosh-bal-soj to fetch him one of the creatures, and here it is. It is hoped that it may be from another world and hold the secret of the *cos-ata-lus*."

The Wieroos approached boldly to take Bradley's "hatchet" from him, their leader having indicated the pistol hanging in its holster at the Englishman's hip, but the first one went reeling backward against his fellows from the blow to the chin which Bradley followed up with a rush and the intention to clean up the room in record time; but he had reckoned without the opening in the roof. Two were down and a great wailing and moaning was arising when reinforcements appeared from above. Bradley did not see them; but the girl did, and though she cried out a warning, it came too late for him to avoid a large Wieroo who dived headforemost for him, striking him between the shoulders and bearing him to the floor. Instantly a dozen more were piling on top of him. His pistol was wrenched from its holster and he was securely pinioned down by the weight of numbers.

At a word from the Wieroo of the yellow slashing who evidently was a person of authority, one left and presently returned with fiber ropes with which Bradley was tightly bound.

"Now bear him to the Blue Place of Seven Skulls," directed the chief Wieroo, "and one take the word of all that has passed to Him Who Speaks for Luata."

Each of the creatures raised a hand, the back against its face, as though in salute. One seized Bradley and carried him through the yellow doorway to the roof from whence it rose upon its wide-spread wings and flapped off across the roof-tops of Oo-oh with its heavy burden clutched in its long talons.

Below him Bradley could see the city stretching away to a distance on every hand. It was not as large as he had imagined, though he judged that it was at least three miles square. The houses were piled in indescribable heaps, sometimes to a height of a hundred feet. The streets and alleys were short and crooked and there were many areas where buildings had been wedged in so closely that no light could possibly reach the lowest tiers, the entire surface of the ground being packed solidly with them.

The colors were varied and startling, the architecture amazing. Many roofs were cup or saucer-shaped with a small hole in the center of each, as though they had been constructed to catch rain-water and conduct it to a reservoir beneath; but nearly all the others had the large opening in the top that Bradley had seen used by these flying men in lieu of doorways. At all levels were the myriad poles surmounted by grinning skulls; but the two most prominent features of the city were the round tower of human skulls that Bradley had noted earlier in the day and another and much larger edifice near the center of the city.

As they approached it, Bradley saw that it was a huge building rising a hundred feet in height from the ground and that it stood alone in the center of what might have been called a plaza in some other part of the world. Its various parts, however, were set together with the same strange irregularity that marked the architecture of the city as a whole; and it was capped by an enormous saucer-shaped roof which projected far beyond the eaves, having the appearance of a colossal Chinese coolie hat, inverted.

The Wieroo bearing Bradley passed over one corner of the open space about the large building, revealing to the Englishman grass and trees and running water beneath. They passed the building and about five hundred yards beyond the creature alighted on the roof of a square, blue building surmounted by seven poles bearing seven skulls. This then, thought Bradley, is the Blue Place of Seven Skulls.

Over the opening in the roof was a grated covering, and this the Wieroo removed. The thing then tied a piece of fiber rope to one of Bradley's ankles and rolled him over the edge of the opening. All was dark below and for an instant the Englishman came as near to experiencing real terror as he had ever come in his life before. As he rolled off into the black abyss he felt the rope tighten about his ankle and an instant later he was stopped with a sudden jerk to swing pendulum-like, head downward. Then the creature lowered away until Bradley's head came in sudden and painful contact with the floor below, after which the Wieroo let loose of the rope entirely and the Englishman's body crashed to the wooden planking. He felt the free end of the rope dropped upon him and heard the grating being slid into place above him.

3

alf-stunned, Bradley lay for a minute as he had fallen and then slowly and painfully wriggled into a less uncomfortable position. He could see nothing of his surroundings in the gloom about him until after a few minutes his eyes became accustomed to the dark interior when he rolled them from side to side in survey of his prison.

He discovered himself to be in a bare room which was windowless, nor could he see any other opening than that through which he had been lowered. In one corner was a huddled mass that might have been almost anything from a bundle of rags to a dead body.

Almost immediately after he had taken his bearings Bradley commenced working with his bonds. He was a man of powerful physique, and as from the first he had been imbued with a belief that the fiber ropes were too weak to hold him, he worked on with a firm conviction that sooner or later they would part to his strainings. After a matter of five minutes he was positive that the strands about his wrists were beginning to give; but he was compelled to rest then from exhaustion.

As he lay, his eyes rested upon the bundle in the corner, and presently he could have sworn that the thing moved. With eyes straining through the gloom the man lay watching the grim and sinister thing in the corner. Perhaps his overwrought nerves were playing a sorry joke upon him. He thought of this and also that his condition of utter helplessness might still further have stimulated his imagination. He closed his eyes and sought to relax his muscles and his nerves; but when he looked again, he knew that he had not been mistaken—the thing had moved; now it lay in a slightly altered form and farther from the wall. It was nearer him.

With renewed strength Bradley strained at his bonds, his fascinated gaze still glued upon the shapeless bundle. No longer was there any doubt that it moved—he saw it rise in the center several inches and then creep closer to him. It sank and arose again—a headless, hideous, monstrous thing of menace. Its very silence rendered it the more terrible.

Bradley was a brave man; ordinarily his nerves were of steel; but to be at the mercy of some unknown and nameless horror, to be unable to defend himself—it was these things that almost unstrung him, for at best he was only human. To stand in the open, even with the odds all against him; to be able to use his fists, to put up some sort of defense, to inflict punishment upon his adversary—then he could face death with a smile. It was not death that he feared now—it was that horror of the unknown that is part of the fiber of every son of woman.

Closer and closer came the shapeless mass. Bradley lay motionless and listened. What was that he heard! Breathing? He could not be mistaken—and then from out of the bundle of rags issued a hollow groan. Bradley felt his hair rise upon his head. He struggled with the slowly parting strands that held him. The thing beside him rose up higher than before and the Englishman could have sworn that he saw a single eye peering at him from among the tumbled cloth. For a moment the bundle remained motionless—only the sound of breathing issued from it, then there broke from it a maniacal laugh.

Cold sweat stood upon Bradley's brow as he tugged for liberation. He saw the rags rise higher and higher above him until at last they tumbled upon the floor from the body of a naked man—a thin, a bony, a hideous caricature of man, that mouthed and mummed and, wabbling upon its weak and shaking legs, crumpled to the floor again, still laughing—laughing horribly.

It crawled toward Bradley. "Food! Food!" it screamed. "There is a way out! There is a way out!"

Dragging itself to his side the creature slumped upon the Englishman's breast. "Food!" it shrilled as with its bony fingers and its teeth, it sought the man's bare throat.

"Food! There is a way out!" Bradley felt teeth upon his jugular. He turned and twisted, shaking himself free for an instant; but once more with hideous persistence the thing fastened itself upon him. The weak jaws were unable to send the dull teeth through the victim's flesh; but Bradley felt it pawing, pawing, pawing, like a monstrous rat, seeking his life's blood.

The skinny arms now embraced his neck, holding the teeth to his throat against all his efforts to dislodge the thing. Weak as it was it had strength enough for this in its mad efforts to eat. Mumbling as it worked, it repeated again and again, "Food! Food! There is a way out!" until Bradley thought those two expressions alone would drive him mad.

And all but mad he was as with a final effort backed by almost maniacal strength he tore his wrists from the confining bonds and grasping the repulsive thing upon his breast hurled it halfway across the room. Panting like a spent hound Bradley worked at the thongs about his ankles while the maniac lay quivering and mumbling where it had fallen. Presently the Englishman leaped to his feet—freer than he had ever before felt in all his life, though he was still hopelessly a prisoner in the Blue Place of Seven Skulls.

With his back against the wall for support, so weak the reaction left him, Bradley stood watching the creature upon the floor. He saw it move and slowly raise itself to its hands and knees, where it swayed to and fro as its eyes roved about in search of him; and when at last they found him, there broke from the drawn lips the mumbled words: "Food! Food! There is a way out!" The pitiful supplication in the tones touched the Englishman's heart. He knew that this could be no Wieroo, but possibly once a man like himself who had been cast into this pit of solitary confinement with this hideous result that might in time be his fate, also.

And then, too, there was the suggestion of hope held out by the constant reiteration of the phrase, "There is a way out." Was there a way out? What did this poor thing know?

"Who are you and how long have you been here?" Bradley suddenly demanded.

For a moment the man upon the floor made no response, then mumblingly came the words: "Food! Food!"

"Stop!" commanded the Englishman—the injunction might have been barked from the muzzle of a pistol. It brought the man to a sitting posture, his hands off the ground. He stopped swaying to and fro and appeared to be startled into an attempt to master his faculties of concentration and thought.

Bradley repeated his questions sharply.

"I am An-Tak, the Galu," replied the man. "Luata alone knows how long I have been here—maybe ten moons, maybe ten moons three times"—it was the Caspakian equivalent of thirty. "I was young and strong when they brought me here. Now I am old and very weak. I am *cos-ata-lu*—that is why they have not killed me. If I tell them the secret of becoming *cos-ata-lu* they will take me out; but how can I tell them that which Luata alone knows?

"What is *cos-ata-lu*?" demanded Bradley.

"Food! Food! There is a way out!" mumbled the Galu.

Bradley strode across the floor, seized the man by his shoulders and shook him.

"Tell me," he cried, "what is *cos-ata-lu*?"

"Food!" whimpered An-Tak.

Bradley bethought himself. His haversack had not been taken from him. In it besides his razor and knife were odds and ends of equipment and a small quantity of dried meat. He tossed a small strip of the latter to the starving Galu. An-Tak seized upon it and devoured it ravenously. It instilled new life in the man.

"What is *cos-ata-lu?*" insisted Bradley again.

An-Tak tried to explain. His narrative was often broken by lapses of concentration during which he reverted to his plaintive mumbling for food and recurrence to the statement that there was a way out; but by firmness and patience the Englishman drew out piece-meal a more or less lucid exposition of the remarkable scheme of evolution that rules in Caspak. In it he found explanations of the hitherto inexplicable. He discovered why he had seen no babes or children among the Caspakian tribes with which he had come in contact; why each more northerly tribe evinced a higher state of development than those south of them; why each tribe included individuals ranging in physical and mental characteristics from the highest of the next lower race to the lowest of the next higher, and why the women of each tribe immersed themselves morning for an hour or more in the warm pools near which the habitations of their people always were located; and, too, he discovered why those pools were almost immune from the attacks of carnivorous animals and reptiles.

He learned that all but those who were *cos-ata-lu* came up *cor-sva-jo*, or *from the beginning*. The egg from which they first developed into tadpole form was deposited, with millions of others, in one of the warm pools and with it a poisonous serum that the carnivora instinctively shunned. Down the warm stream from the pool floated the countless billions of eggs and tadpoles, developing as they drifted slowly toward the sea. Some became tadpoles in the pool, some in the sluggish stream and some not until they reached the great inland sea. In the next stage they became fishes or reptiles, An-Tak was not positive which, and in this form, always developing, they swam far to the south, where, amid the rank and teeming jungles, some of them evolved into amphibians. Always there were those whose development stopped at the first stage, others whose development ceased when they became reptiles, while by far the greater proportion formed the food supply of the ravenous creatures of the deep.

Few indeed were those that eventually developed into baboons and then apes, which was considered by Caspakians the real beginning of evolution. From the egg, then, the individual developed slowly into a higher form, just as the frog's egg develops through various stages from a fish with gills to a frog with lungs. With that thought in mind Bradley discovered that it was not difficult to believe in the possibility of such a scheme—there was nothing new in it.

From the ape the individual, if it survived, slowly developed into the lowest order of man—the Alu—and then by degrees to Bo-lu, Sto-lu, Band-lu, Kro-lu and finally to Galu. And in each stage countless millions of other eggs were deposited in the warm pools of the various races and floated down to the great sea to go through a similar process of evolution outside the womb as develops our own young within; but in Caspak the scheme is much more inclusive, for it combines not only individual development but the evolution of species and genera. If an egg survives it goes through all the stages of development that man has passed through during the unthinkable eons since life first moved upon the earth's face.

The final stage—that which the Galus have almost attained and for which all hope—is *cos-ata-lu*, which literally, means no-egg-man, or one who is born directly as are the young of the outer world of mammals. Some of the Galus produce *cos-ata-lu* and *cos-ata-lo* both; the Weiroos only *cos-ata-lu*—in other words all Wieroos are born male, and so they prey upon the Galus for their women and sometimes capture and torture the Galu men who are *cos-ata-lu* in an endeavor to learn the secret which they believe will give them unlimited power over all other denizens of Caspak.

No Wieroos come up from the beginning—all are born of the Wieroo fathers and Galu mothers who are *cos-ata-lo*, and there are very few of the latter owing to the long and precarious stages of development. Seven generations of the same ancestor must come up from the beginning before a *cos-ata-lu* child may be born; and when one considers the frightful dangers that surround the vital spark from the moment it leaves the warm pool where it has been deposited to float down to the sea amid the voracious creatures that swarm the surface and the deeps and the almost equally unthinkable trials of its effort to survive after it once becomes a land animal and starts northward through the horrors of the Caspakian jungles and forests, it is plainly a wonder that even a single babe has ever been born to a Galu woman.

Seven cycles it requires before the seventh Galu can complete the seventh danger-infested circle since its first Galu ancestor achieved the state of Galu. For ages before, the ancestors of this first Galu may have developed from a Band-lu or Bo-lu egg without ever once completing the whole circle—that is from a Galu egg, back to a fully developed Galu.

Bradley's head was whirling before he even commenced to grasp the complexities of Caspakian evolution; but as the truth slowly filtered into his understanding—as gradually it became possible for him to visualize the scheme, it appeared simpler. In fact, it seemed even less difficult of comprehension than that with which he was familiar.

For several minutes after An-Tak ceased speaking, his voice having trailed off weakly into silence, neither spoke again. Then the Galu recommenced his, "Food! Food! There is a way out!" Bradley tossed him another bit of dried meat, waiting patiently until he had eaten it, this time more slowly.

"What do you mean by saying there is a way out?" he asked.

"He who died here just after I came, told me," replied An-Tak. "He said there was a way out, that he had discovered it but was too weak to use his knowledge. He was trying to tell me how to find it when he died. Oh, Luata, if he had lived but a moment more!"

"They do not feed you here?" asked Bradley.

"No, they give me water once a day—that is all."

"But how have you lived, then?"

"The lizards and the rats," replied An-Tak. "The lizards are not so bad; but the rats are foul to taste. However, I must eat them or they would eat me, and they are better than nothing; but of late they do not come so often, and I have not had a lizard for a long time. I shall eat though," he mumbled. "I shall eat now, for you cannot remain awake forever." He laughed, a cackling, dry laugh. "When you sleep, An-Tak will eat."

It was horrible. Bradley shuddered. For a long time each sat in silence. The Englishman could guess why the other made no sound— he awaited the moment that sleep should overcome his victim. In the long silence there was born upon Bradley's ears a faint, monotonous sound as of running water. He listened intently. It seemed to come from far beneath the floor.

"What is that noise?" he asked. "That sounds like water running through a narrow channel."

"It is the river," replied An-Tak. "Why do you not go to sleep? It passes directly beneath the Blue Place of Seven Skulls. It runs through the temple grounds, beneath the temple and under the city. When we die, they will cut off our heads and throw our bodies into the river. At the mouth of the river await many large reptiles. Thus do they feed. The Wieroos do likewise with their own dead, keeping only the skulls and the wings. Come, let us sleep."

"Do the reptiles come up the river into the city?" asked Bradley.

"The water is too cold—they never leave the warm water of the great pool," replied An-Tak.

"Let us search for the way out," suggested Bradley.

An-Tak shook his head. "I have searched for it all these moons," he said. "If I could not find it, how would you?"

Bradley made no reply but commenced a diligent examination of the walls and floor of the room, pressing over each square foot and tapping with his knuckles. About six feet from the floor he discovered a sleeping-perch near one end of the apartment. He asked An-Tak about it, but the Galu said that no Weiroo had occupied the place since he had been incarcerated there. Again and again Bradley went over the floor and walls as high up as he could reach. Finally he swung himself to the perch, that he might examine at least one end of the room all the way to the ceiling.

In the center of the wall close to the top, an area about three feet square gave forth a hollow sound when he rapped upon it. Bradley felt over every square inch of that area with the tips of his fingers. Near the top he found a small round hole a trifle larger in diameter than his forefinger, which he immediately stuck into it. The panel, if such it was, seemed about an inch thick, and beyond it his finger encountered nothing. Bradley crooked his finger upon the opposite side of the panel and pulled toward him, steadily but with considerable force. Suddenly the panel flew inward, nearly precipitating the man to the floor. It was hinged at the bottom, and when lowered the outer edge rested upon the perch, making a little platform parallel with the floor of the room.

Beyond the opening was an utterly dark void. The Englishman leaned through it and reached his arm as far as possible into the blackness but touched nothing. Then he fumbled in his haversack for a match, a few of which remained to him. When he struck it, An-Tak gave a cry of terror. Bradley held the light far into the opening before him and in its flickering rays saw the top of a ladder descending into a black abyss below. How far down it extended he could not guess; but that he should soon know definitely he was positive.

"You have found it! You have found the way out!" screamed An-Tak. "Oh, Luata! And now I am too weak to go. Take me with you! Take me with you!"

"Shut up!" admonished Bradley. "You will have the whole flock of birds around our heads in a minute, and neither of us will escape. Be quiet, and I'll go ahead. If I find a way out, I'll come back and help you, if you'll promise not to try to eat me up again."

"I promise," cried An-Tak. "Oh, Luata! How could you blame me? I am half crazed of hunger and long confinement and the horror of the lizards and the rats and the constant waiting for death."

"I know," said Bradley simply. "I'm sorry for you, old top. Keep a stiff upper lip." And he slipped through the opening, found the ladder with his feet, closed the panel behind him, and started downward into the darkness.

Below him rose more and more distinctly the sound of running water. The air felt damp and cool. He could see nothing of his surroundings and felt nothing but the smooth, worn sides and rungs of the ladder down which he felt his way cautiously lest a broken rung or a misstep should hurl him downward.

As he descended thus slowly, the ladder seemed interminable and the pit bottomless, yet he realized when at last he reached the bottom that he could not have descended more than fifty feet. The bottom of the ladder rested on a narrow ledge paved with what felt like large round stones, but what he knew from experience to be human skulls. He could not but marvel as to where so many countless thousands of the things had come from, until he paused to consider that the infancy of Caspak dated doubtlessly back into remote ages, far beyond what the outer world considered the beginning of earthly time. For all these eons the Wieroos might have been collecting human skulls from their enemies and their own dead—enough to have built an entire city of them.

Feeling his way along the narrow ledge, Bradley came presently to a blank wall that stretched out over the water swirling beneath him, as far as he could reach. Stooping, he groped about with one hand, reaching down toward the surface of the water, and discovered that the bottom of the wall arched above the stream. How much space there was between the water and the arch he could not tell, nor how deep the former. There was only one way in which he might learn these things, and that was to lower himself into the stream. For only an instant he hesitated weighing his chances. Behind him lay almost certainly the horrid fate of An-Tak; before him nothing worse than a comparatively painless death by drowning. Holding his haversack above his head with one hand he lowered his feet slowly over the edge of the narrow platform. Almost immediately he felt the swirling of cold water about his ankles, and then with a silent prayer he let himself drop gently into the stream.

Great was Bradley's relief when he found the water no more than waist deep and beneath his feet a firm, gravel bottom. Feeling his way cautiously he moved downward with the current, which was not so strong as he had imagined from the noise of the running water.

Beneath the first arch he made his way, following the winding curvatures of the right-hand wall. After a few yards of progress his hand came suddenly in contact with a slimy thing clinging to the wall—a thing that hissed and scuttled out of reach. What it was, the man could not know; but almost instantly there was a splash in the water just ahead of him and then another.

On he went, passing beneath other arches at varying distances, and always in utter darkness. Unseen denizens of this great sewer, disturbed by the intruder, splashed into the water ahead of him and wriggled away. Time and again his hand touched them and never for an instant could he be sure that at the next step some gruesome thing might not attack him. He had strapped his haversack about his neck, well above the surface of the water, and in his left hand he carried his knife. Other precautions there were none to take.

The monotony of the blind trail was increased by the fact that from the moment he had started from the foot of the ladder he had counted his every step. He had promised to return for An-Tak if it proved humanly possible to do so, and he knew that in the blackness of the tunnel he could locate the foot of the ladder in no other way.

He had taken two hundred and sixty-nine steps—afterward he knew that he should never forget that number—when something bumped gently against him from behind. Instantly he wheeled about and with knife ready to defend himself stretched forth his right hand to push away the object that now had lodged against his body. His fingers feeling through the darkness came in contact with something cold and clammy—they passed to and fro over the thing until Bradley knew that it was the face of a dead man floating upon the surface of the stream. With an oath he pushed his gruesome companion out into mid-stream to float on down toward the great pool and the awaiting scavengers of the deep.

At his four hundred and thirteenth step another corpse bumped against him—how many had passed him without touching he could not guess; but suddenly he experienced the sensation of being surrounded by dead faces floating along with him, all set in hideous grimaces, their dead eyes glaring at this profaning alien who dared intrude upon the waters of this river of the dead—a horrid escort, pregnant with dire forebodings and with menace.

Though he advanced very slowly, he tried always to take steps of about the same length; so that he knew that though considerable time had elapsed, yet he had really advanced no more than four hundred yards when ahead he saw a lessening of the pitch-darkness, and at the next turn of the stream his surroundings became vaguely discernible. Above him was an arched roof and on either hand walls pierced at intervals by apertures covered with wooden doors. Just ahead of him in the roof of the aqueduct was a round, black hole about thirty inches in diameter. His eyes still rested upon the opening when there shot downward from it to the water below the naked body of a human being which almost immediately rose to the surface again and floated off down the stream. In the dim light Bradley saw that it was a dead Wieroo from which the wings and head had been removed. A moment later another headless body floated past, recalling what An-Tak had told him of the skull-collecting customs of the Wieroo. Bradley wondered how it happened that the first corpse he had encountered in the stream had not been similarly mutilated.

The farther he advanced now, the lighter it became. The number of corpses was much smaller than he had imagined, only two more passing him before, at six hundred steps, or about five hundred yards, from the point he had taken to the stream, he came to the end of the tunnel and looked out upon sunlit water, running between grassy banks.

One of the last corpses to pass him was still clothed in the white robe of a Wieroo, blood-stained over the headless neck that it concealed.

Drawing closer to the opening leading into the bright daylight, Bradley surveyed what lay beyond. A short distance before him a large building stood in the center of several acres of grass and tree-covered ground, spanning the stream which disappeared through an opening in its foundation wall. From the large saucer-shaped roof and the vivid colorings of the various heterogeneous parts of the structure he recognized it as the temple past which he had been borne to the Blue Place of Seven Skulls.

To and fro flew Wieroos, going to and from the temple. Others passed on foot across the open grounds, assisting themselves with their great wings, so that they barely skimmed the earth. To leave the mouth of the tunnel would have been to court instant discovery and capture; but by what other avenue he might escape, Bradley could not guess, unless he retraced his steps up the stream and sought egress from the other end of the city. The thought of traversing that dark and horror-ridden tunnel for perhaps miles he could not entertain—there must be some other way. Perhaps after dark he could steal through the temple grounds and continue on downstream until he had come beyond the city; and so he stood and waited until his limbs became almost paralyzed with cold, and he knew that he must find some other plan for escape.

A half-formed decision to risk an attempt to swim under water to the temple was crystallizing in spite of the fact that any chance Wieroo flying above the stream might easily see him, when again a floating object bumped against him from behind and lodged across his back. Turning quickly he saw that the thing was what he had immediately guessed it to be—a headless and wingless Wieroo corpse. With a grunt of disgust he was about to push it from him when the white garment enshrouding it suggested a bold plan to his resourceful brain. Grasping the corpse by an arm he tore the garment from it and then let the body float downward toward the temple. With great care he draped the robe about him; the bloody blotch that had covered the severed neck he arranged about his own head. His haversack he rolled as tightly as possible and stuffed beneath his coat over his breast. Then he fell gently to the surface of the stream and lying upon his back floated downward with the current and out into the open sunlight.

Through the weave of the cloth he could distinguish large objects. He saw a Wieroo flap dismally above him; he saw the banks of the stream float slowly past; he heard a sudden wail upon the right-hand shore, and his heart stood still lest his ruse had been discovered; but never by a move of a muscle did he betray that aught but a cold lump of clay floated there upon the bosom of the water, and soon, though it seemed an eternity to him, the direct sunlight was blotted out, and he knew that he had entered beneath the temple.

Quickly he felt for bottom with his feet and as quickly stood erect, snatching the bloody, clammy cloth from his face. On both sides were blank walls and before him the river turned a sharp corner and disappeared. Feeling his way cautiously forward he approached the turn and looked around the corner. To his left was a low platform about a foot above the level of the stream, and onto this he lost no time in climbing, for he was soaked from head to foot, cold and almost exhausted.

As he lay resting on the skull-paved shelf, he saw in the center of the vault above the river another of those sinister round holes through which he momentarily expected to see a headless corpse shoot downward in its last plunge to a watery grave. A few feet along the platform a closed door broke the blankness of the wall. As he lay looking at it and wondering what lay behind, his mind filled with fragments of many wild schemes of escape, it opened and a white-robed Wieroo stepped out upon the platform. The creature carried a large wooden basin filled with rubbish. Its eyes were not upon Bradley, who drew himself to a squatting position and crouched as far back in the corner of the niche in which the platform was set as he could force himself. The Wieroo stepped to the edge of the platform and dumped the rubbish into the stream. If it turned away from him as it started to retrace its steps to the doorway, there was a small chance that it might not see him; but if it turned toward him there was none at all. Bradley held his breath.

The Wieroo paused a moment, gazing down into the water, then it straightened up and turned toward the Englishman. Bradley did not move. The Wieroo stopped and stared intently at him. It approached him questioningly. Still Bradley remained as though carved of stone. The creature was directly in front of him. It stopped. There was no chance on earth that it would not discover what he was.

With the quickness of a cat, Bradley sprang to his feet and with all his great strength, backed by his heavy weight, struck the Wieroo upon the point of the chin. Without a sound the thing crumpled to the platform, while Bradley, acting almost instinctively to the urge of the first law of nature, rolled the inanimate body over the edge into the river.

Then he looked at the open doorway, crossed the platform and peered within the apartment beyond. What he saw was a large room, dimly lighted, and about the side rows of wooden vessels stacked one upon another. There was no Wieroo in sight, so the Englishman entered. At the far end of the room was another door, and as he crossed toward it, he glanced into some of the vessels, which he found were filled with dried fruits, vegetables and fish. Without more ado he stuffed his pockets and his haversack full, thinking of the poor creature awaiting his return in the gloom of the Place of Seven Skulls.

When night came, he would return and fetch An-Tak this far at least; but in the meantime it was his intention to reconnoiter in the hope that he might discover some easier way out of the city than that offered by the chill, black channel of the ghastly river of corpses.

Beyond the farther door stretched a long passageway from which closed doorways led into other parts of the cellars of the temple. A few yards from the storeroom a ladder rose from the corridor through an aperture in the ceiling. Bradley paused at the foot of it, debating the wisdom of further investigation against a return to the river; but strong within him was the spirit of exploration that has scattered his race to the four corners of the earth. What new mysteries lay hidden in the chambers above? The urge to know was strong upon him though his better judgment warned him that the safer course lay in retreat. For a moment he stood thus, running his fingers through his hair; then he cast discretion to the winds and began the ascent.

In conformity with such Wieroo architecture as he had already observed, the well through which the ladder rose continually canted at an angle from the perpendicular. At more or less regular stages it was pierced by apertures closed by doors, none of which he could open until he had climbed fully fifty feet from the river level. Here he discovered a door already ajar opening into a large, circular chamber, the walls and floors of which were covered with the skins of wild beasts and with rugs of many colors; but what interested him most was the occupants of the room—a Wieroo, and a girl of human proportions. She was standing with her back against a column which rose from the center of the apartment from floor to ceiling—a hollow column about forty inches in diameter in which he could see an opening some thirty inches across. The girl's side was toward Bradley, and her face averted, for she was watching the Wieroo, who was now advancing slowly toward her, talking as he came.

Bradley could distinctly hear the words of the creature, who was urging the girl to accompany him to another Wieroo city. "Come with me," he said, "and you shall have your life; remain here and He Who Speaks for Luata will claim you for his own; and when he is done with you, your skull will bleach at the top of a tall staff while your body feeds the reptiles at the mouth of the River of Death. Even though you bring into the world a female Wieroo, your fate will be the same if you do not escape him, while with me you shall have life and food and none shall harm you."

He was quite close to the girl when she replied by striking him in the face with all her strength. "Until I am slain," she cried, "I shall fight against you all." From the throat of the Wieroo issued that dismal wail that Bradley had heard so often in the past—it was like a scream of pain smothered to a groan—and then the thing leaped upon the girl, its face working in hideous grimaces as it clawed and beat at her to force her to the floor.

The Englishman was upon the point of entering to defend her when a door at the opposite side of the chamber opened to admit a huge Wieroo clothed entirely in red. At sight of the two struggling upon the floor the newcomer raised his voice in a shriek of rage. Instantly the Wieroo who was attacking the girl leaped to his feet and faced the other.

"I heard," screamed he who had just entered the room. "I heard, and when He Who Speaks for Luata shall have heard——" He paused and made a suggestive movement of a finger across his throat.

"He shall not hear," returned the first Wieroo as, with a powerful motion of his great wings, he launched himself upon the red-robed figure. The latter dodged the first charge, drew a wicked-looking curved blade from beneath its red robe, spread its wings and dived for its antagonist. Beating their wings, wailing and groaning, the two hideous things sparred for position. The white-robed one being unarmed sought to grasp the other by the wrist of its knife-hand and by the throat, while the latter hopped around on its dainty white feet, seeking an opening for a mortal blow. Once it struck and missed, and then the other rushed in and clinched, at the same time securing both the holds it sought. Immediately the two commenced beating at each other's heads with the joints of their wings, kicking with their soft, puny feet and biting, each at the other's face.

In the meantime the girl moved about the room, keeping out of the way of the duelists, and as she did so, Bradley caught a glimpse of her full face and immediately recognized her as the girl of the place of the yellow door. He did not dare intervene now until one of the Wieroo had overcome the other, lest the two should turn upon him at once, when the chances were fair that he would be defeated in so unequal a battle as the curved blade of the red Wieroo would render it, and so he waited, watching the white-robed figure slowly choking the life from him of the red robe. The protruding tongue and the popping eyes proclaimed that the end was near and a moment later the red robe sank to the floor of the room, the curved blade slipping from nerveless fingers. For an instant longer the victor clung to the throat of his defeated antagonist and then he rose, dragging the body after him, and approached the central column. Here he raised the body and thrust it into the aperture where Bradley saw it drop suddenly from sight. Instantly there flashed into his memory the circular openings in the roof of the river vault and the corpses he had seen drop from them to the water beneath.

As the body disappeared, the Wieroo turned and cast about the room for the girl. For a moment he stood eying her. "You saw," he muttered, "and if you tell them, He Who Speaks for Luata will have my wings severed while still I live and my head will be severed and I shall be cast into the River of Death, for thus it happens even to the highest who slay one of the red robe. You saw, and you must die!" he ended with a scream as he rushed upon the girl.

Bradley waited no longer. Leaping into the room he ran for the Wieroo, who had already seized the girl, and as he ran, he stooped and picked up the curved blade. The creature's back was toward him as, with his left hand, he seized it by the neck. Like a flash the great wings beat backward as the creature turned, and Bradley was swept from his feet, though he still retained his hold upon the blade. Instantly the Wieroo was upon him. Bradley lay slightly raised upon his left elbow, his right arm free, and as the thing came close, he cut at the hideous face with all the strength that lay within him. The blade struck at the junction of the neck and torso and with such force as to completely decapitate the Wieroo, the hideous head dropping to the floor and the body falling forward upon the Englishman.

Pushing it from him he rose to his feet and faced the wide-eyed girl.

"Luata!" she exclaimed. "How came you here?"

Bradley shrugged. "Here I am," he said; "but the thing now is to get out of here—both of us."

The girl shook her head. "It cannot be," she stated sadly.

"That is what I thought when they dropped me into the Blue Place of Seven Skulls," replied Bradley. "Can't be done. I did it.—Here! You're mussing up the floor something awful, you." This last to the dead Wieroo as he stooped and dragged the corpse to the central shaft, where he raised it to the aperture and let it slip into the tube. Then he picked up the head and tossed it after the body. "Don't be so glum," he admonished the former as he carried it toward the well; "smile!"

"But how can he smile?" questioned the girl, a half-puzzled, half-frightened look upon her face. "He is dead."

"That's so," admitted Bradley, "and I suppose he does feel a bit cut up about it."

The girl shook her head and edged away from the man—toward the door.

"Come!" said the Englishman. "We've got to get out of here. If you don't know a better way than the river, it's the river then."

The girl still eyed him askance. "But how could he smile when he was dead?"

Bradley laughed aloud. "I thought we English were supposed to have the least sense of humor of any people in the world," he cried; "but now I've found one human being who hasn't any. Of course you don't know half I'm saying; but don't worry, little girl; I'm not going to hurt you, and if I can get you out of here, I'll do it."

Even if she did not understand all he said, she at least read something in his smiling, countenance—something which reassured her. "I do not fear you," she said; "though I do not understand all that you say even though you speak my own tongue and use words that I know. But as for escaping"—she sighed—"alas, how can it be done?"

"I escaped from the Blue Place of Seven Skulls," Bradley reminded her. "Come!" And he turned toward the shaft and the ladder that he had ascended from the river. "We cannot waste time here."

The girl followed him; but at the doorway both drew back, for from below came the sound of some one ascending. Bradley tiptoed to the door and peered cautiously into the well; then he stepped back beside the girl. "There are half a dozen of them coming up; but possibly they will pass this room."

"No," she said, "they will pass directly through this room—they are on their way to Him Who Speaks for Luata. We may be able to hide in the next room—there are skins there beneath which we may crawl. They will not stop in that room; but they may stop in this one

284

for a short time—the other room is blue."

"What's that go to do with it?" demanded the Englishman.

"They fear blue," she replied. "In every room where murder has been done you will find blue—a certain amount for each murder. When the room is all blue, they shun it. This room has much blue; but evidently they kill mostly in the next room, which is now all blue."

"But there is blue on the outside of every house I have seen," said Bradley.

"Yes," assented the girl, "and there are blue rooms in each of those houses—when all the rooms are blue then the whole outside of the house will be blue as is the Blue Place of Seven Skulls. There are many such here."

"And the skulls with blue upon them?" inquired Bradley. "Did they belong to murderers?"

"They were murdered—some of them; those with only a small amount of blue were murderers—known murderers. All Wieroos are murderers. When they have committed a certain number of murders without being caught at it, they confess to Him Who Speaks for Luata and are advanced, after which they wear robes with a slash of some color—I think yellow comes first. When they reach a point where the entire robe is of yellow, they discard it for a white robe with a red slash; and when one wins a complete red robe, he carries such a long, curved knife as you have in your hand; after that comes the blue slash on a white robe, and then, I suppose, an all blue robe. I have never seen such a one."

As they talked in low tones they had moved from the room of the death shaft into an all blue room adjoining, where they sat down together in a corner with their backs against a wall and drew a pile of hides over themselves. A moment later they heard a number of Wieroos enter the chamber. They were talking together as they crossed the floor, or the two could not have heard them. Half-way across the chamber they halted as the door toward which they were advancing opened and a dozen others of their kind entered the apartment.

Bradley could guess all this by the increased volume of sound and the dismal greetings; but the sudden silence that almost immediately ensued he could not fathom, for he could not know that from beneath one of the hides that covered him protruded one of his heavy army shoes, or that some eighteen large Wieroos with robes either solid red or slashed with red or blue were standing gazing at it. Nor could he hear their stealthy approach.

The first intimation he had that he had been discovered was when his foot was suddenly seized, and he was yanked violently from beneath the hides to find himself surrounded by menacing blades. They would have slain him on the spot had not one clothed all in red held them back, saying that He Who Speaks for Luata desired to see this strange creature.

As they led Bradley away, he caught an opportunity to glance back toward the hides to see what had become of the girl, and, to his gratification, he discovered that she still lay concealed beneath the hides. He wondered if she would have the nerve to attempt the river trip alone and regretted that now he could not accompany her. He felt rather all in, himself, more so than he had at any time since he had been captured by the Wieroo, for there appeared not the slightest cause for hope in his present predicament. He had dropped the curved blade beneath the hides when he had been jerked so violently from their fancied security. It was almost in a spirit of resigned hopelessness that he quietly accompanied his captors through various chambers and corridors toward the heart of the temple.

4

he farther the group progressed, the more barbaric and the more sumptuous became the decorations. Hides of leopard and tiger predominated, apparently because of their more beautiful markings, and decorative skulls became more and more numerous. Many of the latter were mounted in precious metals and set with colored stones and priceless gems, while thick upon the hides that covered the walls were golden ornaments similar to those worn by the girl and those which had filled the chests he had examined in the storeroom of Fosh-bal-soj, leading the Englishman to the conviction that all such were spoils of war or theft, since each piece seemed made for personal adornment, while in so far as he had seen, no Wieroo wore ornaments of any sort.

And also as they advanced the more numerous became the Wieroos moving hither and thither within the temple. Many now were the solid red robes and those that were slashed with blue—a veritable hive of murderers.

At last the party halted in a room in which were many Wieroos who gathered about Bradley questioning his captors and examining him and his apparel. One of the party accompanying the Englishman spoke to a Wieroo that stood beside a door leading from the room. "Tell Him Who Speaks for Luata," he said, "that Fosh-bal-soj we could not find; but that in returning we found this creature within the temple, hiding. It must be the same that Fosh-bal-soj captured in the Sto-lu country during the last darkness. Doubtless He Who

Speaks for Luata would wish to see and question this strange thing."

The creature addressed turned and slipped through the doorway, closing the door after it, but first depositing its curved blade upon the floor without. Its post was immediately taken by another and Bradley now saw that at least twenty such guards loitered in the immediate vicinity. The doorkeeper was gone but for a moment, and when he returned, he signified that Bradley's party was to enter the next chamber; but first each of the Wieroos removed his curved weapon and laid it upon the floor. The door was swung open, and the party, now reduced to Bradley and five Wieroos, was ushered across the threshold into a large, irregularly shaped room in which a single, giant Wieroo whose robe was solid blue sat upon a raised dais.

The creature's face was white with the whiteness of a corpse, its dead eyes entirely expressionless, its cruel, thin lips tight-drawn against yellow teeth in a perpetual grimace. Upon either side of it lay an enormous, curved sword, similar to those with which some of the other Wieroos had been armed, but larger and heavier. Constantly its clawlike fingers played with one or the other of these weapons.

The walls of the chamber as well as the floor were entirely hidden by skins and woven fabrics. Blue predominated in all the colorations. Fastened against the hides were many pairs of Wieroo wings, mounted so that they resembled long, black shields. Upon the ceiling were painted in blue characters a bewildering series of hieroglyphics and upon pedestals set against the walls or standing out well within the room were many human skulls.

As the Wieroos approached the figure upon the dais, they leaned far forward, raising their wings above their heads and stretching their necks as though offering them to the sharp swords of the grim and hideous creature.

"O Thou Who Speakest for Luata!" exclaimed one of the party. "We bring you the strange creature that Fosh-bal-soj captured and brought thither at thy command."

So this then was the godlike figure that spoke for divinity! This arch-murderer was the Caspakian representative of God on Earth! His blue robe announced him the one and the seeming humility of his minions the other. For a long minute he glared at Bradley. Then he began to question him—from whence he came and how, the name and description of his native country, and a hundred other queries.

"Are you *cos-ata-lu*?" the creature asked.

Bradley replied that he was and that all his kind were, as well as every living thing in his part of the world.

"Can you tell me the secret?" asked the creature.

Bradley hesitated and then, thinking to gain time, replied in the affirmative.

"What is it?" demanded the Wieroo, leaning far forward and exhibiting every evidence of excited interest.

Bradley leaned forward and whispered: "It is for your ears alone; I will not divulge it to others, and then only on condition that you carry me and the girl I saw in the place of the yellow door near to that of Fosh-bal-soj back to her own country."

The thing rose in wrath, holding one of its swords above its head.

"Who are you to make terms for Him Who Speaks for Luata?" it shrilled. "Tell me the secret or die where you stand!"

"And if I die now, the secret goes with me," Bradley reminded him. "Never again will you get the opportunity to question another of my kind who knows the secret." Anything to gain time, to get the rest of the Wieroos from the room, that he might plan some scheme for escape and put it into effect.

The creature turned upon the leader of the party that had brought Bradley.

"Is the thing with weapons?" it asked.

"No," was the response.

"Then go; but tell the guard to remain close by," commanded the high one.

The Wieroos salaamed and withdrew, closing the door behind them. He Who Speaks for Luata grasped a sword nervously in his right hand. At his left side lay the second weapon. It was evident that he lived in constant dread of being assassinated. The fact that he permitted none with weapons within his presence and that he always kept two swords at his side pointed to this.

Bradley was racking his brain to find some suggestion of a plan whereby he might turn the situation to his own account. His eyes wandered past the weird figure before him; they played about the walls of the apartment as though hoping to draw inspiration from the dead skulls and the hides and the wings, and then they came back to the face of the Wieroo god, now working in anger.

"Quick!" screamed the thing. "The secret!"

"Will you give me and the girl our freedom?" insisted Bradley.

For an instant the thing hesitated, and then it grumbled "Yes." At the same instant Bradley saw two hides upon the wall directly back of the dais separate and a face appear in the opening. No change of expression upon the Englishman's countenance betrayed that he had seen aught to surprise him, though surprised he was for the face in the aperture was that of the girl he had but just left hidden beneath the hides in another chamber. A white and shapely arm now pushed past the face into the room, and in the hand, tightly clutched, was the curved blade, smeared with blood, that Bradley had dropped beneath the hides at the moment he had been discovered and drawn from his concealment.

"Listen, then," said Bradley in a low voice to the Wieroo. "You shall know the secret of *cos-ata-lu* as well as do I; but none other may hear it. Lean close—I will whisper it into your ear."

He moved forward and stepped upon the dais. The creature raised its sword ready to strike at the first indication of treachery, and Bradley stooped beneath the blade and put his ear close to the gruesome face. As he did so, he rested his weight upon his hands, one upon either side of the Wieroo's body, his right hand upon the hilt of the spare sword lying at the left of Him Who Speaks for Luata.

"This then is the secret of both life and death," he whispered, and at the same instant he grasped the Wieroo by the right wrist and with his own right hand swung the extra blade in a sudden vicious blow against the creature's neck before the thing could give even a single cry of alarm; then without waiting an instant Bradley leaped past the dead god and vanished behind the hides that had hidden the girl.

Wide-eyed and panting the girl seized his arm. "Oh, what have you done?" she cried. "He Who Speaks for Luata will be avenged by Luata. Now indeed must you die. There is no escape, for even though we reached my own country Luata can find you out."

"Bosh!" exclaimed Bradley, and then: "But you were going to knife him yourself."

"Then I alone should have died," she replied.

Bradley scratched his head. "Neither of us is going to die," he said; "at least not at the hands of any god. If we don't get out of here though, we'll die right enough. Can you find your way back to the room where I first came upon you in the temple?"

"I know the way," replied the girl; "but I doubt if we can go back without being seen. I came hither because I only met Wieroos who knew that I am supposed now to be in the temple; but you could go elsewhere without being discovered."

Bradley's ingenuity had come up against a stone wall. There seemed no possibility of escape. He looked about him. They were in a small room where lay a litter of rubbish—torn bits of cloth, old hides, pieces of fiber rope. In the center of the room was a cylindrical shaft with an opening in its face. Bradley knew it for what it was. Here the arch-fiend dragged his victims and cast their bodies into the river of death far below. The floor about the opening in the shaft and the sides of the shaft were clotted thick with a dried, dark brown substance that the Englishman knew had once been blood. The place had the appearance of having been a veritable shambles. An odor of decaying flesh permeated the air.

The Englishman crossed to the shaft and peered into the opening. All below was dark as pitch; but at the bottom he knew was the river. Suddenly an inspiration and a bold scheme leaped to his mind. Turning quickly he hunted about the room until he found what he sought—a quantity of the rope that lay strewn here and there. With rapid fingers he unsnarled the different lengths, the girl helping him, and then he tied the ends together until he had three ropes about seventy-five feet in length. He fastened these together at each end and without a word secured one of the ends about the girl's body beneath her arms.

"Don't be frightened," he said at length, as he led her toward the opening in the shaft. "I'm going to lower you to the river, and then I'm coming down after you. When you are safe below, give two quick jerks upon the rope. If there is danger there and you want me to draw you up into the shaft, jerk once. Don't be afraid—it is the only way."

"I am not afraid," replied the girl, rather haughtily Bradley thought, and herself climbed through the aperture and hung by her hands waiting for Bradley to lower her.

As rapidly as was consistent with safety, the man paid out the rope. When it was about half out, he heard loud cries and wails suddenly arise within the room they had just quitted. The slaying of their god had been discovered by the Wieroos. A search for the slayer would begin at once.

Lord! Would the girl never reach the river? At last, just as he was positive that searchers were already entering the room behind him, there came two quick tugs at the rope. Instantly Bradley made the rest of the strands fast about the shaft, slipped into the black tube and began a hurried descent toward the river. An instant later he stood waist deep in water beside the girl. Impulsively she reached toward him and grasped his arm. A strange thrill ran through him at the contact; but he only cut the rope from about her body and lifted her to the little shelf at the river's side.

"How can we leave here?" she asked.

"By the river," he replied; "but first I must go back to the Blue Place of Seven Skulls and get the poor devil I left there. I'll have to wait until after dark, though, as I cannot pass through the open stretch of river in the temple gardens by day."

"There is another way," said the girl. "I have never seen it; but often I have heard them speak of it—a corridor that runs beside the river from one end of the city to the other. Through the gardens it is below ground. If we could find an entrance to it, we could leave here at once. It is not safe here, for they will search every inch of the temple and the grounds."

"Come," said Bradley. "We'll have a look for it, anyway." And so saying he approached one of the doors that opened onto the skull-paved shelf.

They found the corridor easily, for it paralleled the river, separated from it only by a single wall. It took them beneath the gardens and the city, always through inky darkness. After they had reached the other side of the gardens, Bradley counted his steps until he had retraced as many as he had taken coming down the stream; but though they had to grope their way along, it was a much more rapid trip than the former.

When he thought he was about opposite the point at which he had descended from the Blue Place of Seven Skulls, he sought and found a doorway leading out onto the river; and then, still in the blackest darkness, he lowered himself into the stream and felt up and down upon the opposite side for the little shelf and the ladder. Ten yards from where he had emerged he found them, while the girl waited upon the opposite side.

To ascend to the secret panel was the work of but a minute. Here he paused and listened lest a Wieroo might be visiting the prison in search of him or the other inmate; but no sound came from the gloomy interior. Bradley could not but muse upon the joy of the man on the opposite side when he should drop down to him with food and a new hope for escape. Then he opened the panel and looked into the room. The faint light from the grating above revealed the pile of rags in one corner; but the man lay beneath them, he made no response to Bradley's low greeting.

The Englishman lowered himself to the floor of the room and approached the rags. Stooping he lifted a corner of them. Yes, there was the man asleep. Bradley shook him—there was no response. He stooped lower and in the dim light examined An-Tak; then he stood up with a sigh. A rat leaped from beneath the coverings and scurried away. "Poor devil!" muttered Bradley.

He crossed the room to swing himself to the perch preparatory to quitting the Blue Place of Seven Skulls forever. Beneath the perch he paused. "I'll not give them the satisfaction," he growled. "Let them believe that he escaped."

Returning to the pile of rags he gathered the man into his arms. It was difficult work raising him to the high perch and dragging him through the small opening and thus down the ladder; but presently it was done, and Bradley had lowered the body into the river and cast it off. "Good-bye, old top!" he whispered.

A moment later he had rejoined the girl and hand in hand they were following the dark corridor upstream toward the farther end of the city. She told him that the Wieroos seldom frequented these lower passages, as the air here was too chill for them; but occasionally they came, and as they could see quite as well by night as by day, they would be sure to discover Bradley and the girl.

"If they come close enough," she said, "we can see their eyes shining in the dark—they resemble dull splotches of light. They glow, but do not blaze like the eyes of the tiger or the lion."

The man could not but note the very evident horror with which she mentioned the creatures. To him they were uncanny; but she had been used to them for a year almost, and probably all her life she had either seen or heard of them constantly.

"Why do you fear them so?" he asked. "It seems more than any ordinary fear of the harm they can do you."

She tried to explain; but the nearest he could gather was that she looked upon the Wieroo almost as supernatural beings. "There is a legend current among my people that once the Wieroo were unlike us only in that they possessed rudimentary wings. They lived in villages in the Galu country, and while the two peoples often warred, they held no hatred for one another. In those days each race came up from the beginning and there was great rivalry as to which was the higher in the scale of evolution. The Wieroo developed the first *cos-ata-lu* but they were always male—never could they reproduce woman. Slowly they commenced to develop certain attributes of the mind which, they considered, placed them upon a still higher level and which gave them many advantages over us, seeing which they thought only of mental development—their minds became like stars and the rivers, moving always in the same manner, never varying. They called this *tas-ad*, which means doing everything the right way, or, in other words, the Wieroo way. If foe or friend, right or wrong, stood in the way of *tas-ad*, then it must be crushed.

"Soon the Galus and the lesser races of men came to hate and fear them. It was then that the Wieroos decided to carry *tas-ad* into every part of the world. They were very warlike and very numerous, although they had long since adopted the policy of slaying all those among them whose wings did not show advanced development.

"It took ages for all this to happen—very slowly came the different changes; but at last the Wieroos had wings they could use. But by reason of always making war upon their neighbors they were hated by every creature of Caspak, for no one wanted their *tas-ad*, and so they used their wings to fly to this island when the other races turned against them and threatened to kill them all. So cruel had they become and so bloodthirsty that they no longer had hearts that beat with love or sympathy; but their very cruelty and wickedness kept them from conquering the other races, since they were also cruel and wicked to one another, so that no Wieroo trusted another.

"Always were they slaying those above them that they might rise in power and possessions, until at last came the more powerful than the others with a *tas-ad* all his own. He gathered about him a few of the most terrible Wieroos, and among them they made laws which took from all but these few Wieroos every weapon they possessed.

"Now their *tas-ad* has reached a high plane among them. They make many wonderful things that we cannot make. They think great thoughts, no doubt, and still dream of greatness to come, but their thoughts and their acts are regulated by ages of custom—they are all alike—and they are most unhappy."

As the girl talked, the two moved steadily along the dark passageway beside the river. They had advanced a considerable distance when there sounded faintly from far ahead the muffled roar of falling water, which increased in volume as they moved forward until at last it filled the corridor with a deafening sound. Then the corridor ended in a blank wall; but in a niche to the right was a ladder leading aloft, and to the left was a door opening onto the river. Bradley tried the latter first and as he opened it, felt a heavy spray against his face. The little shelf outside the doorway was wet and slippery, the roaring of the water tremendous. There could be but one explanation—they had reached a waterfall in the river, and if the corridor actually terminated here, their escape was effectually cut off, since it was quite evidently impossible to follow the bed of the river and ascend the falls.

As the ladder was the only alternative, the two turned toward it and, the man first, began the ascent, which was through a well similar to that which had led him to the upper floors of the temple. As he climbed, Bradley felt for openings in the sides of the shaft; but he discovered none below fifty feet. The first he came to was ajar, letting a faint light into the well. As he paused, the girl climbed to his side, and together they looked through the crack into a low-ceiled chamber in which were several Galu women and an equal number of hideous little replicas of the full-grown Wieroos with which Bradley was not quite familiar.

He could feel the body of the girl pressed close to his tremble as her eyes rested upon the inmates of the room, and involuntarily his arm encircled her shoulders as though to protect her from some danger which he sensed without recognizing.

"Poor things," she whispered. "This is their horrible fate—to be imprisoned here beneath the surface of the city with their hideous offspring whom they hate as they hate their fathers. A Wieroo keeps his children thus hidden until they are full-grown lest they be murdered by their fellows. The lower rooms of the city are filled with many such as these."

Several feet above was a second door beyond which they found a small room stored with food in wooden vessels. A grated window in one wall opened above an alley, and through it they could see that they were just below the roof of the building. Darkness was coming, and at Bradley's suggestion they decided to remain hidden here until after dark and then to ascend to the roof and reconnoiter.

Shortly after they had settled themselves they heard something descending the ladder from above. They hoped that it would continue on down the well and fairly held their breath as the sound approached the door to the storeroom. Their hearts sank as they heard the door open and from between cracks in the vessels behind which they hid saw a yellow-slashed Wieroo enter the room. Each recognized him immediately, the girl indicating the fact of her own recognition by a sudden pressure of her fingers on Bradley's arm. It was the Wieroo of the yellow slashing whose abode was the place of the yellow door in which Bradley had first seen the girl.

The creature carried a wooden bowl which it filled with dried food from several of the vessels; then it turned and quit the room. Bradley could see through the partially open doorway that it descended the ladder. The girl told him that it was taking the food to the women and the young below, and that while it might return immediately, the chances were that it would remain for some time.

"We are just below the place of the yellow door," she said. "It is far from the edge of the city; so far that we may not hope to escape if we ascend to the roofs here."

"I think," replied the man, "that of all the places in Oo-oh this will be the easiest to escape from. Anyway, I want to return to the place of the yellow door and get my pistol if it is there."

"It is still there," replied the girl. "I saw it placed in a chest where he keeps the things he takes from his prisoners and victims."

"Good!" exclaimed Bradley. "Now come, quickly." And the two crossed the room to the well and ascended the ladder a short distance to its top where they found another door that opened into a vacant room—the same in which Bradley had first met the girl. To find the pistol was a matter of but a moment's search on the part of Bradley's companion; and then, at the Englishman's signal, she followed him to the yellow door.

It was quite dark without as the two entered the narrow passage between two buildings. A few steps brought them undiscovered to the doorway of the storeroom where lay the body of Fosh-bal-soj. In the distance, toward the temple, they could hear sounds as of a great gathering of Wieroos—the peculiar, uncanny wailing rising above the dismal flapping of countless wings.

"They have heard of the killing of Him Who Speaks for Luata," whispered the girl. "Soon they will spread in all directions searching for us."

"And will they find us?"

"As surely as Lua gives light by day," she replied; "and when they find us, they will tear us to pieces, for only the Wieroos may murder—only they may practice *tas-ad*."

"But they will not kill you," said Bradley. "You did not slay him."

"It will make no difference," she insisted. "If they find us together they will slay us both."

"Then they won't find us together," announced Bradley decisively. "You stay right here—you won't be any worse off than before I came—and I'll get as far as I can and account for as many of the beggars as possible before they get me. Good-bye! You're a mighty decent little girl. I wish that I might have helped you."

"No," she cried. "Do not leave me. I would rather die. I had hoped and hoped to find some way to return to my own country. I wanted to go back to An-Tak, who must be very lonely without me; but I know that it can never be. It is difficult to kill hope, though mine is nearly dead. Do not leave me."

"An-Tak!" Bradley repeated. "You loved a man called An-Tak?"

"Yes," replied the girl. "An-Tak was away, hunting, when the Wieroo caught me. How he must have grieved for me! He also was *cos-ata-lu*, twelve moons older than I, and all our lives we have been together."

Bradley remained silent. So she loved An-Tak. He hadn't the heart to tell her that An-Tak had died, or how.

At the door of Fosh-bal-soj's storeroom they halted to listen. No sound came from within, and gently Bradley pushed open the door. All was inky darkness as they entered; but presently their eyes became accustomed to the gloom that was partially relieved by the soft starlight without. The Englishman searched and found those things for which he had come—two robes, two pairs of dead wings and several lengths of fiber rope. One pair of the wings he adjusted to the girl's shoulders by means of the rope. Then he draped the robe about her, carrying the cowl over her head.

He heard her gasp of astonishment when she realized the ingenuity and boldness of his plan; then he directed her to adjust the other pair of wings and the robe upon him. Working with strong, deft fingers she soon had the work completed, and the two stepped out upon the roof, to all intent and purpose genuine Wieroos. Besides his pistol Bradley carried the sword of the slain Wieroo prophet, while the girl was armed with the small blade of the red Wieroo.

Side by side they walked slowly across the roofs toward the north edge of the city. Wieroos flapped above them and several times they passed others walking or sitting upon the roofs. From the temple still rose the sounds of commotion, now pierced by occasional shrill screams.

"The murderers are abroad," whispered the girl. "Thus will another become the tongue of Luata. It is well for us, since it keeps them too busy to give the time for searching for us. They think that we cannot escape the city, and they know that we cannot leave the island—and so do I."

Bradley shook his head. "If there is any way, we will find it," he said.

"There is no way," replied the girl.

Bradley made no response, and in silence they continued until the outer edge of roofs was visible before them. "We are almost there," he whispered.

The girl felt for his fingers and pressed them. He could feel hers trembling as he returned the pressure, nor did he relinquish her hand; and thus they came to the edge of the last roof.

Here they halted and looked about them. To be seen attempting to descend to the ground below would be to betray the fact that they were not Wieroos. Bradley wished that their wings were attached to their bodies by sinew and muscle rather than by ropes of fiber. A Wieroo was flapping far overhead. Two more stood near a door a few yards distant. Standing between these and one of the outer pedestals that supported one of the numerous skulls Bradley made one end of a piece of rope fast about the pedestal and dropped the other end to the ground outside the city. Then they waited.

It was an hour before the coast was entirely clear and then a moment came when no Wieroo was in sight. "Now!" whispered Bradley; and the girl grasped the rope and slid over the edge of the roof into the darkness below. A moment later Bradley felt two quick pulls upon the rope and immediately followed to the girl's side.

Across a narrow clearing they made their way and into a wood beyond. All night they walked, following the river upward toward its source, and at dawn they took shelter in a thicket beside the stream. At no time did they hear the cry of a carnivore, and though many startled animals fled as they approached, they were not once menaced by a wild beast. When Bradley expressed surprise at the absence of the fiercest beasts that are so numerous upon the mainland of Caprona, the girl explained the reason that is contained in one of their ancient legends.

"When the Wieroos first developed wings upon which they could fly, they found this island devoid of any life other than a few reptiles that live either upon land or in the water and these only close to the coast. Requiring meat for food the Wieroos carried to the island such animals as they wished for that purpose. They still occasionally bring them, and this with the natural increase keeps them provided with flesh."

"As it will us," suggested Bradley.

The first day they remained in hiding, eating only the dried food that Bradley had brought with him from the temple storeroom, and the next night they set out again up the river, continuing steadily on until almost dawn, when they came to low hills where the river wound through a gorge—it was little more than rivulet now, the water clear and cold and filled with fish similar to brook trout though much larger. Not wishing to leave the stream the two waded along its bed to a spot where the gorge widened between perpendicular bluffs to a wooded acre of level land. Here they stopped, for here also the stream ended. They had reached its source—many cold springs bubbling up from the center of a little natural amphitheater in the hills and forming a clear and beautiful pool overshadowed by trees upon one side and bounded by a little clearing upon the other.

With the coming of the sun they saw they had stumbled upon a place where they might remain hidden from the Wieroos for a long time and also one that they could defend against these winged creatures, since the trees would shield them from an attack from above and also hamper the movements of the creatures should they attempt to follow them into the wood.

For three days they rested here before trying to explore the neighboring country. On the fourth, Bradley stated that he was going to scale the bluffs and learn what lay beyond. He told the girl that she should remain in hiding; but she refused to be left, saying that whatever fate was to be his, she intended to share it, so that he was at last forced to permit her to come with him. Through woods at the summit of the bluff they made their way toward the north and had gone but a short distance when the wood ended and before them they saw the waters of the inland sea and dimly in the distance the coveted shore.

The beach lay some two hundred yards from the foot of the hill on which they stood, nor was there a tree nor any other form of shelter between them and the water as far up and down the coast as they could see. Among other plans Bradley had thought of constructing a covered raft upon which they might drift to the mainland; but as such a contrivance would necessarily be of considerable weight, it must be built in the water of the sea, since they could not hope to move it even a short distance overland.

"If this wood was only at the edge of the water," he sighed.

"But it is not," the girl reminded him, and then: "Let us make the best of it. We have escaped from death for a time at least. We have food and good water and peace and each other. What more could we have upon the mainland?"

"But I thought you wanted to get back to your own country!" he exclaimed.

She cast her eyes upon the ground and half turned away. "I do," she said, "yet I am happy here. I could be little happier there."

Bradley stood in silent thought. "'We have food and good water and peace and *each other!*'" he repeated to himself. He turned then and looked at the girl, and it was as though in the days that they had been together this was the first time that he had really seen her. The circumstances that had thrown them together, the dangers through which they had passed, all the weird and horrible surround-ings that had formed the background of his knowledge of her had had their effect—she had been but the companion of an adventure; her self-reliance, her endurance, her loyalty, had been only what one man might expect of another, and he saw that he had unconsciously assumed an attitude toward her that he might have assumed toward a man. Yet there had been a difference—he recalled now the strange sensation of elation that had thrilled him upon the occasions when the girl had pressed his hand in hers, and the depression that had followed her announcement of her love for An-Tak.

He took a step toward her. A fierce yearning to seize her and crush her in his arms, swept over him, and then there flashed upon the screen of recollection the picture of a stately hall set amidst broad gardens and ancient trees and of a proud old man with beetling brows—an old man who held his head very high—and Bradley shook his head and turned away again.

They went back then to their little acre, and the days came and went, and the man fashioned spear and bow and arrows and hunted with them that they might have meat, and he made hooks of fish-bone and caught fishes with wondrous flies of his own invention; and the girl gathered fruits and cooked the flesh and the fish and made beds of branches and soft grasses. She cured the hides of the animals he killed and made them soft by much pounding. She made sandals for herself and for the man and fashioned a hide after the manner of those worn by the warriors of her tribe and made the man wear it, for his own garments were in rags.

She was always the same—sweet and kind and helpful—but always there was about her manner and her expression just a trace of wistfulness, and often she sat and looked at the man when he did not know it, her brows puckered in thought as though she were trying to fathom and to understand him.

In the face of the cliff, Bradley scooped a cave from the rotted granite of which the hill was composed, making a shelter for them against the rains. He brought wood for their cook-fire which they used only in the middle of the day—a time when there was little likelihood of Wieroos being in the air so far from their city—and then he learned to bank it with earth in such a way that the embers held until the following noon without giving off smoke.

Always he was planning on reaching the mainland, and never a day passed that he did not go to the top of the hill and look out across the sea toward the dark, distant line that meant for him comparative freedom and possibly reunion with his comrades. The girl always went with him, standing at his side and watching the stern expression on his face with just a tinge of sadness on her own.

"You are not happy," she said once.

"I should be over there with my men," he replied. "I do not know what may have happened to them."

"I want you to be happy," she said quite simply; "but I should be very lonely if you went away and left me here."

304

He put his hand on her shoulder. "I would not do that, little girl," he said gently. "If you cannot go with me, I shall not go. If either of us must go alone, it will be you."

Her face lighted to a wondrous smile. "Then we shall not be separated," she said, "for I shall never leave you as long as we both live."

He looked down into her face for a moment and then: "Who was An-Tak?" he asked.

"My brother," she replied. "Why?"

And then, even less than before, could he tell her. It was then that he did something he had never done before—he put his arms about her and stooping, kissed her forehead. "Until you find An-Tak," he said, "I will be your brother."

She drew away. "I already have a brother," she said, "and I do not want another."

5

ays became weeks, and weeks became months, and the months followed one another in a lazy procession of hot, humid days and warm, humid nights. The fugitives saw never a Wieroo by day though often at night they heard the melancholy flapping of giant wings far above them.

Each day was much like its predecessor. Bradley splashed about for a few minutes in the cold pool early each morning and after a time the girl tried it and liked it. Toward the center it was deep enough for swimming, and so he taught her to swim—she was probably the first human being in all Caspak's long ages who had done this thing. And then while she prepared breakfast, the man shaved—this he never neglected. At first it was a source of wonderment to the girl, for the Galu men are beardless.

When they needed meat, he hunted, otherwise he busied himself in improving their shelter, making new and better weapons, perfecting his knowledge of the girl's language and teaching her to speak and to write English—anything that would keep them both occupied. He still sought new plans for escape, but with ever-lessening enthusiasm, since each new scheme presented some insurmountable obstacle.

And then one day as a bolt out of a clear sky came that which blasted the peace and security of their sanctuary forever. Bradley was just emerging from the water after his morning plunge when from overhead came the sound of flapping wings. Glancing quickly up the man saw a white-robed Wieroo circling slowly above him. That he had been discovered he could not doubt since the creature even dropped to a lower altitude as though to assure itself that what it saw was a man. Then it rose rapidly and winged away toward the city.

For two days Bradley and the girl lived in a constant state of apprehension, awaiting the moment when the hunters would come for them; but nothing happened until just after dawn of the third day, when the flapping of wings apprised them of the approach of Wieroos. Together they went to the edge of the wood and looked up to see five red-robed creatures dropping slowly in ever-lessening spirals toward their little amphitheater. With no attempt at concealment they came, sure of their ability to overwhelm these two fugitives, and with the fullest measure of self-confidence they landed in the clearing but a few yards from the man and the girl.

Following a plan already discussed Bradley and the girl retreated slowly into the woods. The Wieroos advanced, calling upon them to give themselves up; but the quarry made no reply. Farther and farther into the little wood Bradley led the hunters, permitting them to approach ever closer; then he circled back again toward the clearing, evidently to the great delight of the Wieroos, who now followed more leisurely, awaiting the moment when they should be beyond the trees and able to use their wings. They had opened into semicircular formation now with the evident intention of cutting the two off from returning into the wood. Each Wieroo advanced with his curved blade ready in his hand, each hideous face blank and expressionless.

It was then that Bradley opened fire with his pistol—three shots, aimed with careful deliberation, for it had been long since he had used the weapon, and he could not afford to chance wasting ammunition on misses. At each shot a Wieroo dropped; and then the remaining two sought escape by flight, screaming and wailing after the manner of their kind. When a Wieroo runs, his wings spread almost without any volition upon his part, since from time immemorial he has always used them to balance himself and accelerate his running speed so that in the open they appear to skim the surface of the ground when in the act of running. But here in the woods, among the close-set boles, the spreading of their wings proved their undoing—it hindered and stopped them and threw them to the ground, and then Bradley was upon them threatening them with instant death if they did not surrender—promising them their freedom if they did his bidding.

"As you have seen," he cried, "I can kill you when I wish and at a distance. You cannot escape me. Your only hope of life lies in obedience. Quick, or I kill!"

The Wieroos stopped and faced him. "What do you want of us?" asked one.

"Throw aside your weapons," Bradley commanded. After a moment's hesitation they obeyed.

"Now approach!" A great plan—the only plan—had suddenly come to him like an inspiration.

The Wieroos came closer and halted at his command. Bradley turned to the girl. "There is rope in the shelter," he said. "Fetch it!"

She did as he bid, and then he directed her to fasten one end of a fifty-foot length to the ankle of one of the Wieroos and the opposite end to the second. The creatures gave evidence of great fear, but they dared not attempt to prevent the act.

"Now go out into the clearing," said Bradley, "and remember that I am walking close behind and that I will shoot the nearer one should either attempt to escape—that will hold the other until I can kill him as well."

In the open he halted them. "The girl will get upon the back of the one in front," announced the Englishman. "I will mount the other. She carries a sharp blade, and I carry this weapon that you know kills easily at a distance. If you disobey in the slightest, the instructions that I am about to give you, you shall both die. That we must die with you, will not deter us. If you obey, I promise to set you free without harming you.

"You will carry us due west, depositing us upon the shore of the mainland—that is all. It is the price of your lives. Do you agree?"

Sullenly the Wieroos acquiesced. Bradley examined the knots that held the rope to their ankles, and feeling them secure directed the girl to mount the back of the leading Wieroo, himself upon the other. Then he gave the signal for the two to rise together. With loud flapping of the powerful wings the creatures took to the air, circling once before they topped the trees upon the hill and then taking a course due west out over the waters of the sea.

Nowhere about them could Bradley see signs of other Wieroos, nor of those other menaces which he had feared might bring disaster to his plans for escape—the huge, winged reptilia that are so numerous above the southern areas of Caspak and which are often seen, though in lesser numbers, farther north.

Nearer and nearer loomed the mainland—a broad, parklike expanse stretching inland to the foot of a low plateau spread out before them. The little dots in the foreground became grazing herds of deer and antelope and bos; a huge woolly rhinoceros wallowed in a mudhole to the right, and beyond, a mighty mammoth culled the tender shoots from a tall tree. The roars and screams and growls of giant carnivora came faintly to their ears. Ah, this was Caspak. With all of its dangers and its primal savagery it brought a fullness to the throat of the Englishman as to one who sees and hears the familiar sights and sounds of home after a long absence. Then the Wieroos dropped swiftly downward to the flower-starred turf that grew almost to the water's edge, the fugitives slipped from their backs, and Bradley told the red-robed creatures they were free to go.

When he had cut the ropes from their ankles they rose with that uncanny wailing upon their lips that always brought a shudder to the Englishman, and upon dismal wings they flapped away toward frightful Oo-oh.

When the creatures had gone, the girl turned toward Bradley. "Why did you have them bring us here?" she asked. "Now we are far from my country. We may never live to reach it, as we are among enemies who, while not so horrible, will kill us just as surely as would the Wieroos should they capture us, and we have before us many marches through lands filled with savage beasts."

"There were two reasons," replied Bradley. "You told me that there are two Wieroo cities at the eastern end of the island. To have passed near either of them might have been to have brought about our heads hundreds of the creatures from whom we could not possibly have escaped. Again, my friends must be near this spot—it cannot be over two marches to the fort of which I have told you. It is my duty to return to them. If they still live we shall find a way to return you to your people."

"And you?" asked the girl.

"I escaped from Oo-oh," replied Bradley. "I have accomplished the impossible once, and so I shall accomplish it again—I shall escape from Caspak."

He was not looking at her face as he answered her, and so he did not see the shadow of sorrow that crossed her countenance. When he raised his eyes again, she was smiling.

"What you wish, I wish," said the girl.

Southward along the coast they made their way following the beach, where the walking was best, but always keeping close enough to trees to insure sanctuary from the beasts and reptiles that so often menaced them. It was late in the afternoon when the girl suddenly seized Bradley's arm and pointed straight ahead along the shore. "What is that?" she whispered. "What strange reptile is it?"

Bradley looked in the direction her slim forefinger indicated. He rubbed his eyes and looked again, and then he seized her wrist and drew her quickly behind a clump of bushes.

"What is it?" she asked.

"It is the most frightful reptile that the waters of the world have ever known," he replied. "It is a German U-boat!"

An expression of amazement and understanding lighted her features. "It is the thing of which you told me," she exclaimed, "—the thing that swims under the water and carries men in its belly!"

"It is," replied Bradley.

"Then why do you hide from it?" asked the girl. "You said that now it belonged to your friends."

"Many months have passed since I knew what was going on among my friends," he replied. "I cannot know what has befallen them. They should have been gone from here in this vessel long since, and so I cannot understand why it is still here. I am going to investigate first before I show myself. When I left, there were more Germans on the *U-33* than there were men of my own party at the fort, and I have had sufficient experience of Germans to know that they will bear watching—if they have not been properly watched since I left."

Making their way through a fringe of wood that grew a few yards inland the two crept unseen toward the U-boat which lay moored to the shore at a point which Bradley now recognized as being near the oil-pool north of Dinosaur. As close as possible to the vessel they halted, crouching low among the dense vegetation, and watched the boat for signs of human life about it. The hatches were closed—no one could be seen or heard. For five minutes Bradley watched, and then he determined to board the submarine and investigate. He had risen to carry his decision into effect when there suddenly broke upon his ear, uttered in loud and menacing tones, a volley of German oaths and expletives among which he heard *Englische schweinhunde* repeated several times. The voice did not come from the direction of the U-boat; but from inland. Creeping forward Bradley reached a spot where, through the creepers hanging from the trees, he could see a party of men coming down toward the shore.

He saw Baron Friedrich von Schoenvorts and six of his men—all armed—while marching in a little knot among them were Olson, Brady, Sinclair, Wilson, and Whitely.

Bradley knew nothing of the disappearance of Bowen Tyler and Miss La Rue, nor of the perfidy of the Germans in shelling the fort and attempting to escape in the *U-33*; but he was in no way surprised at what he saw before him.

The little party came slowly onward, the prisoners staggering beneath heavy cans of oil, while Schwartz, one of the German noncommissioned officers cursed and beat them with a stick of wood, impartially. Von Schoenvorts walked in the rear of the column, encouraging Schwartz and laughing at the discomfiture of the Britishers. Dietz, Heinz, and Klatz also seemed to enjoy the entertainment immensely; but two of the men—Plesser and Hindle— marched with eyes straight to the front and with scowling faces.

Bradley felt his blood boil at sight of the cowardly indignities being heaped upon his men, and in the brief span of time occupied by the column to come abreast of where he lay hidden he made his plans, foolhardy though he knew them. Then he drew the girl close to him. "Stay here," he whispered. "I am going out to fight those beasts; but I shall be killed. Do not let them see you. Do not let them take you alive. They are more cruel, more cowardly, more bestial than the Wieroos."

The girl pressed close to him, her face very white. "Go, if that is right," she whispered; "but if you die, I shall die, for I cannot live without you."

He looked sharply into her eyes. "Oh!" he ejaculated. "What an idiot I have been! Nor could I live without you, little girl." And he drew her very close and kissed her lips. "Good-bye." He disengaged himself from her arms and looked again in time to see that the rear of the column had just passed him. Then he rose and leaped quickly and silently from the jungle.

Suddenly von Schoenvorts felt an arm thrown about his neck and his pistol jerked from its holster. He gave a cry of fright and warning, and his men turned to see a half-naked white man holding their leader securely from behind and aiming a pistol at them over his shoulder.

"Drop those guns!" came in short, sharp syllables and perfect German from the lips of the newcomer. "Drop them or I'll put a bullet through the back of von Schoenvorts' head."

The Germans hesitated for a moment, looking first toward von Schoenvorts and then to Schwartz, who was evidently second in command, for orders.

"It's the English pig, Bradley," shouted the latter, "and he's alone—go and get him!"

"Go yourself," growled Plesser. Hindle moved close to the side of Plesser and whispered something to him. The latter nodded. Suddenly von Schoenvorts wheeled about and seized Bradley's pistol arm with both hands, "Now!" he shouted. "Come and take him, quick!"

Schwartz and three others leaped forward; but Plesser and Hindle held back, looking questioningly toward the English prisoners. Then Plesser spoke. "Now is your chance, *Engländer*," he called in low tones. "Seize Hindle and me and take our guns from us—we will not fight hard."

Olson and Brady were not long in acting upon the suggestion. They had seen enough of the brutal treatment von Schoenvorts accorded his men and the especially venomous attentions he had taken great enjoyment in according Plesser and Hindle to understand that these two might be sincere in a desire for revenge. In another moment the two Germans were unarmed and Olson and Brady were running to the support of Bradley; but already it seemed too late.

Von Schoenvorts had managed to drag the Englishman around so that his back was toward Schwartz and the other advancing Germans. Schwartz was almost upon Bradley with gun clubbed and ready to smash down upon the Englishman's skull. Brady and Olson were charging the Germans in the rear with Wilson, Whitely, and Sinclair supporting them with bare fists. It seemed that Bradley was doomed when, apparently out of space, an arrow whizzed, striking Schwartz in the side, passing half-way through his body to crumple him to earth. With a shriek the man fell, and at the same time Olson and Brady saw the slim figure of a young girl standing at the edge of the jungle coolly fitting another arrow to her bow.

Bradley had now succeeded in wrestling his arm free from von Schoenvorts' grip and in dropping the latter with a blow from the butt of his pistol. The rest of the English and Germans were engaged in a hand-to-hand encounter. Plesser and Hindle standing aside from the mêlée and urging their comrades to surrender and join with the English against the tyranny of von Schoenvorts. Heinz and Klatz, possibly influenced by their exhortation, were putting up but a half-hearted resistance; but Dietz, a huge, bearded, bull-necked Prussian, yelling like a maniac, sought to exterminate the *Englische schweinhunde* with his bayonet, fearing to fire his piece lest he kill some of his comrades.

It was Olson who engaged him, and though unused to the long German rifle and bayonet, he met the bull-rush of the Hun with the cold, cruel precision and science of English bayonet-fighting. There was no feinting, no retiring and no parrying that was not also an attack. Bayonet-fighting today is not a pretty thing to see—it is no artistic fencing-match in which men give and take—it is slaughter inevitable and quickly over.

Dietz lunged once madly at Olson's throat. A short point, with just a twist of the bayonet to the left sent the sharp blade over the Englishman's left shoulder. Instantly he stepped close in, dropped his rifle through his hands and grasped it with both hands close below the muzzle and with a short, sharp jab sent his blade up beneath Dietz's chin to the brain. So quickly was the thing done and so quick the withdrawal that Olson had wheeled to take on another adversary before the German's corpse had toppled to the ground.

But there were no more adversaries to take on. Heinz and Klatz had thrown down their rifles and with hands above their heads were crying "*Kamerad! Kamerad!*" at the tops of their voices. Von Schoenvorts still lay where he had fallen. Plesser and Hindle were explaining to Bradley that they were glad of the outcome of the fight, as they could no longer endure the brutality of the U-boat commander.

The remainder of the men were looking at the girl who now advanced slowly, her bow ready, when Bradley turned toward her and held out his hand.

"Co-Tan," he said, "unstring your bow—these are my friends, and yours." And to the Englishmen: "This is Co-Tan. You who saw her save me from Schwartz know a part of what I owe her."

The rough men gathered about the girl, and when she spoke to them in broken English, with a smile upon her lips enhancing the charm of her irresistible accent, each and every one of them promptly fell in love with her and constituted himself henceforth her guardian and her slave.

A moment later the attention of each was called to Plesser by a volley of invective. They turned in time to see the man running toward von Schoenvorts who was just rising from the ground. Plesser carried a rifle with bayonet fixed, that he had snatched from the side of Dietz's corpse. Von Schoenvorts' face was livid with fear, his jaws working as though he would call for help; but no sound came from his blue lips.

"You struck me," shrieked Plesser. "Once, twice, three times, you struck me, pig. You murdered Schwerke—you drove him insane by your cruelty until he took his own life. You are only one of your kind—they are all like you from the Kaiser down. I wish that you were the Kaiser. Thus would I do!" And he lunged his bayonet through von Schoenvorts' chest. Then he let his rifle fall with the dying man and wheeled toward Bradley. "Here I am," he said. "Do with me as you like. All my life I have been kicked and cuffed by such as that, and yet always have I gone out when they commanded, singing, to give up my life if need be to keep them in power. Only lately have I come to know what a fool I have been. But now I am no longer a fool, and besides, I am avenged and Schwerke is avenged, so you can kill me if you wish. Here I am."

"If I was after bein' the king," said Olson, "I'd pin the V.C. on your noble chist; but bein' only an Irishman with a Swede name, for which God forgive me, the bist I can do is shake your hand."

"You will not be punished," said Bradley. "There are four of you left—if you four want to come along and work with us, we will take you; but you will come as prisoners."

"It suits me," said Plesser. "Now that the captain-lieutenant is dead you need not fear us. All our lives we have known nothing but to obey his class. If I had not killed him, I suppose I would be fool enough to obey him again; but he is dead. Now we will obey you— we must obey some one."

"And you?" Bradley turned to the other survivors of the original crew of the U-33. Each promised obedience.

The two dead Germans were buried in a single grave, and then the party boarded the submarine and stowed away the oil.

Here Bradley told the men what had befallen him since the night of September 14th when he had disappeared so mysteriously from the camp upon the plateau. Now he learned for the first time that Bowen J. Tyler, Jr., and Miss La Rue had been missing even longer than he and that no faintest trace of them had been discovered.

Olson told him of how the Germans had returned and waited in ambush for them outside the fort, capturing them that they might be used to assist in the work of refining the oil and later in manning the *U-33*, and Plesser told briefly of the experiences of the German crew under von Schoenvorts since they had escaped from Caspak months before—of how they lost their bearings after having been shelled by ships they had attempted to sneak farther north and how at last with provisions gone and fuel almost exhausted they had sought and at last found, more by accident than design, the mysterious island they had once been so glad to leave behind.

"Now," announced Bradley, "we'll plan for the future. The boat has fuel, provisions and water for a month, I believe you said, Plesser; there are ten of us to man it. We have a last sad duty here—we must search for Miss La Rue and Mr. Tyler. I say a sad duty because we know that we shall not find them; but it is none the less our duty to comb the shore-line, firing signal shells at intervals, that we at least may leave at last with full knowledge that we have done all that men might do to locate them."

None dissented from this conviction, nor was there a voice raised in protest against the plan to at least make assurance doubly sure before quitting Caspak forever.

And so they started, cruising slowly up the coast and firing an occasional shot from the gun. Often the vessel was brought to a stop, and always there were anxious eyes scanning the shore for an answering signal. Late in the afternoon they caught sight of a number of Band-lu warriors; but when the vessel approached the shore and the natives realized that human beings stood upon the back of the strange monster of the sea, they fled in terror before Bradley could come within hailing distance.

That night they dropped anchor at the mouth of a sluggish stream whose warm waters swarmed with millions of tiny tad-polelike organisms—minute human spawn starting on their precarious journey from some inland pool toward "the beginning"—a

317

journey which one in millions, perhaps, might survive to complete. Already almost at the inception of life they were being greeted by thousands of voracious mouths as fish and reptiles of many kinds fought to devour them, the while other and larger creatures pursued the devourers, to be, in turn, preyed upon by some other of the countless forms that inhabit the deeps of Caprona's frightful sea.

The second day was practically a repetition of the first. They moved very slowly with frequent stops and once they landed in the Kro-lu country to hunt. Here they were attacked by the bow-and-arrow men, whom they could not persuade to palaver with them. So belligerent were the natives that it became necessary to fire into them in order to escape their persistent and ferocious attentions.

"What chance," asked Bradley, as they were returning to the boat with their game, "could Tyler and Miss La Rue have had among such as these?"

But they continued on their fruitless quest, and the third day, after cruising along the shore of a deep inlet, they passed a line of lofty cliffs that formed the southern shore of the inlet and rounded a sharp promontory about noon. Co-Tan and Bradley were on deck alone, and as the new shoreline appeared beyond the point, the girl gave an exclamation of joy and seized the man's hand in hers.

"Oh, look!" she cried. "The Galu country! The Galu country! It is my country that I never thought to see again."

"You are glad to come again, Co-Tan?" asked Bradley.

"Oh, so glad!" she cried. "And you will come with me to my people? We may live here among them, and you will be a great warrior—oh, when Jor dies you may even be chief, for there is none so mighty as my warrior. You will come?"

Bradley shook his head. "I cannot, little Co-Tan," he answered. "My country needs me, and I must go back. Maybe someday I shall return. You will not forget me, Co-Tan?"

She looked at him in wide-eyed wonder. "You are going away from me?" she asked in a very small voice. "You are going away from Co-Tan?"

Bradley looked down upon the little bowed head. He felt the soft cheek against his bare arm; and he felt something else there too—hot drops of moisture that ran down to his very finger-tips and splashed, but each one wrung from a woman's heart.

He bent low and raised the tear-stained face to his own. "No, Co-Tan," he said, "I am not going away from you—for you are going with me. You are going back to my own country to be my wife. Tell me that you will, Co-Tan." And he bent still lower yet from his height and kissed her lips. Nor did he need more than the wonderful new light in her eyes to tell him that she would go to the end of the world with him if he would but take her. And then the gun-crew came up from below again to fire a signal shot, and the two were brought down from the high heaven of their new happiness to the scarred and weather-beaten deck of the *U-33*.

An hour later the vessel was running close in by a shore of wondrous beauty beside a parklike meadow that stretched back a mile inland to the foot of a plateau when Whitely called attention to a score of figures clambering downward from the elevation to the lowland below. The engines were reversed and the boat brought to a stop while all hands gathered on deck to watch the little party coming toward them across the meadow.

"They are Galus," cried Co-Tan; "they are my own people. Let me speak to them lest they think we come to fight them. Put me ashore, my man, and I will go meet them."

The nose of the U-boat was run close in to the steep bank; but when Co-Tan would have run forward alone, Bradley seized her hand and held her back. "I will go with you, Co-Tan," he said; and together they advanced to meet the oncoming party.

There were about twenty warriors moving forward in a thin line, as our infantry advance as skirmishers. Bradley could not but notice the marked difference between this formation and the moblike methods of the lower tribes he had come in contact with, and he commented upon it to Co-Tan.

"Galu warriors always advance into battle thus," she said. "The lesser people remain in a huddled group where they can scarce use their weapons the while they present so big a mark to us that our spears and arrows cannot miss them; but when they hurl theirs at our warriors, if they miss the first man, there is no chance that they will kill some one behind him.

"Stand still now," she cautioned, "and fold your arms. They will not harm us then."

Bradley did as he was bid, and the two stood with arms folded as the line of warriors approached. When they had come within some fifty yards, they halted and one spoke. "Who are you and from whence do you come?" he asked; and then Co-Tan gave a little, glad cry and sprang forward with out-stretched arms.

"Oh, Tan!" she exclaimed. "Do you not know your little Co-Tan?"

The warrior stared, incredulous, for a moment, and then he, too, ran forward and when they met, took the girl in his arms. It was then that Bradley experienced to the full a sensation that was new to him—a sudden hatred for the strange warrior before him and a desire to kill without knowing why he would kill. He moved quickly to the girl's side and grasped her wrist.

"Who is this man?" he demanded in cold tones.

Co-Tan turned a surprised face toward the Englishman and then of a sudden broke forth into a merry peal of laughter. "This is my father, Brad-lee," she cried.

"And who is Brad-lee?" demanded the warrior.

"He is my man," replied Co-Tan simply.

"By what right?" insisted Tan.

And then she told him briefly of all that she had passed through since the Wieroos had stolen her and of how Bradley had rescued her and sought to rescue An-Tak, her brother.

"You are satisfied with him?" asked Tan.

"Yes," replied the girl proudly.

It was then that Bradley's attention was attracted to the edge of the plateau by a movement there, and looking closely he saw a horse bearing two figures sliding down the steep declivity. Once at the bottom, the animal came charging across the meadowland at a rapid run. It was a magnificent animal—a great bay stallion with a white-blazed face and white forelegs to the knees, its barrel encircled by a broad surcingle of white; and as it came to a sudden stop beside Tan, the Englishman saw that it bore a man and a girl—a tall man and a girl as beautiful as Co-Tan. When the girl espied the latter, she slid from the horse and ran toward her, fairly screaming for joy.

The man dismounted and stood beside Tan. Like Bradley he was garbed after the fashion of the surrounding warriors; but there was a subtle difference between him and his companion. Possibly he detected a similar difference in Bradley, for his first question was, "From what country?" and though he spoke in Galu Bradley thought he detected an accent.

"England," replied Bradley.

A broad smile lighted the newcomer's face as he held out his hand. "I am Tom Billings of Santa Monica, California," he said. "I know all about you, and I'm mighty glad to find you alive."

"How did you get here?" asked Bradley. "I thought ours was the only party of men from the outer world ever to enter Caprona."

"It was, until we came in search of Bowen J. Tyler, Jr.," replied Billings. "We found him and sent him home with his bride; but I was kept a prisoner here."

Bradley's face darkened—then they were not among friends

after all. "There are ten of us down there on a German sub with small-arms and a gun," he said quickly in English. "It will be no trick to get away from these people."

"You don't know my jailer," replied Billings, "or you'd not be so sure. Wait, I'll introduce you." And then turning to the girl who had accompanied him he called her by name. "Ajor," he said, "permit me to introduce Lieutenant Bradley; Lieutenant, Mrs. Billings— my jailer!"

The Englishman laughed as he shook hands with the girl. "You are not as good a soldier as I," he said to Billings. "Instead of being taken prisoner myself I have taken one—Mrs. Bradley, this is Mr. Billings."

Ajor, quick to understand, turned toward Co-Tan. "You are going back with him to his country?" she asked. Co-Tan admitted it.

"You dare?" asked Ajor. "But your father will not permit it— Jor, my father, High Chief of the Galus, will not permit it, for like me you are *cos-ata-lo*. Oh, Co-Tan, if we but could! How I would love to see all the strange and wonderful things of which my Tom tells me!"

Bradley bent and whispered in her ear. "Say the word and you may both go with us."

Billings heard and speaking in English, asked Ajor if she would go.

"Yes," she answered, "If you wish it; but you know, my Tom, that if Jor captures us, both you and Co-Tan's man will pay the penalty with your lives—not even his love for me nor his admiration for you can save you."

Bradley noticed that she spoke in English—broken English like Co-Tan's but equally appealing. "We can easily get you aboard the ship," he said, "on some pretext or other, and then we can steam away. They can neither harm nor detain us, nor will we have to fire a shot at them."

And so it was done, Bradley and Co-Tan taking Ajor and Billings aboard to "show" them the vessel, which almost immediately raised anchor and moved slowly out into the sea.

"I hate to do it," said Billings. "They have been fine to me. Jor and Tan are splendid men and they will think me an ingrate; but I can't waste my life here when there is so much to be done in the outer world."

As they steamed down the inland sea past the island of Oo-oh, the stories of their adventures were retold, and Bradley learned that Bowen Tyler and his bride had left the Galu country but a fortnight before and that there was every reason to believe that the *Toreador* might still be lying in the Pacific not far off the subterranean mouth of the river which emitted Caprona's heated waters into the ocean.

Late in the second day, after running through swarms of hideous reptiles, they submerged at the point where the river entered beneath the cliffs and shortly after rose to the sunlit surface of the Pacific; but nowhere as far as they could see was sign of another craft. Down the coast they steamed toward the beach where Billings had made his crossing in the hydro-aeroplane and just at dusk the lookout announced a light dead ahead. It proved to be aboard the *Toreador*, and a half-hour later there was such a reunion on the deck of the trig little yacht as no one there had ever dreamed might be possible. Of the Allies there were only Tippet and James to be mourned, and no one mourned any of the Germans dead nor Benson, the traitor, whose ugly story was first told in Bowen Tyler's manuscript.

Tyler and the rescue party had but just reached the yacht that afternoon. They had heard, faintly, the signal shots fired by the *U-33* but had been unable to locate their direction and so had assumed that they had come from the guns of the *Toreador*.

It was a happy party that sailed north toward sunny, southern California, the old *U-33* trailing in the wake of the *Toreador* and flying with the latter the glorious Stars and Stripes beneath which she had been born in the shipyard at Santa Monica. Three newly married couples, their bonds now duly solemnized by the master of the ship, joyed in the peace and security of the untracked waters of the south Pacific and the unique honeymoon which, had it not been for stern duty ahead, they could have wished protracted till the end of time.

And so they came one day to dock at the shipyard which Bowen Tyler now controlled, and here the *U-33* still lies while those who passed so many eventful days within and because of her, have gone their various ways.

MAP OF CASPAK

(Edgar Rice Burroughs, 1917)

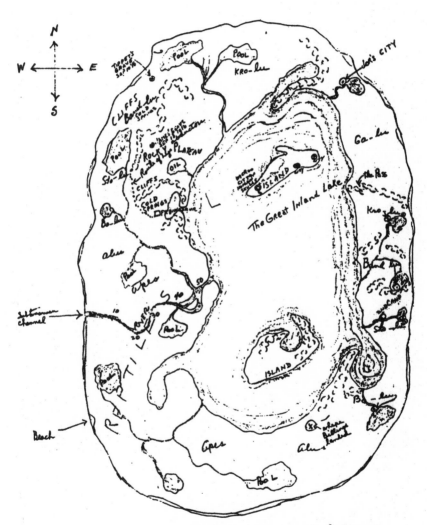

MAP of <u>CASPAK</u> on the Island of <u>Caprona</u>

LAND 130 mi. x 180 mi Lake 60 mi. x 120mi.   Scale: 0   10   20   30

GLOSSARY

PEOPLE

Ahm (or Am): A Bo-lu who was captured by Bowen's first hunting expedition.

Ajor: A female Galu who marries Billings.

Al-tan (also Altan): Chief of the Kro-lu of the east.

Alu: Lowest form of human life on Caspak, having neither language nor weapons.

An-Tak: A Galu who was imprisoned along with Bradley. Brother of Co-Tan.

Band-lu: The spear people. Above the Sto-lu on the evolutionary scale, but below the Kro-lu. Similar to Cro-Magnons, they had primitive stone weapons and some language skills.

Batu: A Caspak human of any type who has reached the end of the evolutionary process and cannot rise any higher.

Benson: Member of the tugboat who, after being shot by Lys La Rue confesses to spying for the Germans.

Billings, Tom: Cowboy and lifelong friend of Bowen Tyler who organizes his rescue mission. Protagonist of *The People That Time Forgot*.

Bo-lu (also Bolu): Club men. Above the Alu on the evolutionary scale, but below the Sto-lu.

Bradley, John: Mate of the tugboat. Protagonist of *Out of Time's Abyss*.

Brady: Irish crewmember of the tugboat.

Caproni: The Italian explorer who originally found Caspak and named it Caprona.

Chal-az: A Kro-lu warrior of the west.

Co-Tan: A Ga-lu female. Rescued from Weirwoo captivity on Oo-oh by Bradley.

Cos-ata-lo: A woman who did not come from an egg, and hence is considered at the top of the evolutionary scale. This is only possible among the Galus.

Dietz: Prussian crewmember of the *U-33*.

Du-seen (also Duseen): An ambitious Galu warrior and Ajor's spurned suitor.

Fosh-bal-soj: Bradley's Weiroo captor.

Galu: People of the rope. The highest form of human life on the evolutionary scale in Caspak. Reproduce like normal humans.

Hatcher and Holland: Paleontologists mentioned in *The People That Time Forgot*.

Heinz: Crewmember of the *U-33*.

Him Who Speaks For Luata: Weiroo leader.

Hindle: Crewmember of the *U-33*.

Hollis, Jimmy: Crewmember of the *Toreador*.

James, William: Crewmember of the tugboat.

Jor: Chief of the Galu.

Kho: A Sto-lu of the tribe of Tsa. Second kidnapper of Lys La Rue.

Klatz: Crewmember of the *U-33*.

Kro-lu (also Krolu): The bow people. The second-highest form of human life on the evolutionary scale—below the Galu.

La Rue, Lys: American passenger on the ship sunk by the *U-33*.

Glossary

Olson: Irish engineer of the tugboat.

Plesser: German crewmember of the *U-33*.

Schoenvorts, Baron Fredriech von: Commander of the *U-33*.

Schwartz: Crewmember of the *U-33*.

Schwerke: Crewmember of the *U-33*.

Short, Colin: Crewmember of the *Toreador*.

Sinclair: Crewmember of the tugboat.

So-al: Kro-lu woman saved by Billings.

So-ta: Band-lu female who becomes Kro-lu.

Sto-lu: The hatchet people. Above the Bo-lu but below the Band-lu on the evolutionary scale. Rudimentary language skills and had knowledge of fire.

Tan: Galu male. Co-Tan's father.

Tippet, John: Crewmember of the tugboat.

To-jo: Chief of the Band-lu.

To-mar: Band-lu who becomes Kro-lu.

Tsa: Sto-lu who attempted to marry Lys La Rue.

Tyler Sr., Bowen J.: Bowen's father. Died aboard the *Toreador*.

Tyler, Bowen: Executive at his father's ship-building company. Protagonist of *The Land That Time Forgot*.

Wieroo (also Weiroo): The all-male, flying human inhabitants of Oo-oh.

Whitely: Crewmember of the tugboat.

Wilson: Crewmember of the tugboat.

PLACES

Blue Place of Seven Skulls: Bradley's prison on Oo-oh.

Cape Farewell: Where Tyler's manuscript in a bottle was found in Greenland.

Caprona: Island continent located in the South Pacific Ocean, protected by large cliffs that surround a protected eco-system with many strange forms of animal and human life.

Caspak: Native name for Caprona.

City of Human Skulls, The: Bradley's name for Oo-oh.

Coslupak: The no man's land "between the Band-lu and the Kro-lu."

Fort Dinosaur: Bowen's village about two miles from the harbor.

Inland Sea: Body of water within Caprona.

Oo-oh: Northern island of the inland sea and home of the Wieroo.

River of Death: River the flows underneath the City of Human Skulls.

Toward the beginning: Mouth of the underground river (south). Where life begins.

CASPAK TERMS

Ata: Eggs, life, young, and/or reproduction.

Atis: Wooly rhinoceros.

Cor sva jo: From the beginning. (The evolutionary process experienced by most people of Caspak.)

Cos: Not.

Cos-ata-lo(lu): One who did not come from an egg. Human.

Ecca: Small horse (about the size of a rabbit).

Ga: Rope.

Ho-lu: Apes.

Jaal-lu: A derogatory name. Literally, hyena-man.

Jo-oo: Pterodactyl.

Ju: Stop.

Kazor: Beware.

Lo: Woman.

Lu: Man.

Lua: Sun.

Luata: God of heat and life.

Tas-ad: Doing everything the right way. The Wieroo way of thinking.

OTHER NAMES *and* TERMS

Ace: Billings's horse.

Crown Prince Nobbler: Tyler's Airedale.

*Toreador***:** The Tyler family yacht, which was used to rescue Bowen Tyler.

Tugboat: Ship that rescued Bowen and Lys.

*U-33***:** German submarine captured by Bowen.

About the Author

orn on September 1, 1875, into a well-to-do family in Chicago, Edgar Rice Burroughs enjoyed a privileged upbringing and education. He tried his hand at several business ventures, but found himself drawn more to an itinerant life of adventure than to a life in the boardroom.

In 1912, after many failed business ventures, the thirty-six-year-old Burroughs published his first story, "Under the Moons of Mars," in the pulp magazine *All-Story*. It was so successful that he turned soon thereafter to writing full-time. He would write nearly 70 novels and numerous short stories before his death in 1950. Although best known for his immensely popular *Tarzan* novels—he later bought an estate near where the films were shot in Southern California that he named Tarzana—Burroughs didn't confine himself to a single genre, and also wrote medieval romances, westerns, and mainstream novels.

Among his many science-fiction works, Burroughs wrote eleven novels in the John Carter of Mars series, the titular final installment of which was published fourteen years after his death.